GW00775640

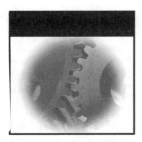

Installing and Configuring Web Servers Using Apache

Melanie Hoag

Gearhead Press™

Wiley Computer Publishing

John Wiley & Sons, Inc.

NEW YORK · CHICHESTER · WEINHEIM · BRISBANE · SINGAPORE · TORONTO

Publisher: Robert Ipsen
Editor: Theresa Hudson
Consulting Editor: Donis Marshall
Developmental Editor: Kathryn A. Malm
Managing Editor: Angela Smith
Text Design & Composition: Benchmark Productions, Inc.

Designations used by companies to distinguish their products are often claimed as trademarks. In all instances where John Wiley & Sons, Inc., is aware of a claim, the product names appear in initial capital or all capital letters. Readers, however, should contact the appropriate companies for more complete information regarding trademarks and registration.

This book is printed on acid-free paper. ∞

Published by John Wiley & Sons, Inc., New York

Published simultaneously in Canada.

This publication is designed to provide accurate and authoritative information in regard to the subject matter covered. It is sold with the understanding that the publisher is not engaged in professional services. If professional advice or other expert assistance is required, the services of a competent professional person should be sought.

The Gearhead Press trademark is the exclusive property of Gearhead Group Corporation.

Library of Congress Cataloging-in-Publication Data:

Hoag, Melanie
  Installing and configuring Web servers using Apache / Melanie Hoag.
    p. cm.
    ISBN 0-471-07155-2
    1. Apache (Computer file : Apache Group) 2. Web servers—Computer programs. I. Title.
TK105.8885.A63 H63 2001
005.7'13769—dc21   2001006063

Printed in the United States of America.

10 9 8 7 6 5 4 3 2 1

A Note from Gearhead Press

Gearhead Press is dedicated to publishing technical books for experienced Information Technology professionals—network engineers, developers, system administrators, and others—who need to update their skills, learn how to use technology more effectively, or simply want a quality reference to the latest technology.

Gearhead Press emerged from my experience with professional trainers of engineers and developers: people who truly understand first-hand the needs of working professionals. Gearhead Press authors are the crème de la crème of industry trainers, working at the companies that define the technology revolution. For this reason, Gearhead Press authors are regularly in the trenches with the developers and engineers that have changed the world through innovative products. Drawing from this experience in IT training, our books deliver superior technical content with a unique perspective that is based on real-world experience.

Now, as an imprint of John Wiley & Sons, Inc., Gearhead Press will continue to bring you, the reader, the level of quality that Wiley has delivered consistently for nearly 200 years.

Thank you.

Donis Marshall
Founder, Gearhead Press
Consulting Editor, Wiley Computer Publishing

Gearhead Press Books in Print

(For complete information about current and upcoming titles, go to www.wiley
.com/compbooks/)

Books in the Gearhead Press *Point to Point* Series

Migrating to Microsoft Exchange 2000
by Stan Reimer
ISBN: 0-471-06116-6

Installing and Configuring Web Servers Using Apache
by Melanie Hoag
ISBN: 0-471-07155-2

VoiceXML: 10 Projects to Voice Enable Your Website
by Mark Miller
ISBN: 0-471-20737-3

Books in the Gearhead Press *In the Trenches* Series

Windows 2000 Automated Deployment
by Ted Malone and Rolly Perraux
ISBN: 0-471-06114-X

Robust Linux: Assuring High Availability
by Iain Campbell
ISBN: 0-471-07040-8

Programming Directory Services for Windows 2000
by Donis Marshall
ISBN: 0-471-15216-1

Programming ADO.NET
by Richard Hundhausen and Steven Borg
ISBN: 0-471-20187-1

Designing .NET Web Services Using ADO.NET and XML
by Richard Hundhausen and Steven Borg
ISBN: 0-471-20186-3

Contents

Acknowledgments

Several people have helped with the development of this book and without them, it would not have been possible.

My appreciation to Donis Marshall (www.gearheadgroup.com), who gave me the opportunity to create this book–thank you. Donis is an efficient project manager who somehow managed to keep track of this project in addition to all of the other "stuff" he does! Also, my thanks to Ben Ryan and the crew at John Wiley & Sons, Inc., (www.wiley.com) who, with their "magic," did all the wonderful "publisher things." I also want to recognize the folks at RT Computer Graphics for permission to use their fantastic artwork in the web pages created for this book. If you ever need high quality Native American, Western, or Petroglyph designs, check out their web site at www.rtcomputer.com.

My gratitude and heartfelt thanks to my husband, Bob Bliss, for creating all of the web pages for the sites used throughout this book. Somehow, he managed, as he always does, to make my scribbles and scrawled notes into wonderful web sites. I also want to thank my daughter, Lee Ann Bliss, who spent many hours of her summertime between first and second grade helping Mama do her "computer work." I thank you both for your time, support, encouragement, and love.

God bless,

Melanie

About the Author

Melanie Hoag, Ph.D., holds LCI (Linux Certified Instructor), LCP (Linux Certified Professional), MCT (Microsoft Certified Instructor), MCSE (Microsoft Certified System Engineer), MCNI (Master Certified Novell Instructor), MCNE (Master Certified Novell Engineer), and CTT (Certified Technical Trainer) certifications.

Melanie began her computer career in 1983 at Drexel University in Philadelphia. She was involved in a variety of activities and projects ranging from software design and construction, courseware development, technical presentation and consulting. After Drexel, Melanie ran a small software development company with her husband. Her roles ranged from managing the business to software development to conference presentations. Since 1995, Melanie has been teaching vendor certified courses, developing training materials, and supplying network design and administration services.

In addition to consulting and teaching, Melanie has authored and co-authored two NetWare 5 certification exam preparation books and is one of three authors of *Linux for Dummies 3rd Edition*. When she's not busy with her computer activities (www.packetsandpings.com), Melanie and her family raise and show Texas Longhorns and try to keep up with their cattle, chickens, and two golden retrievers outside Hutto, Texas.

Contact Melanie at melhoag@packetsandpings.com

Introduction

Web servers play an important role in the exchange and presentation of information throughout the world. In the last few years, Web servers have replaced or supplemented paper, radio, and other media for the transfer of information. There are over 28 million Web servers on the Internet today, with more and more added every day. These numbers, reported by Netcraft, only represent Web servers that are accessible from a public Internet connection. There are also thousands, and perhaps millions, of Web servers on Intranets for the private use of companies and the individuals authorized to access them

When a user accesses a Web site from their browser, HTTP (HyperText Transmission Protocol) is used to send information back and forth between the server and the browser. This protocol was designed to deliver static content from the Web server to the user's browser. When Web servers first became readily accessible on the Internet, most of the information delivered to the users was static content. If the information needed to be changed, it was up to the Web site maintenance team to make changes to the Web site and upload the new content to the Web servers. As the number and usage of Web servers increased, more organizations needed a means to have their Web content dynamically change in response to browser requests or from other information sources such as databases. These needs drove the development of other protocols, such as CGI (Common Gateway Interface) and PHP (Personal Home Page). In general, both protocols manipulate data or programs on the Web server and then deliver the content to the browser. These techniques allow the Web content to be customized to the preferences of the user browsing the Web site. One nice feature of these types of protocols is that the user's browser does not need to know the content has been composed dynamically on the server. Other technologies that enable dynamic page information include Java, JavaScript, Perl, C/C++, and ASP.

Dynamic page generation is a very popular feature for Web sites that operate like a storefront. A customer shopping at the store's Web page, receives customized information reflecting their preferences, geographical area, or other information which makes their experience more personal. Along with window shopping at a store's Web front comes the possibility of product purchases. Since the user cannot pass cash across the Internet, credit cards are the principal method used for financial transactions. Most people do not freely exchange their credit card information with strangers and will not send credit card information to a Web site unless they know their information is protected. Potential buyers need to know that transmission and storage of their credit card information is secure and only authorized personnel have access to this sensitive information. These types of concerns of eCommerce have lead to technologies that enable secure transmission and storage of private information. HTTPS (HyperText Transmission Protocol Secure) is one mechanism to enable secure transmission between the user's browser and Web server across an unsecured network such as the Internet. Once the sensitive information is delivered to the Web server, the data must also be secured so unauthorized access is not permitted.

Web Server Roles

Web servers are generally categorized as public or private. An Intranet, or private Web server, typically contains information available only to individuals in the organization or company that owns the Intranet Web server. Placing the private Web server on the company's network is usually designed to provide access only to users on the company's network. Even with Intranet Web servers, some information may be off-limits to certain individuals in the organization. Some information on a private Intranet Web site can be public to all employees while other information is secured and only accessible by authorized individuals. Intranet Web servers are typically located on the private or company side of a firewall. The firewall between the Intranet Web server and the Internet eliminates or reduces access to the private Web server from a public network.

Web servers that are placed on the Internet and outside companies' firewalls are referred to as public Web servers. The information accessible on a public Web server may be for public consumption and therefore anybody is free to view the content. On some public Web servers, there may be information that is not for the general public and access to information must be controlled. In these cases, software components running on the Web server provide restricted access to the information for the individuals permitted to view the content.

Introducing Ouray Mountain Water:
Our Scenario Company

Throughout this book we will follow a small company as it develops and implements Web servers to provide more services for their employees and customers. Ouray Mountain Water, our scenario company, bottles Colorado pure mountain water and ships their product around the world. They started as a family business in 1954 and over the past seven years have greatly expanded their business. The company's headquarters is located in Ouray, Colorado and employs thirty people. The headquarters provides all of the company's employee services and is also the bottling facility. Ouray Mountain Water has four warehouses in the United States—Ouray, Tujunga Canyon (California), Hutto (Texas), and Malvern (Pennsylvania). The three warehouses outside of Colorado where added six years ago to handle the increased growth of sales. Each of the warehouses outside Colorado employs about ten full-time employees. During holiday seasons and summer months, each warehouse typically adds on an average of five temporary employees.

Ouray Mountain Water has been distributing information to their employees and customers through paper and electronic mail media. The employees receive a monthly newsletter, which contains information on benefit changes, awards, meetings, company parties, and activities. Electronic mail is currently used to deliver time dependent information that cannot wait for the next edition of the newsletter. Changes to employee policies and benefits are printed by each department and distributed through meetings or placed in the employees' mailboxes. Product and pricing information is sent to clients and prospective purchasers in the form of pamphlets and mailings. Information is also sent to customers using electronic mail with attachments outlining product details and pricing. In order to keep up with the daily mailings and inquiries, Ouray Mountain Water will have to add more employees or implement another solution. The company has decided to investigate using Web servers for distributing employee information and for product and pricing information. Since the company does not have any employees skilled in these areas, Ouray Mountain Water has hired your firm to design and implement the needed Web based solutions.

After spending a week at Ouray Mountain Water's headquarters and collecting data from the company's other locations, you have developed a Web server plan to improve the company's information exchange. One Web server will host all of the information for running the daily business and will only be accessible from within the company's network. Access to this Intranet server will not be permitted from outside the company's network. Another Web site will provide information about the company's products and is accessible to anyone on the Internet. This public information Web server will also allow customers to request product information over the Internet. A third Web server will contain information for employees such as available benefits, changes in policies, and other internal information. This Web server will be accessible from both the company's network and the Internet and will employ security tools to protect the private information. Each Web server will run Apache and other add-on components to provide additional capabilities.

Getting Started with Apache

The Apache Web server grew out of a development project of the NCSA (National Center for Supercomputing Applications) at the University of Illinois in Urbana-Champaign. In the early 1990's, Rob McCool developed a basic Web server software component designed to run as a daemon on an existing Unix based platform. This early implementation performed some very basic functions and when Rob McCool left NCSA in mid-1994, NCSA didn't do much with the project and it eventually disappeared. During the early days of the project, and after McCool left NCSA, many developers fixed errors and added their own extensions. Unfortunately, with no standards and people working independently, different flavors of the HTTP daemon developed that were not compatible with each other. Then a small group of these developers got together to organize their corrections and extensions. The developers used the phrase "a patchy" Web server to refer to their product. The term "a patchy" stuck and shortly evolved into the word Apache. Within one year, the Apache team had assembled and tested the extensions and fixes. In December 1995, Apache 1.0 was released. By early 1996, Apache had become the most popular Web server on the Internet.

Even though Apache evolved from a series of patches and fixes, it is a solid, robust product that draws a lot of respect among the Web server community. According to Netcraft (www.netcraft.com/survey/), an organization that tracks Internet Web server information, nearly eighteen million of the over twenty-eight million Internet Web servers are running Apache. Many of these Apache Web servers also have add-on modules or products to provide additional features. We will cover some of these add-on components later in this book.

Basics of the Apache Web Server

Apache runs on most versions of Unix and Linux, Windows NT/2000, NetWare 5.x, Windows 9x and OS/2. Although these underlying operating systems may be dramatically different, Apache is remarkably similar in architecture and configuration. However, because of operating system differences, some of the Apache structure is different but the Apache modular concept and configuration files are very similar. This common architectural concept is very useful because once you are familiar with Apache under one operating system, setting up Apache on another operating system is not much different.

The basic design model of Apache is a modular system. This allows you to add and remove modules so your Apache system matches the needs of your environment. The controls and settings for Apache are done through a set of configuration files. On both Linux and Windows platforms, you can recompile Apache for optimization and fine-tuning. Since Apache evolved on a Unix platform, the product's stability and reliability have not been extensively tested and are not well known on Windows and other platforms. Apache is also available for Novell's NetWare 5.x, HP's MPE/iX, SCO's (Caldera) UnixWare, and IBM's EBCDIC-based TPF (Transaction Processing Facility) operating system. In this book, we will concentrate on Apache for Linux and Windows 2000 Server.

Linux Platforms

Apache is included with most Linux distributions and can be installed when you initially setup your Linux system. Apache can also be added later to your Linux system. The default locations of the Apache components are different in the Linux file system when Apache is installed at the time the operating system is installed. For example, on RedHat 7.1 Linux systems, the Apache configuration files are located in /etc/httpd/conf, the log files are found in /var/log/httpd, the modules are stored in /usr/lib/apache, and the Web content is under /var/www. When Apache is installed after the operating system is in place, the default location for all the Web server's files are typically located at /usr/var/apache. We will go into details on the files and architecture of Apache and Linux later in this book.

Windows Platforms

Apache for Windows is a relatively new product and is available for download from the Apache Software Foundation's Web site, www.apache.org. The version for Windows is designed for Windows NT 4.0 Server, Windows 2000 Server, and Windows 2000 Advanced Server platforms. You can install Apache on other Windows operating systems, such as Windows 98, Windows ME, and Windows 2000 Professional, but it is not recommended to run a production Apache Web server on these operating systems.

Apache for Windows is installed through the Microsoft Installer version 1.10 application. On Windows platforms, the default location for all the Apache components is C:\Program Files\Apache Group\Apache. You can specify a different directory at installation time. Later in this book we will take a closer look at the details of Apache under Windows 2000.

Apache Add-Ons for Linux and Windows

There are a number of add-ons, enhancements, and additional modules for Apache that can be used in your environment. Some components are for Linux and others are only for Windows. Also, some products are commercial and may carry a purchase price and/or licensing fee. The following table summarizes some of the Apache additional components. We will address some of these add-ons in more detail later in this book.

NAME	PLATFORM	DESCRIPTION
ActiveScripting for Apache	Windows	Use ActiveScripting in place of Active Server Pages (ASP)
Apache::ASP	Linux	Port of Active Server Pages done with Perl scripting
Apache Interface to OpenSSL	Linux	Adds SSL v2/v3 (Secure Sockets Layer) and TLS v1 (Transport Layer Security) security features
Apache/Python Integration	Linux	Incorporates a Python language interpreter in the Apache environment
Apache-SSL	Linux	An encrypting Apache Web server that uses SSL

Introduction

One of the most important development tasks for a new Web site is planning. This is crucial for both the content and the operating system components of your Web sites. The operating system platform and Web server that host your Web sites are very important for your Web site's overall performance. These are the areas we will concentrate on in this chapter. The development of the flow and artistic design of your Web site is outside the scope of this book and there are numerous resources available in bookstores and on the Internet that address these topics.

Our scenario company, Ouray Mountain Water, has decided to implement three Web sites. One Web site will be public and accessible to anyone on the Internet. This site will contain information about the company's products and services. Another Web site will contain information for employees and will be accessible from the Internet and the company's internal network. The third Web site's content will include information used internally for day-to-day running of the company. This Web site will be accessible only from the company's private network and not the Internet.

Public Web Site

Ouray Mountain Water's public Web site will host information about the company's products and services. Since this will be a public Web site, the information is accessible to anyone on the Internet. Because this Web site may get a lot of access, the system hosting the Web site must be capable of handling many simultaneous requests. In addition, if the Web site is successful, the computer system for this Web server must also be able to handle future growth.

Exploring the Company's Public Web Site

The main purpose of this Web site is to provide easy access to the public to information about Ouray Mountain Water. On the initial opening page, users will be able to navigate to the other main areas of the Web site. These areas include links to Ouray Mountain Water's products and local area information. Figures 1.1 through 1.4 illustrate the content of the pubic Web site's opening page. The entire content does not fit on one browser screen so the content is displayed across four screen shots.

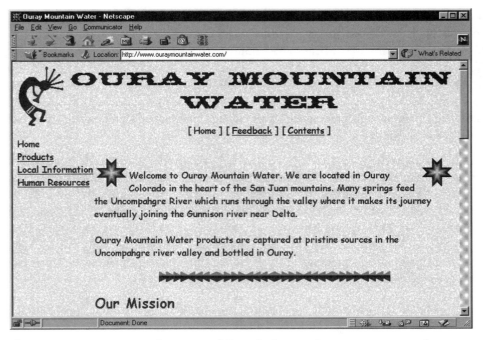

Figure 1.1   Ouray Mountain Water public Web site opening page, screen 1 of 4.

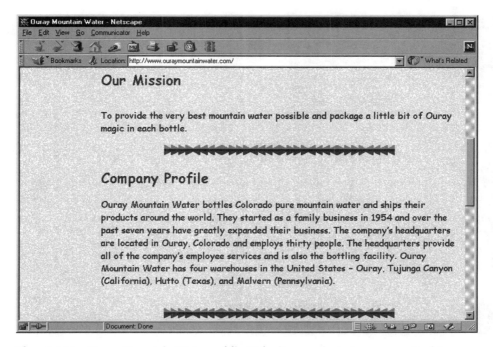

Figure 1.2   Ouray Mountain Water public Web site opening page, screen 2 of 4.

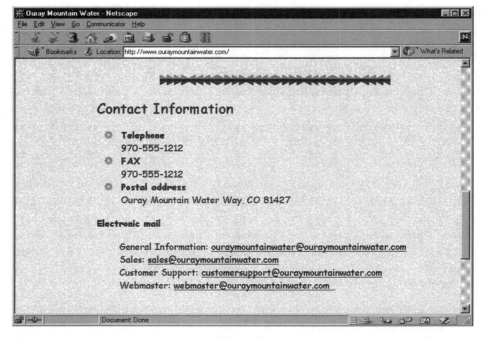

Figure 1.3   Ouray Mountain Water public Web site opening page, screen 3 of 4.

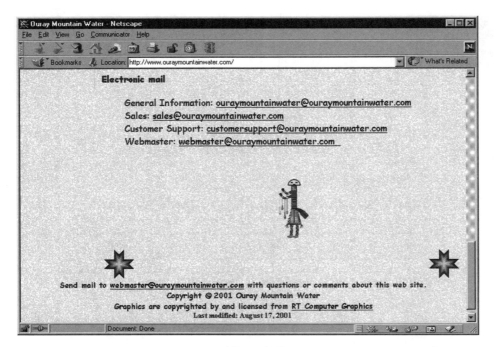

Figure 1.4   Ouray Mountain Water public Web site opening page, screen 4 of 4.

Each of the Web site's main areas is on a separate page and contains links so the user can navigate to any of the other pages. The Products Web page contains information about the company's different products. The main Products page contains links to separate pages, which contain details about each of Ouray Mountain Water's products. Figures 1.5 and 1.6 illustrate the main Product page for the company's public Web site. The content will not fit within one browser window so two figures are used to show the entire Web page content.

The individual Product pages include fields the user can fill out to request information about the different products. Figures 1.7 through 1.9 show one of Ouray Mountain Water's specific product information pages. The style of the Product Detail pages is the same for each product, the only differences being the content that makes each product unique. Since the content of one of the Product Detail pages does not fit in one browser, three figures are used to illustrate the Web page content.

The Local Information page contains information about the area surrounding the Ouray Mountain Water's main location in Colorado. Figure 1.10 illustrates the content of the Local Information page found on the public Web site.

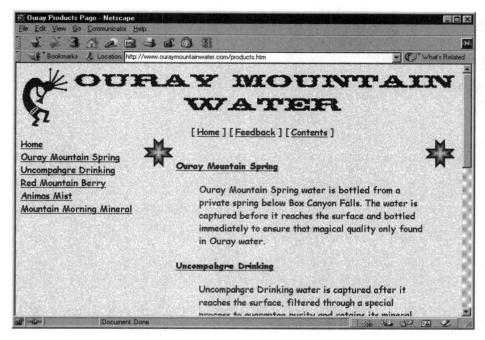

Figure 1.5   Ouray Mountain Water public Web site Product page, screen 1 of 2.

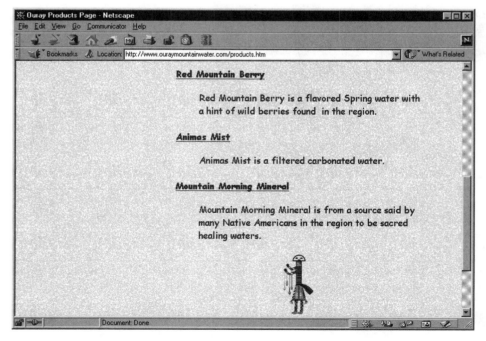

Figure 1.6   Ouray Mountain Water public Web site Product page, screen 2 of 2.

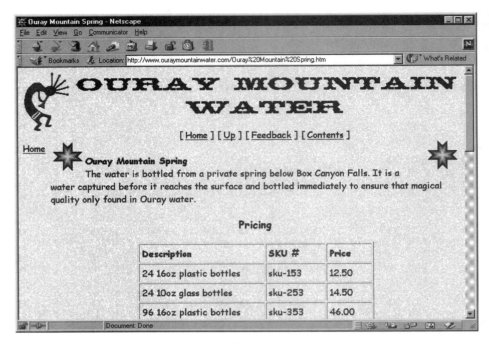

Figure 1.7 Ouray Mountain Water public Web site Product Detail page, screen 1 of 3.

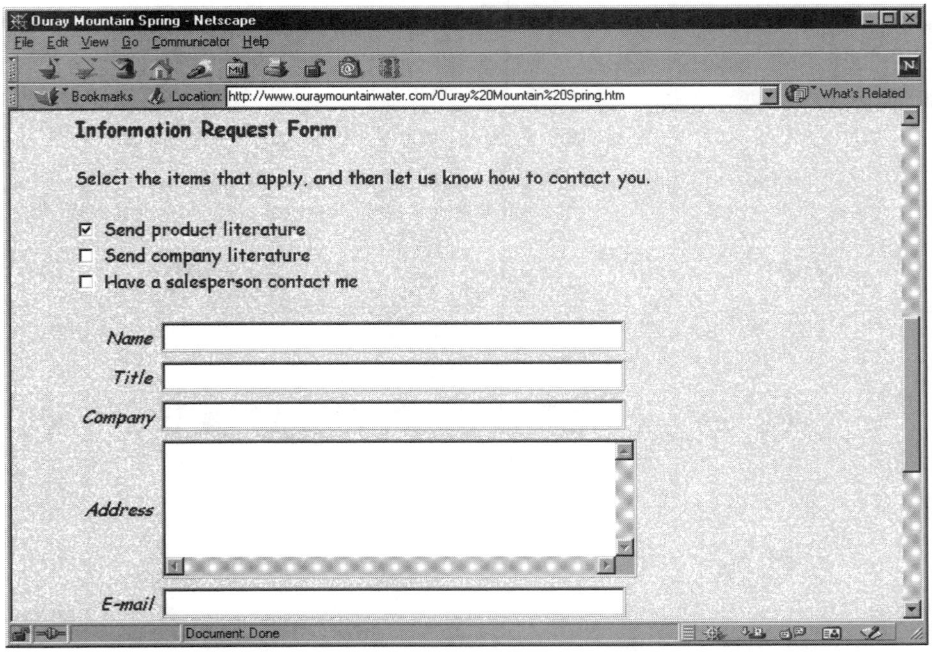

Figure 1.8 Ouray Mountain Water public Web site Product Detail page, screen 2 of 3.

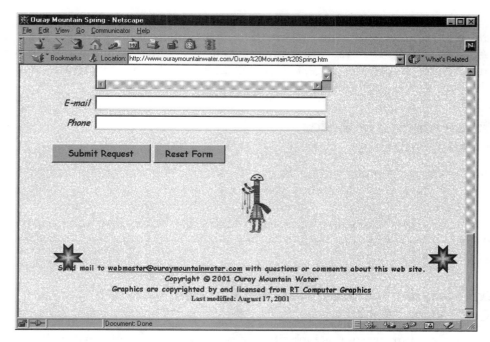

Figure 1.9   Ouray Mountain Water public Web site Product Detail page, screen 3 of 3.

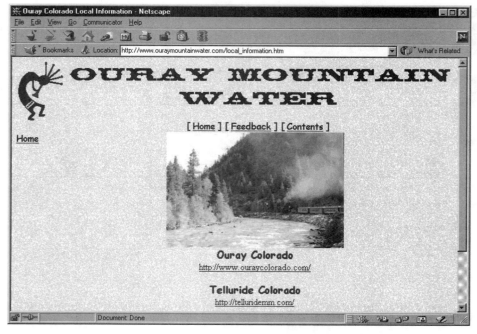

Figure 1.10   Ouray Mountain Water public Web site Local Information page.

The Feedback page presents a mechanism so users browsing the Web site can send comments or other information about different areas of the public Web site. Figures 1.11 and 1.12 show the content of Ouray Water Mountain's public Web site Feedback page. Figure 1.13 illustrates the three content areas to which users may provide feedback.

Ouray Mountain Water Private Web Sites

Ouray Mountain Water will develop two different and separate private Web sites. The employee information private Web site will contain links to company policies and procedures. It will also host Human Resource content such as forms and benefits. The second private Web site contains details about manufacturing and warehousing and is only available to employees who need access to the information.

Exploring the Company's Private Employee Information Web Site

The primary purpose of this Web site is to provide access to information that is applicable to all employees of the Ouray Mountain Water company. This Web

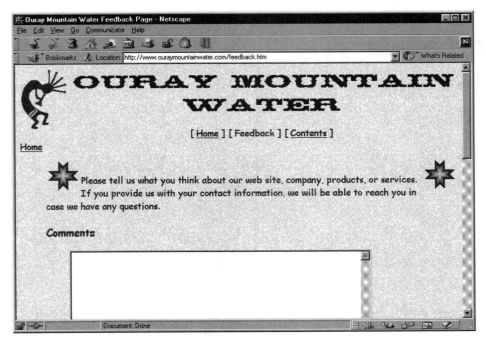

Figure 1.11   Ouray Mountain Water public Web site Feedback page, screen 1 of 2.

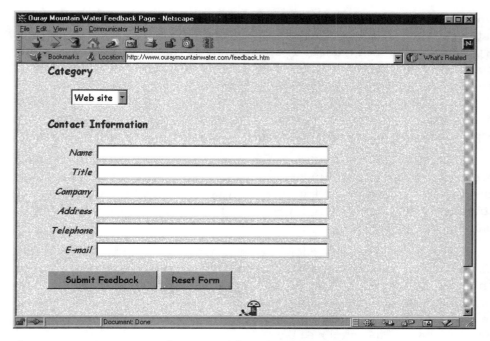

Figure 1.12   Ouray Mountain Water public Web site Feedback page, screen 2 of 2.

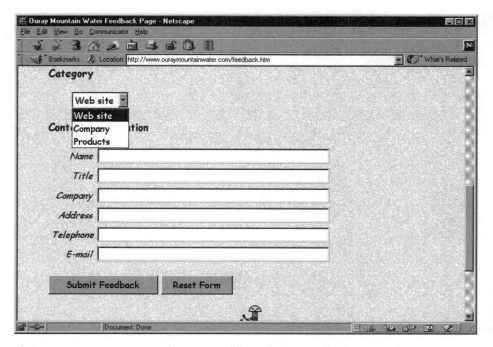

Figure 1.13   Ouray Mountain Water public Web site Feedback page selection areas.

site will be available to employees from the company's network and from the Internet. When the user attempts to access this Web site from the Internet, they will need to enter their name and password. Access to the Web site from a computer on the company's network does not require an account and password. The entire content of the Web site is contained on secure pages so the information transmitted across the Internet and Intranet is encrypted. This secure connection will slow down the Web site's response but the security is necessary, especially for an Internet connection.

The initial Welcome employee Web site page contains links to company events, information, and Human Resources. Figure 1.14 shows the initial login and password page of the employee private Web site. Figure 1.15 demonstrates the first page the employee sees after they have successfully logged onto the private Web site.

The Events page is a collection of company sponsored or endorsed events. These are organized by location and event name. When an employee clicks on an event, information about the activity is displayed on a separate details page. The Human Resource sections of the Web site gives access to pertinent information for the employee. Figure 1.16 illustrates the initial Human Resource page of the employee Web site.

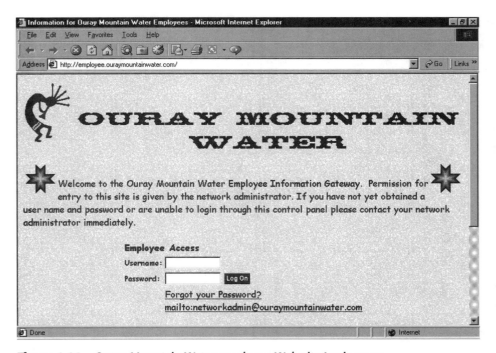

Figure 1.14   Ouray Mountain Water employee Web site Login page.

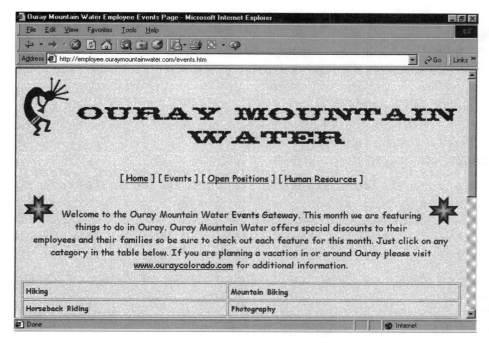

Figure 1.15   Ouray Mountain Water employee Web site Welcome page.

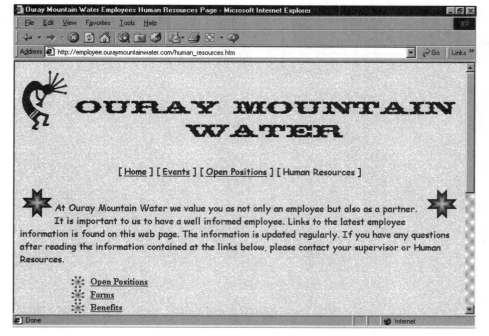

Figure 1.16   Ouray Mountain Water employee Web site Human Resource opening page.

The Open Positions section of the Web site lists any open jobs available throughout the company's locations. When the user clicks on a job entry, the job description and any other pertinent information is displayed. The employee can also find out the contact information for the open position they selected. Figures 1.17 and 1.18 illustrate samples of the Open Positions page on the employee Web site.

Exploring the Company's Intranet Manufacturing and Warehousing Web Site

The second private Web site Ouray Mountain Water will develop is for the manufacturing and warehouse departments—the Production Web server. Since the information is not needed by all employees, the initial Welcome page will contain two fields so the user can enter their name and password. Figure 1.19 shows the opening page of the Production Web site.

Once the employee has successfully logged into the Web site, the next page displays links to manufacturing and warehouses at the different locations. Figure 1.20 illustrates the Web page on the Production Web server that gives access to the manufacturing and warehouse locations.

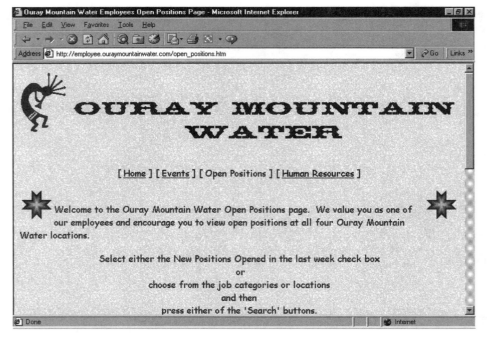

Figure 1.17   Ouray Mountain Water employee Web site Open Positions page, screen 1 of 2.

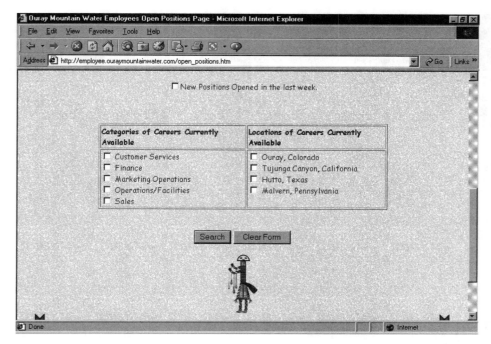

Figure 1.18   Ouray Mountain Water employee Web site Open Positions page, screen 2 of 2.

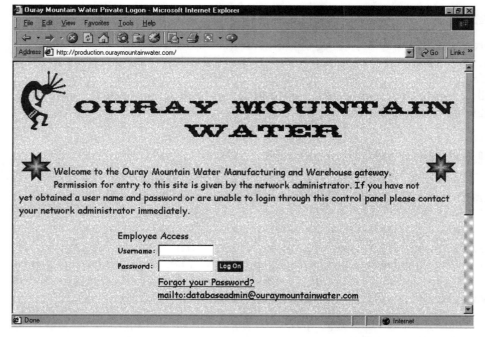

Figure 1.19   Ouray Mountain Water private Web site Welcome page for Manufacturing and Warehouses.

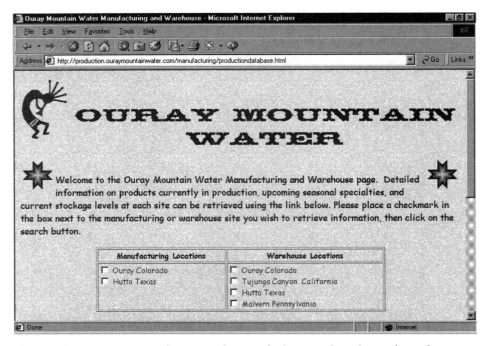

Figure 1.20 Ouray Mountain Water private Web site Manufacturing and Warehouses page.

These links will lead to additional pages that contain details about what products are currently being manufactured and the items in stock at the warehouses. These Web pages are a front end to a database that stores all the manufacturing and warehouse details. Providing a browser interface to the data allows employees to access the information without the need to install the database's client software on their machine.

Hardware Requirements

The hardware requirements for setting up your Apache Web servers are divided into two main areas. One category includes installing Apache with the operating system. For these situations, the majority of your hardware concerns revolve around the operating system needs. The second category covers installing Apache on an existing operating system or upgrading Apache from a previous version. Hopefully, in this last category, the majority of the hardware requirements have already been addressed and satisfied.

When you are installing Apache on an existing running operating system, the major hardware issues revolve around the following:

- Can the existing hardware architecture handle the addition of components when future growth requires more hardware?

- Is there sufficient disk storage space available to hold the content of the Web site? This also includes adequate space to handle anticipated growth of the Web site content.

- Is there sufficient memory to handle delivery of the Web site content to the users? This includes proper performance so the users don't get frustrated.

- Does the network card or cards have sufficient "horsepower" to handle all the incoming and outgoing requests to the Web site? Keep in mind that while the existing network cards may be managing existing traffic quite well, the question is will these cards be able to handle increases in demands? Adding additional network cards may have to be considered.

While it is difficult to predict the future and know how much your new Web sites will be used, it is important to keep in mind the ability to handle growth. This is an important consideration for installing Apache on existing systems as well as when installing the operating system and Apache. For example, your Apache Web server's network card may be quite adequate to handle today's existing activity. However, within a year or two you may need to add an additional network card. If the Web server computer has open slots to add another network card, the time it takes to add the new hardware is less than the time it takes to set up a new system, move all your data to the new system, and then reconfigure the system. The less time your Web sites are not available, the less your customers are inconvenienced.

Of course, there is always the possibility that you may need to replace all the hardware within a year or two. This may be due to the current age of your hardware and the quality of your hardware. If you decide that your current hardware is not sufficient or that it may only *last* a few more months, it may be better to make a new hardware investment before installing Apache and setting up your Web sites.

In general, for your servers, it is better to invest in server grade hardware rather than hardware designed for desktops. While it may be more expensive than a desktop system, over time, server grade hardware is a better investment. One of the typical architectural differences between server and desktop systems is the storage system. For server type systems, SCSI architecture is recommended over IDE. If you anticipate doing a lot of disk access on your Web servers then SCSI provides better performance and reliability. In addition, if you need to add more hard drives or other storage devices, you can place more devices in a SCSI system. If you anticipate running a database service, such as Oracle or MySQL, your system may have a lot of disk activity. Also, if you are considering RAID 5 for fault tolerance, most RAID 5 systems are SCSI based.

Another server hardware consideration is the architecture of the motherboard and interface cards. For server systems, PCI is recommended over ISA. Since PCI is newer then ISA, it addresses and overcomes some of the limitations of the ISA architecture. Some of these limitations include the speed of data transfer along the hardware communication channels. Most mid- to low-level systems contain PCI and ISA interface slots and you should not use any ISA cards in a server system. Some of the newer and/or higher end systems have only PCI slots and no ISA slots.

For new operating system and Apache installations, you need to take into account what the operating system needs so the server provides good performance. Then you need to consider what Apache needs and "add" that to the basic server needs. For both Linux and Windows NT/2000, there are hardware compatibility lists available on the Internet. These lists let you know what hardware has been tested and works with the operating system. Microsoft maintains hardware compatibility lists for their operating systems on their Web site (www.microsoft.com/windows2000/server/howtobuy/upgrading/compat/default.asp). Since Linux is not "owned" by anybody, there are several places that have hardware compatibility (and incompatibility) lists. One Linux hardware compatibility location is www.ibiblio.org/pub/Linux/docs/howto/Hardware-HOWTO.

In addition to typical hardware, such as the mouse, keyboard, floppy drive, CD drive (SCSI or ATAPI), and NIC (network interface card), you need to be aware of the specifications of your video system. Both Linux and Windows can get "hung up" on detecting the correct video hardware. When you are installing Windows or Linux you may need to use generic VGA settings if the video card cannot, or is not, properly detected. Before you begin installing the operating system, make a note of the type of video card you have, the amount of memory, and the supported resolutions. If your video card is "generic" or is imbedded in the motherboard, it may emulate a brand name or slot-based video card. In these cases, note the emulation or chip set information in addition to the memory and supported resolutions. Nothing is worse than when you're halfway through the install and the screen goes black because the system thinks the video is something different! In addition to the video card, make sure you know the capabilities of the video monitor. Make a note of the vertical and horizontal frequencies and the refresh rate capabilities of your monitor.

One final hardware issue to address is the backup hardware. If you plan on connecting the backup hardware to the Apache system, make sure the backup hardware is supported by the Linux or Windows 2000 operating system. In general, if the backup device is SCSI based, and was manufactured within the last two years, odds are it will work on your system. If you plan on backing up your Web site's data and/or the Linux or Windows 2000 system from another system on the network, verify that the backup software supports Linux and/or Windows 2000. In addition, make sure you are comfortable with the network connection and reliability when backing data up across the network. If your backup solution backs the data up (and restores the data) across a WAN connection, take into account the impact on the WAN traffic. Depending on how many Apache servers you have, how much Web site data there is, and if you are also backing up the operating system, there might be a significant impact on your WAN traffic. If your network experiences a lot of traffic and/or suffers from poor connections, you will probably want to attach the backup hardware to your Apache servers.

In addition to accounting for the amount of data scheduled for backup, you need to determine the best part of the day to perform the backups. If your organization is not a 24/7 facility (that is, not 24 hours a day for all seven days of the week) you will want to arrange the start and finish time of the backups to occur when there is little activity on the network and servers. Most backup programs also provide for different types of backups—full, differential and incremental. A full backup backs up all the data at every scheduled period to the selected backup storage media. A differential backup backs up the data that has changed since the last full backup. In a differential backup solution, a full backup is usually performed once a week. The incremental backup only backs up changed data since the last time data was backed up. In an incremental backup solution, a full backup is usually performed once a week. Each of these types of backups takes a different amount of time to backup the data and to restore the information. If the data does not change a lot each day then you may find an incremental or differential backup may be your preferred solution. On the other hand, if your data is constantly changing, then a full backup may be the most effective.

Now that we have discussed all of these hardware issues, how can you determine what hardware you actually have? One place to look is the documentation that came with your system. If you have recently purchased the hardware, the hardware documentation may *not* be on paper. Most current systems come with several CDs and one may contain the documentation. Hopefully, the manufacturer has placed the documentation in a cross-platform format, such as Adobe Acrobat PDF files, which can be read on either a Linux or Windows system. If the documentation is not included with your system or you cannot read the files, check out the vendor's Web site. Some computer manufacturer Web sites allow you to put in the system's serial number or asset number. When this information is entered you can usually navigate around the Web site and find the hardware specifications.

If your computer system information is not available you can find out your hardware specifications through other means. One method is to look at the current operating system running on the computer. If the system you plan on installing Linux or Windows 2000 on is already running an operating system, look at the hardware information the current operating system is using. If the computer is not currently running an operating system, observe the information on the screen as the system is powered on and look at the BIOS (Basic Input/Output System) information. You may need to step through several BIOS screens but you can find quite a bit about your hardware in the BIOS.

Once you have found all the hardware information you can about your system, write it down! Having ready access to the hardware specifications will be very handy in the future for upgrades, adding hardware, and hardware troubleshooting.

Linux

The hardware specifications for installing a basic Linux system are very small. In addition, you can use almost any type of PC hardware from an old 386 to the newest of the Pentium and related families, such as AMD (Advanced Micro Devices). The minimum amount of memory to run Linux is 2 MB but that is not realistic for an Apache server system. In addition, if you plan to run the Linux X Window or GUI (graphical user interface) system, more memory is required for this environment. For a server system to perform well and provide the necessary services, 64MB would be a starting point. Any "left-over" memory not used by the operating system and the services will be used to cache data. For production servers, you want to have relatively new hardware and plenty of memory for Linux and Apache.

Most Linux distributions are available on CD so your system will need a CDROM drive. You can start the installation from a floppy disk but after getting started the installation will need access to the Linux CD. You can install Linux over a network connection but this takes quite a bit of work and time to set-up and configure. If you have access to the Internet and a CDROM burner, you can download Linux and burn the images on CDs. Some Linux distributions can take several CDs for the operating system plus all the extra goodies. Most of the current CD delivered Linux distributions can be installed directly from the CD. If your system's hardware supports booting from a CD, make sure the system is set to boot from a CD. For IDE based systems, check the BIOS to make sure the CD is set to be the first boot device. For SCSI based systems, the default is usually set to boot from a CD if it is in the drive when the system is powered on. You will typically see a prompt and information on the screen indicating the CD was found. On SCSI systems there is usually an option to bypass booting from the CD. If your system cannot boot from a CD or the Linux installation CD cannot boot the computer, you will need access to either a Linux or UNIX system, or a DOS/Windows machine. This is necessary so you can create the installation boot floppy disk. If you have purchased Linux "in-a-box," the boot or install floppy may be included in the materials. The process for creating the boot floppy is covered in the Linux installation section later in the book (see Chapter 2, "Installing Linux and Apache").

Most current Linux distributions support either a text-based or graphical-based installation process. If you plan to use the graphical installation interface and/or will be running the X Window system on the server, you will need a mouse. Linux supports most serial and PS/2 type mice and does a very good job of detecting the type of mouse and number of buttons.

One of the areas that can give you hardware headaches is the video. In the past, many video card manufacturers did not make the hardware specifications readily available to the general public. This made it very difficult for programmers to write Linux video card drivers and whenever the manufacturer changed the specifications, existing video card drivers often did not work and had to be rewritten. More recently, the video card manufacturers have made the hardware specifications available so most current Linux distributions contain support for lots of different video cards. Also, the installation process does a good job of detecting the video hardware but it is a *really* good idea to have your video card specifications on hand in case you need to change a setting.

Related to the video card is the monitor. Again, most current Linux distributions contain support for a lot of current monitors but again, you should know your video monitor's specifications. When you are installing Linux you have the option to set the monitor's scan frequencies. Please note that if you set these values higher than what your monitor can handle you can actually physically destroy your monitor! This is a very important issue for older monitors. Newer monitors may have built into them a protection mechanism in the event there is an attempt to "overdrive" the monitor. When this happens, you may see a message on the monitor similar to "signal out of range." But, to be on the safe side, make a note of what your monitor's scan frequencies are in the event the monitor is not detected or is not listed as an available monitor.

The amount of disk space needed to install Linux can be quite small. It all depends on what you choose to install on the system. For most distributions, if you choose to install all of the software that is included on the CDs, the amount of disk space used is around 800MB to 1GB. When Apache is installed, it takes just over 4MB of disk space. In addition to the disk space used by Linux and Apache, you need to take into account the space needed for your Web site content.

Linux's development revolved around the Internet and networks. Because of this, Linux has good support for network cards and chances are Linux will support your network card if it is PCI-based.

Windows

Apache can run on Windows 95 and higher. However, for a production Web server, you will want to use either Windows NT 4 Server, Windows 2000 Server, or Windows 2000 Advanced Server. These systems are designed to support multiple connections and services. Windows 9x, Windows NT Workstation, Windows ME, and Windows 2000 Professional are primarily designed for client activities and were developed to access other servers and service providers. To get the best performance of Apache on Windows NT or Windows 2000 server systems, the computer should not be tasked with other activities or services. For example, if you install Apache on a domain controller, the operating system has to split its resources between serving Web site requests and user account authentication processing. It is recommended that you designate your Windows systems as member servers and not run other services, such as printing, on the same system.

The minimum hardware requirements for Windows 2000 Server and Windows 2000 Advanced Server are primarily the same. According to Microsoft, the minimum processor is a Pentium 133 but in reality a much faster and Pentium III type processor or greater is needed. The minimum memory is 128MB but Microsoft recommends 256MB to start with. Once again, more memory is really needed in the neighborhood of 512MB or higher. The amount of disk space to install Windows 2000 Server or Advanced Server is 2GB with 1GB of free space. One disk space consideration to keep in mind is the swap file that Windows automatically creates when you install the operating system. In general, the size of the swap file is the same as the amount of memory, so make sure you have enough disk space to hold the operating system plus the swap file. When you install Apache on the Windows system, it takes about 4MB of storage space. Then on top of these disk space requirements, add on the size of your Web site content.

A CDROM drive is required to install Windows 2000 Server and Advanced Server. The installation CDs are bootable so if your computer can boot to a CD, you can start off the installation directly from the CD. If your system cannot boot from a CD, you will need to boot the system from a DOS based disk that contains CDROM drivers. Note that if you use a pre-Windows 95-based DOS, such as DOS 6.22, the size of the initial disk partition you create will be limited to 2GB. If you want to make this larger, use a version of DOS that supports larger partition sizes. Microsoft does indicate that Windows 2000 can be installed across the network. Similar to the Linux network install, it takes quite a bit of time and expertise to set-up network installations.

Since Windows installations are graphical, a mouse is needed to perform the installation. Both PS/2 and serial mice are supported by Windows 2000. Video is also an important issue because once Windows is installed, a graphical interface is always present. If your video card and monitor are relatively current, odds are Windows 2000 will support your hardware. If you are not sure your video card is supported, take a look at the video card manufacturer's Web site to determine if Windows 2000 supports the video hardware.

Windows 2000 supports a number of PCI network cards. To verify the compatibility of your NIC, check out Microsoft's hardware compatibility list or the vendor of the network card's Web site.

Software Requirements

Apache on Linux and Windows does not have many software requirements but there are a few items to consider. Your Apache Web server must have IP (Internet Protocol) functioning on the network card(s) that will be used to accept incoming requests. Furthermore, the IP number(s) for your Web server(s) should be manually assigned and NOT configured using DHCP (Dynamic Host Configuration Protocol). If DHCP is used to delivery the IP address(es) to your Apache servers, the next time the server is restarted or the current IP address is released and renewed, the system may receive a different IP address. You would then need to find all the places the old IP address was specified and change them to the current IP address. This will also create additional work to change DNS server configuration. The administrator would need to go into the DNS server records and change any entries with the old IP address to the current IP address. This change would then need to "populate" to the other DNS servers on the Internet. In the meantime, some users would be able to get to your Web site and other users would not. DDNS or Dynamic DNS can help alleviate some of these issues by allowing the DNS records to update automatically when a change occurs. However, this does not help in situations where other services or users are looking for a device by its IP address instead of by its name. To prevent these types of headaches, it is recommended that you manually assign IP numbers to your Apache servers (and all servers) and not use DHCP. Note that for some Linux distributions and Windows systems, DHCP is the default for the IP configuration. In both platforms, you can choose not to use DHCP at installation time or later.

Another important factor that can affect the server's software performance is time. You want to make sure the time on your servers is correct so any software that uses timestamps to track events is accurate. Databases and accounting software typically use time to mark events and activities. If you anticipate running software such as MySQL with your Apache Web server, you'll want to make sure the time on the server is reliable and accurate. You can configure both Linux and Windows 2000 systems to use external time sources to maintain an accurate system clock. There are many publicly accessible time servers on the Internet that you can use to synchronize time on your systems.

Linux

You can run a Linux and Apache system entirely from the command line without using the X Window system or graphical interface. However, if you do plan to use X, you'll want to make sure the mouse and video are configured properly. These can be configured when you install Linux or they can be setup after the Linux system is up and running. Also, if you plan on supporting a graphical interface, make sure you have sufficient memory and processor speed so the other services on the system, such as Apache, are not affected by launching the X Window environment.

Windows

On the Windows platform, Apache is designed to run on Window NT 4 Server, Windows 2000 Server, or Windows 2000 Advanced Server. Apache's configuration and functions are the same on these different Windows platforms. However, there are some issues to keep in mind based on the operating system you are using. For Windows NT 4, Service Pack 3 or 6 is recommended. Service Pack 4 has problems with the TCP/IP WinSock which have been fixed in newer Service Packs. If you will be using Apache 1.3.7 or later, WinSock 2 is required. Throughout the remainder of this book, we will be using Windows 2000 Server for the Apache Windows servers.

Windows 2000 Server installation requires a CDROM drive and the system is capable of booting from the CD. The installation process does not include the ability to create a floppy boot installation disk. However, if you have another Windows system, such as Windows 98, you can create a floppy system boot disk. This boot floppy allows you to startup the computer and contains drivers to access an IDE CDROM drive. If you are using SCSI on your Apache server, you may need to add the SCSI CDROM drivers to the floppy system boot disk.

Apache is best run as a service on Windows NT 4 and Windows 2000 server systems. This allows Apache to keep running when you logout of Windows 2000 or NT 4. In addition, when the system is rebooted, Apache will startup automatically without the need for user intervention. You can also start Apache from a command window instead of running it as a service. This is useful for testing your Apache configuration but it is not recommended to use this method when you release the Web server for production use. If you start Apache from a command window, whenever the current account logs off the machine, the Web server is shut down. Also, if the machine is restarted, the Apache server will not load automatically. Note: Depending on how the software is coded and the syntax of the command used to start the service, a service launched at a command line can remain running when the user logs off and it can be restarted automatically when the system reboots.

Storage Space Requirements

Apache uses very little disk space to store its components. Installing Apache on Linux and Windows takes about 4MB. As you begin to add content to your Web server, additional space will be needed. You do have the option to separate your Web content from the Apache operating files. This is recommended when you expect the Web content to be large and/or change frequently.

Both Linux and Windows operating systems can be installed on one physical disk or across multiple drives. For multiple disk environments, make sure the first drive and partition is large enough to hold the operating system files. In addition, verify that you have adequate free space to store updates and patches you add to the system.

Linux and Windows 2000 use swap space and virtual memory to allow more applications to run. Windows 2000 uses a swap file or files for virtual memory. In order to run properly, the size of the swap file should be the same or slightly larger than the amount of physical memory in the system. You can place the swap file across different partitions but this will decrease the performance of your system. Linux can use either swap partitions or swap files. The preferred method is a swap partition or partitions because the system is more efficient accessing a file system designed specifically for swapping data between memory and disk space. Maintaining a swap file introduces the overhead of the file system optimized for working with files rather than swapped memory content. The recommended size of the Linux swap partition is equivalent to the amount of memory in your system. However, on systems with a lot of physical memory you will not need a large swap partition. For example, a system with 500MB or more physical memory will not need to have a 500MB or larger swap partition.

How and Where Do You Get Apache and the Documentation?

Most Linux distributions that include Apache also contain the Apache documentation. On some distributions, the installation process will add a shortcut or link to the documentation on the vendor's Web site or the Apache Software Foundation's Web site. If your Linux distribution does not include Apache or you want to use a different version than what is included in your bundle, Apache and the documentation can be downloaded from the Internet.

Both the Linux and Windows versions of Apache can be obtained from the Apache Software Foundation's Web site at www.apache.org. The size of the download is only a few megabytes in size and typically includes the documentation.

How and Where Do You Get Apache Add-Ons and the Documentation?

Many of the add-ons for Apache are listed on the Apache Software Foundation's Web site, www.apache.org. Their Web site contains links to the vendor or the developer of the add-on product. Note that, at this point in time, most of the add-on products are designed for the Linux environment since the primary operating system for Apache is Linux. However, as Apache on Windows grows, there will probably be more add-on products for the Windows operating systems.

Installing Linux and Apache

In this chapter, we cover installing Apache on a new Linux system and an existing system. For a new Linux system, we discuss the basic Linux installation steps. Depending on the Linux distribution you are using, the installation interface may be different. However, whatever Linux distribution you decide to use, the installation and configuration of Apache is the same.

Some Linux distributions offer a graphical installation and others do not. For example, RedHat, Caldera, and Corel all have the option to use a graphical installation interface but others, like Debian, do not include a graphical interface installation option. All Linux distributions support a text or command line installation interface. Some of the text or command interfaces probe for hardware and use, or suggest, default settings and options while others do not do hardware probing or install default components. Throughout this book, we use the RedHat 7.1 Linux distribution for the Linux based Apache Web servers. In addition, we use the command line or text interface by default. We chose this method because most Linux servers do not have the X Window or GUI environment installed. If you do have the GUI environment installed, some applications and their configurations can be accomplished using the X Window system.

How Can I Tell if I Already Have Apache Running?

Apache runs as a process in the Linux operating system. If you are logged into the Linux system, one of the quickest ways to determine if Apache is already running is to check the currently running processes. The ps command with the –e parameter will display a list of all running processes. If the results fill more than one screen, you can use the more option with the ps command. For example:

```
ps -e | more
```

The process for the Apache Web server is:

```
httpd
```

There may be several instances of this process running. That is "okay" and "normal" and we will cover these details later in the book.

Another mechanism to determine if Apache is running is to see if you can access the Web server from a browser. In the URL area of a browser, either on the Linux system or from another system that can communicate with the Linux server, enter in the IP address of the Linux system. For example, if the Linux system's IP address is 172.16.3.2, enter the following in the browser's URL field:

```
http://172.16.3.2
```

If the Apache Web server is running and it has been configured properly, you should see the default Apache Web page. Figure 2.1 is an example of a default Apache Web server page.

What Version Am I Running and Do I Need to Upgrade?

On Linux systems, you can very easily determine the version of Apache that is running. At a command prompt (terminal window) enter in the following:

```
httpd -v
```

The output will indicate the version of Apache that is running and the date and time the Linux server operating system was compiled or "built."

If you are using RedHat or another distribution that uses RPM (RedHat Package Manager) you can enter the following at a command prompt:

```
rpm -q apache
```

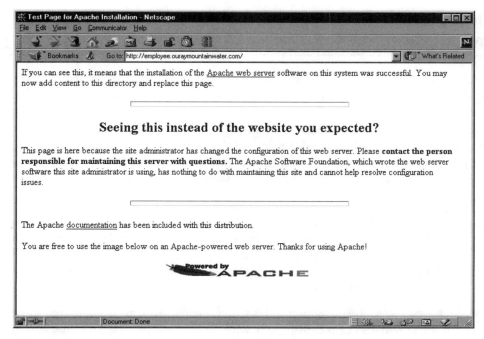

Figure 2.1   Sample Apache Web server default Web page.

The –q option performs a query of the RMP database for the package specified. The RPM command's output will display the version of Apache that is running. For more verbose feedback, use the following:

```
rpm -qi apache
```

Keep in mind that whoever assembled the RMP file determines where the various Apache files and components are placed in your system. To determine where the files are, use the following rpm command:

```
rpm -ql apache | more
```

The –l option lists all the files in the package and their locations.

In addition to the major release number, e.g., 1.3, a minor release number is also indicated. Ideally, you will want to use the latest minor release number. As of August 2001, the current minor release number was 20. If you are using version 1.2 or earlier, consider upgrading Apache to version 1.3. The Apache FAQ (Frequently Asked Questions) is a good reference for differences and changes between Apache 1.3 and earlier versions (http://httpd.apache.org/docs/misc/FAQ.html).

Downloading and Locating the Apache Installation Files

The Apache installation files can be downloaded from the Internet at the Apache Software Foundation's Web site, www.apache.org. If your Linux distribution included Apache, you can install the software from the Linux distribution CDs. However, instead of hunting for the software on the Linux CDs, you may want to go ahead and download the software. This will also give you the latest released version of the software. Even for recent Linux packaged or downloaded distributions, the Apache software may not be the latest.

Some Linux distributions use software managers as a mechanism to install and update software. One popular tool used by RedHat and others is RPM or RedHat Package Manager. This tool has both a command line and graphical (X Window) interface. The first task that must be accomplished is to locate the Apache RPM file. Search for a file that begins with apache and ends with .rpm on your Linux installation media.

Apache can also be downloaded as a binary (application) and installed without the need to compile the software. You can find the Apache binary packages at http://httpd.apache.org/dist/httpd/binaries/linux.

The third way Apache software is bundled contains all the source code and documentation. These are compressed files where the name contains the version of Apache. For example, the file labeled apache_1.3.10.tar.gz is Apache 1.3.20.

Installing Linux and Apache at the Same Time

Most Linux distributions include Apache and it can be installed at the same time you install Linux. Some Linux installations have the option of choosing the role of the Linux system. Typically, these include categories such as Workstation, Server, and Custom. The Workstation choice is designed for Linux systems that will be accessing and using services. Typically, this installation option will install the X Window environment and user type applications. The Workstation choice does not install services, such as FTP, DNS, and Apache, and is not recommended for a Linux Apache Web server. The Server option typically does not install the X Window system but does install services such as FTP, DNS, Apache, and others. This is a good choice for a basic server system without the graphical environment. The Custom option allows you to choose exactly what applications and services you want to install. Most administrators prefer this option since it gives them the greatest flexibility.

Whatever choice you decide to use, you can always add or remove applications and services at a later time.

Another installation option to consider is whether to use the text or graphical installation interface. The text install usually takes less time than the graphical interface. In addition, if Linux has trouble detecting your video environment or selects the incorrect settings, you may not be able to use the graphical interface. As an example, in this section, RedHat 7.1 Linux and Apache are installed at the same time using the text interface method.

RedHat 7.1 Linux can be installed directly from the CD or from a floppy disk and the CD. Whether you boot the system from the floppy disk or the CD, the installation process is the same. The first installation screen displays the different ways you can install Linux. The available choices are:

graphical. This is the default and if you don't type anything, the installation will start automatically using this mode. The graphical installation uses 16-bit color, 800 × 600 resolution, and a video framebuffer.

text. This interface uses the keyboard. The mouse and the graphical interface are not used. If you are not sure about the compatibility of your system's video architecture, you should choose the text option.

lowres. A graphical installation that uses 640 × 480 resolution. If you are attempting to use the default graphical installation but the system cannot handle 800 × 600 resolution, try the lowres option.

nofb. This disables framebuffer mode in the graphical installation. If you are attempting to use the default graphical installation but the system cannot use a framebuffer, try the nofb choice.

expert. This installation does not use autoprobing to determine the hardware. The expert option gives you complete control but you must know all the hardware specifications. This option allows you to include additional modules.

linux rescue. This can be used when your installed Linux system does not boot properly. This option gives you access to many utilities and tools for recovery.

linux dd. Use this choice if you have a separate driver disk (dd).

To start the text installation interface, type text at the prompt. A "mini" version of Linux is loaded and the system starts the process of detecting the hardware.

The Language Selection screen allows you to specify the language of your Linux system. English (US) is the default and there are many available languages to choose from. The Keyboard Selection window allows you to specify the keyboard attached to the system. The default is US and there are many keyboard configurations supported by Linux. The next screen, Welcome, contains generic information including where to obtain help about Linux.

The next screen allows you to choose the role of you Linux system. The Installation Type window provides five options:

- Workstation
- Server System
- Laptop
- Custom System
- Upgrade Existing Installation

For our example in this chapter, the Custom System installation type is selected. The next configuration area is the layout of your disk partitions. Two options are available in the Automatic Partition screen:

Continue. This will automatically erase any existing Linux partitions. If Workstation installation type was selected earlier, this will remove any existing Linux partitions. If Server System was selected earlier, this will remove ALL partitions of any type.

Manually Partition. This allows you to specify the partitions and file system types on your disks.

For our example installation in this chapter, Manually Partition is selected. This choice then advances to the Partition screen.

Two tools are available to partition the disk space, Disk Druid and fdisk. Disk Druid uses a text screen interface to create partitions. fdisk is a command line utility and requires more experience to use than Disk Druid. For our example in this section, Disk Druid is selected. In Disk Druid, to create a partition, choose the Add option. In the Edit New Partition screen, enter in the name of the mount point, the size of the partition, and the type of partition. When you create the swap partition, a mount point is not specified. After you create the partitions, the next step is to format the new partitions. The Filesystem Formatting screen gives you the option to verify your media. If you are using relatively new and reliable drives, the verification option is probably not necessary.

After you create and format your partitions, the next installation screen is LILO Configuration. LILO or LInux LOader, is a program that uses a configuration file or settings to install a system boot loader. If you have any special settings that need to be used to create the boot loader program, you can specify those items in the LILO Configuration screen. In most cases you will not need to specify anything for LILO Configuration and you can continue onto the next step. The system boot loader can be installed on the MBR or Master Boot

Record of your start up disk drive. It can also be installed on the first sector of the boot partition. This option may be necessary if you will be installing multiple operating systems on the same storage devices and the other operating systems use a different boot loader. For our Linux Apache Web servers, they will only be running Linux so the boot loader will be placed on the MBR. The next LILO Configuration option specifies what other operating systems the Linux boot loader can load. Again, since the Apache Web servers will only have Linux installed, there will only be one operating system listed. The operating system is given a boot label name. If you don't like the label the installation process suggests, edit the label and enter the label you prefer. Otherwise, just accept the defaults and continue on.

The next installation step is Network Configuration. The Network Configuration screen allows you to specify the method of IP address assignment to your network card or cards. It is highly recommended that you DO NOT use DHCP to deliver the information to your Linux server. Instead, enter in the "permanent" IP address, subnet mask (netmask), default gateway, and nameserver(s) for the network card.

The Hostname Setup area allows you to give a name to your Web servers. This name, along with the domain name, will typically be used by users to access your Web site. The hostname should reflect the functional identity of the Web server. For example, the name of the public Web server for Ouray Mountain Water will be www. This way users can enter in www.ouraymountainwater.com and go right to the Web site. In addition, most browsers default to a www in front of the domain name if the user just enters the name of the domain. Note that the hostname is just the name of the Web server and does not include the domain name.

RedHat 7.1 includes a Firewall Configuration screen that allows you to specify a security level. Since Ouray Mountain Water will be using a separate firewall system to protect their systems, we will choose No firewall at the Firewall Configuration screen.

The next area is the Mouse Configuration. Even if you do not plan on using the X Window system, the mouse can be used in some text interface utilities. The Mouse Configuration options allow you to specify the type of mouse, the number of buttons, and if you want to emulate three buttons for a two button mouse. For serial mouse, the Mouse Configuration may ask you to specify the communication's port for the mouse. Once you have made your selections, continue with the installation.

The Language Support area defaults to USA English. However, Linux includes a lot of support for different languages' time and date configurations. Choose the appropriate language for your system.

The Time Zone Setup screen allows you to specify the time zone for the server and if the computer's system clock is set to GMT. Most new Linux installs do not use GMT for the hardware clock.

Once you have specified your system's time zone, the Root Password selection is next. Make sure to use a unique and not-easy-to-figure-out password for the root account. This is very important because the root account has access to everything on the system and can do anything to the system.

After you specify the root account's password, you have the option to add other user accounts. During installation it is a good idea to create at least one additional account for yourself. You can create other accounts at this time or later. At the Authentication settings screen, it is recommended that you choose to Use Shadow Passwords and Enable MD5 Passwords. Both of these provide more security for password storage and password length.

In our example installation for this chapter, we chose Custom so the next area to configure is Package Groups. If you chose a Workstation or Server type system, you will not encounter the Package Groups installation screen. Linux categorizes applications and tools into product groups called packages. For our Linux Apache Web server, we will not install much besides the Web server so the system resources are dedicated to servicing browser requests and not other tasks. If you plan on compiling Apache, the operating system, or any other software component, make sure you include the development tools and environment. These will not use any additional resources other than consumption of disk space. Depending on the packages you have selected, you may get one or more Package Dependencies screens. These usually pop up when a package you have selected has components it needs in another package that you have not selected to install. So that everything runs correctly, it is highly suggested that you choose the option to Install packages to satisfy dependencies.

If you have decided to install the X Window system, the installation process will attempt to probe your video card for you. If the probed results are correct, you can accept what the X Configuration screen displays and continue on.

The Installation Begins screen mentions a log of the installation process is placed on the system. The installation process creates a log file which can be examined after installation. If you encounter a problem during installation, the log file may help determine the cause of the problem. The Installation Begins screen indicates the location of the log file which is typically in the /tmp directory. The name of the log file is called something like install.log. This phase of the installation may take several minutes. The overall time depends on the number of packages you have selected and the system's hardware.

After all the items have been installed, the procedure goes through a post install process. This includes the option to create a boot disk. It is highly recommended that you create a custom boot disk for each Linux system you are installing. After the boot disk is created, the installation process will attempt to probe for your monitor if you selected earlier to install the X Window environment. If the settings match your monitor you can proceed to the next step. If the probed values do not match your monitor, make the appropriate changes. Remember, do *not* enter any values that are outside the capability of your monitor. If you do, you risk the possibility of physically destroying your monitor. The next few screens will display probed values for the video card's RAM and clockchip value (if needed). Finally, you will be presented with a screen to select the color depth and resolution. You can choose several values but make sure they are within the capabilities of your video card. After you make these selections, the Xconfigurator application will attempt to start the X Window environment using the settings you have specified. If all works out okay, you will see a confirmation dialog box and another to choose if you want to start the Linux system up in X. It is recommended for a Linux server system that you do not start the computer up into graphical mode.

The final step is to reboot the new Linux system.

Installing Apache on an Existing Linux System

Apache can be installed easily and quickly on an existing Linux system. In addition, there are several different ways you can install Apache which range from the "easy and quick" to the "more involved but customized" flavors. If you are already familiar with compiling Linux applications then the "more involved but customized" method may not be all that involved!

Preparing to Install Apache

Before you plunge into installing Apache on a system that is currently running and providing services to users, there are a few things you need to do. First, make sure you have a current backup of the system. We don't expect the Apache installation process to "break" anything but whenever you plan on making a change to the system, it is always a good idea to have a recent backup of all the data, important applications, and the operating system. If you have never installed a Linux application before, you may want to set up an "experimental" Linux system to practice on. Once you are comfortable with the process, you can then move on to the "real" Linux servers.

A second item to consider is the impact of the Apache installation process on the system's resources. Apache can be launched and unloaded without the need to bring down the Linux system or stop other services. If you decide to compile Apache, the compiler will use CPU and memory resources so make sure the system is not already using a lot of CPU or memory resources. If it is, you should consider doing the compilation process during times when the system is not heavily used.

Basic/Typical Apache Installation Details

Apache can be installed several different ways. One method uses the RedHat Package Manager (RPM). If your Linux distribution uses or supports RPM you can install the version of Apache included on the Linux installation CDs. Once you have located the Apache RPM file, change to the directory where the RPM file is stored, and run the rpm command. For example, to install Apache version 1.3.20, execute the following at a command prompt or terminal window:

```
rpm -iv apache-1.3.20.i386.rpm
```

If you are installing a different version or the name of the package file is different, use the correct name of the file in the rpm command. The -i option indicates install and the -v option gives verbose feedback so you can see what is happening. Once the rpm process has installed Apache you can immediately start the Web server. Navigate to the directory where the httpd application is located. Then execute the following:

```
./httpd start
```

You will receive a message that the server name is not defined and 127.0.0.1 will be used as the server name. This is okay for now. Later in this chapter we will cover how to "fix" this. Even with this message, you can still browse your Web server on the same machine. If you have installed X Window on the system, start up the GUI and load Netscape or whatever Web browser you prefer. In the location or URL field, go to:

```
http://127.0.0.1
```

You should see the default opening page for the new Apache server you have just installed. If you don't have the X Window system installed, the system may have a text Web browser, such as lynx, available. For those browsers, use the URL address 127.0.0.1 to view the default page of your new Web server.

If you are not using RPM, there are two other ways to install Apache. One method is to download the Apache binary or application. This option includes a precompiled Apache file using all of the default components or modules. It also includes all of the source code and directions in case you would like to recompile the Apache binary. However, keep in mind that the latest, current version of Apache may not be available in binary package format. For example, as of August 2001, version 1.3.14 was the latest version of an Apache binary bundle you could download. Note that some of the Linux distributions available in August 2001 include newer versions of Apache. Before you decide to opt for the binary package, make sure you are comfortable with the version of Apache contained in the binary.

The remaining installation method involves compiling the Apache source code. If you have never compiled code before...*don't* worry! It is not as bad as it may seem. In fact, you can immediately compile the code after you have downloaded it without having to modify any of the configuration files. You do though have the ability to edit the compilation configuration files so the Apache you compile is customized for your system and services. However, to compile Apache you do have some requirements to satisfy.

Compiling code takes additional disk space because you have both the source code and the resultant Apache binary and associated files to account for. Make sure you have at least 12MB of free disk space available. About 7MB to 8MB is the size of the source files and all supporting elements. The remaining 3MB to 4MB is the size of the compiled Apache binary and files you will generate. If you decide to customize your Apache compilation and include additional modules, such as some of the Apache add-ons, you may need additional disk space.

The second requirement involves the compiler used to create the Apache binary. Make sure you have an ANSI-C compiler installed in your system. Most of the software development for UNIX and Linux is done in C or C++. The default, standard Linux compiler in most distributions is gcc (GNU C Compiler). gcc is a very powerful and advanced compiler. It supports the ANSI C standard as well as all the modern C standards currently in use. In addition to being a C compiler, gcc can also handle C++ and Objective-C. You also need to make sure you have a minimal version of gcc. To check what version of gcc your system uses, execute the following:

```
gcc -v
```

Make sure you are using 2.72 or higher. Some Linux distributions also include egcs. egcs is based on gcc and one of egcs' major advantages is its support of newer C++ features.

To compile a program into a Linux executable involves several steps. Here we will present a brief overview so you have an idea what is going on when you compile Apache or any other Linux application including the kernel itself. The first thing is the file or files that contain the source code—the programming language instructions. The source code files are text files created with a text editor such as vi. To make sure the gcc compiler can recognize the source code files, the name of the files must have .c at the end. For example, http_main.c, is one of the source code files for Apache. Next, an object file must be generated by the compiler from the source code file. The contents of the object file are the machine code commands that correspond to the C commands in the source code. To distinguish a source code file from an object code file, a .o is used at the end of an object code file name. For example, the compiler would create a http_main.o object code file from the http_main.c source code file.

The next step in the process is to link the object files created by the compiler with the appropriate pieces of code from the library files on the system. Libraries consist of collections of object files that define actions and functions that are common to many programs. So, instead of every programmer writing code for the same action, a common repository for these code "pieces" is located in the libraries. Libraries come in two forms, static and shared. For static libraries, the linker places a copy of the library code with the object files of the application you are building. In a shared library structure, the linker places a piece of "stub" code in your application that references the shared library code. Essentially, what this stub code is doing is telling your compiled application to use the code in the shared library. Using shared libraries provides more flexibility when a new release or update of the libraries is available. To use the new features in the shared libraries, you do not need to recompile the application. If static libraries are used, you will need to recompile the code if you want to take advantage of the newer elements in the libraries. Once the linker, which is actually a separate application (ld), has finished its actions, you will have an executable application.

Many applications, including Apache, are built from different source files. If you were to manually compile each source file one step at a time, whenever you changed any one of the files, you would need to recompile all of the files all over again. A much more efficient way would be to recompile only the changed source code files and then have the linker link the new object files with the unchanged object files. This method is available on Linux by using a project manager called make. make uses makefiles, which specify how an application is built and uses time stamps to decide which source files have been changed. The syntax of a makefile can be a bit of a challenge for the new, but fortunately, most applications that you'll compile come with a makefile. Now that we have a little bit of background about compiling Linux applications, lets go ahead and compile Apache.

The first way to compile Apache is to use a "pre-built" process called APACI (Apache 1.3 Autoconf-style Interface). APACI is relatively new and is basically a batch configuration interface that allows you to compile and build Apache quickly and without the need to modify any files. Using this, you can build your new Apache in a matter of minutes and with all the default features and functions available. The first thing you need to do is decide where in the file system you want the Apache files to reside. Some suggested locations for applications that will be used by more than one user are the /usr or /var directories. For our example, we will use the directory /usr/local/apache. The next task is to decompress the Apache file you downloaded or copied to your system. You can use gunzip to decompress the downloaded Apache file. For example, if the file were called apache_1.3.20.tar.gz, the syntax of gunzip would be:

```
gunzip apache_1.3.20.tar.gz
```

The result of the gunzip command generates a tarfile (tarball) of the same name without the .gz extension. For our example, the tarball created is called apache_1.3.20.tar. The next step is to extract the contents of the tarball with the tar command. For example,

```
tar -xvf apache_1.3.20.tar
```

The tar command creates a directory with the same name as the tarball file without the .tar at the end of the name. Inside the directory are files and subdirectories that contain all the source code and necessary elements to compile into the executable Apache application. The next step in the process is to run configure, a script, which defines the compilation environment and settings. But, before we begin the actual compilation lets take a look at where the compilation process will place the various Apache files. Executing the configure script with the show-layout option displays the directory structure:

```
./configure --show-layout | more
```

It is important to know where the files that Apache uses are located. You can change these locations by modifying the configure script. However, successfully changing the configure script is *not* an easy task if you have never done it before!

Now, let's go ahead and run the configure script which is located in the directory that contains the extracted files from the tar command.

```
./configure
```

Processing the script should not take too long. You will notice the informational output of the script indicates several makefiles were generated and which C compiler will be used. The next step is to run the make command:

```
make
```

The make application indicates on the screen what it is doing and you will get several pages of information. Depending on the hardware, the make application may take several minutes to complete. Now you can install Apache by executing:

```
make install
```

After a few seconds, an informational "screen" appears indicating that you should check the Apache configuration file. Based on our example, using the /usr/local/apache directory, the Apache configuration file is located in:

```
/usr/local/apache/conf/httpd.conf
```

In addition, the information "screen" indicates the command to get the Web server running. For our example, using the /usr/local/apache directory, to launch the Web server you would execute:

```
/usr/local/apache/bin/apachectl start
```

apachectl is an Apache control script that can be used to control Apache. Go ahead and try it and see what happens! You'll receive a message saying it could not determine the server's fully qualified domain name so for the time being it is using 127.0.0.1 as the server name. Later in this chapter we will cover how to change the name of the server so you can access the Web server from another machine. For now, if you have installed the X Window system on the Linux system where you have just compiled Apache, go into the GUI and launch a Web browser such as Netscape. Enter the following into the location (URL) area of the Web browser:

```
http://127.0.0.1
```

You should see the default Web page included with Apache. If your system does not have the X Window system installed, your system may include a text browser such as lynx. Specify the URL address of 127.0.0.1 in the text Web browser and you should see the default Apache Web server opening page. Congratulations! You have compiled Apache, installed Apache, and now have a running Web server.

The APACI process we have just covered addresses the "quick and easy" way to compile Apache by accepting all the defaults. If you don't want to use the defaults, then you will need to edit some of the files before starting the process. A good place to start is to read and review the contents of the README.configure file. This file is located in the directory where you extracted the files with the tar command. This will help you understand the sections of the configure script. Once you are comfortable with compiling and installing Apache using the "quick and easy" way, you may want to begin experimenting and customizing the compilation process.

NOTE Make sure you always retain a copy of any files you modify in case you need to go back to the way things were before you started "experimenting!"

Upgrading an Existing Apache System

A newer version of Apache can be installed on a Linux system that already has Apache running. Since the server may be hosting Web sites, it is very important that you consider the impact of changing the engine behind your Web sites. If possible, you may want to set up a separate experimental Linux system and test the effects of upgrading Apache. Once you are satisfied with what the upgrade process will involve, you can then move to the "real" production Web server.

Preparing to Upgrade Apache

One of the most important items to take into account is the Web site content. You want to make sure that the upgrade process does NOT remove or replace any of your Web content. Thus, it is very important that you have a recent, reliable backup of your Web site. Secondly, the Web service will need to be shutdown while you switch to the new Apache. Of course, if any users are currently browsing the Web site, stopping the Apache server will abruptly stop the ability of the users to access the Web site!

In order not to interfere with the current Web site, it is typically suggested you install the newer or different version of Apache in a different file system location. This also allows you to switch back and forth between the new and the old in the event there is a problem. In addition, if you have specified your Linux system to automatically start up the Web server when the Linux system is started, you may need to make the appropriate changes to use the new Apache engine.

In addition to the above-mentioned items, keep in mind that if you decide to compile Apache, the compilation process will use some of your system's resources. Although the compilation process is short, it will use CPU and memory resources. Make sure you are comfortable with the effects of compiling on an active, service-providing system.

Once you have all your preparation tasks accomplished, install the new version of Apache using whatever method you prefer—RPM, binary, or compilation.

Required Minimal Configuration Necessary for the Web Server to Work

If you have just installed and/or launched Apache for the first time, you may receive a message that the server name was not defined and 127.0.0.1 is being used. While 127.0.0.1 is a legal IP address that refers to the local machine, it is not very practical to keep this name because users on other systems would not be able to access the Web server. All that needs to be done is to specify the name of the Web server in the Web server's configuration file. The configuration file is called httpd.conf and is located in a directory called conf in the location where Apache is installed. For example, if Apache is installed in the directory /usr/local/apache, the httpd.conf file would be in the /usr/local/apache/conf directory. Note that if Apache was installed at the same time you installed Linux, the location of the httpd.conf file may be different. For example, with RedHat 7.1, httpd.conf is located in the /etc/httpd/conf directory. The httpd.conf is a long file and the details of this file are covered in Chapter 4, "Apache Architecture."

Open the httpd.conf file with your favorite text editor and look for a line that begins with:

```
#ServerName
```

After the ServerName entry, there may be the address 127.0.0.1 or the hostname of your Linux system. To set a valid ServerName, remove the pound sign (#) at the beginning of the line and enter the name of your Web server. The name of the Web server is what users will enter, along with the name of your domain, in the URL field in their Web browser. For example, if the Web server is the public Web server for Ouray Mountain Water, then the name of the Web server would be www. This way users can put www.ouraymountainwater.com in their Web browsers and go to the Web site for the Ouray Mountain Water company.

> **NOTE**   Enter just the name of the Web server and do not include the domain name for ServerName in the httpd.conf file. Otherwise users would need to put in www.ouraymountainwater.com.ouraymountainwater.com as the URL. Not too friendly! In addition, make sure any DNS servers that contain the address of your Web server are appropriately updated.

Once you have made the adjustment in the httpd.conf file, you will need to restart the Web server. If the server was loaded using the httpd command, you can restart the service with the command:

```
./httpd restart
```

If you have used the apachectl command to start the server then the command would be:

```
./apachectl restart
```

Now you should be able to access the Web server from another machine by entering in the name of the Web server followed by the domain name. If the DNS servers have not been updated to reflect the name of the Web server, you can put the IP number of the Web server in the URL field of your browser.

Managing and Setting Up User Accounts

When Apache is started, it runs as a service using a user account. When Apache is installed with the Linux operating systems, the distribution may create an account and group for the Apache server. For example, installing Apache while installing RedHat 7.1 creates a user account called apache and a group called apache. The apache user account is a member of the group apache and the Apache Web services runs under the user account apache. Using a unique user account and/or group for the Apache server is helpful if you ever have a security issue and you are tracking which user account affected the system. If you have configured and installed Apache from the source code, typically the Apache server runs as the user nobody which is a member of the group nobody. It is not a good idea to keep the user as nobody because other processes may use the same user account and it makes it difficult, if not impossible, to determine which nobody affected the Web server. You can change the name of the account and group either when you compile the server or in the httpd.conf file. To change the name of the account and group before you compile the Apache source code you will need to edit the configure script. Add the following text where, in this example, apache is the name of the user and group:

```
--server-uid=apache
--server-gid=apache
```

If you have already compiled Apache, find the two lines in the httpd.conf file that contain:

```
User nobody
Group nobody
```

Change the nobody to the name of the account and group you have decided to use for Apache. Make sure the account and group are already created in the system. Once you make the change to the httpd.conf file, you will need to restart the Web server.

Since Apache was installed while you were logged in as the root account, most of the files used by Apache and the default Web content are owned by root. While this may not create any problems, you may want to change the ownership of the Apache files to the name of the account the Web server runs under.

Web servers primarily have two types of users who need access to the Web server. The first category includes users who need to access the content of the Web browser and will not be adding any content or making changes. The other classification involves those individuals who are responsible for maintaining the Web server and the content. For these users, accounts and possibly groups are necessary so the user can write and modify Apache information as appropriate.

Web Server Administrators

The individuals who may need to stop and start the Web service for mainte-nance or changes will need to have the proper permissions. You can accomplish this by creating a Web server administrator account and specifying the proper permission. If there will be several Web administrators you may want to create a Web server administrator group and add the user accounts to the group. Then you can specify the proper permissions to the group. The necessary permis-sions include the ability to read and execute the httpd or apachectl files and the ability to read the Apache log files. If the Web server administrators will be making changes to any files, such as httpd.conf, make sure the Web adminis-trator account or group has the write permission to the appropriate files.

Web Designers

The individuals who create the content for your Web site will need the capa-bility to add the Web content to the Web server. For these users, their user accounts, or a Web designer group, need to have write access to the folder and subfolders where the Web content is located. They will not need to modify any of the Apache configuration files, just the Web content itself. Also, if you do not want new Web pages to overwrite existing Web site content, you may need to create subdirectories for the new Web content and only assign the designer accounts permission to the new Web content directories and not to the existing Web content locations.

Web Site Users

User accounts are not needed for ordinary Web browsing capabilities. As long as their system and browser can get to the Web server, they can browse the contents. For private Web servers that allow access from outside the organiza-tion's network, user accounts and passwords will need to be set up so only authorized users can gain access to the Web server content. Web servers that run other applications, such as Oracle, use accounts and passwords to limit access to the data managed by the other applications. Often, these types of server applications have their own accounts and passwords which are only used for the application and are not used by Apache.

Verifying that the Apache Web Server Is Working

One of the best ways to determine if your Web server is running is to browse it! If you can browse the Web server content, odds are it is working properly. However, be careful that the user's browser has not cached the Web server's pages and that you aren't therefore viewing the content from saved files. Also, if there is a proxy or caching server between the user and your Web server, the user may be viewing the pages from the proxy or caching server. This is not an unusual instance when accessing Web sites from large commercial Internet providers such as AOL, CompuServe, and so on. To make sure you are actually viewing the contents of the Web server, set the Web browser to always "download" the Web pages. If it is not convenient to launch a Web browser, you can check your running processes. If you see several listings of httpd, then the Web server is running.

A Few Quick Things to Check if You Cannot Browse Your Web Server

There are several things that may prevent a user from browsing your Web server. The first thing is to make sure the service is actually running! If it is not, then restart the service. If there is a problem when the service attempts to restart you will see an error message on the screen. You can also check the Apache server log files.

If the service is running okay, maybe the user's browser cannot resolve the name of the Web server. Use the ping command with the Web server's name to see if the user's machine can resolve the name. For example, if the DNS name of the Web server is www.ouraymountainwater.com, the ping command syntax would be:

```
ping www.ouraymountainwater.com
```

If the name can be resolved, most ping commands echo back the device's IP number, the number of bytes sent and the transit time. If you don't get a response from the ping command it may mean the user's machine cannot resolve the name. In that case, try to ping your Web server with the IP number of the Web server. If you can ping the number but not the name, then the problem is probably in the user's machine DNS setup and/or the DNS server(s) configuration.

Installing Windows 2000 Server and Apache

In this chapter we cover installing Apache on a Windows 2000 server. In addition to Apache, we also address installing Windows 2000 Server. Note that if you plan on installing Windows NT 4, the installation steps are very similar to a Windows 2000 Server installation. The Apache Web server software is installed in the same manner on Windows 2000 and Windows NT.

Downloading and Locating the Apache Installation Files

The Apache installation file for Windows can be downloaded from the Internet from the Apache Software Foundation's Web site, www.apache.org. The Apache software comes in two forms—one with the source code and one without the source code. If you think you may be recompiling Apache or doing some programming, download the file that contains the source code. The size of the file without the source code is about 1.8 MB. With the source code it is approximately 3MB.

The Windows Apache installation process is an MSI file and uses the Microsoft Windows Installer application. The Microsoft Windows Installer or

MSI application is included with Windows 2000 operating systems. If you will be using Windows NT 4, you will need to download the MSI application from Microsoft's ftp site: ftp://ftp.microsoft.com/developr/platformsdk/oct2000/msi/winnt/x86/instmsi.exe. The MSI application is not included with Windows NT 4. To compile the Apache source for Windows, you will need Microsoft's Visual Studio or Visual C++ version 5.0 or greater.

Installing Windows 2000

Windows 2000 Server installation must be started by booting the computer from the CD or with a bootable disk that can access the CD drive. If you boot the computer from the Windows 2000 Server installation CD the installation process starts immediately. If you are starting the installation from a floppy disk, run the application called SETUP.EXE that is located at the root of the Windows 2000 Server installation CD.

The initial portion of the Windows 2000 installation is text oriented and the mouse is not used. The first phase loads various driver files for the hardware. At the Welcome to Setup screen you have the option to install Windows 2000, repair a Windows 2000 installation, or quit the installation. For a new install of Windows 2000 we will select to set up Windows 2000. The Windows 2000 Licensing Agreement appears and you must accept it to continue on. If you do not accept the license agreement, the install process is aborted and the computer reboots.

The next step is to define the disk partitions. You can choose to create one or multiple partitions. To create a new partition, type a C and the next screen will request the size of the partition. Once you have the partition or partitions created, you will need to select which one you want to install Windows 2000 on. The next configuration specification is the file system type for the partition Windows 2000 will reside on. The NTFS file system type gives you the best choices for security and the best use of disk space. The FAT file system cannot be secured for local access and you do not have as many security options when the system is accessed from the network. In addition, the FAT file system is "old" and does not efficiently work with large partitions and disk drives. Since we want to secure our Windows 2000 Apache Web server, we will choose NTFS. Depending on the size of the partition for Windows 2000, it may take several minutes to format the partition. After the formatting is completed, the install process will check the disk space and then the file copy phase starts. Depending on the speed of your hardware, the file copy process may take several minutes. After the file copy process, the system will reboot to begin the next phase of the installation.

The remaining portions of the installation are performed in a graphical environment. After the system reboots, the set up process detects and installs device drivers, such as the mouse, keyboard, video, and others. The screen may flicker several times when the video detection is occurring. Depending on the system's hardware and speed, this may take several minutes. After the device drivers are set up, the next configuration item is Regional Settings. The default settings are for US English and US keyboard and you can customize the environment to match your regional settings. The next step allows you to Personalize Your Software. This is where you enter the name and organization the Windows 2000 software is registered to.

Windows 2000 provides two types of licensing modes. Per Server specifies the permitted number of active connections on the server you are installing. Each machine that connects to the server to access its resources must have a Client Access License. The second method, Per Seat licensing, is primarily used in environments that only have one Windows based server. Per Seat licensing also requires each computer accessing the server to have a Client Access License. If you are not sure of the type of licensing your organization purchased, check with the proper individuals before proceeding further in the installation. For our example installation of Windows 2000, we will be using Per Server licensing. When this option is used, the number of permitted licensed connections must be specified. The default is 5 and you may need to change the value to match your organization's licensing scheme.

The Windows 2000 server, and every Windows machine, must have a unique computer name. This is used by users and other services to identify and locate the system. The name you specify should be short but descriptive. Also, avoid the use of any "odd" characters and stick with letters and numbers. Non-alphanumeric characters could potentially "confuse" a service or cause compatibility problems in the future. Note that this is the name of the computer and does not include the domain name. In the Computer Name and Administrator Password set up screen, you must also enter the password for the Administrator's account. The Administrator's account has full access to the Windows 2000 system so make sure you use a password that is not common or easy to figure out. Also, remember that Windows 2000 passwords are case sensitive.

The Windows 2000 Components window allows you to specify what components you want installed on the system. These are standard Windows 2000 Server components and do not include non-Microsoft software such as Apache. You may choose to install just the bare necessities on the system so resources are not tied up doing non-Web server tasks. Please note that Microsoft's Web server, IIS (Internet Information Services), is selected by default. Since we will only be running one Web server on the Windows 2000 system, make sure you deselect IIS. You may want to consider selecting some of the Management and Monitoring Tools.

Adjust as necessary in the Date and Time Settings window the values to match your local date and time.

The next major installation step is configuring the system's network environment. At the Networking Settings window there are two installation options. The Typical settings choice is designed more for systems that will be accessing other services and systems. The Typical settings will use DHCP to obtain IP addressing information. As a reminder, DHCP is not recommended for server based systems. The second choice, Custom settings, gives you complete control over all of your network parameters. The Custom settings option is recommended for servers since it allows you to chose the services and values you want. For our example Windows 2000 server installation, we will choose Custom settings. In the first Custom settings screen, you have the option to choose protocols and services. The default options are:

Client for Microsoft Networks. This is needed if you plan on using the Windows 2000 Apache server to access other Windows systems using Window's networking services. Since our example Windows 2000 Apache Web server will not be using Microsoft Networking, we will deselect this service.

File and Printer Sharing for Microsoft Networks. This service is necessary if other systems will be accessing any shared folders or printers on the Windows 2000 Apache Web server. Since our example Windows 2000 will not be sharing its resources by using Microsoft's services, we will deselect this service.

Internet Protocol (TCP/IP). This protocol must be enabled and configured so others can access the Web server. To specify the IP information, select the protocol and choose the Properties button. The default method for the IP address information is DHCP. You can set the IP address and related information in the Internet Protocol (TCP/IP) Properties window.

When you are finished setting your custom network properties, the installation returns to the Networking Components window. If you need to add another protocol or service that is not listed, the Install button allows you to choose additional Clients, Services, and/or Protocols. For our example Apache Windows 2000 server, we will not be adding other protocols and services.

The next step is to specify the role your Apache Windows 2000 server will have in a Windows domain or workgroup environment. If you do not want to, or need to add the Apache server to a domain, choose the option labeled No, this computer is not on a network, or is on a network without a domain. Even though you are on a network and there may be Microsoft domains, choose the No option. When this is selected you need to indicate a name for a Workgroup even if you will not be using a Workgroup. If you choose to make the Apache server a member of a domain, you will need to supply the name of a valid domain. For our example Apache Web server, we will choose the No option and enter OURAYWATER as the Workgroup name. Once this step is completed, the next item is installing more components and copying files. This step may take several minutes to complete.

When the file copying is completed, the next portion of the install process is Performing Final Tasks. This section covers installing the Start menu items, registering the components, saving the system's settings, and removing any temporary files. This process may take several minutes to complete. The final step is to remove the installation CD and restart the computer.

When you log onto the system for the first time, you are presented with a Windows 2000 Configure Your Server window. Since we don't need to do any configuration at this point, you can choose I will configure this server later. To access this window again, go to the Start menu, choose Programs | Adminstrative Tools | Configure Your Computer. If you don't want the reminder window to appear when you log on to the system each time, deselect the option to Show this screen at startup and then close the window. There is no OK button.

Installing Apache on a Windows 2000 Server

Installing Apache uses Microsoft's MSI application, which presents a graphical interface (wizard) to the installation process. Before you begin the installation, you will need to decide where you want the installer to place the Apache files. It is recommended that you place the Web server and the content on a partition that is using the NTFS file system so access can be secured both locally and remotely. This also gives you more flexibility for setting up different levels of access for Web administrators and Web designers.

Preparing to Install Apache

One *very* important preparation task that *must* be done before you install Apache is to make sure IIS is not running or installed. If IIS is installed, stop the service and uninstall IIS. Installing Apache on a system that is running IIS, or has IIS installed, confuses both IIS and Apache. As with anything that modifies the system, it is a good idea to make sure you have a recent and reliable backup of the Windows 2000 operating system, data, and important applications. The installation process should not "damage" anything but it is a good idea to be on the safe side in the event of a failure.

Running the MSI application does not greatly impact computer resources but it will use some CPU and memory resources. Make sure you are comfortable with the ability of your system to handle the momentary increase in demand without negatively affecting any other services that the Windows 2000 server may be providing. Ideally, if you have an experimental Windows 2000 Server, you can "practice" all of your Apache installations and configurations before doing it on a "live" production server.

In this chapter we cover the installation of Apache using the MSI application. You can also compile the Apache source code if you are familiar with compiling Windows 2000 applications. Compiling Windows 2000 applications requires another product that is not included with the Windows 2000 Server installation CDs. Microsoft's Visual Studio or Visual C++ version 5.0 or higher are commercial products. One of these products will need to be purchased and installed on your system in order to compile Apache for Windows.

Basic/Typical Apache Installation Details

To begin the installation process, locate the Apache file you downloaded—it should end with a .msi extension—and run the installation file. The first screen presented is a Welcome screen. To continue, click on the Next button. The license agreement screen appears and you will need to choose the option to accept the license agreement. If you do not, the Next button is grayed out and you cannot continue to install the software. The Read This First page contains a list of some items about the recommended Windows versions, where to look for documentation, and so on. When you have finished reading the information use the Next button to advance to the next step.

The Server Information page contains several fields to complete. The field labeled Network Domain is the name of the domain your Web server will reside in. For example, if we were installing the Intranet production Web server for Ouray Mountain Water, the Network Domain would be:

```
ouraymountainwater.com
```

The next field is the Server Name. If the name of our Ouray Mountain Water private Intranet server were production, the Server Name would be:

```
production.ouraymountainwater.com
```

The last entry field is the email address of the administrator of the Web server.

At the bottom of the page are two radio buttons:

```
Run as a service for All Users - Recommended
Run when started manually, only for me
```

It is highly recommended you choose the first option, to run as a service. This way the Web server will run when the system is restarted and whether or not somebody is logged onto the Web server system.

The next page is the Setup type. The type Complete will install all the program features but it does not allow you to specify the location of the files. The Custom option allows you install what you want and where you want them. For our example Ouray Mountain Water company Web server, we will choose the Custom option. The Custom Setup screen displays the features you can choose to install. If you have downloaded the Apache MSI file that includes the source code there are three features you can install:

```
Apache Runtime
Apache Documentation
Apache Source Code
```

If you are using the MSI file that does not contain the source code then the third option is not available. Without the source code, the amount of disk space the installation will occupy is about 6MB. With the source code the total size is about 10MB. Make sure you have both the Apache Runtime and Apache Documentation enabled to install these features on the local hard drive. You can choose to install the source code now or at a later time.

At the bottom of the Custom Setup screen is the location where Apache will be installed. The default location is

```
C:\Program Files\Apache Group\
```

For our example Web server we are going to change the location to:

```
G:\Apache\
```

The next screen is the Ready to Install the Program window. When you are ready, click on the Install button. Depending on your system, this may take several minutes to install. You may see a momentary flicker of a command window when the installation process starts the Apache Web server. When it is completed, the installation wizard displays a completion screen. To exit the installer program click on the Finish button.

If all of the information was correctly entered in the installation wizard you should be able to immediately access the Web server. Assuming the DNS servers are aware of the new Web server, enter in the name of the Web server in the URL field of your browser and you should see the default Apache Web server opening page. Figure 3.1 is an example of the default Web page for Apache 1.3.20 running on a Windows 2000 Server system.

Apache for Windows can also be compiled. This allows you to customize what components or modules are included in the Web server. Make sure that when you choose to install Apache you also select to install the source code files. As an example in this chapter we will use Microsoft's Visual C++, which is part of Visual Studio, to compile Apache.

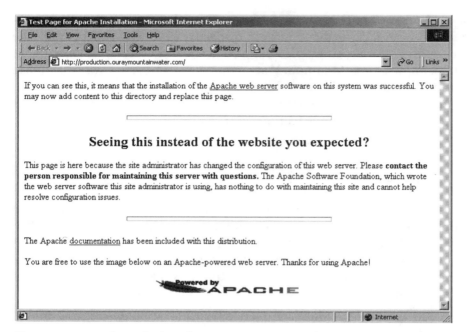

Figure 3.1   Apache Default Web Server Page on a Windows 2000 Server.

The source code for Apache is located in the src directory under the apache directory that was created when you ran the MSI application. In our example, where we specified the path of G:\Apache, the source code is located in:

```
G:\Apache\apache\src\
```

The src directory contains a Project Workspace document called Apache.dsw. In the Visual C++ application open up the Apache.dsw document. To create the Apache application, choose Build Apache.exe from the Build menu. This process may take several minutes depending on your system's hardware. The compiled application is placed in a subdirectory called debug which is located in the src directory.

Managing and Setting Up User Accounts

For maintenance of the Web server you may need to create some additional accounts and/or groups. Also you need to consider the permissions needed by the content designers for adding and/or changing Web content.

Web Server Administrators

Individuals who are responsible for starting and stopping the Web server for maintenance will need the appropriate rights. Placing the Web server administrators as members of the Power Users group will give the Web administrators the ability to stop and start the Apache Web server.

Web Designers

The users who will be creating the Web content will need the ability to publish the new information to the Web server. If the Web designers will be adding the new content from a different machine, the user's account must be able to access the system from the network. This may involve sharing the Web content directory and setting NTFS permissions so the user can write to the folders.

Web Site Users

Once the Web server is up and running, "ordinary" users can access it without the need for a user account. For private Web servers that allow access from outside the organization's network, user accounts and passwords need to be set up so only authorized users can gain access to the Web server content. Web servers that run other applications, such as Oracle, use accounts and passwords to restrict access to the data managed by these applications. Often, these types of server applications have their own accounts and passwords which are only used for the application and are not used by Apache.

Verifying that the
Apache Web Server Is Working

There are several things you can do to determine if your Web server is working properly. One way is to determine if the Apache service is actually running. Accessing the Services management component in Windows 2000 displays all the services the system is running and could run. If you see the status as Started for the entry titled Apache, then the Web server is running.

You can also use the net command to view the running services. In a command window, execute the following:

```
net start
```

All of the running services are listed alphabetically. If you see Apache in the list, then the Apache Web server is running.

Browsing Your New Web Server

Another quick way to determine if the Web server is running is to use a Web browser. If you are at the Web server itself, run Internet Explorer and put the name of the Web server in the Address or URL field. If DNS is not set up for your new Web server, use the IP address instead of the name of the server. If you see the default Apache Web page, then your Web server is running.

A Few Quick Things to Check if You Cannot Browse Your Web Server

If you cannot access your Web server from a Web browser, make sure the Web server is running. In the Services management component, if the status field is empty for Apache, then the Web server is not running. Double click on the Apache line to bring up the Apache Properties window. Click on the Start button to activate the Web server. You can also execute

```
net start apache
```

in a command window to start the Apache Web server.

If the server is running and you cannot browse the Web server from the same machine, check to make sure there were no error messages when the Web server attempted to start. Investigate the Event Viewer's system and application events and also look at the error.log file in the logs directory under the Apache installation location for any information that may indicate why the service cannot be started properly.

If the service is running okay, the user's browser may not be able to resolve the name of the Web server. Use the ping command with the Web server's name to see if the user's machine can resolve the name. For example, if the DNS name of the Web server were production.ouraymountainwater.com, the ping command syntax would be:

```
ping production.ouraymountainwater.com
```

If the name can be resolved, most ping commands echo back the device's IP number, the number of bytes sent, and the transit time. If you don't get a response from the ping command, it may mean the user's machine cannot resolve the name. In that case, try to ping your Web server with the IP number of the Web server. If you can ping the number but not the name, then the problem is probably either in the user's machine DNS set up and/or the DNS server(s) configuration.

CHAPTER

4

Apache Architecture

The Apache Web server is composed of several files that perform different actions and functions. The main program that handles and processes the users' requests is a compiled application that is referred to as the Apache binary. On Linux systems, the Apache binary is typically called httpd, although some distributions name it apache. On Windows 2000 systems, the Apache binary is named apache.exe.

On Linux systems, Apache runs as a process and it replicates itself into several "child" processes. The child processes do the actual "work" of the Web server and deliver the content to the users' browsers. When a request comes into the Web server, Apache will assign an idle child process to handle the new request. When the request has been satisfied and the child process has nothing else to do, the process goes into an idle state and is available for the next Web server request.

On Windows 2000 systems, Apache can run as a service or an application. It is recommended that you run Apache as a service so the Web server is always available regardless of who is logged onto the system. Using Apache as a service also allows the Web server to start automatically when the Windows 2000 system is started. A Windows 2000 service is an application that has been specifically coded to run as a service. Service applications do not have a user interface and they are designed to interact with the system. When the Apache service is started on a Windows 2000 system, it runs as a multithreaded application. It does not "spin" off multiple copies of itself to process Web server requests. Instead, there are two Apache processes running on Windows 2000. One process is the parent process, or the process created when Apache is started. The second process is a generated child process, which handles all the Web server requests. Within the child process, a separate thread is used to handle each Web server request.

Overview of Apache Design

The Apache binary is compiled from a collection of other components (files) called modules. Each of these modules performs a specific task and, for the most part, operates independent of each other. This modular approach allows new features and improved functions to be added without the need to change code in the other modules. This design also makes it easier to plug in and unplug those features that you do not need or want. There are hundreds of modules available for Apache. To keep track of which module does what, most modules are registered with the Apache Software Foundation. To find out more about the modules available for Apache, go to http://modules.apache.org. Because there are so many modules available, and things can get complex awfully fast, the Apache included in a Linux distribution and those that are downloaded, come with a collection of default modules. These modules provide the necessary functions for most Web server needs.

The modules that are included in the compiled Apache binary are specified in a file called Configuration, which is located in the src directory. The content of the Configuration file that is included in the Apache source code is identical on both Linux and Windows platforms. The file is processed from top to bottom and the order in which the modules are listed in the Configuration file is important. An entry at the end of the file may override a previous entry. The order of the statements in the Configuration file included with the source code is the recommended order. The Configuration file contains many comments that briefly explain the purpose of each entry. It is recommended that you read through this file before making changes. Below is the Configuration file included with the source code for Apache 1.3.20; it has not been modified.

```
# Config file for the Apache httpd.

# Configuration.tmpl is the template for Configuration. Configuration should
# be edited to select the modules to be included as well as various flags
# for Makefile.

# The template should only be changed when a new system or module is added,
```

```
# or an existing one modified. This will also most likely require some minor
# changes to Configure to recognize those changes.

# There are 5 types of lines here:

# '#' comments, distinguished by having a '#' as the first non-blank character
#
# Makefile options, such as CC=gcc, etc...
#
# Rules, distinguished by having "Rule" at the front. These are used to
# control Configure's behavior as far as how to create Makefile.
#
# Module selection lines, distinguished by having 'AddModule' at the front.
# These list the configured modules, in priority order (highest priority
# last).  They're down at the bottom.
#
# Optional module selection lines, distinguished by having `%Module'
# at the front.  These specify a module that is to be compiled in (but
# not enabled).  The AddModule directive can be used to enable such a
# module.  By default no such modules are defined.


################################################################
# Makefile configuration
#
# These are added to the general flags determined by Configure.
# Edit these to work around Configure if needed. The EXTRA_* family
# will be added to the regular Makefile flags. For example, if you
# want to compile with -Wall, then add that to EXTRA_CFLAGS. These
# will be added to whatever flags Configure determines as appropriate
# and needed for your platform.
#
# You can also set the compiler (CC) and optimization (OPTIM) used here as
# well.  Settings here have priority; If not set, Configure will attempt to
# guess the C compiler, looking for gcc first, then cc.
#
# Optimization note:
# Be careful when adding optimization flags (like -O3 or -O6) on the OPTIM
# entry, especially when using some GCC variants. Experience showed that using
# these for compiling Apache is risky. If you don't want to see Apache dumping
# core regularly then at most use -O or -O2.
#
# The EXTRA_DEPS can be used to add extra Makefile dependencies to external
# files (for instance third-party libraries) for the httpd target. The effect
# is that httpd is relinked when those files are changed.
#
EXTRA_CFLAGS=
EXTRA_LDFLAGS=
EXTRA_LIBS=
EXTRA_INCLUDES=
EXTRA_DEPS=
```

```
#CC=
#CPP=
#OPTIM=
#RANLIB=

################################################################
# Name of the installed Apache HTTP webserver.
#
#TARGET=

################################################################
# Dynamic Shared Object (DSO) support
#
# There is experimental support for compiling the Apache core and
# the Apache modules into dynamic shared object (DSO) files for
# maximum runtime flexibility.
#
# The Configure script currently has only limited built-in
# knowledge on how to compile these DSO files because this is
# heavily platform-dependent. The current state of supported and
# explicitly unsupported platforms can be found in the file
# "htdocs/manual/dso.html", under "Supported Platforms".
#
# For other platforms where you want to use the DSO mechanism you
# first have to make sure it supports the pragmatic dlopen()
# system call and then you have to provide the appropriate
# compiler and linker flags below to create the DSO files on your
# particular platform.
#
# The placement of the Apache core into a DSO file is triggered
# by the SHARED_CORE rule below while support for building
# individual Apache Modules as DSO files and loading them under
# runtime without recompilation is triggered by `SharedModule'
# commands. To be able to use the latter one first enable the
# module mod_so (see corresponding 'AddModule' command below).
# Then enable the DSO feature for particular modules individually
# by replacing their 'AddModule' command with 'SharedModule' and
# change the filename extension from '.o' to '.so'.
#
# Sometimes the DSO files need to be linked against other shared
# libraries to explicitly resolve symbols from them when the
# httpd program not already contains references to them. For
# instance when buidling mod_auth_db as a DSO you need to link
# the DSO against the libdb explicity because the Apache kernel
# has no references for this library. But the problem is that
# this "chaining" is not supported on all platforms. Although one
# usually can link a DSO against another DSO without linker
# complains the linkage is not really done on these platforms.
# So, when you receive "unresolved symbol" errors under runtime
# when using the LoadModule directive for a particular module try
```

```
# to enable the SHARED_CHAIN rule below.

#CFLAGS_SHLIB=
#LD_SHLIB=
#LDFLAGS_SHLIB=
#LDFLAGS_SHLIB_EXPORT=

Rule SHARED_CORE=default
Rule SHARED_CHAIN=default

####################################################################
# Rules configuration
#
# These are used to let Configure know that we want certain
# functions. The format is: Rule RULE=value
#
# At present, only the following RULES are known: WANTHSREGEX, SOCKS4,
# SOCKS5, IRIXNIS, IRIXN32, PARANOID, and DEV_RANDOM.
#
# For all Rules except DEV_RANDOM, if set to "yes"- then Configure knows
# we want that capability and does what is required to add it in. If set
# to "default" then Configure makes a "best guess"; if set to anything
# else, or not present, then nothing is done.
#
# SOCKS4:
#  If SOCKS4 is set to 'yes', be sure that you add the socks library
#  location to EXTRA_LIBS, otherwise Configure will assume
#  "-L/usr/local/lib -lsocks"
#
# SOCKS5:
#  If SOCKS5 is set to 'yes', be sure that you add the socks5 library
#  location to EXTRA_LIBS, otherwise Configure will assume
#  "-L/usr/local/lib -lsocks5"
#
# IRIXNIS:
#  Only takes effect if Configure determines that you are running
#  SGI IRIX.  If you are using a (ancient) 4.x version of IRIX, you
#  need this if you are using NIS and Apache needs access to it for
#  things like mod_userdir.  This is not required on 5.x and later
#  and you should not enable it on such systems.
#
# IRIXN32:
#  If you are running a version of IRIX and Configure detects
#  n32 libraries, it will use those instead of the o32 ones.
#
# PARANOID:
#  New with version 1.3, during Configure modules can run
#  pre-programmed shell commands in the same environment that
#  Configure runs in. This allows modules to control how Configure
#  works. Normally, Configure will simply note that a module
#  is performing this function. If PARANOID is set to yes, it will
```

```
#   actually print-out the code that the modules execute
#
# EXPAT:
#  Include James Clark's Expat package into Apache, for use by the
#  modules. The "default" is to include it if the lib/expat-lite/
#  directory is present. This rule will always be interpreted as "no"
#  if the directory is not present.
#

Rule SOCKS4=no
Rule SOCKS5=no
Rule IRIXNIS=no
Rule IRIXN32=yes
Rule PARANOID=no
Rule EXPAT=default

# DEV_RANDOM:
#  Note: this rule is only used when compiling mod_auth_digest.
#  mod_auth_digest requires a cryptographically strong random seed for its
#  random number generator. It knows two ways of getting this: 1) from
#  a file or device (such as "/dev/random"), or 2) from the truerand
#  library. If this rule is set to 'default' then Configure will choose
#  to use /dev/random if it exists, else /dev/urandom if it exists,
#  else the truerand library. To override this behaviour set DEV_RANDOM
#  either to 'truerand' (to use the library) or to a device or file
#  (e.g. '/dev/urandom'). If the truerand library is selected, Configure
#  will assume "-L/usr/local/lib -lrand".
Rule DEV_RANDOM=default

# The following rules should be set automatically by Configure. However, if
# they are not set by Configure (because we don't know the correct value for
# your platform), or are set incorrectly, you may override them here.
# If you have to do this, please let us know what you set and what your
# platform is, by filling out a problem report form at the Apache web site:
# <http://bugs.apache.org/>.  If your browser is forms-incapable, you
# can get the information to us by sending mail to apache-bugs@apache.org.
#
# WANTHSREGEX:
#  Apache requires a POSIX regex implementation. Henry Spencer's
#  excellent regex package is included with Apache and can be used
#  if desired. If your OS has a decent regex, you can elect to
#  not use this one by setting WANTHSREGEX to 'no' or commenting
#  out the Rule. The "default" action is "yes" unless overruled
#  by OS specifics

Rule WANTHSREGEX=default

##################################################################
# Module configuration
#
# Modules are listed in reverse priority order--the ones that come
```

```
# later can override the behavior of those that come earlier.  This
# can have visible effects; for instance, if UserDir followed Alias,
# you couldn't alias out a particular user's home directory.

# The configuration below is what we consider a decent default
# configuration.  If you want the functionality provided by a particular
# module, remove the "#" sign at the beginning of the line. But remember,
# the more modules you compile into the server, the larger the executable
# is and the more memory it will take, so if you are unlikely to use the
# functionality of a particular module you might wish to leave it out.

## mod_mmap_static is an experimental module, you almost certainly
## don't need it.  It can make some webservers faster.  No further
## documentation is provided here because you'd be foolish
## to use mod_mmap_static without reading the full documentation.

# AddModule modules/experimental/mod_mmap_static.o

## mod_vhost_alias provides support for mass virtual hosting
## by dynamically changing the document root and CGI directory
## based on the host header or local IP address of the request.
## See "../htdocs/manual/vhosts/mass.html".

# AddModule modules/standard/mod_vhost_alias.o

##
## Config manipulation modules
##
## mod_env sets up additional or restricted environment variables to be
## passed to CGI/SSI scripts.  It is listed first (lowest priority) since
## it does not do per-request stuff.

AddModule modules/standard/mod_env.o

##
## Request logging modules
##

AddModule modules/standard/mod_log_config.o

## Optional modules for NCSA user-agent/referer logging compatibility
## We recommend, however, that you just use the configurable access_log.

# AddModule modules/standard/mod_log_agent.o
# AddModule modules/standard/mod_log_referer.o

##
## Type checking modules
##
## mod_mime_magic determines the type of a file by examining a few bytes
## of it and testing against a database of filetype signatures.  It is
```

```
## based on the unix file(1) command.
## mod_mime maps filename extensions to content types, encodings, and
## "magic" type handlers (the latter is obsoleted by mod_actions, and
## don't confuse it with the previous module).
## mod_negotiation allows content selection based on the Accept* headers.

# AddModule modules/standard/mod_mime_magic.o
AddModule modules/standard/mod_mime.o
AddModule modules/standard/mod_negotiation.o

##
## Content delivery modules
##
## The status module allows the server to display current details about
## how well it is performing and what it is doing.  Consider also enabling
## the 'ExtendedStatus On' directive to allow full status information.
## Please note that doing so can result in a palpable performance hit.

AddModule modules/standard/mod_status.o

## The Info module displays configuration information for the server and
## all included modules. It's very useful for debugging.

# AddModule modules/standard/mod_info.o

## mod_include translates server-side include (SSI) statements in text files.
## mod_autoindex handles requests for directories which have no index file
## mod_dir handles requests on directories and directory index files.
## mod_cgi handles CGI scripts.

AddModule modules/standard/mod_include.o
AddModule modules/standard/mod_autoindex.o
AddModule modules/standard/mod_dir.o
AddModule modules/standard/mod_cgi.o

## The asis module implements ".asis" file types, which allow the embedding
## of HTTP headers at the beginning of the document.  mod_imap handles internal
## imagemaps (no more cgi-bin/imagemap/!).  mod_actions is used to specify
## CGI scripts which act as "handlers" for particular files, for example to
## automatically convert every GIF to another file type.

AddModule modules/standard/mod_asis.o
AddModule modules/standard/mod_imap.o
AddModule modules/standard/mod_actions.o

##
## URL translation modules.
##

## The Speling module attempts to correct misspellings of URLs that
## users might have entered, namely by checking capitalizations
```

```
## or by allowing up to one misspelling (character insertion / omission /
## transposition/typo). This catches the majority of misspelled requests.
## If it finds a match, a "spelling corrected" redirection is returned.

# AddModule modules/standard/mod_speling.o

## The UserDir module for selecting resource directories by user name
## and a common prefix, e.g., /~<user> , /usr/web/<user> , etc.

AddModule modules/standard/mod_userdir.o

## The Alias module provides simple URL translation and redirection.

AddModule modules/standard/mod_alias.o

## The URL rewriting module allows for powerful URI-to-URI and
## URI-to-filename mapping using a regular expression based
## rule-controlled rewriting engine.

# AddModule modules/standard/mod_rewrite.o

##
## Access control and authentication modules.
##
AddModule modules/standard/mod_access.o
AddModule modules/standard/mod_auth.o

## The anon_auth module allows for anonymous-FTP-style username/
## password authentication.

# AddModule modules/standard/mod_auth_anon.o

## db_auth and dbm_auth work with Berkeley DB files make sure there
## is support for DBM files on your system.  You may need to grab the GNU
## "gdbm" package if not and possibly adjust EXTRA_LIBS. (This may be
## done by Configure at a later date)

# AddModule modules/standard/mod_auth_dbm.o
# AddModule modules/standard/mod_auth_db.o

## "digest" implements HTTP Digest Authentication rather than the less
## secure Basic Auth used by the other modules.  This is the old version.

# AddModule modules/standard/mod_digest.o

## "auth_digest" implements HTTP/1.1 Digest Authentication (RFC 2617)
## rather than the less secure Basic Auth used by the other modules.
## This is an updated version of mod_digest, but it is not as well tested
## and is therefore marked experimental.  Use either the one above, or
## this one below, but not both digest modules.
## Note: If you add this module in then you might also need the
```

```
## truerand library (available for example from
## ftp://research.att.com/dist/mab/librand.shar) see the Rule
## DEV_RANDOM above for more info.
##
## Must be added above (run later than) the proxy module because the
## WWW-Authenticate and Proxy-Authenticate headers are parsed in the
## post-read-request phase and it needs to know if this is a proxy request.

# AddModule modules/experimental/mod_auth_digest.o

## Optional Proxy
##
## The proxy module enables the server to act as a proxy for outside
## http and ftp services. It's not as complete as it could be yet.
## NOTE: You do not want this module UNLESS you are running a proxy;
##       it is not needed for normal (origin server) operation.

# AddModule modules/proxy/libproxy.a

## Optional response header manipulation modules.
##
## cern_meta mimics the behavior of the CERN web server with regards to
## metainformation files.

# AddModule modules/standard/mod_cern_meta.o

## The expires module can apply Expires: headers to resources,
## as a function of access time or modification time.

# AddModule modules/standard/mod_expires.o

## The headers module can set arbitrary HTTP response headers,
## as configured in server, vhost, access.conf or .htaccess configs.

# AddModule modules/standard/mod_headers.o

## Miscellaneous modules
##
## mod_usertrack is the new name for mod_cookies.  This module
## uses Netscape cookies to automatically construct and log
## click-trails from Netscape cookies, or compatible clients who
## aren't coming in via proxy.
##
## You do not need this, or any other module to allow your site
## to use Cookies.  This module is for user tracking only.

# AddModule modules/standard/mod_usertrack.o

## The example module, which demonstrates the use of the API.  See
## the file modules/example/README for details.  This module should
## only be used for testing--DO NOT ENABLE IT on a production server.
```

```
# AddModule modules/example/mod_example.o

## mod_unique_id generates unique identifiers for each hit, which are
## available in the environment variable UNIQUE_ID.  It may not work on all
## systems, hence it is not included by default.

# AddModule modules/standard/mod_unique_id.o

## mod_so lets you add modules to Apache without recompiling.
## This is an experimental feature at this stage and only supported
## on a subset of the platforms we generally support.
## Don't change this entry to a 'SharedModule' variant (Bootstrapping!)

# AddModule modules/standard/mod_so.o

## mod_setenvif lets you set environment variables based on the HTTP header
## fields in the request; this is useful for conditional HTML, for example.
## Since it is also used to detect buggy browsers for workarounds, it
## should be the last (highest priority) module.

AddModule modules/standard/mod_setenvif.o
```

The AddModule entries indicate the modules that will be included in the Apache binary when Apache is compiled. The # (pound sign) in front of a line indicates a comment and the text following the # will not be processed. Therefore, if there is a # in front of AddModule, that module is not included in the compiled Apache. For example:

```
# AddModule modules/standard/mod_mime_magic.o
AddModule modules/standard/mod_mime.o
AddModule modules/standard/mod_negotiation.o
```

The two modules, mod_mime and mod_negotiation, are contained in the Apache binary and mod_mime_magic is not included in the binary. If you want to enable or disable a module, you will need to make the appropriate change in the Configuration file. Once you have modified the Configuration file, you will need to recompile Apache for your changes to be in effect. The behavior, features, and functions of the modules included in the Apache binary are controlled through directives. In the Configuration File Details section of this chapter we cover the directives that are important for your Web servers.

The following is a list of the modules included in the Apache "package." The modules have been organized by their function using the same categories defined by the Apache Software Foundation. All of the modules, except for core, follow a naming convention. The mod_ label indicates it is a module and the remaining portion of the name indicates its function. If you plan on developing an Apache module, make sure you register your module with the Apache Software Foundation so there are no conflicts with other modules.

CORE

Core This is the "heart" of Apache and it defines the basic Web server features. This module provides support for really basic server operations, including options and commands which control the operation of other modules.

ENVIRONMENT CREATION

mod_env This module allows for control of the environment that will be provided to CGI scripts and SSI pages. Environment variables may be passed from the environment which started the Apache application. Environment variables can also be set in the Apache configuration file, httpd.conf.

mod_setenvif This module lets you set environment variables based on the HTTP header fields in the request. You can set environment variables according to whether different aspects of the request match regular expressions you specify. These environment variables can be used by other parts of the server to make decisions about actions to be taken. Regular expressions are a way of describing a pattern, for example, "all the words that begin with the letter A" or "every 10-digit phone number" or even "Every sentence with two commas in it, and no capital letter Q." Regular expressions (regex) are useful in Apache because they let you apply certain attributes against collections of files or resources in a variety of ways.

mod_unique_id This module generates unique identifiers for each Web server request. These unique values are available in the environment variable UNIQUE_ID. The module provides a "magic" token for each request which guarantees each request is unique across all requests. The unique identifier is unique across multiple machines in a properly configured cluster of machines. The mod_unique_id module may not work on all systems. This module is not enabled by default and is not compiled into the Apache binary.

CONTENT TYPE DECISIONS

mod_mime This module maps filename extensions to content types, encodings, and "magic" type handlers. mod_mime is used to determine various bits of "meta information" about documents. This information relates to the content of the document and is returned to the browser or used in content-negotiation within the server. In addition, a "handler" can be set for a document, which determines how the document will be processed within the server

mod_mime_magic This module determines the type of file by examining a few bytes of it and testing it against a database of filetype signatures. This module is intended as a "second line of defense" for situations that mod_mime can't resolve. This module is derived from a free version of the file(1) command for Unix, which uses "magic numbers" and other hints from a file's contents to figure out what the contents are. This module is not enabled by default and is not compiled into the Apache binary.

mod_negotiation This module allows content selection based on the Accept headers. Content selection, or content negotiation, is the selection of the document from several available documents that best matches the clients' browsers' capabilities. There are two implementations of content negotiation.

- A type map, which explicitly lists the files containing the variants.
- A MultiViews search where the server does an implicit filename pattern match, and chooses from the results found.

URL MAPPING

mod_alias The Alias module provides simple URL translation and redirection. The directives (controls) contained in this module allow for manipulation and control of URLs as requests arrive at the server. The Alias and ScriptAlias directives are used to map between URLs and filesystem paths. This allows for content which is not directly under the Web server's root document directory (DocumentRoot) to be served as part of the Web document tree. The ScriptAlias directive gives you the ability to identify a directory as containing only a certain type of file. For example, you can use ScriptAlias to "mark" a directory called scripts as only containing CGI scripts. The Redirect directives are used to instruct clients to make a new request with a different URL. They are often used when a resource has moved to a new location. A more powerful and flexible set of directives for manipulating URLs is contained in the mod_rewrite module.

mod_rewrite The URL rewriting module allows for powerful URL-to-URL and URL-to-filename mapping. This module uses a rule-based rewriting engine (based on a regular-expression parser) to rewrite requested URLs on the fly. It supports an unlimited number of rules and an unlimited number of attached rule conditions for each rule. This methodology provides a very flexible and powerful URL manipulation mechanism. The URL manipulations can depend on various tests; for instance, server variables, environment variables, HTTP headers, time stamps, and even external database lookups in various formats can be used to achieve very granular URL matching. This module is very complex and detailed and, as the Apache Software Foundation states, "don't expect to understand this entire module in just one day."

mod_userdir This module provides support for user home directories. The UserDir module is for selecting resource directories by user name and a common prefix. The UserDir directive sets the real directory to a user's home directory to use when a request for a document for a user is received.

mod_speling This module automatically corrects minor typographical errors in URLs. The mod_speling module attempts to correct misspellings of URLs that users might have entered. The module performs its functions by checking capitalization or by allowing up to one misspelling in the URL. When a misspelling is detected, the module will scan the contents of the directory the user is attempting to access.

- If no matching document is found, Apache proceeds as usual and returns a "document not found" error.
- If only one document is found that "almost" matches the request, it is returned in the form of a redirection response.
- If more than one document with a close match is found, the list of the matches is returned to the client, and the client can select the document they want.

This module is not enabled by default and is not compiled into the Apache binary.

mod_vhost_alias If the Web server will be hosting more than one Web site, this module dynamically changes the document root and CGI directory based on the incoming request's host header or IP address. This module is not enabled by default and is not compiled into the Apache binary.

DIRECTORY HANDLING

mod_dir This module handles requests on directories and directory index files. The mod_dir module provides for "trailing slash" redirects and serving directory index files. The index of a directory can come from one of two sources:

- A file written by the Web designer which is typically called index.html. The DirectoryIndex directive of mod_dir sets the name of this file.
- A listing generated by the server. This function is provided by the mod_autoindex module.

A "trailing slash" redirect is issued when the server receives a request for a URL. For example, if the URL entered for a directory were www .ouraymountainwater/about/offices, the mod_dir module would issue a redirect to www.ouraymountainwater/about/offices/.

mod_autoindex This module handles requests for directories that have no index file and provides for automatic directory indexing. The index of a directory can come from one of two sources:

- A file written by the Web designer which is typically called index.html. The DirectoryIndex directive of the mod_dir module sets the name of this file.

- A listing generated by the server. Automatic index generation is enabled with the core module's Options directive.

If FancyIndexing is enabled, or the FancyIndexing keyword is present in the IndexOptions directive, the column headers are links that control the order of the display.

The two modules, mod_dir and mod_autoindex, are separated so that, if preferred, you can remove automatic index generation.

ACCESS CONTROL

mod_access This module provides access control based on the client's host-name, IP address, or other characteristics of the client request (browser). The directives provided by mod_access are used in the core module to control access to particular parts of the server. The Allow and Deny directives are used to specify which clients are or are not allowed access to the server, while the Order directive sets the default access state, and configures how the Allow and Deny directives interact with each other. Both host-based access restrictions and password-based authentication may be implemented simultaneously. In general, access restriction directives apply to all access methods. This is the desired behavior in most cases. However, it is possible to restrict some methods, while leaving other methods unrestricted.

mod_auth This module provides for user authentication by using HTTP Basic Authentication to restrict access by looking up users in password and group text files. Similar functionality and greater flexibility is provided by mod_auth_dbm and mod_auth_db. The mod_auth_digest module provides HTTP Digest Authentication.

mod_auth_dbm This module allows for user authentication using DBM files. It provides for HTTP Basic Authentication where the usernames and passwords are stored in DBM type database files. It is an alternative to the plain text password files provided by mod_auth and the Berkely DB password files provided by mod_auth_db. Make sure there is support for DBM files on your system before using this module. This module is not enabled by default and is not compiled into the Apache binary.

mod_auth_db This module allows for user authentication using Berkeley DB files. It provides an alternative to DBM files for those systems which support DB and not DBM. This module is not enabled by default and is not compiled into the Apache binary.

mod_auth_anon This module allows "anonymous" user access to authenticated areas of the Web server. This module performs access control in a manner similar to anonymous-ftp sites with an anonymous user name and the email address of the user as the password. The email addresses used as passwords can be logged. Combining this module with other (database) access control methods allows for effective user tracking and customization while still keeping the site open for anonymous users. One advantage of using mod_auth_anon based user tracking is that it is completely browser independent. This module is not enabled by default and is not compiled into the Apache binary.

mod_auth_digest This module provides for user authentication using MD5 Digest Authentication. MD5 implements HTTP/1.1 Digest Authentication (RFC 2617) rather than the less secure HTTP Basic Authentication used by other modules. MD5 authentication provides a more secure password system than HTTP Basic Authentication but it only works with supporting browsers. This module is an updated version of mod_digest, but it is not as well tested and is therefore marked experimental. Use either this module or mod_digest, but do not use both digest modules at the same time. This module is not enabled by default and is not compiled into the Apache binary.

mod_digest This module implements an older version of the MD5 Digest Authentication specification and it may not work with some newer browsers. Refer to mod_auth_digest for a module that implements the most recent version of the MD5 standard. This module is not enabled by default and is not compiled into the Apache binary.

HTTP RESPONSE

mod_headers This module provides a directive to control the sending of HTTP headers. Headers can be merged, replaced or removed. This module is not enabled by default and is not compiled into the Apache binary.

mod_cern_meta This module emulates the CERN HTTPD Meta file semantics. Meta files are HTTP headers that can be output in addition to the normal range of headers for each file accessed. They appear like the Apache .asis files, and provide an elementary way of influencing the Expires: header, as well as providing other items. There are many ways to manage meta information, and this one was included because there are already a large number of CERN users who can use this module. This module is not enabled by default and is not compiled into the Apache binary.

mod_expires This module controls the setting of the Expires HTTP header in server responses. The expiration date can be set to be relative to either the time the source file was last modified or to the time of the client access. The Expires HTTP header is an instruction to the browser about the document's validity and persistence. If cached, the document may be retrieved from the cache rather than from the source until the specified time has passed. After that, the cache copy is considered "expired" and invalid, and a new copy must be obtained from the source. This module is not enabled by default and is not compiled into the Apache binary.

mod_asis This module provides the handler send-as-is, which directs Apache to send the document without adding most of the usual HTTP headers. This feature can be used to send any kind of data from the server, including redirects and other special HTTP responses, without requiring a cgi script or a nph script. For compatibility with older environments, this module will also process any file with the mime type httpd/send-as-is.

DYNAMIC CONTENT

mod_include This module provides support for documents with Server Side Includes (SSI) and translates SSI statements in text files. mod_include provides a handler that will process files before they are sent to the browser. This processing is controlled by specially formatted SGML comments, referred to as elements. These elements allow conditional text, the inclusion of other files or programs, as well as the setting and display of environment variables.

mod_cgi This module handles CGI scripts. Any file that has the mime type application/x-httpd-cgi or handler cgi-script is processed as a CGI script by the server and the output is returned to the user's browser. Files are defined as a CGI type by either having a name containing an extension defined by the AddType directive in the mod_mime module or by being located in a ScriptAlias directory. Files that are not in a ScriptAlias directory, but which are of type application/x-httpd-cgi as defined by the AddType directive, will not be executed by the server unless Options ExecCGI is enabled. See the core module's Options directive for more details.

mod_actions This module is used to specify CGI scripts which act as "handlers" for particular files. For example, this module can be used to automatically convert every GIF to another file type. This module has two directives. The Action directive lets you run CGI scripts whenever a file of a certain type is requested. The Script directive lets you run CGI scripts whenever a particular method is used in a request. This makes it much easier to execute scripts that process files.

INTERNAL CONTENT HANDLERS

mod_status The Status module allows you to find out how well the Web server is performing. An HTML page is presented that gives the current server statistics in an easily readable form. This status page can be made to automatically refresh. The details presented are:

- The number of children (Web server child process) serving requests
- The number of idle children
- The status of each child, the number of requests that child has performed, and the total number of bytes served by the child

- The total number of accesses and byte count delivered
- The time the server was started/restarted and its running time
- Average values for the number of requests per second, the number of bytes served per second and the average number of bytes per request
- The current percentage CPU used by each child and the total used by Apache
- The current hosts and requests being processed

This module is not enabled by default on the Windows version of Apache and is not compiled into apache.exe.

mod_info This module provides a comprehensive overview of the server configuration including all installed modules and directives in the configuration files. It's very useful for debugging and you will probably only want to enable this if you are developing or modifying code. This module is not enabled by default and is not compiled into the Apache binary.

LOGGING

mod_log_config This module provides for logging of the requests made to the server using the Common Log Format or a user-specified format. Logs may be written directly to a file, or to an external program. Conditional logging is provided so that individual requests may be included or excluded from the logs based on characteristics of the request. Three directives are provided by this module: TransferLog to create a log file, LogFormat to set a custom format, and CustomLog to define a log file and format in one step. The TransferLog and CustomLog directives can be used multiple times in each server to cause each request to be logged to multiple files.

mod_log_agent This module is provided for compatibility with NCSA httpd, which is no longer used in newer systems. It is recommended you use mod_log_config instead. The mod_log_agent module provides for logging of the client user agents. This module is not enabled by default and is not compiled into the Apache binary.

mod_log_referrer This module is provided for compatibility with NCSA httpd, which is no longer used in newer systems. It is recommended that you use mod_log_config instead. The mod_log_referer module provides for logging of documents that reference other documents on the server. This module is not enabled by default and is not compiled into the Apache binary.

mod_usertrack Earlier releases of Apache included a module which generated a "clickstream" log of user activity on a site using cookies. This was called the "cookies" module or mod_cookies. In Apache 1.2 and later this module has been renamed the "user tracking" module, mod_usertrack. You do not need this, or any other module, to allow your site to use cookies. The mod_usertrack module is not enabled by default and is not compiled into the Apache binary.

MISCELLANEOUS

mod_imap This module processes .map files which replaces the functionality of the imagemap CGI program. Any directory or document type configured to use the handler imap-file will be processed by this module. This module provides for server-side imagemap processing.

mod_proxy The proxy module enables the server to act as a proxy. It implements proxying capabilities for FTP, CONNECT (for SSL), HTTP/0.9, and HTTP/1.0. The module can be configured to connect to other proxy modules. Note that you do not want to include this module unless you are running a proxy. It is not needed for normal, Web server operation. This module is not enabled by default and is not compiled into the Apache binary.

mod_so This module lets you add modules to Apache without recompiling the binary. You can dynamically load executable code and modules into the Web server at start up or restart. This module uses the Dynamic Shared Object (DSO) mechanism. On Linux, the loaded code typically comes from shared object files (usually with .so extension). On Windows this module loads DLL files. The mod_so module is only available in Apache 1.3 and greater. This is an experimental module and is only available on a subset of the platforms the Apache Software Foundation generally supports. This module is not enabled by default on Linux and it is not compiled into the Apache Linux binary. This module is enabled by default on Windows and is available in apache.exe.

mod_mmap_static This module provides mmap()ing of a statically configured list of frequently requested unchanged files. This mmap()ing is done only when the Web server is started or restarted. Whenever one of the mapped files changes in the filesystem you have to restart the server. This is an experimental module and should be used carefully. This module is not enabled by default and is not compiled into the Apache binary.

DEVELOPMENT

mod_example This example module demonstrates the use of the Apache API (Application Programming Interface). See the README file in the example directory for details. This module illustrates many aspects of the Apache API and demonstrates the manner in which module callbacks are triggered by the server. This module should only be used for testing—*Do not enable it* on a production server! The mod_example module is not enabled by default and is not compiled into the Apache binary.

For Windows 2000 systems, there is one module unique to the Apache Windows environment.

DYNAMIC CONTENT

mod_isapi This Windows module provides ISAPI Extension support. It allows Internet Server extensions (e.g. ISAPI .dll modules) to be served by Apache for Windows. ISAPI extension modules are written by third party individuals and the Apache Software Foundation does not provide support for them. For assistance, you will need to contact the ISAPI's author.

You can determine what modules are included in your Apache binary. In a command window on your Linux system, navigate to the bin directory located under the Apache main directory. Execute the following at the command prompt:

```
./httpd -l
```

In a Command Prompt window on your Windows 2000 system, navigate to the main Apache directory. Execute the following at the command prompt:

```
apache -l
```

Both of these commands display a list of the modules included in the Apache binary.

Names and Locations of Apache Files and Directories

The files that are used to start the Apache Web server and the content of the Web server are typically located under one directory. This directory is specified when you compile Apache. You always have the option to move the Apache directory to another location. If Apache is installed along with Linux, the various Apache files may be sprinkled around the system in different directories. In this book we are assuming that all the Apache related files are in one location and that none of the files or subdirectories have been renamed or moved. Throughout the different examples in this book, we refer to a directory called apache where all of the Apache files and directories are installed.

On a Linux system, under the main apache directory, the following subdirectories are found:

```
bin
cgi-bin
conf
```

```
htdocs
icons
include
libexec
logs
man
proxy
```

If you have extracted the contents of the downloaded Apache file in the same location, another subdirectory will be present. The default name for the extracted files directory is apache followed by the revision number. For example, Apache 1.3.20 generates the directory apache_1.3.20. Within the extracted files directory are several files and subdirectories. The subdirectory src in this extracted files subdirectory contains the Apache source code.

On a Windows system, under the main apache directory, the following subdirectories are found:

```
bin
cgi-bin
conf
htdocs
icons
include
lib
libexec
logs
modules
proxy
src
```

The src directory is present if you downloaded a copy of Apache for Windows that contains the source code. The src directory contains the source code for the Windows version of Apache.

For the most part, the files contained in the Apache directories are identical and perform the same functions on Linux and Windows. Due to the differences in the nature of the operating systems, the file types and portions of the file names maybe different. In the following paragraphs, we cover the key files that are involved in running and configuring Apache. In all instances we are referencing a Linux and Windows 2000 system where all of Apache has been installed under a directory called apache. Files that participate in monitoring and optimizing Apache are covered in Chapter 7, "Monitoring and Optimizing Apache."

The bin directory contains several files that are involved in the initial launching of Apache. On a Linux system, this includes the Apache binary, httpd, and apachectl. apachectl is an Apache specific script that provides a command line interface for controlling Apache. On a Windows 2000 environment, the Apache binary, apache.exe, is located directly under the Apache root directory; e.g. apache. Usage of the Linux apachectl file is discussed later in this chapter.

On a Linux system, the bin directory also includes a file called ab. The ab program is an Apache server benchmarking tool. You can gather information about your server, such as, how many requests per second can the Web server handle. On both Linux and Windows, the other bin files, dbmmanage, htdigest, and htpasswd, are used in systems that require users to authenticate before they can access the Web server's content. Logresolve and rotatelogs are used to manipulate and work with the log files generated by Apache. The cgi-bin directory can be used to place all of the Web server's CGI programs.

The conf directory contains the configuration files used by Apache when the Web server is started. The primary configuration file is httpd.conf. The other two configuration files, access.conf and srm.conf, are no longer used. They are present for historical reasons and their content reminds the administrator to do everything in httpd.conf. The contents of these two unused configuration files are essentially the same for Linux and Windows. For your reference, the content of the Linux access.conf file is:

```
##
## access.conf -- Apache HTTP server configuration file
##

#
# This is the default file for the AccessConfig directive in httpd.conf.
# It is processed after httpd.conf and srm.conf.
#
# To avoid confusion, it is recommended that you put all of your
# Apache server directives into the httpd.conf file and leave this
# one essentially empty.
#
```

The content of the access.conf file for Windows is:

```
#
# This is the default file for the AccessConfig directive in httpd.conf.
# It is processed after httpd.conf and srm.conf.
#
# To avoid confusion, it is recommended that you put all of your
# Apache server directives into the httpd.conf file and leave this
# one essentially empty.
#
```

The content of the srm.conf file for Linux is:

```
##
## srm.conf -- Apache HTTP server configuration file
##


#
# This is the default file for the ResourceConfig directive in httpd.conf.
# It is processed after httpd.conf but before access.conf.
#
# To avoid confusion, it is recommended that you put all of your
# Apache server directives into the httpd.conf file and leave this
# one essentially empty.
#
```

For Windows the srm.conf content is:

```
#
# This is the default file for the ResourceConfig directive in httpd.conf.
# It is processed after httpd.conf but before access.conf.
#
# To avoid confusion, it is recommended that you put all of your
# Apache server directives into the httpd.conf file and leave this
# one essentially empty.
#
```

The magic file in the conf directory is used by the mod_mime_magic module. This module uses a database of filetype signatures to determine the type of file. The mime.types file contains a list of the media types that correspond to different file extensions. There is a registry for the Internet media types at ftp://ftp.iana.org/in-notes/iana/assignments/media-types/. There are hundreds of them!

The htdocs directory is the default directory for your Web site content. The htdocs directory contains a default Apache index page and the Apache manual. Several copies of the manual and default index page are present in htdocs in different languages. In all likelihood, you will want to move this directory some place else in your file system for security and content management concerns. We address these issues in the next section of this chapter.

The icons directory contains a collection of pictures and icons used by the default Apache index page and the manual. On a Linux system, the main Apache directory contains another directory called man. This subdirectory contains the man pages for Apache. The two manual page categories available in the man directory are user commands (man1) and system administration (man8).

The include directory contains the header files used by the C compiler when you compile Apache. Most of these files are the same on Linux and Windows but some are different, such as os.h, because of the different operating systems.

The lib directory is generated when you compile Apache and contains libraries of routines. The libexec is also generated when you compile Apache. It is used when compiling Apache on Windows. The include directory is empty on Linux systems. The modules directory on a Windows system contains modules that are not compiled in the binary but can be loaded through the DSO (Dynamic Shared Object) support. By default, none of the modules in the Windows' modules directory are loaded into Apache. These DSO modules will not appear in a Linux system unless you have compiled Apache to support DSO. For more information about DSO options for Linux take a look at the Configuration file in the src directory.

The logs directory contains various logs generated by the system. The two log files typically found are access.log and error.log. We will cover the details of the log files in Chapter 7.

Configuration File Details

Apache is controlled by commands, which are called directives. Directives have a specific syntax which is basically:

```
Directive [option [option]]
```

Depending on the nature of the directive, there may be one or more options available. Some directives are self-explanatory while others may be somewhat obscure. For example, the directive:

```
ServerName www.ouraymountainwater.com
```

is a directive that specifies the name of the Web server. In this example, the role of the directive is pretty obvious. However, the function of the directive:

```
IndexIgnore .??* *~ *# HEADER* README* RCS CVS *,v *,t
```

may not be very obvious. By the way, the IndexIgnore directive is the set of file-names which directory indexing should ignore. The directives used to control Apache are specified in the Apache configuration file, httpd.conf, which is located in the conf directory. Most of the over 200 directives are the same for Linux and Windows 2000. However, because of the differences in the way Apache runs on the different platforms, there are a few directives that apply only to Windows and others that are only for Linux. For a complete listing of the directives, definitions, and options, go to http://httpd.apache.org/docs/mod/directives.html.

The directives and settings are contained in the httpd.conf file. This text file, which we discuss later in this section, allows you to control and specify settings for your Web server. Each directive supports a specific syntax and parameters. Many modules support several directives and some can be quite involved. Most of the directives have a default setting. As an example of the directives for a module, lets take a look at the mod_dir module. This module provides for "trailing slash" redirects and serving directory index files. This module supports one directive:

DirectoryIndex. The DirectoryIndex directive defines the list of Web page documents to look for when the browser requests an index of the directory by specifying a / at the end of the directory name.

The syntax of the DirectoryIndex directive is:

```
DirectoryIndex local-url [local-url] ...
```

In this example, the local-url is either the name of the document in the Web server's root directory or a path relative to the Web server's root directory. For example, on the www.ouraymountainwater.com Web server, if the name of the Web page were index.html, then the syntax would be:

```
DirectoryIndex index.html
```

If the user entered www.ouraymountainwater.com in their Web browser, the index.html file would be displayed.

Directives also have a scope which indicates the area the item will affect. For example, directives can affect the entire server or just a portion, such as a directory or location. The different supported scopes are:

Directory. The listed directives only apply to the specified directory and its subdirectories.

DirectoryMatch. This scope is similar to Directory except that the expression used to represent the directories uses a different syntax.

Files. The listed directives only apply to the specified file or files. You can also use wildcards to indicate a list of files that match a particular pattern.

FilesMatch. This scope is similar to Files except that the expression used to represent the files uses a different syntax.

Location. This scope defines a specific URL. Wildcards are supported by the Location scope so you can include several URLs.

LocationMatch. This scope is similar to Location except that the expression used to represent the locations uses a different syntax.

VirtualHost. If the Web server is hosting different Web sites, this scope allows you to specify the directives for a particular host site.

Scopes and their directives use a specific syntax. For example, the following scope:

```
<Directory "/usr/local/apache/icons">
    Options Indexes MultiViews
    AllowOverride None
    Order allow,deny
    Allow from all
</Directory>
```

is a Directory scope. Between the <Directory "/usr/local/apache/icons"> and </Directory> lines there are four directives that apply to the icons subdirectory.

The Apache configuration file, httpd.conf, is "read" and used when the Web server is started. In earlier versions of Apache (<1.3.4), there were three separate configuration files—access.conf, httpd.conf, and srm.conf. Two of these files are no longer used to configure Apache. These two files, access.conf and srm.conf, are still physically present in the conf directory but they don't do anything. The access.conf file was used to control access to the Web server documents or content. The srm.conf file indicated what type or kind of documents the Web server could serve. All of the controls and features that were done with access.conf and srm.conf are now done in httpd.conf.

The httpd.conf file contains quite a bit of documentation within it and it is highly recommended that you read the file. The httpd.conf file for Apache 1.3.20 for both Linux and Windows are included in this chapter. Note that the httpd.conf files in this section are from functioning Web servers. The only changes to the files were to set the server name and change the user and group assignments. These modifications are covered in Chapters 2 and 3 as the minimal changes necessary to make the Web server work and be accessible. In this section we cover other suggested changes to the httpd.conf file. When you make changes to the httpd.conf file you can verify its syntax and references on a Linux system by using the configtest parameter with apachectl. For Windows environments, choose the Test Configuration menu item (Start | Programs | Apacehhttpd Server | Configure Apache Server | Test Configuration).

The httpd.conf file is divided into three sections:

Section 1: Global Environment. These directives affect the overall operation of Apache.

Section 2: Main Server Configuration. These directives apply to all Web sites on the server.

Section 3: Virtual Hosts. This section allows you to specify directives for each Web site your Web server is hosting.

The beginning of the httpd.conf file before Section 1 is identical for both Linux and Windows. The information outlines the role of the httpd.conf file and syntax information. For Windows systems, there is a very important syntax item to keep in mind. Instead of using the backslash to separate directories when defining a path, you use forward slashes. For example, instead of using:

```
G:\apache\apache\htdocs
```

to refer to the Web content directory, use:

```
G:/apache/apache/htdocs
```

Drive letters are used as expected to specify the partition the directory is located on.

Section 1: Global Environment specifies directives that apply to all of Apache. In other words, the scope of these directives is Web server wide. The ServerType directive is only applicable to Linux platforms. You can run Apache as either a daemon (standalone) or it can be started by the system process inetd (inetd). The daemon choice is highly recommended. If you choose to use inetd, then each time a request comes into the Web server a new copy of the Web server is launched. This introduces a lot of overhead in the system when creating and closing down the application. The default setting in the httpd.conf file for ServerType is standalone.

The ServerRoot setting indicates the location of the Apache binary, configuration, and log files. If you move the Apache directory, you will need to modify this setting to reflect the new directory location. Please note that the ServerRoot directory is not referring to the Web server's content.

Another specification included in Section 1 is disabling the use of the access.conf and srm.conf files.

```
#ResourceConfig conf/srm.conf
#AccessConfig conf/access.conf
```

These two files were used in previous version of Apache but since there was no standard as to what settings were in which file, a lot of inconsistency between systems developed. As you can see, the # (pound sign) in front prevents the use of the two outdated files.

Section 2: Main Server Configuration contains directives and settings that apply to all of the Web sites hosted by the server. If the Web server is hosting one

Web site, then these settings will apply to the single Web site. If the Web server is hosting multiple sites, virtual hosting, then these settings will apply to all the Web sites hosted by the server. The port setting specifies what TCP/IP port number the Web server will "listen on" for incoming requests. The default port used by Web browsers is 80. If you specify a different port number in the httpd.conf file, you will need to tell all your users what port number to attach to the end of their URL. For example, if you changed the port number to 50000 for the Ouray Mountain Water company's production Web site, then the users would need to put in their browser's URL:

```
http://production.ouraymountainwater.com:50000
```

The ServerAdmin setting allows you to indicate the email address of the individual that should receive messages concerning server related items. This email address may be for the Web administrator or the server administrator. Whatever is appropriate for your environments.

On a Linux system, the User and Group entry allows you to specify the account under which the server runs. For more details on these settings, refer to Chapter 2, "Installing Linux and Apache."

The ServerName definition indicates the name of the Web server. This is the name users will enter in their browsers to access the Web site. This can either be the name of the server or the complete name of the server—that is name and domain name. For example, you could specify www or www .ouraymountainwater.com. If you specify just the name of the server, make sure the Linux or Windows system is in the same domain as the Web server. If the name of the domain where the server resides may change, or if it is different from the domain of the Web server, it is probably "safer" to indicate the complete name of the server for the ServerName parameter.

The DocumentRoot value defines the location of the Web server content. The default location is htdocs under the main Apache directory. It is a good idea for security reasons to move the content directory some place different than the directory where the Apache binary and configuration files are located. Also, remember to take into account the amount of disk space the Web site content will consume. For those reasons, you may want to move the directory so you don't impact disk space for other critical items. You will also need to make this same change to reflect the new document directory location in the <Directory "…"> statement. This <Directory "…"> line immediately follows the comment, "This should be changed to whatever you set DocumentRoot to." The statements between the <Directory "…"> and the next </Directory> indicate settings and directives for the Web site's content directory. These statements include who can access the Web site and if the specifications in the .htaccess file can override any options. The default is to allow everybody the ability to access the Web site and security settings cannot be replaced with values in the .htaccess file. The .htaccess file gives the ability to control access to individual directories so you can have different access permissions for different directories. We cover the .htaccess file usage in Chapter 7.

The UserDir area is used to support users' directories on the Web server. If you plan on allowing the Web server users to read and/or store their own data, you will need to specify the location of the user directories. For example, imagine we decided to support users' directories located under a directory called users on the employee.ouraymountainwater.com private server. For leeann, a user, to access her user directory, she would enter the following URL in her browser:

```
http://employee.ouraymountainwater.com/~leeann
```

The user leeann would then view the default Web page in her directory. The UserDir specification defines the parent directory under which the users' directories are stored. On Linux systems the default user's parent directory is set relative to the $HOME environment variable. If the user's directories are different than their Linux home directories, you will need to specify the path to the parent Web user directories. Also, if you want to make sure the path is defined independent of a variable, which may change, specify the full path to the Web user directories' parent directory. On a Windows 2000 system, there may or may not be home directories in use. You will need to specify the complete path to the location of the parent directory of the Web user directories.

The DirectoryIndex allows you to specify the name or names of HTML files which will be displayed when a user goes to a directory on the Web server with their browser. If you use more than one filename, you can specify each filename separated by a space. For example, in some directories the filename may be index.html and at other locations the name is home.html. To specify both instances, the appropriate entry for DirectoryIndex would be:

```
DirectoryIndex index.html home.html
```

If the directory contains both an index.html and a home.html file, the file listed first in the DirectoryIndex specification is displayed.

The AccessFilename section is designed to specify the name of the file containing directory access information. The default name for this support is .htaccess but you can change this if you wish. Following this entry in the httpd.conf file are a few lines of comments and commands to hide viewing of the .htaccess file from users. This is highly recommended because if a user can view the contents of the .htaccess and the related .htpasswd files then the security of your Web server would be compromised.

The Aliases section allows you to specify aliases for content types and the file locations for the files. You can have as many aliases as you need. The httpd.conf file contains some aliases for icons and cgi scripts.

There are other sections of the httpd.conf file you may want to explore on your own. We have covered in this section those areas where you will most likely be making adjustments for your Web server.

Linux

Listed below is the httpd.conf file from our sample company's public Linux Internet Apache Web server—www.ouraymountainwater.com. The only change to this document from the original is the ServerName, User, and Group settings. Everything else is untouched.

```
##
## httpd.conf -- Apache HTTP server configuration file
##


#
# Based upon the NCSA server configuration files originally by Rob McCool.
#
# This is the main Apache server configuration file.  It contains the
# configuration directives that give the server its instructions.
# See <URL:http://www.apache.org/docs/> for detailed information about
# the directives.
#
# Do NOT simply read the instructions in here without understanding
# what they do.  They're here only as hints or reminders.  If you are unsure
# consult the online docs. You have been warned.
#
# After this file is processed, the server will look for and process
# /usr/local/apache/conf/srm.conf and then /usr/local/apache/conf/access.conf
# unless you have overridden these with ResourceConfig and/or
# AccessConfig directives here.
#
# The configuration directives are grouped into three basic sections:
#  1. Directives that control the operation of the Apache server process as a
#     whole (the 'global environment').
#  2. Directives that define the parameters of the 'main' or 'default' server,
#     which responds to requests that aren't handled by a virtual host.
#     These directives also provide default values for the settings
#     of all virtual hosts.
#  3. Settings for virtual hosts, which allow Web requests to be sent to
#     different IP addresses or hostnames and have them handled by the
#     same Apache server process.
#
# Configuration and logfile names: If the filenames you specify for many
# of the server's control files begin with "/" (or "drive:/" for Win32), the
```

```
# server will use that explicit path.  If the filenames do *not* begin
# with "/", the value of ServerRoot is prepended -- so "logs/foo.log"
# with ServerRoot set to "/usr/local/apache" will be interpreted by the
# server as "/usr/local/apache/logs/foo.log".
#

### Section 1: Global Environment
#
# The directives in this section affect the overall operation of Apache,
# such as the number of concurrent requests it can handle or where it
# can find its configuration files.
#

#
# ServerType is either inetd, or standalone.  Inetd mode is only supported on
# Unix platforms.
#
ServerType standalone

#
# ServerRoot: The top of the directory tree under which the server's
# configuration, error, and log files are kept.
#
# NOTE!  If you intend to place this on an NFS (or otherwise network)
# mounted filesystem then please read the LockFile documentation
# (available at <URL:http://www.apache.org/docs/mod/core.html#lockfile>);
# you will save yourself a lot of trouble.
#
ServerRoot "/usr/local/apache"

#
# The LockFile directive sets the path to the lockfile used when Apache
# is compiled with either USE_FCNTL_SERIALIZED_ACCEPT or
# USE_FLOCK_SERIALIZED_ACCEPT. This directive should normally be left at
# its default value. The main reason for changing it is if the logs
# directory is NFS mounted, since the lockfile MUST BE STORED ON A LOCAL
# DISK. The PID of the main server process is automatically appended to
# the filename.
#
#LockFile /usr/local/apache/logs/httpd.lock

#
# PidFile: The file in which the server should record its process
# identification number when it starts.
#
PidFile /usr/local/apache/logs/httpd.pid

#
# ScoreBoardFile: File used to store internal server process information.
# Not all architectures require this.  But if yours does (you'll know because
# this file will be  created when you run Apache) then you *must* ensure that
```

```
# no two invocations of Apache share the same scoreboard file.
#
ScoreBoardFile /usr/local/apache/logs/httpd.scoreboard


#
# In the standard configuration, the server will process httpd.conf (this
# file, specified by the -f command line option), srm.conf, and access.conf
# in that order.  The latter two files are now distributed empty, as it is
# recommended that all directives be kept in a single file for simplicity.
# The commented-out values below are the built-in defaults.  You can have the
# server ignore these files altogether by using "/dev/null" (for Unix) or
# "nul" (for Win32) for the arguments to the directives.
#
#ResourceConfig conf/srm.conf
#AccessConfig conf/access.conf


#
# Timeout: The number of seconds before receives and sends time out.
#
Timeout 300


#
# KeepAlive: Whether or not to allow persistent connections (more than
# one request per connection). Set to "Off" to deactivate.
#
KeepAlive On


#
# MaxKeepAliveRequests: The maximum number of requests to allow
# during a persistent connection. Set to 0 to allow an unlimited amount.
# We recommend you leave this number high, for maximum performance.
#
MaxKeepAliveRequests 100


#
# KeepAliveTimeout: Number of seconds to wait for the next request from the
# same client on the same connection.
#
KeepAliveTimeout 15


#
# Server-pool size regulation.  Rather than making you guess how many
# server processes you need, Apache dynamically adapts to the load it
# sees --- that is, it tries to maintain enough server processes to
# handle the current load, plus a few spare servers to handle transient
# load spikes (e.g., multiple simultaneous requests from a single
# Netscape browser).
#
# It does this by periodically checking how many servers are waiting
# for a request.  If there are fewer than MinSpareServers, it creates
# a new spare.  If there are more than MaxSpareServers, some of the
```

```
# spares die off.  The default values are probably OK for most sites.
#
MinSpareServers 5
MaxSpareServers 10


#
# Number of servers to start initially --- should be a reasonable ballpark
# figure.
#
StartServers 5


#
# Limit on total number of servers running, i.e., limit on the number
# of clients who can simultaneously connect --- if this limit is ever
# reached, clients will be LOCKED OUT, so it should NOT BE SET TOO LOW.
# It is intended mainly as a brake to keep a runaway server from taking
# the system with it as it spirals down...
#
MaxClients 150


#
# MaxRequestsPerChild: the number of requests each child process is
# allowed to process before the child dies.  The child will exit so
# as to avoid problems after prolonged use when Apache (and maybe the
# libraries it uses) leak memory or other resources.  On most systems, this
# isn't really needed, but a few (such as Solaris) do have notable leaks
# in the libraries. For these platforms, set to something like 10000
# or so; a setting of 0 means unlimited.
#
# NOTE: This value does not include keepalive requests after the initial
#       request per connection. For example, if a child process handles
#       an initial request and 10 subsequent "keptalive" requests, it
#       would only count as 1 request towards this limit.
#
MaxRequestsPerChild 0


#
# Listen: Allows you to bind Apache to specific IP addresses and/or
# ports, in addition to the default. See also the <VirtualHost>
# directive.
#
#Listen 3000
#Listen 12.34.56.78:80


#
# BindAddress: You can support virtual hosts with this option. This directive
# is used to tell the server which IP address to listen to. It can either
# contain "*", an IP address, or a fully qualified Internet domain name.
# See also the <VirtualHost> and Listen directives.
#
#BindAddress *
```

```
#
# Dynamic Shared Object (DSO) Support
#
# To be able to use the functionality of a module which was built as a DSO you
# have to place corresponding 'LoadModule' lines at this location so the
# directives contained in it are actually available _before_ they are used.
# Please read the file README.DSO in the Apache 1.3 distribution for more
# details about the DSO mechanism and run 'httpd -l' for the list of already
# built-in (statically linked and thus always available) modules in your httpd
# binary.
#
# Note: The order in which modules are loaded is important.  Don't change
# the order below without expert advice.
#
# Example:
# LoadModule foo_module libexec/mod_foo.so


#
# ExtendedStatus controls whether Apache will generate "full" status
# information (ExtendedStatus On) or just basic information (ExtendedStatus
# Off) when the "server-status" handler is called. The default is Off.
#
#ExtendedStatus On


### Section 2: 'Main' server configuration
#
# The directives in this section set up the values used by the 'main'
# server, which responds to any requests that aren't handled by a
# <VirtualHost> definition.  These values also provide defaults for
# any <VirtualHost> containers you may define later in the file.
#
# All of these directives may appear inside <VirtualHost> containers,
# in which case these default settings will be overridden for the
# virtual host being defined.
#


#
# If your ServerType directive (set earlier in the 'Global Environment'
# section) is set to "inetd", the next few directives don't have any
# effect since their settings are defined by the inetd configuration.
# Skip ahead to the ServerAdmin directive.
#


#
# Port: The port to which the standalone server listens. For
# ports < 1023, you will need httpd to be run as root initially.
#
Port 80


#
```

```
# If you wish httpd to run as a different user or group, you must run
# httpd as root initially and it will switch.
#
# User/Group: The name (or #number) of the user/group to run httpd as.
#  . On SCO (ODT 3) use "User nouser" and "Group nogroup".
#  . On HPUX you may not be able to use shared memory as nobody, and the
#    suggested workaround is to create a user www and use that user.
#  NOTE that some kernels refuse to setgid(Group) or semctl(IPC_SET)
#  when the value of (unsigned)Group is above 60000;
#  don't use Group nobody on these systems!
#
User apache
Group apache


#
# ServerAdmin: Your address, where problems with the server should be
# e-mailed.  This address appears on some server-generated pages, such
# as error documents.
#
ServerAdmin root@www


#
# ServerName allows you to set a host name which is sent back to clients for
# your server if it's different than the one the program would get (i.e., use
# "www" instead of the host's real name).
#
# Note: You cannot just invent host names and hope they work. The name you
# define here must be a valid DNS name for your host. If you don't understand
# this, ask your network administrator.
# If your host doesn't have a registered DNS name, enter its IP address here.
# You will have to access it by its address (e.g., http://123.45.67.89/)
# anyway, and this will make redirections work in a sensible way.
#
# 127.0.0.1 is the TCP/IP local loop-back address, often named localhost. Your
# machine always knows itself by this address. If you use Apache strictly for
# local testing and development, you may use 127.0.0.1 as the server name.
#
ServerName www.ouraymountainwater.com


#
# DocumentRoot: The directory out of which you will serve your
# documents. By default, all requests are taken from this directory, but
# symbolic links and aliases may be used to point to other locations.
#
DocumentRoot "/usr/local/apache/htdocs"


#
# Each directory to which Apache has access, can be configured with respect
# to which services and features are allowed and/or disabled in that
# directory (and its subdirectories).
#
```

```
# First, we configure the "default" to be a very restrictive set of
# permissions.
#
<Directory />
    Options FollowSymLinks
    AllowOverride None
</Directory>

#
# Note that from this point forward you must specifically allow
# particular features to be enabled - so if something's not working as
# you might expect, make sure that you have specifically enabled it
# below.
#

#
# This should be changed to whatever you set DocumentRoot to.
#
<Directory "/usr/local/apache/htdocs">

#
# This may also be "None", "All", or any combination of "Indexes",
# "Includes", "FollowSymLinks", "ExecCGI", or "MultiViews".
#
# Note that "MultiViews" must be named *explicitly* --- "Options All"
# doesn't give it to you.
#
    Options Indexes FollowSymLinks MultiViews

#
# This controls which options the .htaccess files in directories can
# override. Can also be "All", or any combination of "Options", "FileInfo",
# "AuthConfig", and "Limit"
#
    AllowOverride None

#
# Controls who can get stuff from this server.
#
    Order allow,deny
    Allow from all
</Directory>

#
# UserDir: The name of the directory which is appended onto a user's home
# directory if a ~user request is received.
#
<IfModule mod_userdir.c>
    UserDir public_html
</IfModule>
```

```
#
# Control access to UserDir directories.  The following is an example
# for a site where these directories are restricted to read-only.
#
#<Directory /home/*/public_html>
#     AllowOverride FileInfo AuthConfig Limit
#     Options MultiViews Indexes SymLinksIfOwnerMatch IncludesNoExec
#     <Limit GET POST OPTIONS PROPFIND>
#         Order allow,deny
#         Allow from all
#     </Limit>
#     <LimitExcept GET POST OPTIONS PROPFIND>
#         Order deny,allow
#         Deny from all
#     </LimitExcept>
#</Directory>


#
# DirectoryIndex: Name of the file or files to use as a pre-written HTML
# directory index.  Separate multiple entries with spaces.
#
<IfModule mod_dir.c>
    DirectoryIndex index.html
</IfModule>


#
# AccessFileName: The name of the file to look for in each directory
# for access control information.
#
AccessFileName .htaccess


#
# The following lines prevent .htaccess files from being viewed by
# Web clients.  Since .htaccess files often contain authorization
# information, access is disallowed for security reasons.  Comment
# these lines out if you want Web visitors to see the contents of
# .htaccess files.  If you change the AccessFileName directive above,
# be sure to make the corresponding changes here.
#
# Also, folks tend to use names such as .htpasswd for password
# files, so this will protect those as well.
#
<Files ~ "^\.ht">
    Order allow,deny
    Deny from all
</Files>


#
# CacheNegotiatedDocs: By default, Apache sends "Pragma: no-cache" with each
# document that was negotiated on the basis of content. This asks proxy
# servers not to cache the document. Uncommenting the following line disables
```

```
# this behavior, and proxies will be allowed to cache the documents.
#
#CacheNegotiatedDocs


#
# UseCanonicalName:  (new for 1.3)  With this setting turned on, whenever
# Apache needs to construct a self-referencing URL (a URL that refers back
# to the server the response is coming from) it will use ServerName and
# Port to form a "canonical" name.  With this setting off, Apache will
# use the hostname:port that the client supplied, when possible.  This
# also affects SERVER_NAME and SERVER_PORT in CGI scripts.
#
UseCanonicalName On


#
# TypesConfig describes where the mime.types file (or equivalent) is
# to be found.
#
<IfModule mod_mime.c>
    TypesConfig /usr/local/apache/conf/mime.types
</IfModule>


#
# DefaultType is the default MIME type the server will use for a document
# if it cannot otherwise determine one, such as from filename extensions.
# If your server contains mostly text or HTML documents, "text/plain" is
# a good value.  If most of your content is binary, such as applications
# or images, you may want to use "application/octet-stream" instead to
# keep browsers from trying to display binary files as though they are
# text.
#
DefaultType text/plain


#
# The mod_mime_magic module allows the server to use various hints from the
# contents of the file itself to determine its type.  The MIMEMagicFile
# directive tells the module where the hint definitions are located.
# mod_mime_magic is not part of the default server (you have to add
# it yourself with a LoadModule [see the DSO paragraph in the 'Global
# Environment' section], or recompile the server and include mod_mime_magic
# as part of the configuration), so it's enclosed in an <IfModule> container.
# This means that the MIMEMagicFile directive will only be processed if the
# module is part of the server.
#
<IfModule mod_mime_magic.c>
    MIMEMagicFile /usr/local/apache/conf/magic
</IfModule>


#
# HostnameLookups: Log the names of clients or just their IP addresses
# e.g., www.apache.org (on) or 204.62.129.132 (off).
```

```
# The default is off because it'd be overall better for the net if people
# had to knowingly turn this feature on, since enabling it means that
# each client request will result in AT LEAST one lookup request to the
# nameserver.
#
HostnameLookups Off


#
# ErrorLog: The location of the error log file.
# If you do not specify an ErrorLog directive within a <VirtualHost>
# container, error messages relating to that virtual host will be
# logged here.  If you *do* define an error logfile for a <VirtualHost>
# container, that host's errors will be logged there and not here.
#
ErrorLog /usr/local/apache/logs/error_log


#
# LogLevel: Control the number of messages logged to the error_log.
# Possible values include: debug, info, notice, warn, error, crit,
# alert, emerg.
#
LogLevel warn


#
# The following directives define some format nicknames for use with
# a CustomLog directive (see below).
#
LogFormat "%h %l %u %t \"%r\" %>s %b \"%{Referer}i\" \"%{User-Agent}i\""
combined
LogFormat "%h %l %u %t \"%r\" %>s %b" common
LogFormat "%{Referer}i -> %U" referer
LogFormat "%{User-agent}i" agent


#
# The location and format of the access logfile (Common Logfile Format).
# If you do not define any access logfiles within a <VirtualHost>
# container, they will be logged here.  Contrariwise, if you *do*
# define per-<VirtualHost> access logfiles, transactions will be
# logged therein and *not* in this file.
#
CustomLog /usr/local/apache/logs/access_log common


#
# If you would like to have agent and referer logfiles, uncomment the
# following directives.
#
#CustomLog /usr/local/apache/logs/referer_log referer
#CustomLog /usr/local/apache/logs/agent_log agent


#
# If you prefer a single logfile with access, agent, and referer information
```

```
# (Combined Logfile Format) you can use the following directive.
#
#CustomLog /usr/local/apache/logs/access_log combined


#
# Optionally add a line containing the server version and virtual host
# name to server-generated pages (error documents, FTP directory listings,
# mod_status and mod_info output etc., but not CGI generated documents).
# Set to "EMail" to also include a mailto: link to the ServerAdmin.
# Set to one of:  On | Off | EMail
#
ServerSignature On


# EBCDIC configuration:
# (only for mainframes using the EBCDIC codeset, currently one of:
# Fujitsu-Siemens' BS2000/OSD, IBM's OS/390 and IBM's TPF)!!
# The following default configuration assumes that "text files"
# are stored in EBCDIC (so that you can operate on them using the
# normal POSIX tools like grep and sort) while "binary files" are
# stored with identical octets as on an ASCII machine.
#
# The directives are evaluated in configuration file order, with
# the EBCDICConvert directives applied before EBCDICConvertByType.
#
# If you want to have ASCII HTML documents and EBCDIC HTML documents
# at the same time, you can use the file extension to force
# conversion off for the ASCII documents:
# > AddType        text/html .ahtml
# > EBCDICConvert Off=InOut .ahtml
#
# EBCDICConvertByType  On=InOut text/* message/* multipart/*
# EBCDICConvertByType  On=In    application/x-www-form-urlencoded
# EBCDICConvertByType  On=InOut application/postscript model/vrml
# EBCDICConvertByType Off=InOut */*


#
# Aliases: Add here as many aliases as you need (with no limit). The format is
# Alias fakename realname
#
<IfModule mod_alias.c>

    #
    # Note that if you include a trailing / on fakename then the server will
    # require it to be present in the URL.  So "/icons" isn't aliased in this
    # example, only "/icons/".  If the fakename is slash-terminated, then the
    # realname must also be slash terminated, and if the fakename omits the
    # trailing slash, the realname must also omit it.
    #
    Alias /icons/ "/usr/local/apache/icons/"
```

```
<Directory "/usr/local/apache/icons">
    Options Indexes MultiViews
    AllowOverride None
    Order allow,deny
    Allow from all
</Directory>


#
# ScriptAlias: This controls which directories contain server scripts.
# ScriptAliases are essentially the same as Aliases, except that
# documents in the realname directory are treated as applications and
# run by the server when requested rather than as documents sent to the
client.
# The same rules about trailing "/" apply to ScriptAlias directives as to
# Alias.
#
ScriptAlias /cgi-bin/ "/usr/local/apache/cgi-bin/"


#
# "/usr/local/apache/cgi-bin" should be changed to whatever your
ScriptAliased
# CGI directory exists, if you have that configured.
#
<Directory "/usr/local/apache/cgi-bin">
    AllowOverride None
    Options None
    Order allow,deny
    Allow from all
</Directory>


</IfModule>
# End of aliases.


#
# Redirect allows you to tell clients about documents which used to exist in
# your server's namespace, but do not anymore. This allows you to tell the
# clients where to look for the relocated document.
# Format: Redirect old-URI new-URL
#


#
# Directives controlling the display of server-generated directory listings.
#
<IfModule mod_autoindex.c>

    #
    # FancyIndexing is whether you want fancy directory indexing or standard
    #
    IndexOptions FancyIndexing

    #
```

```
# AddIcon* directives tell the server which icon to show for different
# files or filename extensions.  These are only displayed for
# FancyIndexed directories.
#
AddIconByEncoding (CMP,/icons/compressed.gif) x-compress x-gzip

AddIconByType (TXT,/icons/text.gif) text/*
AddIconByType (IMG,/icons/image2.gif) image/*
AddIconByType (SND,/icons/sound2.gif) audio/*
AddIconByType (VID,/icons/movie.gif) video/*

AddIcon /icons/binary.gif .bin .exe
AddIcon /icons/binhex.gif .hqx
AddIcon /icons/tar.gif .tar
AddIcon /icons/world2.gif .wrl .wrl.gz .vrml .vrm .iv
AddIcon /icons/compressed.gif .Z .z .tgz .gz .zip
AddIcon /icons/a.gif .ps .ai .eps
AddIcon /icons/layout.gif .html .shtml .htm .pdf
AddIcon /icons/text.gif .txt
AddIcon /icons/c.gif .c
AddIcon /icons/p.gif .pl .py
AddIcon /icons/f.gif .for
AddIcon /icons/dvi.gif .dvi
AddIcon /icons/uuencoded.gif .uu
AddIcon /icons/script.gif .conf .sh .shar .csh .ksh .tcl
AddIcon /icons/tex.gif .tex
AddIcon /icons/bomb.gif core

AddIcon /icons/back.gif ..
AddIcon /icons/hand.right.gif README
AddIcon /icons/folder.gif ^^DIRECTORY^^
AddIcon /icons/blank.gif ^^BLANKICON^^

#
# DefaultIcon is which icon to show for files which do not have an icon
# explicitly set.
#
DefaultIcon /icons/unknown.gif

#
# AddDescription allows you to place a short description after a file in
# server-generated indexes.  These are only displayed for FancyIndexed
# directories.
# Format: AddDescription "description" filename
#
# AddDescription "GZIP compressed document" .gz
# AddDescription "tar archive" .tar
# AddDescription "GZIP compressed tar archive" .tgz

#
# ReadmeName is the name of the README file the server will look for by
```

```
      # default, and append to directory listings.
      #
      # HeaderName is the name of a file which should be prepended to
      # directory indexes.
      #
      # If MultiViews are amongst the Options in effect, the server will
      # first look for name.html and include it if found.  If name.html
      # doesn't exist, the server will then look for name.txt and include
      # it as plaintext if found.
      #
      ReadmeName README
      HeaderName HEADER

      #
      # IndexIgnore is a set of filenames which directory indexing should ignore
      # and not include in the listing.  Shell-style wildcarding is permitted.
      #
      IndexIgnore .??* *~ *# HEADER* README* RCS CVS *,v *,t

</IfModule>
# End of indexing directives.

#
# Document types.
#
<IfModule mod_mime.c>

      #
      # AddEncoding allows you to have certain browsers (Mosaic/X 2.1+) uncompress
      # information on the fly. Note: Not all browsers support this.
      # Despite the name similarity, the following Add* directives have nothing
      # to do with the FancyIndexing customization directives above.
      #
      AddEncoding x-compress Z
      AddEncoding x-gzip gz tgz

      #
      # AddLanguage allows you to specify the language of a document. You can
      # then use content negotiation to give a browser a file in a language
      # it can understand.
      #
      # Note 1: The suffix does not have to be the same as the language
      # keyword --- those with documents in Polish (whose net-standard
      # language code is pl) may wish to use "AddLanguage pl .po" to
      # avoid the ambiguity with the common suffix for perl scripts.
      #
      # Note 2: The example entries below illustrate that in quite
      # some cases the two character 'Language' abbreviation is not
      # identical to the two character 'Country' code for its country,
      # E.g. 'Danmark/dk' versus 'Danish/da'.
      #
```

```
# Note 3: In the case of 'ltz' we violate the RFC by using a three char
# specifier. But there is 'work in progress' to fix this and get
# the reference data for rfc1766 cleaned up.
#
# Danish (da) - Dutch (nl) - English (en) - Estonian (ee)
# French (fr) - German (de) - Greek-Modern (el)
# Italian (it) - Korean (kr) - Norwegian (no)
# Portugese (pt) - Luxembourgeois* (ltz)
# Spanish (es) - Swedish (sv) - Catalan (ca) - Czech(cz)
# Polish (pl) - Brazilian Portuguese (pt-br) - Japanese (ja)
# Russian (ru)
#
AddLanguage da .dk
AddLanguage nl .nl
AddLanguage en .en
AddLanguage et .ee
AddLanguage fr .fr
AddLanguage de .de
AddLanguage el .el
AddLanguage he .he
AddCharset ISO-8859-8 .iso8859-8
AddLanguage it .it
AddLanguage ja .ja
AddCharset ISO-2022-JP .jis
AddLanguage kr .kr
AddCharset ISO-2022-KR .iso-kr
AddLanguage no .no
AddLanguage pl .po
AddCharset ISO-8859-2 .iso-pl
AddLanguage pt .pt
AddLanguage pt-br .pt-br
AddLanguage ltz .lu
AddLanguage ca .ca
AddLanguage es .es
AddLanguage sv .se
AddLanguage cz .cz
AddLanguage ru .ru
AddLanguage zh-tw .tw
AddLanguage tw .tw
AddCharset Big5         .Big5    .big5
AddCharset WINDOWS-1251 .cp-1251
AddCharset CP866        .cp866
AddCharset ISO-8859-5   .iso-ru
AddCharset KOI8-R       .koi-r
AddCharset UCS-2        .ucs2
AddCharset UCS-4        .ucs4
AddCharset UTF-8        .utf8


# LanguagePriority allows you to give precedence to some languages
# in case of a tie during content negotiation.
#
```

```
# Just list the languages in decreasing order of preference. We have
# more or less alphabetized them here. You probably want to change this.
#
<IfModule mod_negotiation.c>
    LanguagePriority en da nl et fr de el it ja kr no pl pt pt-br ru ltz ca
    es sv tw
</IfModule>


#
# AddType allows you to tweak mime.types without actually editing it, or to
# make certain files to be certain types.
#
# For example, the PHP 3.x module (not part of the Apache distribution - see
# http://www.php.net) will typically use:
#
#AddType application/x-httpd-php3 .php3
#AddType application/x-httpd-php3-source .phps
#
# And for PHP 4.x, use:
#
#AddType application/x-httpd-php .php
#AddType application/x-httpd-php-source .phps

AddType application/x-tar .tgz


#
# AddHandler allows you to map certain file extensions to "handlers",
# actions unrelated to filetype. These can be either built into the server
# or added with the Action command (see below)
#
# If you want to use server side includes, or CGI outside
# ScriptAliased directories, uncomment the following lines.
#
# To use CGI scripts:
#
#AddHandler cgi-script .cgi


#
# To use server-parsed HTML files
#
#AddType text/html .shtml
#AddHandler server-parsed .shtml


#
# Uncomment the following line to enable Apache's send-asis HTTP file
# feature
#
#AddHandler send-as-is asis


#
# If you wish to use server-parsed imagemap files, use
```

```
    #
    #AddHandler imap-file map

    #
    # To enable type maps, you might want to use
    #
    #AddHandler type-map var

</IfModule>
# End of document types.

#
# Action lets you define media types that will execute a script whenever
# a matching file is called. This eliminates the need for repeated URL
# pathnames for oft-used CGI file processors.
# Format: Action media/type /cgi-script/location
# Format: Action handler-name /cgi-script/location
#

#
# MetaDir: specifies the name of the directory in which Apache can find
# meta information files. These files contain additional HTTP headers
# to include when sending the document
#
#MetaDir .web

#
# MetaSuffix: specifies the file name suffix for the file containing the
# meta information.
#
#MetaSuffix .meta

#
# Customizable error response (Apache style)
#   these come in three flavors
#
#     1) plain text
#ErrorDocument 500 "The server made a boo boo.
#  n.b.  the single leading (") marks it as text, it does not get output
#
#     2) local redirects
#ErrorDocument 404 /missing.html
#  to redirect to local URL /missing.html
#ErrorDocument 404 /cgi-bin/missing_handler.pl
#  N.B.: You can redirect to a script or a document using server-side-includes.
#
#     3) external redirects
#ErrorDocument 402 http://some.other_server.com/subscription_info.html
#  N.B.: Many of the environment variables associated with the original
#  request will *not* be available to such a script.
```

```
#
# Customize behaviour based on the browser
#
<IfModule mod_setenvif.c>

    #
    # The following directives modify normal HTTP response behavior.
    # The first directive disables keepalive for Netscape 2.x and browsers that
    # spoof it. There are known problems with these browser implementations.
    # The second directive is for Microsoft Internet Explorer 4.0b2
    # which has a broken HTTP/1.1 implementation and does not properly
    # support keepalive when it is used on 301 or 302 (redirect) responses.
    #
    BrowserMatch "Mozilla/2" nokeepalive
    BrowserMatch "MSIE 4\.0b2;" nokeepalive downgrade-1.0 force-response-1.0

    #
    # The following directive disables HTTP/1.1 responses to browsers which
    # are in violation of the HTTP/1.0 spec by not being able to grok a
    # basic 1.1 response.
    #
    BrowserMatch "RealPlayer 4\.0" force-response-1.0
    BrowserMatch "Java/1\.0" force-response-1.0
    BrowserMatch "JDK/1\.0" force-response-1.0

</IfModule>
# End of browser customization directives

#
# Allow server status reports, with the URL of http://servername/server-status
# Change the ".your_domain.com" to match your domain to enable.
#
#<Location /server-status>
#    SetHandler server-status
#    Order deny,allow
#    Deny from all
#    Allow from .your_domain.com
#</Location>

#
# Allow remote server configuration reports, with the URL of
# http://servername/server-info (requires that mod_info.c be loaded).
# Change the ".your_domain.com" to match your domain to enable.
#
#<Location /server-info>
#    SetHandler server-info
#    Order deny,allow
#    Deny from all
#    Allow from .your_domain.com
#</Location>
```

```
#
# There have been reports of people trying to abuse an old bug from pre-1.1
# days.  This bug involved a CGI script distributed as a part of Apache.
# By uncommenting these lines you can redirect these attacks to a logging
# script on phf.apache.org.  Or, you can record them yourself, using the script
# support/phf_abuse_log.cgi.
#
#<Location /cgi-bin/phf*>
#    Deny from all
#    ErrorDocument 403 http://phf.apache.org/phf_abuse_log.cgi
#</Location>


#
# Proxy Server directives. Uncomment the following lines to
# enable the proxy server:
#
#<IfModule mod_proxy.c>
#    ProxyRequests On

#    <Directory proxy:*>
#        Order deny,allow
#        Deny from all
#        Allow from .your_domain.com
#    </Directory>

    #
    # Enable/disable the handling of HTTP/1.1 "Via:" headers.
    # ("Full" adds the server version; "Block" removes all outgoing Via: headers)
    # Set to one of: Off | On | Full | Block
    #
#    ProxyVia On

    #
    # To enable the cache as well, edit and uncomment the following lines:
    # (no cacheing without CacheRoot)
    #
#    CacheRoot "/usr/local/apache/proxy"
#    CacheSize 5
#    CacheGcInterval 4
#    CacheMaxExpire 24
#    CacheLastModifiedFactor 0.1
#    CacheDefaultExpire 1
#    NoCache a_domain.com another_domain.edu joes.garage_sale.com

#</IfModule>
# End of proxy directives.

### Section 3: Virtual Hosts
#
# VirtualHost: If you want to maintain multiple domains/hostnames on your
# machine you can setup VirtualHost containers for them. Most configurations
```

```
# use only name-based virtual hosts so the server doesn't need to worry about
# IP addresses. This is indicated by the asterisks in the directives below.
#
# Please see the documentation at <URL:http://www.apache.org/docs/vhosts/>
# for further details before you try to setup virtual hosts.
#
# You may use the command line option '-S' to verify your virtual host
# configuration.

#
# Use name-based virtual hosting.
#
#NameVirtualHost *

#
# VirtualHost example:
# Almost any Apache directive may go into a VirtualHost container.
# The first VirtualHost section is used for requests without a known
# server name.
#
#<VirtualHost *>
#      ServerAdmin webmaster@dummy-host.example.com
#      DocumentRoot /www/docs/dummy-host.example.com
#      ServerName dummy-host.example.com
#      ErrorLog logs/dummy-host.example.com-error_log
#      CustomLog logs/dummy-host.example.com-access_log common
#</VirtualHost>
```

Windows

Listed below is the httpd.conf file from our sample company's Windows 2000 private Apache Web server—production.ouraymountainwater.com. The only change to this document from the original is the ServerName settings. Everything else is untouched.

```
#
# Based upon the NCSA server configuration files originally by Rob McCool.
#
# This is the main Apache server configuration file.  It contains the
# configuration directives that give the server its instructions.
# See <URL:http://www.apache.org/docs/> for detailed information about
# the directives.
#
# Do NOT simply read the instructions in here without understanding
# what they do.  They're here only as hints or reminders.  If you are unsure
# consult the online docs. You have been warned.
#
# After this file is processed, the server will look for and process
# G:/Apache/Apache/conf/srm.conf and then G:/Apache/Apache/conf/access.conf
```

```
# unless you have overridden these with ResourceConfig and/or
# AccessConfig directives here.
#
# The configuration directives are grouped into three basic sections:
#  1. Directives that control the operation of the Apache server process as a
#     whole (the 'global environment').
#  2. Directives that define the parameters of the 'main' or 'default' server,
#     which responds to requests that aren't handled by a virtual host.
#     These directives also provide default values for the settings
#     of all virtual hosts.
#  3. Settings for virtual hosts, which allow Web requests to be sent to
#     different IP addresses or hostnames and have them handled by the
#     same Apache server process.
#
# Configuration and logfile names: If the filenames you specify for many
# of the server's control files begin with "/" (or "drive:/" for Win32), the
# server will use that explicit path.  If the filenames do *not* begin
# with "/", the value of ServerRoot is prepended -- so "logs/foo.log"
# with ServerRoot set to "/usr/local/apache" will be interpreted by the
# server as "/usr/local/apache/logs/foo.log".
#
# NOTE: Where filenames are specified, you must use forward slashes
# instead of backslashes (e.g., "c:/apache" instead of "c:\apache").
# If a drive letter is omitted, the drive on which Apache.exe is located
# will be used by default.  It is recommended that you always supply
# an explicit drive letter in absolute paths, however, to avoid
# confusion.
#


### Section 1: Global Environment
#
# The directives in this section affect the overall operation of Apache,
# such as the number of concurrent requests it can handle or where it
# can find its configuration files.
#


#
# ServerType is either inetd, or standalone.  Inetd mode is only supported on
# Unix platforms.
#
ServerType standalone


#
# ServerRoot: The top of the directory tree under which the server's
# configuration, error, and log files are kept.
#
ServerRoot "G:/Apache/Apache"


#
# PidFile: The file in which the server should record its process
# identification number when it starts.
```

```
#
PidFile logs/httpd.pid

#
# ScoreBoardFile: File used to store internal server process information.
# Not all architectures require this.  But if yours does (you'll know because
# this file will be  created when you run Apache) then you *must* ensure that
# no two invocations of Apache share the same scoreboard file.
#
ScoreBoardFile logs/apache_runtime_status

#
# In the standard configuration, the server will process httpd.conf (this
# file, specified by the -f command line option), srm.conf, and access.conf
# in that order.  The latter two files are now distributed empty, as it is
# recommended that all directives be kept in a single file for simplicity.
# The commented-out values below are the built-in defaults.  You can have the
# server ignore these files altogether by using "/dev/null" (for Unix) or
# "nul" (for Win32) for the arguments to the directives.
#
#ResourceConfig conf/srm.conf
#AccessConfig conf/access.conf

#
# Timeout: The number of seconds before receives and sends time out.
#
Timeout 300

#
# KeepAlive: Whether or not to allow persistent connections (more than
# one request per connection). Set to "Off" to deactivate.
#
KeepAlive On

#
# MaxKeepAliveRequests: The maximum number of requests to allow
# during a persistent connection. Set to 0 to allow an unlimited amount.
# We recommend you leave this number high, for maximum performance.
#
MaxKeepAliveRequests 100

#
# KeepAliveTimeout: Number of seconds to wait for the next request from the
# same client on the same connection.
#
KeepAliveTimeout 15

#
# Apache on Win32 always creates one child process to handle requests.  If it
# dies, another child process is created automatically.  Within the child
# process multiple threads handle incoming requests.  The next two
```

```
# directives control the behaviour of the threads and processes.
#

#
# MaxRequestsPerChild: the number of requests each child process is
# allowed to process before the child dies.  The child will exit so
# as to avoid problems after prolonged use when Apache (and maybe the
# libraries it uses) leak memory or other resources.  On most systems, this
# isn't really needed, but a few (such as Solaris) do have notable leaks
# in the libraries.  For Win32, set this value to zero (unlimited)
# unless advised otherwise.
#
# NOTE: This value does not include keepalive requests after the initial
#       request per connection. For example, if a child process handles
#       an initial request and 10 subsequent "keptalive" requests, it
#       would only count as 1 request towards this limit.
#
MaxRequestsPerChild 0

#
# Number of concurrent threads (i.e., requests) the server will allow.
# Set this value according to the responsiveness of the server (more
# requests active at once means they're all handled more slowly) and
# the amount of system resources you'll allow the server to consume.
#
ThreadsPerChild 50

#
# Listen: Allows you to bind Apache to specific IP addresses and/or
# ports, in addition to the default. See also the <VirtualHost>
# directive.
#
#Listen 3000
#Listen 12.34.56.78:80

#
# BindAddress: You can support virtual hosts with this option. This directive
# is used to tell the server which IP address to listen to. It can either
# contain "*", an IP address, or a fully qualified Internet domain name.
# See also the <VirtualHost> and Listen directives.
#
#BindAddress *

#
# Apache Modules compiled into the standard Windows build
#
# The following modules are bound into the standard Apache binary distribution
# for Windows.  To change the standard behavior, uncomment the following lines
# and modify the list of those specific modules to be enabled in the server.
#
# WARNING: This is an advanced option that may render your server inoperable!
```

```
# Do not use these directives without expert guidance.
#
#ClearModuleList
#AddModule mod_so.c mod_mime.c mod_access.c mod_auth.c mod_negotiation.c
#AddModule mod_include.c mod_autoindex.c mod_dir.c mod_cgi.c mod_userdir.c
#AddModule mod_alias.c mod_env.c mod_log_config.c mod_asis.c mod_imap.c
#AddModule mod_actions.c mod_setenvif.c mod_isapi.c


#
# Dynamic Shared Object (DSO) Support
#
# To be able to use the functionality of a module which was built as a DSO you
# have to place corresponding 'LoadModule' lines at this location so the
# directives contained in it are actually available _before_ they are used.
# Please read the file README.DSO in the Apache 1.3 distribution for more
# details about the DSO mechanism and run 'apache -l' for the list of already
# built-in (statically linked and thus always available) modules in your Apache
# binary.
#
# Note: The order in which modules are loaded is important.  Don't change
# the order below without expert advice.
#
#LoadModule anon_auth_module modules/mod_auth_anon.so
#LoadModule dbm_auth_module modules/mod_auth_dbm.so
#LoadModule digest_auth_module modules/mod_auth_digest.so
#LoadModule cern_meta_module modules/mod_cern_meta.so
#LoadModule digest_module modules/mod_digest.so
#LoadModule expires_module modules/mod_expires.so
#LoadModule headers_module modules/mod_headers.so
#LoadModule proxy_module modules/mod_proxy.so
#LoadModule rewrite_module modules/mod_rewrite.so
#LoadModule speling_module modules/mod_speling.so
#LoadModule info_module modules/mod_info.so
#LoadModule status_module modules/mod_status.so
#LoadModule usertrack_module modules/mod_usertrack.so


#
# ExtendedStatus controls whether Apache will generate "full" status
# information (ExtendedStatus On) or just basic information (ExtendedStatus
# Off) when the "server-status" handler is called. The default is Off.
#
#ExtendedStatus On

### Section 2: 'Main' server configuration
#
# The directives in this section set up the values used by the 'main'
# server, which responds to any requests that aren't handled by a
# <VirtualHost> definition.  These values also provide defaults for
# any <VirtualHost> containers you may define later in the file.
#
# All of these directives may appear inside <VirtualHost> containers,
```

```
# in which case these default settings will be overridden for the
# virtual host being defined.
#


#
# Port: The port to which the standalone server listens.  Certain firewall
# products must be configured before Apache can listen to a specific port.
# Other running httpd servers will also interfere with this port.  Disable
# all firewall, security, and other services if you encounter problems.
# To help diagnose problems use the Windows NT command NETSTAT -a
#
Port 80

#
# ServerAdmin: Your address, where problems with the server should be
# e-mailed.  This address appears on some server-generated pages, such
# as error documents.
#
ServerAdmin administrator@ouraywatermountain.com

#
# ServerName allows you to set a host name which is sent back to clients for
# your server if it's different than the one the program would get (i.e., use
# "www" instead of the host's real name).
#
# Note: You cannot just invent host names and hope they work. The name you
# define here must be a valid DNS name for your host. If you don't understand
# this, ask your network administrator.
# If your host doesn't have a registered DNS name, enter its IP address here.
# You will have to access it by its address (e.g., http://123.45.67.89/)
# anyway, and this will make redirections work in a sensible way.
#
# 127.0.0.1 is the TCP/IP local loop-back address, often named localhost. Your
# machine always knows itself by this address. If you use Apache strictly for
# local testing and development, you may use 127.0.0.1 as the server name.
#
ServerName production.ouraymountainwater.com


#
# DocumentRoot: The directory out of which you will serve your
# documents. By default, all requests are taken from this directory, but
# symbolic links and aliases may be used to point to other locations.
#
DocumentRoot "G:/Apache/Apache/htdocs"

#
# Each directory to which Apache has access, can be configured with respect
# to which services and features are allowed and/or disabled in that
# directory (and its subdirectories).
#
```

```
# First, we configure the "default" to be a very restrictive set of
# permissions.
#
<Directory />
    Options FollowSymLinks
    AllowOverride None
</Directory>


#
# Note that from this point forward you must specifically allow
# particular features to be enabled - so if something's not working as
# you might expect, make sure that you have specifically enabled it
# below.
#


#
# This should be changed to whatever you set DocumentRoot to.
#
<Directory "G:/Apache/Apache/htdocs">

#
# This may also be "None", "All", or any combination of "Indexes",
# "Includes", "FollowSymLinks", "ExecCGI", or "MultiViews".
#
# Note that "MultiViews" must be named *explicitly* --- "Options All"
# doesn't give it to you.
#
    Options Indexes FollowSymLinks MultiViews

#
# This controls which options the .htaccess files in directories can
# override. Can also be "All", or any combination of "Options", "FileInfo",
# "AuthConfig", and "Limit"
#
    AllowOverride None

#
# Controls who can get stuff from this server.
#
    Order allow,deny
    Allow from all
</Directory>


#
# UserDir: The name of the directory which is appended onto a user's home
# directory if a ~user request is received.
#
# Under Win32, we do not currently try to determine the home directory of
# a Windows login, so a format such as that below needs to be used.  See
# the UserDir documentation for details.
#
```

```
<IfModule mod_userdir.c>
    UserDir "G:/Apache/Apache/users/"
</IfModule>


#
# Control access to UserDir directories.  The following is an example
# for a site where these directories are restricted to read-only.
#
#<Directory "G:/Apache/Apache/users">
#    AllowOverride FileInfo AuthConfig Limit
#    Options MultiViews Indexes SymLinksIfOwnerMatch IncludesNoExec
#    <Limit GET POST OPTIONS PROPFIND>
#        Order allow,deny
#        Allow from all
#    </Limit>
#    <LimitExcept GET POST OPTIONS PROPFIND>
#        Order deny,allow
#        Deny from all
#    </LimitExcept>
#</Directory>


#
# DirectoryIndex: Name of the file or files to use as a pre-written HTML
# directory index.  Separate multiple entries with spaces.
#
<IfModule mod_dir.c>
    DirectoryIndex index.html
</IfModule>


#
# AccessFileName: The name of the file to look for in each directory
# for access control information.
#
AccessFileName .htaccess


#
# The following lines prevent .htaccess files from being viewed by
# Web clients.  Since .htaccess files often contain authorization
# information, access is disallowed for security reasons.  Comment
# these lines out if you want Web visitors to see the contents of
# .htaccess files.  If you change the AccessFileName directive above,
# be sure to make the corresponding changes here.
#
# Also, folks tend to use names such as .htpasswd for password
# files, so this will protect those as well.
#
<Files ~ "^\.ht">
    Order allow,deny
    Deny from all
</Files>
```

```
#
# CacheNegotiatedDocs: By default, Apache sends "Pragma: no-cache" with each
# document that was negotiated on the basis of content. This asks proxy
# servers not to cache the document. Uncommenting the following line disables
# this behavior, and proxies will be allowed to cache the documents.
#
#CacheNegotiatedDocs


#
# UseCanonicalName:  (new for 1.3)  With this setting turned on, whenever
# Apache needs to construct a self-referencing URL (a URL that refers back
# to the server the response is coming from) it will use ServerName and
# Port to form a "canonical" name.  With this setting off, Apache will
# use the hostname:port that the client supplied, when possible.  This
# also affects SERVER_NAME and SERVER_PORT in CGI scripts.
#
UseCanonicalName On


#
# TypesConfig describes where the mime.types file (or equivalent) is
# to be found.
#
<IfModule mod_mime.c>
    TypesConfig conf/mime.types
</IfModule>


#
# DefaultType is the default MIME type the server will use for a document
# if it cannot otherwise determine one, such as from filename extensions.
# If your server contains mostly text or HTML documents, "text/plain" is
# a good value.  If most of your content is binary, such as applications
# or images, you may want to use "application/octet-stream" instead to
# keep browsers from trying to display binary files as though they are
# text.
#
DefaultType text/plain


#
# The mod_mime_magic module allows the server to use various hints from the
# contents of the file itself to determine its type.  The MIMEMagicFile
# directive tells the module where the hint definitions are located.
# mod_mime_magic is not part of the default server (you have to add
# it yourself with a LoadModule [see the DSO paragraph in the 'Global
# Environment' section], or recompile the server and include mod_mime_magic
# as part of the configuration), so it's enclosed in an <IfModule> container.
# This means that the MIMEMagicFile directive will only be processed if the
# module is part of the server.
#
<IfModule mod_mime_magic.c>
    MIMEMagicFile conf/magic
</IfModule>
```

```
#
# HostnameLookups: Log the names of clients or just their IP addresses
# e.g., www.apache.org (on) or 204.62.129.132 (off).
# The default is off because it'd be overall better for the net if people
# had to knowingly turn this feature on, since enabling it means that
# each client request will result in AT LEAST one lookup request to the
# nameserver.
#
HostnameLookups Off


#
# ErrorLog: The location of the error log file.
# If you do not specify an ErrorLog directive within a <VirtualHost>
# container, error messages relating to that virtual host will be
# logged here.  If you *do* define an error logfile for a <VirtualHost>
# container, that host's errors will be logged there and not here.
#
ErrorLog logs/error.log


#
# LogLevel: Control the number of messages logged to the error.log.
# Possible values include: debug, info, notice, warn, error, crit,
# alert, emerg.
#
LogLevel warn


#
# The following directives define some format nicknames for use with
# a CustomLog directive (see below).
#
LogFormat "%h %l %u %t \"%r\" %>s %b \"%{Referer}i\" \"%{User-Agent}i\""
combined
LogFormat "%h %l %u %t \"%r\" %>s %b" common
LogFormat "%{Referer}i -> %U" referer
LogFormat "%{User-agent}i" agent


#
# The location and format of the access logfile (Common Logfile Format).
# If you do not define any access logfiles within a <VirtualHost>
# container, they will be logged here.  Contrariwise, if you *do*
# define per-<VirtualHost> access logfiles, transactions will be
# logged therein and *not* in this file.
#
CustomLog logs/access.log common


#
# If you would like to have agent and referer logfiles, uncomment the
# following directives.
#
#CustomLog logs/referer.log referer
```

```
#CustomLog logs/agent.log agent

#
# If you prefer a single logfile with access, agent, and referer information
# (Combined Logfile Format) you can use the following directive.
#
#CustomLog logs/access.log combined

#
# Optionally add a line containing the server version and virtual host
# name to server-generated pages (error documents, FTP directory listings,
# mod_status and mod_info output etc., but not CGI generated documents).
# Set to "EMail" to also include a mailto: link to the ServerAdmin.
# Set to one of:  On | Off | EMail
#
ServerSignature On

#
# Apache parses all CGI scripts for the shebang line by default.
# This comment line, the first line of the script, consists of the symbols
# pound (#) and exclamation (!) followed by the path of the program that
# can execute this specific script.  For a perl script, with perl.exe in
# the C:\Program Files\Perl directory, the shebang line should be:

   #!c:/program files/perl/perl

# Note you _must_not_ indent the actual shebang line, and it must be the
# first line of the file.  Of course, CGI processing must be enabled by
# the appropriate ScriptAlias or Options ExecCGI directives for the files
# or directory in question.
#
# However, Apache on Windows allows either the Unix behavior above, or can
# use the Registry to match files by extention.  The command to execute
# a file of this type is retrieved from the registry by the same method as
# the Windows Explorer would use to handle double-clicking on a file.
# These script actions can be configured from the Windows Explorer View menu,
# 'Folder Options', and reviewing the 'File Types' tab.  Clicking the Edit
# button allows you to modify the Actions, of which Apache 1.3 attempts to
# perform the 'Open' Action, and failing that it will try the shebang line.
# This behavior is subject to change in Apache release 2.0.
#
# Each mechanism has it's own specific security weaknesses, from the means
# to run a program you didn't intend the Website owner to invoke, and the
# best method is a matter of great debate.
#
# To enable the this Windows specific behavior (and therefore -disable- the
# equivilant Unix behavior), uncomment the following directive:
#
#ScriptInterpreterSource registry
#
# The directive above can be placed in individual <Directory> blocks or the
```

```
# .htaccess file, with either the 'registry' (Windows behavior) or 'script'
# (Unix behavior) option, and will override this server default option.
#


#
# Aliases: Add here as many aliases as you need (with no limit). The format is
# Alias fakename realname
#
<IfModule mod_alias.c>

    #
    # Note that if you include a trailing / on fakename then the server will
    # require it to be present in the URL.  So "/icons" isn't aliased in this
    # example, only "/icons/".  If the fakename is slash-terminated, then the
    # realname must also be slash terminated, and if the fakename omits the
    # trailing slash, the realname must also omit it.
    #
    Alias /icons/ "G:/Apache/Apache/icons/"

    <Directory "G:/Apache/Apache/icons">
        Options Indexes MultiViews
        AllowOverride None
        Order allow,deny
        Allow from all
    </Directory>

    #
    # ScriptAlias: This controls which directories contain server scripts.
    # ScriptAliases are essentially the same as Aliases, except that
    # documents in the realname directory are treated as applications and
    # run by the server when requested rather than as documents sent to the client.
    # The same rules about trailing "/" apply to ScriptAlias directives as to
    # Alias.
    #
    ScriptAlias /cgi-bin/ "G:/Apache/Apache/cgi-bin/"

    #
    # "G:/Apache/Apache/cgi-bin" should be changed to whatever your ScriptAliased
    # CGI directory exists, if you have that configured.
    #
    <Directory "G:/Apache/Apache/cgi-bin">
        AllowOverride None
        Options None
        Order allow,deny
        Allow from all
    </Directory>

</IfModule>
# End of aliases.

#
```

```
# Redirect allows you to tell clients about documents which used to exist in
# your server's namespace, but do not anymore. This allows you to tell the
# clients where to look for the relocated document.
# Format: Redirect old-URI new-URL
#


#
# Directives controlling the display of server-generated directory listings.
#
<IfModule mod_autoindex.c>

    #
    # FancyIndexing is whether you want fancy directory indexing or standard
    #
    # Note, add the option TrackModified to the IndexOptions default list only
    # if all indexed directories reside on NTFS volumes.  The TrackModified flag
    # will report the Last-Modified date to assist caches and proxies to properly
    # track directory changes, but it does _not_ work on FAT volumes.
    #
    IndexOptions FancyIndexing

    #
    # AddIcon* directives tell the server which icon to show for different
    # files or filename extensions.  These are only displayed for
    # FancyIndexed directories.
    #
    AddIconByEncoding (CMP,/icons/compressed.gif) x-compress x-gzip

    AddIconByType (TXT,/icons/text.gif) text/*
    AddIconByType (IMG,/icons/image2.gif) image/*
    AddIconByType (SND,/icons/sound2.gif) audio/*
    AddIconByType (VID,/icons/movie.gif) video/*

    AddIcon /icons/binary.gif .bin .exe
    AddIcon /icons/binhex.gif .hqx
    AddIcon /icons/tar.gif .tar
    AddIcon /icons/world2.gif .wrl .wrl.gz .vrml .vrm .iv
    AddIcon /icons/compressed.gif .Z .z .tgz .gz .zip
    AddIcon /icons/a.gif .ps .ai .eps
    AddIcon /icons/layout.gif .html .shtml .htm .pdf
    AddIcon /icons/text.gif .txt
    AddIcon /icons/c.gif .c
    AddIcon /icons/p.gif .pl .py
    AddIcon /icons/f.gif .for
    AddIcon /icons/dvi.gif .dvi
    AddIcon /icons/uuencoded.gif .uu
    AddIcon /icons/script.gif .conf .sh .shar .csh .ksh .tcl
    AddIcon /icons/tex.gif .tex
    AddIcon /icons/bomb.gif core

    AddIcon /icons/back.gif ..
```

```
        AddIcon /icons/hand.right.gif README
        AddIcon /icons/folder.gif ^^DIRECTORY^^
        AddIcon /icons/blank.gif ^^BLANKICON^^

        #
        # DefaultIcon is which icon to show for files which do not have an icon
        # explicitly set.
        #
        DefaultIcon /icons/unknown.gif

        #
        # AddDescription allows you to place a short description after a file in
        # server-generated indexes.  These are only displayed for FancyIndexed
        # directories.
        # Format: AddDescription "description" filename
        #
        #AddDescription "GZIP compressed document" .gz
        #AddDescription "tar archive" .tar
        #AddDescription "GZIP compressed tar archive" .tgz

        #
        # ReadmeName is the name of the README file the server will look for by
        # default, and append to directory listings.
        #
        # HeaderName is the name of a file which should be prepended to
        # directory indexes.
        #
        # If MultiViews are amongst the Options in effect, the server will
        # first look for name.html and include it if found.  If name.html
        # doesn't exist, the server will then look for name.txt and include
        # it as plaintext if found.
        #
        ReadmeName README
        HeaderName HEADER

        #
        # IndexIgnore is a set of filenames which directory indexing should ignore
        # and not include in the listing.  Shell-style wildcarding is permitted.
        #
        IndexIgnore .??* *~ *# HEADER* README* RCS CVS *,v *,t

</IfModule>
# End of indexing directives.

#
# Document types.
#
<IfModule mod_mime.c>

        #
        # AddEncoding allows you to have certain browsers (Mosaic/X 2.1+) uncompress
```

```
# information on the fly. Note: Not all browsers support this.
# Despite the name similarity, the following Add* directives have nothing
# to do with the FancyIndexing customization directives above.
#
AddEncoding x-compress Z
AddEncoding x-gzip gz tgz
#
# AddLanguage allows you to specify the language of a document. You can
# then use content negotiation to give a browser a file in a language
# it can understand.
#
# Note 1: The suffix does not have to be the same as the language
# keyword --- those with documents in Polish (whose net-standard
# language code is pl) may wish to use "AddLanguage pl .po" to
# avoid the ambiguity with the common suffix for perl scripts.
#
# Note 2: The example entries below illustrate that in quite
# some cases the two character 'Language' abbreviation is not
# identical to the two character 'Country' code for its country,
# E.g. 'Danmark/dk' versus 'Danish/da'.
#
# Note 3: In the case of 'ltz' we violate the RFC by using a three char
# specifier. But there is 'work in progress' to fix this and get
# the reference data for rfc1766 cleaned up.
#
# Danish (da) - Dutch (nl) - English (en) - Estonian (ee)
# French (fr) - German (de) - Greek-Modern (el)
# Italian (it) - Korean (kr) - Norwegian (no)
# Portugese (pt) - Luxembourgeois* (ltz)
# Spanish (es) - Swedish (sv) - Catalan (ca) - Czech(cz)
# Polish (pl) - Brazilian Portuguese (pt-br) - Japanese (ja)
# Russian (ru)
#
AddLanguage da .dk
AddLanguage nl .nl
AddLanguage en .en
AddLanguage et .ee
AddLanguage fr .fr
AddLanguage de .de
AddLanguage el .el
AddLanguage he .he
AddCharset ISO-8859-8 .iso8859-8
AddLanguage it .it
AddLanguage ja .ja
AddCharset ISO-2022-JP .jis
AddLanguage kr .kr
AddCharset ISO-2022-KR .iso-kr
AddLanguage no .no
AddLanguage pl .po
AddCharset ISO-8859-2 .iso-pl
AddLanguage pt .pt
```

```
AddLanguage pt-br .pt-br
AddLanguage ltz .lu
AddLanguage ca .ca
AddLanguage es .es
AddLanguage sv .se
AddLanguage cz .cz
AddLanguage ru .ru
AddLanguage tw .tw
AddLanguage zh-tw .tw
AddCharset Big5         .Big5    .big5
AddCharset WINDOWS-1251 .cp-1251
AddCharset CP866         .cp866
AddCharset ISO-8859-5    .iso-ru
AddCharset KOI8-R        .koi8-r
AddCharset UCS-2         .ucs2
AddCharset UCS-4         .ucs4
AddCharset UTF-8         .utf8


# LanguagePriority allows you to give precedence to some languages
# in case of a tie during content negotiation.
#
# Just list the languages in decreasing order of preference. We have
# more or less alphabetized them here. You probably want to change this.
#
<IfModule mod_negotiation.c>
    LanguagePriority en da nl et fr de el it ja kr no pl pt pt-br ru ltz ca
        es sv tw
</IfModule>


#
# AddType allows you to tweak mime.types without actually editing it, or to
# make certain files to be certain types.
#
# For example, the PHP 3.x module (not part of the Apache distribution - see
# http://www.php.net) will typically use:
#
#AddType application/x-httpd-php3 .php3
#AddType application/x-httpd-php3-source .phps
#
# And for PHP 4.x, use:
#
#AddType application/x-httpd-php .php
#AddType application/x-httpd-php-source .phps


AddType application/x-tar .tgz


#
# AddHandler allows you to map certain file extensions to "handlers",
# actions unrelated to filetype. These can be either built into the server
# or added with the Action command (see below)
#
```

```
                # If you want to use server side includes, or CGI outside
                # ScriptAliased directories, uncomment the following lines.
                #
                # To use CGI scripts:
                #
                #AddHandler cgi-script .cgi

                #
                # To use server-parsed HTML files
                #
                #AddType text/html .shtml
                #AddHandler server-parsed .shtml

                #
                # Uncomment the following line to enable Apache's send-asis HTTP file
                # feature
                #
                #AddHandler send-as-is asis

                #
                # If you wish to use server-parsed imagemap files, use
                #
                #AddHandler imap-file map

                #
                # To enable type maps, you might want to use
                #
                #AddHandler type-map var

        </IfModule>
        # End of document types.

        #
        # Action lets you define media types that will execute a script whenever
        # a matching file is called. This eliminates the need for repeated URL
        # pathnames for oft-used CGI file processors.
        # Format: Action media/type /cgi-script/location
        # Format: Action handler-name /cgi-script/location
        #

        #
        # MetaDir: specifies the name of the directory in which Apache can find
        # meta information files. These files contain additional HTTP headers
        # to include when sending the document
        #
        #MetaDir .web

        #
        # MetaSuffix: specifies the file name suffix for the file containing the
        # meta information.
        #
```

```
#MetaSuffix .meta

#
# Customizable error response (Apache style)
#  these come in three flavors
#
#    1) plain text
#ErrorDocument 500 "The server made a boo boo.
# n.b.  the single leading (") marks it as text, it does not get output
#
#    2) local redirects
#ErrorDocument 404 /missing.html
# to redirect to local URL /missing.html
#ErrorDocument 404 /cgi-bin/missing_handler.pl
# N.B.: You can redirect to a script or a document using server-side-includes.
#
#    3) external redirects
#ErrorDocument 402 http://some.other_server.com/subscription_info.html
# N.B.: Many of the environment variables associated with the original
# request will *not* be available to such a script.


#
# Customize behaviour based on the browser
#
<IfModule mod_setenvif.c>

    #
    # The following directives modify normal HTTP response behavior.
    # The first directive disables keepalive for Netscape 2.x and browsers that
    # spoof it. There are known problems with these browser implementations.
    # The second directive is for Microsoft Internet Explorer 4.0b2
    # which has a broken HTTP/1.1 implementation and does not properly
    # support keepalive when it is used on 301 or 302 (redirect) responses.
    #
    BrowserMatch "Mozilla/2" nokeepalive
    BrowserMatch "MSIE 4\.0b2;" nokeepalive downgrade-1.0 force-response-1.0

    #
    # The following directive disables HTTP/1.1 responses to browsers which
    # are in violation of the HTTP/1.0 spec by not being able to grok a
    # basic 1.1 response.
    #
    BrowserMatch "RealPlayer 4\.0" force-response-1.0
    BrowserMatch "Java/1\.0" force-response-1.0
    BrowserMatch "JDK/1\.0" force-response-1.0

</IfModule>
# End of browser customization directives


#
# Allow server status reports, with the URL of http://servername/server-status
```

```
# Change the "ouraymountainwater.com" to match your domain to enable.
#
#<Location /server-status>
#    SetHandler server-status
#    Order deny,allow
#    Deny from all
#    Allow from ouraymountainwater.com
#</Location>


#
# Allow remote server configuration reports, with the URL of
# http://servername/server-info (requires that mod_info.c be loaded).
# Change the "ouraymountainwater.com" to match your domain to enable.
#
#<Location /server-info>
#    SetHandler server-info
#    Order deny,allow
#    Deny from all
#    Allow from ouraymountainwater.com
#</Location>


#
# There have been reports of people trying to abuse an old bug from pre-1.1
# days.  This bug involved a CGI script distributed as a part of Apache.
# By uncommenting these lines you can redirect these attacks to a logging
# script on phf.apache.org.  Or, you can record them yourself, using the script
# support/phf_abuse_log.cgi.
#
#<Location /cgi-bin/phf*>
#    Deny from all
#    ErrorDocument 403 http://phf.apache.org/phf_abuse_log.cgi
#</Location>


#
# Proxy Server directives. Uncomment the following lines to
# enable the proxy server:
#
#<IfModule mod_proxy.c>
#    ProxyRequests On

#    <Directory proxy:*>
#        Order deny,allow
#        Deny from all
#        Allow from ouraymountainwater.com
#    </Directory>

    #
    # Enable/disable the handling of HTTP/1.1 "Via:" headers.
    # ("Full" adds the server version; "Block" removes all outgoing Via:
headers)
    # Set to one of: Off | On | Full | Block
```

```
    #
#    ProxyVia On

    #
    # To enable the cache as well, edit and uncomment the following lines:
    # (no cacheing without CacheRoot)
    #
#    CacheRoot "G:/Apache/Apache/proxy"
#    CacheSize 5
#    CacheGcInterval 4
#    CacheMaxExpire 24
#    CacheLastModifiedFactor 0.1
#    CacheDefaultExpire 1
#    NoCache a_domain.com another_domain.edu joes.garage_sale.com

#</IfModule>
# End of proxy directives.


### Section 3: Virtual Hosts
#
# VirtualHost: If you want to maintain multiple domains/hostnames on your
# machine you can setup VirtualHost containers for them. Most configurations
# use only name-based virtual hosts so the server doesn't need to worry about
# IP addresses. This is indicated by the asterisks in the directives below.
#
# Please see the documentation at <URL:http://www.apache.org/docs/vhosts/>
# for further details before you try to setup virtual hosts.
#
# You may use the command line option '-S' to verify your virtual host
# configuration.


#
# Use name-based virtual hosting.
#
#NameVirtualHost *


#
# VirtualHost example:
# Almost any Apache directive may go into a VirtualHost container.
# The first VirtualHost section is used for requests without a known
# server name.
#
#<VirtualHost *>
#    ServerAdmin webmaster@dummy-host.example.com
#    DocumentRoot /www/docs/dummy-host.example.com
#    ServerName dummy-host.example.com
#    ErrorLog logs/dummy-host.example.com-error_log
#    CustomLog logs/dummy-host.example.com-access_log common
#</VirtualHost>
```

Starting and Stopping the Apache Web Server

Starting and stopping Apache is a relatively fast process. You ideally want to interrupt the Web server when few people (or none) are accessing the Web site. When you make a change to the httpd.conf file, the Web server needs to be restarted so the changed information is reflected in the running Web server. The httpd.conf file is only read when the Web service is started. Also, if you have recompiled Apache, you will need to stop the Web server. In this case, you may also need to move the newly compiled Apache binary to the appropriate directory before restarting the Web server. Note that to stop, start, or restart the Web server does not require any actions on the underlying server operating system. For example, if you have changed the Web content directory you will need to restart the Web server but you do not need to restart Linux or Windows 2000.

Linux

The Apache Web server can be started, stopped, and restarted from the command line. This method is helpful when you are testing the configuration of your Web site. If you have compiled a recent version of Apache, for example 1.3.20, you can use the apachectl script to interact with the Web server. This script is located in the bin directory and the apachectl syntax is:

```
./apachectl (start|stop|restart|fullstatus|status|graceful|configtest|help)
```

Most of these commands are self-explanatory. Fullstatus will display information about the Web server as long as the mod_status module is enabled. The graceful parameter will restart the Web server and will not close down any open connections to the server. It also checks the configuration files before starting Apache by using the configtest parameter. The configtest option will check the configuration files and if all is okay, will report back with Syntax OK. If there is a problem, configtest will indicate there is/are syntax error(s) and at what line or lines in the configuration file. The test will also indicate what configuration file or files the error(s) was/were found in.

You may need to make some adjustments to the apachectl file. For example, if you have moved or renamed the location of the Apache files, you will need to make the appropriate adjustments in the apachectl file. Here is an example of the apachectl file from the employee.ouraymountainwater.com Apache Web server. The file has not been modified except to remove the license information at the end of the file to save space. The license information at the end of the file is the standard Apache software license found in most of the files included with Apache.

```
#!/bin/sh
#
# Apache control script designed to allow an easy command line interface
# to controlling Apache.  Written by Marc Slemko, 1997/08/23
#
# The exit codes returned are:
#     0 - operation completed successfully
#     1 -
#     2 - usage error
#     3 - httpd could not be started
#     4 - httpd could not be stopped
#     5 - httpd could not be started during a restart
#     6 - httpd could not be restarted during a restart
#     7 - httpd could not be restarted during a graceful restart
#     8 - configuration syntax error
#
# When multiple arguments are given, only the error from the _last_
# one is reported.  Run "apachectl help" for usage info
#
#
# |||||||||||||||||||| START CONFIGURATION SECTION  ||||||||||||||||||||
# --------------------                              --------------------
#
# the path to your PID file
PIDFILE=/usr/local/apache/logs/httpd.pid
#
# the path to your httpd binary, including options if necessary
HTTPD=/usr/local/apache/bin/httpd
#
# a command that outputs a formatted text version of the HTML at the
# url given on the command line.  Designed for lynx, however other
# programs may work.
LYNX="lynx -dump"
#
# the URL to your server's mod_status status page.  If you do not
# have one, then status and fullstatus will not work.
STATUSURL="http://localhost/server-status"
#
# --------------------                              --------------------
# |||||||||||||||||||||  END CONFIGURATION SECTION  ||||||||||||||||||||

ERROR=0
ARGV="$@"
if [ "x$ARGV" = "x" ] ; then
    ARGS="help"
fi

for ARG in $@ $ARGS
do
    # check for pidfile
    if [ -f $PIDFILE ] ; then
```

```
    PID='cat $PIDFILE'
    if [ "x$PID" != "x" ] && kill -0 $PID 2>/dev/null ; then
        STATUS="httpd (pid $PID) running"
        RUNNING=1
    else
        STATUS="httpd (pid $PID?) not running"
        RUNNING=0
    fi
else
  STATUS="httpd (no pid file) not running"
  RUNNING=0
fi

case $ARG in
start)
    if [ $RUNNING -eq 1 ]; then
        echo "$0 $ARG: httpd (pid $PID) already running"
        continue
    fi
    if $HTTPD ; then
        echo "$0 $ARG: httpd started"
    else
        echo "$0 $ARG: httpd could not be started"
        ERROR=3
    fi
    ;;
stop)
    if [ $RUNNING -eq 0 ]; then
        echo "$0 $ARG: $STATUS"
        continue
    fi
    if kill $PID ; then
        echo "$0 $ARG: httpd stopped"
    else
        echo "$0 $ARG: httpd could not be stopped"
        ERROR=4
    fi
    ;;
restart)
    if [ $RUNNING -eq 0 ]; then
        echo "$0 $ARG: httpd not running, trying to start"
        if $HTTPD ; then
            echo "$0 $ARG: httpd started"
        else
            echo "$0 $ARG: httpd could not be started"
            ERROR=5
        fi
    else
        if $HTTPD -t >/dev/null 2>&1; then
            if kill -HUP $PID ; then
                echo "$0 $ARG: httpd restarted"
```

```
                else
                    echo "$0 $ARG: httpd could not be restarted"
                    ERROR=6
                fi
            else
                echo "$0 $ARG: configuration broken, ignoring restart"
                echo "$0 $ARG: (run 'apachectl configtest' for details)"
                ERROR=6
            fi
        fi
        ;;
    graceful)
        if [ $RUNNING -eq 0 ]; then
            echo "$0 $ARG: httpd not running, trying to start"
            if $HTTPD ; then
                echo "$0 $ARG: httpd started"
            else
                echo "$0 $ARG: httpd could not be started"
                ERROR=5
            fi
        else
            if $HTTPD -t >/dev/null 2>&1; then
                if kill -USR1 $PID ; then
                    echo "$0 $ARG: httpd gracefully restarted"
                else
                    echo "$0 $ARG: httpd could not be restarted"
                    ERROR=7
                fi
            else
                echo "$0 $ARG: configuration broken, ignoring restart"
                echo "$0 $ARG: (run 'apachectl configtest' for details)"
                ERROR=7
            fi
        fi
        ;;
    status)
        $LYNX $STATUSURL | awk ' /process$/ { print; exit } { print } '
        ;;
    fullstatus)
        $LYNX $STATUSURL
        ;;
    configtest)
        if $HTTPD -t; then
            :
        else
            ERROR=8
        fi
        ;;
    *)
        echo "usage: $0
(start|stop|restart|fullstatus|status|graceful|configtest|help)"
```

```
        cat  <<EOF

start      - start httpd
stop       - stop httpd
restart    - restart httpd if running by sending a SIGHUP or start if
             not running
fullstatus - dump a full status screen; requires lynx and mod_status enabled
status     - dump a short status screen; requires lynx and mod_status enabled
graceful   - do a graceful restart by sending a SIGUSR1 or start if not running
configtest - do a configuration syntax test
help       - this screen

EOF
        ERROR=2
      ;;

      esac

done

exit $ERROR
```

The apachectl file makes reference to Lynx, a common text based browser found on many Linux systems. The status information pages can either be displayed on the Web server's screen through the Lynx application or from another machine's browser. We cover the status information specifics in Chapter 7.

Once you have the Web server configured and ready to go, you will probably want to set up the environment so whenever the Linux server is started, the Web server is also started. This can be accomplished in several different ways but probably the most common is to modify the rc.local file. This file is located in the /etc/directory and, depending on the distribution, may be located under a subdirectory. For example, on a RedHat 7.1 system, rc.local is found under the /etc/rc.d directory. Using your favorite text editor, add an entry at the end of the rc.local file specifying the full path of the apachectl file followed by an appropriate parameter such as start or graceful.

Windows

On the Windows platform, Apache runs as a service so you can stop and start the Web server through the Services administration tool. To start and/or stop the Web server, open the Services tool which is accessible from Start | Programs | Administrative Tools | Services. Near the top of the available services is an entry titled Apache. Double click on the Apache entry to display the Apache Properties window. A Startup type of Automatic indicates the service will start whenever the Windows 2000 system is started. To stop the service (if it is running), click on the Stop button. To start the service (if it is stopped) click on the

Start button. In both instances a Service Control window appears displaying the progress of the action.

The Apache installation process adds several menu items to the Programs menu which allows you to manage the Apache server. The default name of the menu item is Apache httpd Server. The Apache httpd Server menu contains five sub menu items:

Configure Apache Server. Under this menu item are two additional menu items (shortcuts); Edit the Apache httpd.conf Configuration File and Test Configuration.

Control Apache Server. This menu item contains three sub menu items (shortcuts); Restart, Start, and Stop.

Review Server Log Files. Under this menu are two additional entries (shortcuts); Review Access Log and Review Error Log

Apache Docs Online. This menu item (shortcut) points to the http:// httpd.apache.org/docs/ Web site.

Help I'm Stuck. This menu item (shortcut) points to the FAQ (Frequently Asked Questions) document on your Web server. If your Apache Web server is not running and you cannot get to this document, you can also access the information on the Internet at http://httpd.apache.org /docs/misc/FAQ.html.

You can start, stop, and restart the Apache server from the Control Apache Server menu item by selecting either Restart, Start, or Stop. These menu items are essentially the Windows equivalents of using the Restart, Start, and Stop parameters with the Linux apachectl file. Each of these menu items is a short-cut to the Apache executable with various parameters. For example, choosing Start executes:

```
G:\Apache\Apache\Apache.exe -w -n "Apache" -k start
```

Where G:\Apache\Apache is the location of the Apache files. The items before the –k option define the name of the service so the start, stop, and restart functions can operate properly. The Stop menu item executes:

```
G:\Apache\Apache\Apache.exe -w -n "Apache" -k stop
```

and the restart menu option executes:

```
G:\Apache\Apache\Apache.exe -w -n "Apache" -k restart
```

You can execute these commands in a Command window without the need to use the corresponding menu item. There are other options supported by apache.exe. Executing apache –h in a command window will display the various apache.exe parameters.

NOTE You need to be either a member of the Administrators or Power Users group to be able to start, stop or restart the Apache service.

How to Get Started Programming an Apache Module

So you have decided to delve into the world of programming an Apache module! In this section we cover just the bare necessities to start the process. Of course, we are assuming that you are already an "experienced" programmer in one of the C languages. If you have not coded before in C, or any language, it is suggested you investigate and learn programming concepts and one or two programming languages before you begin modifying or writing an Apache module.

In order to compile code, you need a compiler. Linux distributions come with at least one C compiler and some have more than one available. Depending on how you installed Linux, you may or may not have the development tools present. These are necessary so the compiler and code libraries are available for code development and compiling. Make sure you have an ANSI-C compiler installed in your system. The default, standard Linux compiler in most distributions is gcc (GNU C Compiler). gcc is a very powerful and advanced compiler. It supports the ANSI C standard as well as all the modern C standards currently in use. In addition to being a C compiler, gcc can also handle C++ and Objective-C. In addition to the compiler itself you also need to make sure you have a compatible version of gcc. To check what version of gcc your system uses, execute the following at a command prompt:

```
gcc -v
```

Make sure you are using 2.72 or higher. Some Linux distributions also include egcs. egcs is based on gcc and one of egcs' major advantages is its support of newer C++ features.

To compile an Apache module for Windows, you will need Microsoft's Visual Studio or Visual C++ version 5.0 or higher. This is a commercial product and you will need to purchase it and install it on your system in order to develop and compile C code.

If you plan on developing a new module, the next step is to check with the Apache module registry at http://modules.apache.org. You can search the registry to see if a module already exists that satisfies, or partially satisfies, your needs. Instead of reinventing the wheel you may find a module for the complete solution or part of the solution. Since most of the Apache modules available for download are "open source" and covered under GPL (General Public License), you can take existing code, modify it, and then release it to the world. You also need to become very familiar with the GPL license so that you follow the proper guidelines for development and release of your software. For information on GPL and related topics, go to www.gnu.org/copyleft/gpl.html.

The next step is to take a look at the sample module code included with the Apache source code. The objective of this module, mod_example, is to demonstrate the various Apache APIs and the layout of a module. The sample code and associated README file are located in the src directory in the modules/ example/ subdirectory. The mod_example.c file illustrates the different callback mechanisms and the required syntax. Please note that a "real" module would not include all these routines but since this is a sample module, they are all included in the mod_example.c file. This file contains lots of good comments and it is highly suggested that you read through the file before building your own module.

The example module is an actual working module. You can add it to the modules compiled in Apache and when the Web server is accessed, you can see the results of the different callbacks. Please note that if you do include the example module in Apache, do this on an experimental Apache system, not on a production Web server. To enable the example module, you will need to modify the src/Configuration.tmpl or src/Configuration files. Near the bottom of each file is the entry:

```
# AddModule modules/example/mod_example.o
```

Remove the pound sign (#) in front of the line and save the changes to the Configuration file. Then go ahead and compile the Apache binary.

Linux

In a command window, navigate to the directory that contains the Apache files and execute the following (this is usually the directory that contains the extracted files from the Apache TAR file):

```
./configure
```

When that is completed, execute:

```
make
```

and then run:

```
make install
```

Windows

To begin the process of compiling Apache in Visual C++, open the Project Workspace document called Apache.dsw in the src directory. You will need to make additional changes and adjustments in the environment to include the mod_example module. To create the Apache application, choose Rebuild All from the Build menu. This process may take several minutes depending on your system's hardware. The compiled application is placed in a subdirectory called debug, which is located in the src directory.

Using the Example Module

Once you have recompiled Apache to include the example module, you need to modify the httpd.conf file. Below the existing Location scopes positioned near the end of Section 2, add the following Location scope:

```
<Location /example-info>
    SetHandler example-handler
</Location>
```

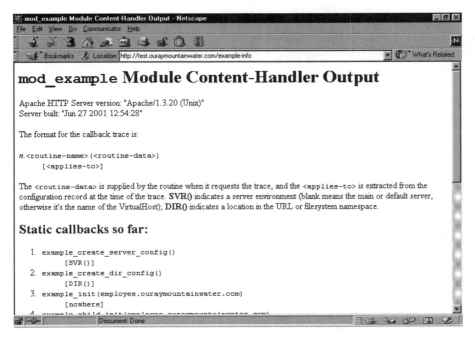

Figure 4.1   Example module browser output.

After you have saved the changes to the httpd.conf file, start the Apache server. To see the example module in action on a test Web server called, for example, test.ouraymountainwater.com, enter the following in the URL of your browser:

```
http://test.ouraymountainwater.com/example-info
```

Figure 4.1 shows the output of the example module.

The top of the display indicates the version of Apache and the date and time when the server was built or compiled. Examining the mod_example.c source file and the resulting output of the module in your browser is a good starting point for understanding the workings of an Apache module.

CHAPTER 5

Preparing to Add Your Web Content

A Web server has two personalities. One is the engine, which provides all the methods and services enabling users' to access and view the Web server's Web site(s) in their browsers. The second personality is the actual content of the Web pages the Web server is doling out. Since we are a very visual animal, the look and feel of your Web sites is as important as the engine behind the scenes. Once the content of your Web sites has been created, the next step is to put the content on the Web server. By the way, we are assuming that you and/or a Web designer has performed all the magic necessary to make your Web pages shine. If the Web content is not "all there yet," you can still setup and test putting up or publishing the Web server's content with sample pages. You can even use the documents in Apache's htdocs directory to start with. In this chapter we use as examples the Web content developed for our scenario company, Ouray Mountain Water. We also cover the different methods and preparation tasks needed before you start publishing your Web site's content to the Web server.

The Different Ways to Add Your Web Content

There are different methods available for adding, or publishing, your Web content to the Web server. These range from easy, to more involved methods that incorporate proprietary elements. Probably the simplest method of getting your Web site's content to the server is copy and paste. If the Web authoring tool is on the same system as your Web server, the Web developer can paste a copy of the Web pages into the Web server's content, or DocumentRoot, directory. While the combination of the Web development tool and the Web server being the same machine is not practical for production servers, it is a convenient option for a test Web server.

If the Web developer is using a different machine than the Web server, the developer needs to be able to move the Web content from one machine to the other. This can be accomplished by using removable media or the network. If the files are not too big, a floppy disk (or two) can be used. For larger Web sites a re/writable CD or ZIP drive are other alternatives for data transport. For network transfers, the available choices depend on the operating systems and available services. In a Windows environment, you can transfer the Web content from the developer's Windows system to the Apache Windows 2000 Web server with Microsoft's networking services. For mixed Windows and Linux environments where Microsoft networking is used on the Windows machines, you can configure the Linux systems to appear as Windows systems. This service is called SAMBA and is used frequently in mixed operating system environments. SAMBA is a useful option in networks that use predominately Windows systems and Microsoft protocols. If the Web developers are using Windows systems and the Apache Web server is on a Linux system, SAMBA allows the Web content directory on the server to be shared and made accessible across the network. For more information on SAMBA, check out www.samba.org.

Probably the most common method of moving Web content from one machine to another across a network is FTP (File Transfer Protocol). FTP is available on almost any operating system you can think of that uses IP as a network protocol. Both Linux and Windows come with an FTP client when the IP protocol is installed on the system. The FTP client allows the system to access an FTP server. The FTP server service is available on both Windows and Linux systems. However, the service needs to be configured to accept connections from FTP clients and to allow copying or uploading of files to the Web server. Once the FTP service is configured on the Web server, you can use a command line or graphical interface FTP client to move the Web content to the Web server.

In addition to FTP client applications, most current Web browsers also allow you to access FTP sites. Usually all that is needed is to specify the communication protocol in the URL. For example, to access Ouray Mountain Water's production Web server using FTP, you would use the following URL:

```
ftp://production.ouraymountainwater.com
```

Some Web development authoring tools support FTP for publishing your Web content to the Web server.

Besides FTP, HTTP can also be used to transfer files. HTTP is most commonly used to access and view Web sites but it can also be used to publish Web content. The HTTP protocol is a request-response protocol. The client (browser) sends a request message to the server and the server sends back to the client a response message. The request message is composed of three elements: the method, the URI (Uniform Resource Identifier), and the headers. The method parameter describes the type of request. There are eight different methods: OPTIONS, GET, HEAD, POST, PUT, DELETE, TRACE, and CONNECT. The GET method is what is sent in the request to the Web server when you attempt to go to a location specified in the URL field in your Web browser. The POST method is used when you fill out a form on a Web page and then send the results to the Web server. The POST method does not modify the contents of the Web page but is used as a mechanism to collect data from the browser and send it to another process, such as a database. In order to modify a Web page itself, the request needs to specify the PUT method. Some Web authoring tools support the PUT method to publish the Web content from the authoring application directly to the Web server. However, in order to complete the operation, the Web server itself has to be able to accept PUT commands. Apache does not come with the built-in capability to accept the HTTP PUT method but you can add this functionality to Apache.

Some Web development applications use proprietary methods to place the Web content onto the server. In addition, some of these tools may require additional software to be placed on your Web server so the Web site can be published properly. A good example of software that fits this category is FrontPage from Microsoft. FrontPage can use either FTP or HTTP (proprietary method) to publish Web content to the Web server. However, in order to use HTTP to publish from FrontPage, the Web server has to have FrontPage extensions installed. Fortunately, FrontPage extensions exist for Apache so you can use FrontPage to develop and publish your Web sites to Apache Linux Web servers.

One of the problems when more than one individual is developing a Web site is making sure that the Web site has the most up-to-date copies of the Web content files from the different authors involved. If two or more Web developers are attempting to publish their data to the Web site at the same time, conflicts and problems can pop up. WebDAV is a protocol that is designed to alleviate these types of problems. It also adds more features and capabilities to the Web publishing environment. WebDAV, or Web-based Distributed Authoring and Versioning, is designed to allow Web developers the ability to collaboratively manage and edit the Web content files on multiple Web servers. WebDAV is not built into Apache versions 1.3.x (or lower) but it is supported natively in Apache 2.0. However, there is a WebDAV module for Apache 1.3.x that you may want to look into and test out. For more information on this module and other WebDAV data, go to www.webdav.org.

Preparing Your Web Server for Publication

In this section we describe the necessary steps to prepare your Web server to accept Web content. The first method we mentioned in the previous section involves a simple copy and paste of the Web content into the Web server's DocumentRoot directory. If the Web developer is working on the same machine as the Web server, they already have the necessary permissions to create and modify files in the locations where the Web developer is saving the Web pages. In order to add the Web pages to the Web server's DocumentRoot directory, the developer needs to have the appropriate permissions on the Web server's content directory. For Linux systems, the developer will need the Read and Write permissions and on Windows 2000, the developer will need the Read, Write, and Modify NTFS permissions.

Local File System Access

Linux permissions to a directory and its contents are typically setup using the chmod command. At a command prompt, navigate to the parent directory of the DocumentRoot directory. For example, if the DocumentRoot directory is /usr/local/content/htdocs, navigate to /usr/local/content, the parent directory. If there is only one Web developer, for example bob, you can set the appropriate permissions to just the owner (Web developer). Before you set permissions for bob, our Web developer, you need to verify that he is the owner of the DocumentRoot directory. To verify the owner of the Document-Root directory, execute the following at a command prompt from the /usr/local/content location:

```
ls -l
```

The –l performs a long listing and in the output you can determine who the owner is (the name on the left side) and the group (the name on the right). If bob is not the owner and you want to change ownership to bob, execute the following at a command prompt—you will need to be logged onto the system as root:

```
chown bob htdocs -v -R
```

The –v gives back verbose feedback so you can see what is happening, and the –R changes ownership on all files and directories recursively below htdocs.

Linux permissions to directories and files are managed as a triplet. One set applies to the owner (user) of the file or directory the second set applies to the group, and the last applies to everybody else. The three available permissions are Read, Write, and Execute. Each of these are represented by a decimal value: Read = 4, Write = 2, and Execute = 1. To set the Read and Execute permissions, you supply the number 5 because Read (4) + Execute (1) = 5. If you don't want to set any permissions, use a value of 0. To set the permissions for the owner, group, and everybody else at the same time, you specify the values for each category as a triplet. For example, we want to give bob Read (r), Write (w), and Execute (x), the group webdev Read (r), Write (w), and Execute (x), and everybody else Read (r) and Execute (x). For bob that would be 7 (4 + 2 + 1), the webdav group would be 7 (4 + 2 + 1), and everybody else gets 5 (4 + 1). So the triplet number to represent those permissions is 775. Now that we've gone through the "math," lets discuss how to use these values to set permissions. To set bob, our Web developer, permissions to the DocumentRoot directory and all files and subdirectories below, we use the chmod command. For example, to allow bob to create and modify files and to permit all others to read and execute the files, the chmod syntax would be:

```
chmod 755 htdocs -v -R
```

By the way, you need to make sure everybody else, besides bob, has just the Read and Execute permission on the DocumentRoot directory and everything below. You only want bob to be able to modify the content (Write), but to view the Web pages in a browser, Read and Execute are necessary for everybody else.

For environments that have more than one Web developer, a group is a good method for assigning permissions. For example, we have set up a group for the Web developers called webdev. Bob and Lee Ann are our web developers and both of their accounts, bob and leeann, are assigned to the webdev group. Lee Ann is the lead designer and we want to make sure she owns the files. To set the user and group ownership for the DocumentRoot directory, we use the chown command but with a slightly different syntax. In a command window at the parent directory (/usr/local/content/) of our DocumentRoot directory (htdocs), the chown command would be:

```
chown leeann:webdev htdocs -v -R
```

Now the htdocs directory, and everything below it (-R), is owned by the user leeann and the group webdev. The next step is to assign the proper permissions (r w x) to the user (leeann) and the group (webdev) while giving everybody else Read and Execute (r x). The syntax for the chmod command would be:

```
chmod 775 htdocs -v -R
```

Another item to keep in mind involves the use of removable media. Make sure the Web developer(s) have the proper permissions to mount and access the contents of the removable media.

Windows 2000 NTFS permissions are typically configured through Windows Explorer. If there is only one Web developer, you can set the appropriate permissions for one account. If your environment has more than one Web developer, it is recommended you create a local group and assign the Web developer accounts as members. To begin assigning the necessary NTFS permissions, navigate to the DocumentRoot directory (folder) in Windows Explorer. Open the properties window for the DocumentRoot directory, e.g. htdocs, and select the Security tab. By default, directories and files "inherit" NTFS permissions from their parent directory. NTFS permissions inherited from the parent are displayed as gray checkboxes with gray checkmarks. By default, the group Everyone has full rights to all directories and files on all the drives. These rights are inherited from the permissions assigned at the root of each drive.

On our htdocs directory, we don't want the group Everyone to have full access to the Web site content, so at the htdocs directory we will turn off the ability to inherit permissions from the parent directory. In the Security area of the DocumentRoot properties window, clear the checkmark next to the item: "Allow inheritable permissions from parent to propagate to this object." When you clear the checkmark another window appears, Security. The Copy option allows you to copy the previously inheritable permissions to the object and the Remove choice will remove all inherited permissions and retain only those permissions explicitly assigned at the htdocs directory. For our example, we select Remove so the Everyone group does not have any permissions on the Web content directory. The next item is to assign permissions to our Web developers on the DocumentRoot directory. In the DocumentRoot properties window choose the Add button and from the list of items displayed add the account name of the Web developer. Make sure you enable Modify and Write in addition to Read & Execute, List Folder Contents, and Read so the Web developer can make the appropriate file system changes. If you have more than one Web developer, add the name of the local group for the Web developers and assign the Modify, Read & Execute, List Folder Contents, Read, and Write permissions. Also, make sure you add the Administrators local group to the list with Full Control permissions. (See Figure 5.1.)

Network Access

For environments that plan on using Microsoft Networking services to transfer files between machines, the DocumentRoot directory needs to be accessible from the network. In order for the Web developer to remotely access the Web

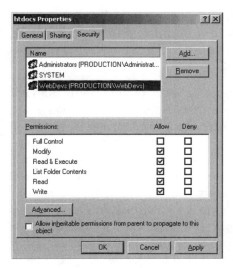

Figure 5.1 NTFS Permissions Window.

server's content directory, the DocumentRoot directory must be shared. Since you don't want everybody else on the Microsoft network to access the content directory through their Windows Explorers, the share permissions will only be assigned to the Web developer(s). Share permissions have no effect on users accessing the Web content through a browser and are only necessary for access to files using Microsoft's networking protocols.

Sharing a folder is typically accomplished through Windows Explorer. Open the properties window of the DocumentRoot directory, e.g. htdocs, and select the Sharing tab. Choose to Share this folder and either accept the name of the default share or enter in the name you wish. The name of the share has to be unique to the machine and it is recommended you choose a share name that makes sense to the Web developers. For our example here, we used the share name of webcontent. The next item is to assign the share permissions. The default share permissions is Full Control (everything) for the Everyone group. In this case this is okay because we have specified that the Everyone group has no NTFS permissions on the DocumentRoot directory. When you access the share, webcontent, from the network, both the Share permissions and the NTFS permissions determine what the user can do. Whatever combination of the Share and NTFS permissions is the most restrictive, that is the effective permissions to the user accessing the directory across the network. In our example, the Everyone group has Full Control share permissions and no NTFS permissions so their effective permissions are nothing. For the Web developer account or group, the Share permissions are Full Control from the Everyone group and the NTFS permissions are Modify, Read & Execute, List Folder Contents, Read, and Write. In this case their effective permissions are Modify, Read & Execute, List Folder Contents, Read and Write—everything except Full Control.

Setting up the FTP client on the Web developer's workstation usually does not require any configuration other than to specify the destination, user name and password. If you have installed the X Window system on Linux, a graphical FTP client is probably available on the system. One common graphical FTP application is gFTP. If you can't find it on one of the menus in the X Window interface, try typing gftp in a command window in the graphical environment and see if the application launches. If you don't have a graphical FTP client, look on your Linux distribution CDs for one or download one from the Internet. On Windows systems, there are several graphical FTP applications available but you will need to download these from the Internet. One product called WS_FTP32, is a fairly common application used by Windows users. The interface for WS_FTP32 and gFTP look very similar. In addition to graphical FTP clients, both Windows and Linux come with command line oriented FTP clients. At a command prompt in either operating system, enter ftp. The command line prompt changes to:

```
ftp>
```

To find out what commands are available, enter help at the ftp> prompt. To get more information about a specific command, enter help followed by the command. For example,

```
help bye
```

indicates the bye command will "terminate ftp session and exit." To connect to another system, enter open followed by the name of the remote system or its IP number. For example, to connect to Ouray Mountain Water company's production server with FTP, at the ftp> prompt enter:

```
open production.ouraymountainwater.com
```

If the remote system's FTP server has been configured to use user names and passwords, the FTP client will then prompt for an account name and password.

Most current Web browsers also support FTP. Basically, all that needs to be done is to specify ftp as the protocol on the URL field. For example, to access the Ouray Mountain Water production server with FTP in a Web browser, enter the following in the URL field:

```
ftp://production.ouraymountainwater.com
```

On some browsers, such as Internet Explorer, the browser will display a dialog box if account and password authentication is required by the FTP service. Some browsers will default to using an anonymous connection and do not present an account and dialog box. With Netscape, to connect with FTP using an account, the account name is placed in the URL. For example, if the Web developer's account is bob, to access the Web server using FTP in Netscape, he would enter in the location (URL):

```
ftp://bob@production.ouraymountainwater.com
```

The browser then presents a dialog box requesting the password for bob. Internet Explorer also supports the option of placing the account name in the address (URL) field for FTP access.

The FTP service on Linux and Windows 2000 must be configured to support connections and data transfer using the FTP protocol. On some Linux distributions, the FTP server software is present but the default is not to enable the service. In Windows 2000, you have a similar situation. Even though the software is installed and the service is running, you must configure the environment to allow access.

Most Linux distributions use an FTP server called WU-FTPD. This FTP server uses two primary configuration files—one to start the service and the other to configure access. The FTP server (daemon) is typically started when the Linux system is loaded and "sits" in the background waiting for incoming requests. To determine if the FTP service is running, enter the following at a command prompt:

```
chkconfig --list
```

or

```
chkconfig --list wu-ftpd
```

If you see the word *on* next to the entry for wu-ftpd then the FTP service is running. If it says *off* then you need to turn on the FTP service. Open the /etc/conf/xinetd.d/wu-ftpd file in your favorite text editor. Note that depending on the version and distribution of Linux you are using, the wu-ftpd file may be in a different location. You should see an entry that says:

```
disable                 = yes
```

Change the yes to no and save the file. This will allow the Linux server to accept incoming FTP requests.

The second item is to set up the environment so the Web developer(s) can access data and send files with FTP. When the FTP service is installed on the Linux Web server, an FTP access configuration file should already be present. The name of the file is ftpaccess and it is located in the /etc directory. You want to check the file to make sure there are no deny statements for the name of the account that will be used to connect to the FTP server. Also, to make sure the FTP server knows where the Linux system accounts are, you may want to place the following in the ftpaccess file:

```
passwd        /etc/passwd
shadow        /etc/shadow
```

In addition to configuring FTP access, make sure the Web developer(s) has/have the proper file system privileges to access the files in the Web content directory. In the previous section, we covered how to set the proper Linux file system permissions for the Web developer(s).

Microsoft provides a suite of IP based services in their IIS (Internet Information Services) product. One of the services available in IIS is an FTP server. This FTP server can be installed when you install Windows 2000 or at another time. To install the IIS FTP server you will need access to the Windows 2000 Server installation CD. In the Control Panel window, open the Add/Remove Programs applet. Select Add/Remove Windows Components and the list of Windows 2000 components installed in your system is presented. Select the entry line Internet Information Services (IIS) but do not enable the checkbox next to the entry. With IIS selected, click on the Details... button. (See Figure 5.2.)

In the Internet Information Services (IIS) window enable only Common Files, File Transfer Protocol (FTP) Server, and Internet Information Services Snap-In. Then choose OK and continue with the installation process with the Next and Finish buttons. Note that if the check box next to IIS is enabled initially and you don't go into the Details for IIS area, several IP based services besides FTP are installed. One of these default IIS services is Microsoft's Web server. You do not want both the IIS Web server and the Apache Web server installed and simultaneously attempting to run on the same machine! If this happens, both Web servers are trying to listen on the same port (80) for incoming requests. Needless to say, this causes confusion on the part of the server and no Web services are provided.

Once the Microsoft IIS FTP service is installed, the FTP server needs to be configured to allow the Web developer to upload files to the Web server. Part of the installation of IIS FTP server is a graphical management tool. From the Start menu choose Programs|Administrative Tools|Internet Services Manager. When you open up this tool for the first time the left pane displays the name of the Windows 2000 server. When you select your server name, or expand the contents of the server, one entry is revealed. The single listing, Default FTP Site,

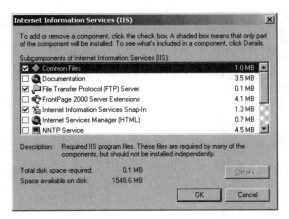

Figure 5.2   IIS FTP Installation Component Selection.

contains the initial configuration of the FTP server. To change the values to reflect the FTP settings you want, open the Properties window of the Default FTP Site. The tab labeled FTP Site allows you to specify the name of the FTP site. You may want to change this to indicate the identity of the FTP server, such as Production FTP Server. In the IP Address section, select the IP address of the network interface the FTP server will be servicing. The default TCP port to listen for FTP activity is 21 and it is recommended that you use the standard port number. You can also specify the maximum number of FTP connections permitted and the maximum idle connection time allowed for each. You can also choose to allow Unlimited FTP connections. The default settings are 100,000 connections with a 900 second (15 minute) idle duration. The timeout settings specifies that after 15 minutes, if there has been no activity on a connection, the FTP server will close down the inactive connection. This is done so the server is not tying up its resources keeping track of idle connections. (See Figure 5.3.)

The Security Accounts tab allows you to specify the name of the account used for anonymous connections and the FTP Site Operators. The Messages tab permits you to create a Welcome message that the user sees when they make a connection to the FTP server. The Exit message is displayed when the user closes the FTP session. The Maximum Connections message will be displayed to the user when they are attempting to access the FTP server and the maximum number of FTP connections has been reached. The Home Directory tab indicates the directory on the file system for the FTP site. In our examples, the FTP server's function is to provide a file transfer method for the Web developers, so we changed the Local Path value to the Web site's Document-

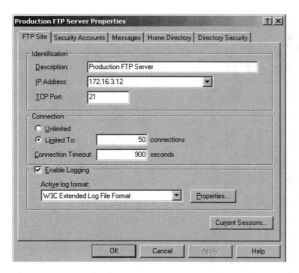

Figure 5.3   Windows FTP Server Configuration Tool.

Root directory. Also, make sure you enable Write in addition to Read and Log visits so the Web developers can add content to the Web site. The Directory Security allows you to indicate who can access the FTP server. This can be defined by individual IP numbers for each permitted computer, or the network address for all the machines on the subnet specified. You can specify machines and/or networks that are denied access to the FTP server.

Some Web authoring tools use HTTP to publish the Web content to the Web server. For example, Netscape supports within its Composer element the ability to Publish Web pages with HTTP to a Web server. Netscape also supports FTP to publish Web pages in addition to HTTP. In order to publish using HTTP to a Web server, the Web server has to accept the HTTP PUT method. Apache does not support this feature by default but you can add this functionality to Apache. There are primarily two ways to enable HTTP PUT support. One method involves scripts and if you are versed in the HTTP protocol and scripts, such as PERL or cgi, then you can develop and implement a PUT script. The other procedure is through the use of a module added to Apache. The mod_put module and information about the module are available at http://hpwww.ec-lyon.fr/~vincent/apache/mod_put.html. For our example, the Web developers working on the private Web site for Ouray Mountain Water, have decided to use Netscape's HTTP method to upload the Web content to the Web server. In order to accomplish this, we have to add the PUT module to Apache and make the method available for use.

The first task we must do after downloading and extracting the PUT module is to place the code in an appropriate place within the Apache source code. There are two files contained in the downloaded mod_put file—mod_put.c and mod_put.html. The mod_put.html file contains the documentation and can be placed anywhere in the file system. The second file, mod_put.c, contains the code to add the PUT capability to Apache. As an example here, we are using Apache 1.3.20. We created a directory called others under the modules directory where we placed the mod_put.c file. The complete path to the mod_put.c file in our example is:

```
/usr/local/apache/apache_1.3.20/src/modules/others/mod_put.c
```

In order to compile the mod-put.c code with the rest of the Apache, we need to create a Makefile.tmpl text file in the same location as the mod_put.c file. The Makefile.tmpl file is not contained in the mod_put package but you should be able to use the one listed here:

```
#Dependencies

$(OBJS) $(OBJS_PIC): Makefile

# DO NOT REMOVE
mod_put.o: mod_put.c $(INCDIR)/httpd.h \
 $(INCDIR)/http_config.h \
 $(INCDIR)/http_core.h $(INCDIR)/http_protocol.h \
 $(INCDIR)/http_log.h
```

The next step in the process is to modify the Configuration.tmpl (or Configuration) file in the src directory to indicate that you want the mod_put module compiled in the Apache binary. At the end of the file add the following line:

```
AddModule modules/others/mod_put.c
```

If you have placed mod_put.c and the associated Makefile.tmpl file at a different location, adjust the path in the AddModule statement to correspond with your file system location. Once you have accomplished these steps, then you can go ahead and compile Apache. To verify that the PUT module was compiled into the Apache binary, execute the following at a command prompt (adjust the path to wherever your httpd file is located):

```
./httpd -l
```

If all compiled okay you will see mod_put.c in the displayed list of compiled-in modules.

The next step in the process is to enable the use of the PUT command in the Apache Web server. To accomplish this, the httpd.conf file needs to be edited to turn on PUT and to specify who can use it. You don't want everybody to be able to modify the Web content so you need to put appropriate restrictions in place. Locate the section in the httpd.conf file that looks similar to the example below:

```
# This should be changed to whatever you set DocumentRoot to.
#
<Directory "/usr/local/content/htdocs">

#
# This may also be "None", "All", or any combination of "Indexes",
# "Includes", "FollowSymLinks", "ExecCGI", or "MultiViews".
#
# Note that "MultiViews" must be named *explicitly* --- "Options All"
# doesn't give it to you.
#
    Options Indexes FollowSymLinks MultiViews

#
# This controls which options the .htaccess files in directories can
# override. Can also be "All", or any combination of "Options", "FileInfo",
# "AuthConfig", and "Limit"
#
    AllowOverride None

#
# Controls who can get stuff from this server.
#
```

Locate the AllowOverride line and change:

```
AllowOverride      None
```

to

```
AllowOverride      Limit
```

Add the following lines, highlighted in bold, below the AllowOverride entry but before the next </Directory> entry:

```
#
# This controls which options the .htaccess files in directories can
# override. Can also be "All", or any combination of "Options", "FileInfo",
# "AuthConfig", and "Limit"
#
    AllowOverride Limit

#
# Controls who can get stuff from this server.
```

```
#
    Order allow,deny
    Allow from all
    EnablePUT On
    <Limit PUT>
      AuthType Basic
      AuthName "Web Publishing"
      AuthUserFile /usr/local/apache/webpasswd
      require valid-user
    </Limit>
</Directory>
```

The EnablePUT statement turns on the acceptance of HTTP PUT commands by Apache. The items enclosed by the Limit statements restrict who can use the PUT command. When an attempt is made to use PUT, the require valid-user statement directs Apache to look in the /usr/local/apache/webpasswd file and check if the user is listed. If the user is not in the list they cannot use the PUT command.

The webpasswd file of permitted users is generated by one of the utilities included with Apache, htpasswd. The htpasswd application is usually located in the same directory as httpd. This first usage of the htpasswd utility is to create the file and add one user to the authorized list. For our examples, bob is the account for one of the Web developers and webpasswd is the name of the PUT permission list. You can use a name other than webpasswd for the name of the file. In our example, at a command prompt at the Apache bin directory, execute the following:

```
./htpasswd -c webpasswd bob
```

At the New password: prompt enter the password for bob. Note that this does not have to be the same password used by bob to log into Linux. You will be asked to verify the password again at the Re-type new password: prompt. To add another Web developer to an existing PUT permission list, use the htpasswd command again but without the –c (create file) option. For example, to add leeann to the webpasswd file, the syntax would be:

```
./htpasswd webpasswd leeann
```

Again·you will be prompted to enter and verify the password for the user you are adding to the PUT permission list. By the way, the passwords are stored in the PUT permission list file in an encrypted format. Once you have added all the Web developers to the file, you need to put the file in the location you specified in the httpd.conf file. Notice in the example above that we did not place the webpasswd file at the same location as the Web content. This was done for security reasons. If the Web developers have permissions to read and write the contents of the Web content directory and the PUT permission list is at the same location, the file could be accidentally, or intentionally, modified. In our example here, the Web developers do not have access to the /usr/local/apache/ directory. Once you have made the appropriate changes to the httpd.conf file, you will need to restart the Apache Web server.

NOTE In order to publish with the mod_put module, the user and/or group ownership of the DocumentRoot directory and all files below must be the same as the User and/or Group specified in the httpd.conf file. If the ownership of the directories and files does not match the User and/or Group in the httpd.conf file, nobody can use the PUT command with the mod_put module to add files to the Web server's content directory.

FrontPage 2000

Some authoring programs implement proprietary methods to publish Web content developed in their tools to the Web server. One commonly used Web development tool is FrontPage 2000 from Microsoft. In addition to FrontPage's proprietary HTTP method, you can also use FTP to publish from FrontPage to an Apache Web server. Additional software called FrontPage Extensions must be installed on the Web server in order for the Web developer to publish from FrontPage using HTTP. Microsoft provides FrontPage extensions for IIS, Apache, and other Web servers.

NOTE The FrontPage Extensions for Windows does not support a Windows 2000 Apache Web server. The Windows FrontPage Extensions support IIS, Netscape FastTrack, Netscape Enterprise, O'Reilly Web Site, and FrontPage Personal Web servers. The Linux/UNIX FrontPage extensions support Apache, NCSA, Netscape FastTrack, Netscape Enterprise, and StrongHold Web servers.

FrontPage displays an informational dialog box when an attempt is made to publish with HTTP from FrontPage to a Web server that does not have the FrontPage Extensions installed. Figure 5.4 is an example of the information displayed.

Figure 5.4 Missing FrontPage Extensions notification window.

If your Web developers plan on using FrontPage to publish with HTTP to an Apache Linux Web server, the FrontPage Extensions must be installed and configured on the Linux Apache Web server. The FrontPage Extensions for Linux systems are available from Microsoft's Web site and other locations on the Internet. For our FrontPage Extensions example, we will be installing the FrontPage 2000 Extensions for an Apache 1.3.20 Web server. The Web server has been installed in the default installation location of /usr/local/apache/ and the Web content directory (DocumentRoot) is located at /usr/local/content/htdocs/. We will be using FrontPage 2000 to publish via HTTP the Ouray Mountain Water's public Web site content to the Linux Apache Web server.

The FrontPage 2000 Extensions for Linux come as a compressed tar package, fp40.linux.tar.Z, which is about 15 MB in size. Place the file someplace suitable in your file system and extract the package contents. For example, place the tar file in the /usr/local/fp2000/ directory and execute the following at a command prompt:

```
gunzip fp40.linux.tar.Z
```

and then unTAR the package with:

```
tar -xvf fp40.linux.tar
```

The extraction process creates the directory structure, frontpage/version4.0/ below where you extracted the package. The version 4.0 directory contains the Extensions software, documentation, and SERK—the Server Extensions Resource Kit. The SERK information is designed to be viewed through a Web browser.

The installation process is started by executing the fp_install.sh script. This script steps you through the installation and we go through the process later in this section. A copy of the fp_install.sh is included below for your reference. You can modify the content as you see fit to meet your needs. Notice that the script is copyrighted so you cannot distribute modified copies to other parties without permission from the copyright holder.

```
#! /bin/sh
#
# Copyright 1998 Microsoft Corporation -- All Rights Reserved.
#
# $Revision: 1.1 $
# $Date: 1998/12/02 21:58:21 $
#


step1()
{
```

```
    echo
    echo "Step 1.  Setting Up Installation Environment"
    echo

    checkuser || error                  # Check to make sure we are root
    banner
    usrlocalexists || error             # Check to make sure that /usr/local exists
    checkforaccess || error             # Check for RWX access to /usr/local
    wheretoinstall || error             # Find out where to install the extensions

}

step2()
{
 echo
 echo "Step 2.  Untarring the Extensions and Checking Protections"
 echo

    untarext   || error                 # Untar the extensions

}

step3()
{
 echo   echo "Step 3.  Upgrading/Installing the extensions"
 echo

    upgradeexistingservers || error     # Check to see if servers need upgrading
    chownexistingservers || error
    installrootweb || error             # Install the root web
    installnewsubwebs $PORT || error    # Install new servers
    installvirtualwebs || error         # Install any virtual webs

}

initialize()
{
  VERSION="4.0"
  PATH=".:/bin:/usr/bin:/sbin:/usr/sbin:/usr/ucb:/etc:/usr/bsd"
  INSTALLDIRDEFAULT="/usr/local/frontpage"

case "`echo 'x\c'`" in
   'x\c')   echo="echo -n"    nnl= ;;        #BSD
   x)       echo="echo"       nnl="\c" ;;  # Sys V
   *)       echo "$0 quitting:  Can't set up echo." ; exit 1 ;;
esac

 TAB="         "
 system=`uname -a`

 case "$system" in
```

```
    OSF1*)               machine="alpha" ;;
    Linux*mips*)         machine="mips-linux" ;;
    Linux*)              machine="linux" ;;
    HP-UX*)              machine="hp700" ;;
    AIX*)                machine="rs6000" ;;
    IRIX*)               machine="sgi" ;;
    SunOS*5.*sun4*)      machine="solaris" ;;
    SunOS*5.*i386*)      machine="solarisx86" ;;
    BSD/OS*)             machine="bsdi" ;;
    SCO_SV*)             machine="sco5" ;;
    FreeBSD*)          machine="freebsd" ;;
    UnixWare\ *\ *\ 7*\ i*)   machine="uware7" ;;
    *)                   echo "ERROR:  Unsupported platform!  Uname is $system."
                         return 1
                           ;;
esac

case "$machine" in
  sunos) functions="function toupper(CHAR) {
                  UPPER = \"ABCDEFGHIJKLMNOPQRSTUVWXYZ\";
                  LOWER = \"abcdefghijklmnopqrstuvwxyz\";
                  if (POS = index(LOWER,CHAR))
                      RETVAL = substr(UPPER,POS,1);
                  else
                      RETVAL = CHAR;

                  return RETVAL

                  }

                  function tolower(CHAR) {
                  UPPER = \"ABCDEFGHIJKLMNOPQRSTUVWXYZ\";
                  LOWER = \"abcdefghijklmnopqrstuvwxyz\";
                  if (POS = index(UPPER,CHAR))
                     RETVAL = substr(LOWER,POS,1);
                  else
                      RETVAL = CHAR;

                  return RETVAL

                  }"
        ;;
      *) functions=""
        ;;
esac

case "$machine" in
     solaris) awk=nawk
              lsg="ls -ld"
              ;;
   solarisx86) awk=nawk
```

```
                            lsg="ls -ld"
                            ;;
                 sgi)  awk=nawk
                            lsg="ls -ld"
                            ;;
             uware7)  awk=nawk
                            lsg="ls -ld"
                            ;;
                   *)  awk=awk
                            lsg="ls -ld"
                            ;;
  esac


}


checkuser()
{
 #
 # Make sure we are not running as root.
 #

whoami=`whoami 2>/dev/null` || whoami=`/usr/bin/id | sed -e ' s/).*//;
s/^.*(//;'`
 retval=0

 echo "Setting umask 002"
 umask 002

 if [ $whoami != "root" ]
 then
     echo "ERROR:  Logged in as $whoami.  Must be root to do this installation!"
     retval=1
 else
     echo "Logged in as root."
 fi

 return $retval


}

banner()
{
cat <<EOF


 fp_install.sh

 Revision$Revision: 1.1 $dummy
 Date$Date: 1998/12/02 21:58:21 $dummy

This script will step the user through upgrading existing and installing
```

new servers and webs. As with any software installation, a backup should be done before continuing. It is recommended that the FrontPage installation directory, server configuration file directory, and all web content be backed up before continuing with this installation.

```
EOF
 myprompt 'yYnN' "Are you satisfied with your backup of the system (y/n)" "N"
 if [ $answer = n ] || [ $answer = N ]
 then
     exit 0
 fi
 echo

 return 0
}

myprompt()
{
 answer="|"
 until echo $1 | grep $answer >/dev/null
 do
     $echo "${2} [${3}]?  ${nnl}"
     read answer
     if [ "$3" != "" ] && [ "$answer" = "" ]
     then
         answer=$3
     fi
 done
}

getpassword()
{
 prompt=$1
 PASSWORD=""
 until [ "$PASSWORD" != "" ]
 do
     $echo "$prompt:  ${nnl}"
     stty -echo
     read password1
     stty echo
     echo
     $echo "Re-enter $prompt:  ${nnl}"
     stty -echo
     read password2
     stty echo
     echo
     if [ "$password1" = "$password2" ]
     then
         PASSWORD=$password1
     fi
```

```
    done

  return 1
}

usrlocalexists()
{
 #
 # Now lets make sure that /usr/local exists.
 #

 localdir="/usr/local"
 prot=755
 retval=0

 if [ ! -d "$localdir" ]
 then
     myprompt 'yYnN' "$localdir does not exist.  Would you like to create it
(y/n)" "Y"
     if [ $answer = y ] || [ $answer = Y ]
     then
         echo "Creating $localdir"
         if mkdir "$localdir"
         then
             echo "Directory $localdir has been created."
             if chmod "$prot" "$localdir"
             then
                 echo "Directory $localdir chmoded to $prot."
             else
                 echo "ERROR:  Unable to chmod $localdir to $prot."
                 retval=1
             fi
         else
             echo "ERROR:  Unable to create $localdir!"
             retval=1
         fi
     else
         echo "ERROR:  Directory $localdir must exist!"
         retval=1
     fi
 else
     if [ ! -d "$localdir" ]
     then
         echo "ERROR:  $localdir exists but is not a directory!"
         retval=1
     else
         echo "Directory $localdir exists."
     fi
 fi

 return $retval
```

```
}


checkforaccess()
{
 #
 # Make sure that we have the correct access to /usr/local
 #

 retval=0

 #
 # Check to make sure that we have read access to the directory
 #
 comma=""
 if [ ! -r /usr/local ]
 then
    noaccess="Read"
    comma=", "
 fi


 #
 # Check to make sure that we have write access to the directory
 #
 if [ ! -w /usr/local ]
 then
    noaccess="$noaccess${comma}Write"
    comma=", "
 fi


 #
 # Check to make sure that we have execute access to the directory
 #
 if [ ! -x /usr/local ]
 then
    noaccess="$noaccess${comma}Execute"
 fi


 if  [ "$noaccess" != "" ]
 then
    echo "ERROR:  Root does not have $noaccess access to /usr/local!"
    retval=1
 else
    echo "Root has necessary access to /usr/local."
 fi

 return $retval

}
```

```
wheretoinstall()
{
 #
 # Find out where to install the extensions and create directory and/or link
 # as necessary.
 #

 retval=0

 echo
 echo "Where would you like to install the FrontPage Extensions.  If you"
 echo "select a location other than /usr/local/frontpage/ then a symbolic"
 echo "link will be created from /usr/local/frontpage/ to the location that"
 echo "is chosen."
 echo
 $echo "FrontPage Extensions directory [/usr/local/frontpage/]:  ${nnl}"
 read installdir

 if [ "$installdir" = "" ]
 then
     installdir=$INSTALLDIRDEFAULT
 fi
 installdir=`dirname $installdir`/`basename $installdir`

 if [ ! -d "$installdir" ]
 then
    echo "Creating $installdir"
    if mkdir "$installdir"
    then
       echo "Directory $installdir has been created."
       if chmod "$prot" "$installdir"
       then
          echo "Directory $installdir chmoded to $prot."
       else
          echo "ERROR:  Unable to chmod $installdir to $prot."
          retval=1
       fi
    else
       echo "ERROR:  Unable to create $installdir!"
       retval=1
    fi
 else
    echo "WARNING:  Directory $installdir already exists."
    echo "Installation will overwrite existing files."
    echo

    myprompt 'yYnN' "Continue the installation (y/n)" "N"
    echo
    if [ $answer = n ] || [ $answer = N ]
    then
       exit 0
```

```
        fi
 fi

 if [ "$installdir" != "/usr/local/frontpage" ]
 then
    if [ ! -d "/usr/local/frontpage" ]
    then
        if ln -s "$installdir" "/usr/local/frontpage"
        then
            echo "Snapped link /usr/local/frontpage --> $installdir"
        else
            echo "ERROR:  Unable to  snap link /usr/local/frontpage -->
$installdir!"
            retval=1
        fi
    else
        echo "ERROR:  Unable to snap link /usr/local/frontpage --> $installdir,
/usr/local/frontpage already exists!"
        retval=1
    fi
 fi

 return $retval

}

untarext()
{
 #
 # Untar the extensions into the installation directory and check permissions
 #
 retval=0

 if [ -d "${installdir}/version${VERSION}" ]
 then
    echo "Version $VERSION FrontPage Server Extensions found."
    myprompt 'yYnN' "Would you like to overwrite? (y/n)" "Y"
    echo
    if [ $answer = n ] || [ $answer = N ]
    then
        echo "No need to un-tar the extensions.  Continuing..."
        return $retval
    else
        echo "Looking for tar file..."
    fi
 else
     echo "Version $VERSION FrontPage Server Extensions not found."
     echo "Looking for tar file..."
 fi

 vtfile="fp40.$machine.tar"
```

```
        echo "Platform is $machine."

        vtfilelocation="`pwd`/"

        getextfilename $vtfilelocation $vtfile || return 1

        olddir=`pwd`

        if [ "$installdir" != "/usr/local/frontpage" ]
        then
            cd $installdir
        else
            cd /usr/local
        fi
        case $fullvtfile in
            *tar) echo "Untarring file $fullvtfile into /usr/local..."
                  tar -xf $fullvtfile ;;
              *Z) echo "Uncompressing/Untarring file $fullvtfile into /usr/local..."
                  zcat $fullvtfile | tar -xf -
                  ;;
             *gz) zcat=""
                  while [ "$zcat" = "" ] || [ ! -f "$zcat" ]
                  do
                      $echo "Where is the zcat which can uncompress gz files? ${nnl}"
                      read zcat
                      base=`basename zcat`
                      case $base in
                         zcat) ;;
                            *) zcat=`dirname $zcat`/`basename $zcat`/zcat ;;
                      esac
                  done
                  echo "Uncompressing/Untarring file $fullvtfile into /usr/local..."
                  $zcat $fullvtfile | tar -xf -
                  ;;
              *) echo "ERROR:  Unknown file type: $fullvtfile"
                 return 1
                 ;;
        esac

        if [ "$installdir" != "/usr/local/frontpage" ]
        then
            mv frontpage/* .
            rm -rf frontpage
        fi

        cd $olddir

        return $retval

    }
```

```
getextfilename()
{
 vtfilelocation=$1
 vtfile=$2
 fullvtfile="${vtfilelocation}${vtfile}"
 if [ ! -f "$fullvtfile" ]
 then
     if [ -f "${fullvtfile}.Z" ]
     then
         fullvtfile="${fullvtfile}.Z"
     else
         if [ -f "${fullvtfile}.gz" ]
         then
             fullvtfile="${fullvtfile}.gz"
         else
          if [ -f "${fullvtfile}.z" ]
          then
              echo "Renaming ${vtfile}.z to ${vtfile}.Z"
              mv "${fullvtfile}.z" "${fullvtfile}.Z"
              fullvtfile="${fullvtfile}.Z"
          else
             echo "Cannot find the FrontPage Extensions tar file in
${vtfilelocation}."
             $echo "Which directory is the file located in (X to cancel)?   ${nnl}"
             read vtfilelocation
             if [ "$vtfilelocation" = "X" ] || [ "$vtfilelocation" = "x" ]
             then
                 return 1
             else

                 vtfilelocation=`echo $vtfilelocation | sed -e 's/\/$//'`

                 if [ ! -d "$vtfilelocation" ]
                 then
                     vtfilelocation=`dirname $vtfilelocation`
                 fi

                 getextfilename $vtfilelocation/ $vtfile
             fi
          fi
         fi
     fi
 fi


}

upgradeexistingservers()
{
 retval=0
```

```
echo "Checking for existing web servers to upgrade..."

upgrade="none"
for file in ${installdir}/*.cnf
do
    if [ "$file" = "${installdir}/*.cnf" ]
    then
        echo "No existing web servers found to upgrade."
        return $retval
    fi

    cat <<EOF

Existing web servers were found.
You can upgrade them later by re-running fp_install.sh and
answering yes to the following question.

EOF
    myprompt 'yYnN' "Would you like to upgrade them now (y/n)" "Y"

    if [ $answer = n ] || [ $answer = N ]
    then
        upgrade="no"
        echo "For details on how to upgrade servers manually, please see"
        echo "the Server Extension Resource Kit (SERK), located in"
        echo "/usr/local/frontpage/version${VERSION}/serk"
        echo
        return $retval
    else
        upgrade="yes"
    fi
    break
done

cat <<EOF

The file ${installdir}/version${VERSION}/upgrade_results.txt will
contain Success/Fail status for the upgrades.  When the upgrade is
complete you should examine this file to make sure that all of the
upgrades completed successfully.

EOF
$echo "Hit enter to continue${nnl}"
read continue
echo

echo "All existing servers will now be upgraded:"
echo " "

createdate=`date`
cat >${installdir}/version${VERSION}/upgrade_results.txt <<EOF
```

```
#
# Server Upgrade Results
#
# Automatically generated by fp_install.sh on $createdate
#
EOF

 for weconfigfile in ${installdir}/*.cnf
 do
    echo
    echo "Upgrading using configuration file:  "$weconfigfile
    if verifywebserver $weconfigfile
    then
        if upgradeserver $weconfigfile
        then
            echo "Upgrade Successful  $weconfigfile" >>
${installdir}/version${VERSION}/upgrade_results.txt
        else
            echo "Upgrade Failed       $weconfigfile" >>
${installdir}/version${VERSION}/upgrade_results.txt
            echo "ERROR:  Server upgrade failed!"
            echo "Continuing with next server."
            $echo "Hit enter to continue${nnl}"
            read continue
        fi
    else
        echo "Cancelling upgrade..."
        echo "Upgrade Failed       $weconfigfile" >>
${installdir}/version${VERSION}/upgrade_results.txt
    fi
 done

 weconfigfile=""

 return $retval
}

verifywebserver()
{
 weconfigfile="$1"

 conf=`basename $weconfigfile`
  port=`echo  $conf | sed -e '
    s/:/:/
    tmulti
    s/.cnf$//
    s/.*[^0-9]//
    q
    :multi
    s/.cnf$//'`
```

```
echo "Verifying web server configuration..."

configfile=`grep -i "^serverconfig:" $weconfigfile | sed -e '
            s/serverconfig://g
            s/fakeconf.*\///'`
if [ ! -f "$configfile" ]
then
    echo "$configfile does not exist."
    return 1
fi

servertype=`grep -i "^servertype:" $weconfigfile | sed -e 's/servertype://g'`
configfiledir=`dirname $configfile`"/"

if [ $servertype = "cern" ]
then
    echo "This version of FrontPage does not suppport cern servers."
    echo "For more information about supported servers, please see"
    echo "the Server Extension Resource Kit (SERK), located in"
    echo "/usr/local/frontpage/version${VERSION}/serk"
    return 1
fi

if [ $servertype = "apache-fp" ]
then
    echo "This server has the Microsoft FrontPage 98 Apache patch installed."
    echo "Be sure to install the FrontPage 2000 Apache patch by running the"
    echo "change_server.sh script, or this web server will not be upgraded to"
    echo "Microsoft FrontPage 2000."
    $echo "Hit enter to continue${nnl}"
    read continue
fi

getdocroot $weconfigfile ||
{
    echo "ERROR:  Unable to get DocumentRoot/UserDir"
    return 1
}

case $servertype in
    *pache*) getHttpDirective $configfile AccessConfig $port
            if [ "$param" != "" ]
            then
                file=`basename $param`
                accessconffile="${configfiledir}${file}"
            else
                accessconffile="${configfiledir}access.conf"
            fi

            if [ ! -f "$accessconffile" ]
            then
```

```
                        echo "$accessconffile does not exist."
                        return 1
                fi
                ;;
        ncsa)  getHttpDirective $configfile AccessConfig $port
                if [ "$param" != "" ]
                then
                        file=`basename $param`
                        accessconffile="${configfiledir}${file}"
                else
                        accessconffile="${configfiledir}access.conf"
                fi

                if [ ! -f "$accessconffile" ]
                then
                        echo "$accessconffile does not exist."
                        return 1
                fi
                ;;
  esac

  servicesfile=${docroot}"/_vti_pvt/services.cnf"

  if [ ! -f "$servicesfile" ]
  then
      echo "There are no services to upgrade for this web."
      return 1
  fi

  return 0
}

chownexistingservers()
{
  retval=0

  if [ "$upgrade" = "yes" ]
  then
      echo
      echo "Preparing to chown webs..."
      cat <<EOF
```

Your webs have been upgraded to use the new FrontPage Server Extensions. The
next step is to chown the web in order to guarantee that the extensions will
work properly. At this point you have two options:

1. This script will prompt you interactively for an owner and group of
   each web and then perform the chown. If you do not have a lot of
   webs you might want to choose this option.

2. This script will generate a script, which you can edit to fill in the

```
            owner and group for each web, to run at a later date.  If you have a
            large number of webs you might want to choose this option.

    EOF

        echo "Would you like to be prompted interactively for"
        myprompt 'yYnN' "each webs owner/group (y/n)" "Y"
        if [ $answer = y ] || [ $answer = Y ]
        then
            chownwebs
        else
            generatechownscript $file  ||
            (
                echo "ERROR:  Server chown failed!  Continuing with next server."
                $echo "Hit enter to continue${nnl}"
                read continue
            )

        fi
        return $retval
    fi
}

chownwebs()
{
 retval=0

 for weconfigfile in ${installdir}/*.cnf
 do
     if grep Failed ${installdir}/version${VERSION}/upgrade_results.txt | grep
${weconfigfile} > /dev/null
     then
         echo
         echo "Upgrade of ${weconfigfile} failed."
         echo "See ${installdir}/version${VERSION}/upgrade_results.txt"
         echo "Skipping chown..."
     else
         chownWeb $weconfigfile
     fi
 done

 weconfigfile=""

 return $retval
}

chownWeb()
{
 weconfigfile=$1

 echo
```

```
conf=`basename $weconfigfile`
webport=`echo  $conf | sed -e '
    s/:/:/
    tmulti
    s/.cnf$//
    s/.*[^0-9]//
    q
    :multi
    s/.cnf$//'`

port=$webport

echo "Processing webs in port $webport..."
echo

servertype=`grep -i "^servertype:" $weconfigfile | sed -e 's/servertype://g'`
configfile=`grep -i "^serverconfig:" $weconfigfile | sed -e '
            s/serverconfig://g
            s/fakeconf.*\///'`
configfiledir=`dirname $configfile`"/"

getdocroot $weconfigfile ||
{
    echo "ERROR:  Unable to get DocumentRoot/UserDir"
    return 1
}

servicesfile=${docroot}"/_vti_pvt/services.cnf"

exec 4<&0
exec <$servicesfile
n=0
while read service
do
    echo
    if [ $service = "/" ]
    then
        webname=""
        webtext="root web"
        web=""
    else
        webname="$service"
        webtext="$service"
        web="-w $webname"
    fi
    exec 5<&0
    exec 0<&4

    getdocroot $weconfigfile ||
    {
        echo "ERROR:  Unable to get DocumentRoot/UserDir"
```

```
        return 1
    }

    case $service in
        /~*)  owner=`echo $service | sed -e 's/\///'`

            webowner=`echo $service | sed -e 's/\/~//'`
            homedir=`finger $webowner | $awk ' { if (NR==2) print $2}'`
            if [ -d "${homedir}/${userdir}" ]
            then
                echo "Web ${webtext} on port ${webport} will be owned by
${webowner}"
                defwebgroup=`$lsg ${homedir}/${userdir} | $awk ' { print $4}'`
                exists=0
            else
                exists="${homedir}/${userdir}"
            fi
            ;;
        *)  if [ -d "${docroot}/${service}" ]
            then
                defwebowner=`$lsg ${docroot}${service} | $awk ' { print $3}'`
                defwebgroup=`$lsg ${docroot}${service} | $awk ' { print $4}'`

                webowner=""
                until [ "$webowner" != "" ]
                do
                    $echo "Who should own web ${webtext} on port ${webport}
[${defwebowner}]:  ${nnl}"
                    read webowner
                    if [ "$webowner" = "" ]
                    then
                        webowner=$defwebowner
                    fi
                done

                exists=0
            else
                exists="${docroot}/${service}"
            fi

            ;;
    esac

    if [ "$exists" = "0" ]
    then
        webgroup=""
        until [ "$webgroup" != "" ]
        do
            $echo "What should the group for web ${webtext} on port ${webport}
be [${defwebgroup}]:  ${nnl}"
            read webgroup
```

```
                if [ "$webgroup" = "" ]
                then
                        webgroup=$defwebgroup
                fi
        done

        /usr/local/frontpage/version${VERSION}/bin/fpsrvadm.exe -o chown -p
$webport $web -xUser $webowner -xGroup $webgroup ||
        {
            echo
            echo "ERROR:  Unable to chown web ${webtext} in port ${webport}"
            $echo "Hit enter to continue${nnl}"
            read continue
        }
    else
        echo "ERROR:  web $service - $exists does not exist!  Skipping to next
web."
    fi
        exec 0<&5
 done
 exec <&4

}

generatechownscript()
{
 retval=0
 scriptout="/usr/local/frontpage/version${VERSION}/fp_chown.sh"
 createdate=`date`

 cat <<EOF

A script will be generated in ${scriptout}
which you can edit to chown your webs at a future date.  You will
need to edit the script and set the owner and group for each web
before running the script.

EOF

 cat >$scriptout <<EOF
#! /bin/sh
#
#
# Copyright 1996 Microsoft Corporation -- All Rights Reserved.
#
#           Automatically generated by fp_install.sh
#
# Automatically generated by fp_install.sh on $createdate
#
# You will need to edit this script before running it.  Change each
# <OWNER> and <GROUP> to reflect the ownership/group that you want
```

```
# set for the web.
#
# Example:  80 /testweb webowner webgroup
#

VERSION="4.0"

chown_web()
{
 port=\$1
 webname=\$2
 webowner=\$3
 webgroup=\$4

 if [ "\$webowner" = "<OWNER>" ] || [ "\$webgroup" = "<GROUP>" ]
 then
     echo "WARNING:  Owner/Group not specified for web \$webname on \$port."
     echo "Skipping to next web..."
 else
     if [ "\$webname" != "/" ]
     then
         webname=\`echo \$webname | sed -e 's%^/%%g'\`
         webtext="\$webname"
         web="-w \$webname"
     else
         webtext="root web"
         web=""
     fi
     echo
     echo "Chowning web \${webtext} in port \${port} to owner \${webowner} group
\${webgroup}"
     /usr/local/frontpage/version4.0/bin/fpsrvadm.exe -o chown -p \$port  \$web
-xUser \$webowner -xGroup \$webgroup
 fi
}

while read port webname webowner webgroup
do
    chown_web \$port \$webname \$webowner \$webgroup
done <<ENDCHOWN
EOF

 for weconfigfile in ${installdir}/*.cnf
 do
     if grep Failed ${installdir}/version${VERSION}/upgrade_results.txt | grep
        ${weconfigfile} > /dev/null
     then
         echo
         echo "Upgrade of ${weconfigfile} failed."
         echo "See ${installdir}/version${VERSION}/upgrade_results.txt"
         echo "Skipping chown..."
```

```
        else
            addChownWeb $weconfigfile
        fi
 done

 echo "ENDCHOWN" >>$scriptout

 chmod 764 $scriptout

 weconfigfile=""
 return $retval
}

addChownWeb()
{

 weconfigfile=$1

 echo
 echo "Processing  $weconfigfile"
 conf=`basename $weconfigfile`
 webport=`echo  $conf | sed -e '
    s/:/:/
    tmulti
    s/.cnf$//
    s/.*[^0-9]//
    q
    :multi
    s/.cnf$//'`

 port=$webport

 echo "Adding webs in port ${webport} to chown script..."
 servertype=`grep -i "^servertype:" $weconfigfile | sed -e 's/servertype://g'`
 configfile=`grep -i "^serverconfig:" $weconfigfile | sed -e '
            s/serverconfig://g
            s/fakeconf.*\///'`
 configfiledir=`dirname $configfile`"/"
 getdocroot $weconfigfile ||
 {
     echo "ERROR:  Unable to get DocumentRoot/UserDir"
     return 1
 }

 servicesfile="${docroot}/_vti_pvt/services.cnf"
 if [ -r $servicesfile ]
 then
     exec 4<&0
     exec <$servicesfile
     n=0
```

```
         while read service
         do
            if [ $service = "/" ]
            then
                webtext="root web"
            else
                webtext="$service"
            fi

            case $service in
               /~*)  owner=`echo $service | sed -e 's/\///'`

                     webowner=`echo $service | sed -e 's/\/~//'`
                     homedir=`finger $webowner |  $awk ' { if (NR==2) print $2}'`
                     if [ -d "${homedir}/${userdir}" ]
                     then
                         webgroup=`$lsg ${homedir}/${userdir} | $awk ' { print $4}'`
                         exists="0"

                     else
                         exists="${homedir}/${userdir}"
                     fi
                     ;;
                  *)  if [ -d "${docroot}/${service}" ]
                      then
                          webowner=`$lsg ${docroot}${service} | $awk ' { print $3}'`
                          webgroup=`$lsg ${docroot}${service} | $awk ' { print $4}'`
                          exists="0"
                      else
                          exists="${docroot}/${service}"
                      fi
                      ;;
            esac


         if [ "$exists" = "0" ]
         then
            echo "web ${webtext}"
            echo "$webport $service $webowner $webgroup" >> $scriptout
         else
            echo "ERROR:  web ${webtext}- Path $exists does not exist!  Skipping to
   next web."
         fi
         done
         exec <&4
    else
         echo "WARNING:  Unable to read $servicesfile!"
         echo "Skipping to next port."
    fi


   }
```

```
upgradeserver()
{
 retval=0
 weconfigfile="$1"

 bindir=$installdir'/version'$VERSION'/bin/'

 conf=`basename $weconfigfile`

 echo "Upgrading server "$port

 /usr/local/frontpage/version${VERSION}/bin/fpsrvadm.exe -o upgrade -p $port

 return $retval
}

installrootweb()
{
 retval=0

 configfile=""
 admin=""
 port=""
 multihost=""
 webname=""
 webowner=""
 servertype=""

 echo
 echo "Note: If you have not installed the root web then you need to do it now."
 echo
 myprompt 'yYnN' "Do you want to install a root web (y/n)" "Y"
 if [ $answer = n ] || [ $answer = N ]
 then
     return $retval
 fi

 echo " "
 echo "Installing the root web..."
 echo " "

 webname="/"

 configfile=""
 while ( [ "$configfile" = "" ] || [ ! -f $configfile ] )
 do
     $echo "Server config filename:  ${nnl}"
     read configfile
 done
```

```
admin=""
until [ "$admin" != "" ]
do
    $echo "FrontPage Administrator's user name:  ${nnl}"
    read admin
done

getparam Port $configfile
port=$param

until [ "$port" != "" ]
do
    $echo "Enter the new servers port number:  ${nnl}"
    read port
done

getparam User $configfile
defwebowner=$param

weconfigfile="${installdir}/we${port}.cnf"

webowner=""
until [ "$webowner" != "" ]
do
    $echo "Unix user name of the owner of this new web:[$defwebowner]  ${nnl}"
    read webowner
    if [ "$webowner" = "" ]
    then
        webowner=$defwebowner
    fi
done

getparam Group $configfile
defgroup=$param
webgroup=""
until [ "$webgroup" != "" ]
do
    echo
    $echo "Unix group of this new web:[$defgroup]  ${nnl}"
    read webgroup
    if [ "$webgroup" = "" ]
    then
        webgroup=$defgroup
    fi
done

until [ "$servertype" != "" ]
do
    echo
    echo "    1.  ncsa"
    echo "    2.  apache"
```

```
       echo "    3.   apache-fp"
       echo "    4.   netscape-fasttrack"
       echo "    5.   netscape-enterprise"
       echo "    6.   stronghold"
       $echo "What type of Server is this:   ${nnl}"
       read servertypenum
       echo

       case $servertypenum in
            "1") servertype="ncsa" ;;
            "2") servertype="apache" ;;
            "3") servertype="apache-fp" ;;
            "4") servertype="netscape-fasttrack" ;;
            "5") servertype="netscape-enterprise" ;;
            "6") servertype="stronghold" ;;
             *) echo "Invalid option!  Please try again."   ;;
       esac
done

multihost="."
if [ "$configfile" = "" ]
then
    configfile="."
fi

PORT=$port

echo "Installing root web into port $port..."
echo
installserver $port $multihost $webname $webowner $webgroup $admin $configfile
    $servertype ||
{
    echo "ERROR:  $webname installation failed."
    $echo "Hit enter to continue${nnl}"
    read continue
    return $retval
}

isItApacheFP
handlelanguage

return $retval
}

isItApacheFP()
{
retval=0

if [ "$servertype" = "apache-fp" ]
then
    apachedir=$installdir'/version'$VERSION'/apache-fp'
```

```
echo
echo "Chowning $apachedir to root..."
chown root $apachedir ||
  (
   echo "ERROR:  Unable to chown $apachedir to root"
   retval=1
  )

echo
echo "Chmoding $apachedir to 711..."
chmod 711 $apachedir ||
  (
   echo "ERROR:  Unable to chown $apachedir to 711"
   retval=1
  )

apachedir=$installdir'/version'$VERSION'/apache-fp/_vti_bin'

echo
echo "Chowning $apachedir to root..."
chown root $apachedir ||
  (
   echo "ERROR:  Unable to chown $apachedir to root"
   retval=1
  )

echo
echo "Chmoding $apachedir to 755..."
chmod 755 $apachedir ||
  (
   echo "ERROR:  Unable to chown $apachedir to 755"
   retval=1
  )

fpexe=$installdir'/version'$VERSION'/apache-fp/_vti_bin/fpexe'

echo
echo "Chowning $fpexe to root..."
chown root $fpexe ||
  (
   echo "ERROR:  Unable to chown $fpexe to root"
   retval=1
  )

echo "Setting $fpexe to SUID..."
chmod u+s $fpexe ||
  (
   echo "ERROR:  Unable to set SUID for "$fpexe
   retval=1
  )
```

```
        rm -f ${installdir}/version${VERSION}/apache-fp/suidkey

        ps=`ps -ea | tail -10` ; echo $ps | sed -e 's/ //g' | cut -c10-137 >
            ${installdir}/version${VERSION}/apache-fp/suidkey

        chown root ${installdir}/version${VERSION}/apache-fp/suidkey
        chmod 600 ${installdir}/version${VERSION}/apache-fp/suidkey
  fi

  return $retval

}

handlelanguage()
{
 retval=0

 until [ "$charencoding" != "" ]
 do
        echo
        echo "    1.  LATIN1 (ISO 8859-1)"
        echo "    2.  LATIN2 (ISO 8859-2)"
        echo "    3.  EUCJP  (Japanese EUC)"
        echo "    4.  EUCKR  (Korean EUC)"
        $echo "Which local character encoding does your system support: [1]  ${nnl}"
        read charencodingnum
        echo

        case $charencodingnum in
            "") charencoding="latin1" ;;
            "1") charencoding="latin1" ;;
            "2") charencoding="latin2" ;;
            "3") charencoding="eucjp" ;;
            "4") charencoding="euckr" ;;
              *) echo "Invalid option!  Please try again."  ;;
        esac
 done

 until [ "$lang" != "" ]
 do
        echo
        echo "    1.  English"
        echo "    2.  French"
        echo "    3.  German"
        echo "    4.  Italian"
        echo "    5.  Japanese"
        echo "    6.  Spanish"
        $echo "What should the default language be: [1] ${nnl}"
        read langnum
        echo
```

```
      case $langnum in
          "") lang="en" ;;
          "1") lang="en" ;;
          "2") lang="fr" ;;
          "3") lang="de" ;;
          "4") lang="it" ;;
          "5") lang="ja" ;;
          "6") lang="es" ;;
            *) echo "Invalid option!  Please try again."  ;;
      esac
  done

  conffile=$installdir'/version'$VERSION'/frontpage.cnf'
  echo "Setting "$conffile" to:"
  echo
  echo "defaultLanguage:${lang}"
  echo "localCharEncoding:${charencoding}"
  echo
  echo "Moving ${conffile} to ${conffile}.orig"
  echo
  mv $conffile ${conffile}.orig ||
  {
      echo "ERROR:  Unable to backup $conffile to ${conffile}.orig!"
      $echo "Hit enter to continue${nnl}"
      read continue
      return 1
  }

  echo "Creating and modifying new ${conffile}..."
  echo
  sed -e "s/defaultLanguage:.*/defaultLanguage:${lang}/g
          s/localCharEncoding:.*/localCharEncoding:${charencoding}/g" \
        ${conffile}.orig > $conffile ||
  {
      echo "ERROR:  Unable to create new $conffile!"
      echo "If the file has been corrupted you should be able to replace it with"
      echo "the backup file (${conffile}.orig)"
      $echo "Hit enter to continue${nnl}"
      read continue
      return 1
  }

 return $retval
}

installvirtualwebs()
{
 retval=0

 echo
```

```
echo "Installing Virtual Webs.."
echo
myprompt 'yYnN' "Do you want to install Virtual Webs (y/n)" "Y"
if [ $answer = n ] || [ $answer = N ]
then
    return $retval
fi

defaultconfigfile=$configfile
configfile=""
while ( [ "$configfile" = "" ] || [ ! -f $configfile ] )
do
    $echo "Server config filename [${defaultconfigfile}]:  ${nnl}"
    read configfile
    if [ "$configfile" = "" ]
    then
        configfile=$defaultconfigfile
    fi
done

getparam Port $configfile
port=$param
getparam User $configfile
webowner=$param

case $configfile in
    *magnus*) echo
            echo "Looking for Netscape virtuals..."
            n=0
            resourcefile=`echo $configfile | sed -e
's/magnus\.conf/obj.conf/'`
            urlhosts=`grep -i \urlhost $resourcefile`
            if [ "$urlhosts" ]
            then
                novirtuals=0
            else
                novirtuals=1
            fi

            while [ "$urlhosts" ]
            do
                urlhost=`echo $urlhosts | sed -e '
                    s/>.*/>/'`
                virtweb=`echo $urlhost | sed -e '
                    s/\"//g
                    s/ *<.*= *//
                    s/ *> *//'`
                n=`expr $n + 1`
                eval virtwebs$n="$virtweb"
                urlhost=`echo $urlhost | sed -e '
                    s/\./\\\./g
```

```
                                    s/\"/\\\"/g'`
                        urlhosts=`echo $urlhosts | sed -e "s/$urlhost *//"`
                done

                virtuals=`grep -i NameTrans $resourcefile | grep -i \address |
                    sed -e "
                        s/\"//g
                        s/.*[Aa][Dd][Dd][Rr][Ee][Ss][Ss]= *//
                        s/ .*//"`

                if [ "$virtuals" ]
                then
                    novirtuals=0
                fi

                for virtweb in $virtuals
                do
                    n=`expr $n + 1`
                    eval virtwebs$n="$virtweb"
                done

                if [ $novirtuals = 1 ]
                then
                    echo "ERROR:  There are no valid virtual webs defined."
                    $echo "Hit enter to continue${nnl}"
                    read continue
                    return 1
                fi
                ;;
        *) virtnames=`cat $configfile | $awk "
                BEGIN {
                    value = \"\"; j=0
                }


                { x=0; y=0; server=\"\"; virtname=\"\" }


                /^[^#]* *<
        *[Vv][Ii][Rr][Tt][Uu][Aa][Ll][Hh][Oo][Ss][Tt][ $TAB]/ {
                    virtname = \\\$2; y=1; j++
                }

                /^[^#]*[Ss][Ee][Rr][Vv][Ee][Rr][Nn][Aa][Mm][Ee][ $TAB]/  {
                    server = \\\$2; y=2
                }

                {
                    if (y == 1) {  gsub(/>/,\"\",virtname); ARRAY[j] =
                        virtname }
                    if (y == 2) { ARRAY[j] = server }
```

```
                                         }

                             END {
                                     for ( i =1; i <= j; i++ ) {
                                            print ARRAY[i] \" \"
                                     }
                             }"`

                     virtnames=`echo $virtnames | sed -e 's/>//g'`
                     n=0
                     for word in $virtnames
                     do
                         n=`expr $n + 1`
                         eval virtwebs$n="$word"
                     done

                     ;;
esac

while echo
     n=1
     val=`eval echo $"virtwebs$n"`
     while [ "$val" != "" ]
     do
         echo "  $n) $val"
         n=`expr $n + 1`
         val=`eval echo $"virtwebs$n"`
     done

     echo
     $echo "Select the virtual web to install (CTRL-D if no more webs): ${nnl}"
     read virtwebno
do
   getparam Port $configfile
   port=$param
   until [ "$port" != "" ]
   do
       $echo "Enter the new servers port number:  ${nnl}"
       read port
   done

   port="`eval echo $"virtwebs$virtwebno"`:$port"

   getHttpVirtualDirective $configfile $port User
   defwebowner=$param

   webowner=""
   until [ "$webowner" != "" ]
   do
       $echo "Unix user name of the owner of this new web:[$defwebowner]  ${nnl}"
```

```
        read webowner
        if [ "$webowner" = "" ]
        then
            webowner=$defwebowner
        fi
done

getHttpVirtualDirective $configfile $port Group
defwebgroup=$param

webgroup=""
until [ "$webgroup" != "" ]
do
    echo
    $echo "Unix group of this new web:[$defgroup]  ${nnl}"
    read webgroup
    if [ "$webgroup" = "" ]
    then
        webgroup=$defgroup
    fi
done

webname="/"

admin=""
until [ "$admin" != "" ]
do
    $echo "FrontPage Administrator's user name:  ${nnl}"
    read admin
done

until [ "$servertype" != "" ]
do
 echo
 echo "    1.  ncsa"
 echo "    2.  apache"
 echo "    3.  apache-fp"
 echo "    4.  netscape-fasttrack"
 echo "    5.  netscape-enterprise"
 echo "    6.  stronghold"
 $echo "What type of Server is this:  ${nnl}"
 read servertypenum
 echo

 case $servertypenum in
     "1") servertype="ncsa" ;;
     "2") servertype="apache" ;;
     "3") servertype="apache-fp" ;;
     "4") servertype="netscape-fasttrack" ;;
     "5") servertype="netscape-enterprise" ;;
     "6") servertype="stronghold" ;;
```

```
                      *) echo "Invalid option!  Please try again."    ;;
            esac
        done

        multihost="`eval echo $"virtwebs$virtwebno"`"
        if [ "$configfile" = "" ]
        then
            configfile="."
        fi
        if [ "$servertype" = "" ]
        then
            servertype="."
        fi


        PORT=$port
        echo "Installing virtual root web into port $port..."
        echo
        installserver $port $multihost $webname $webowner $webgroup $admin
            $configfile $servertype ||
        {
            echo "ERROR:  $webname installation failed."
            $echo "Hit enter to continue${nnl}"
            read continue
            return $retval
        }

        isItApacheFP
        handlelanguage

        weconfigfile=""

        installnewsubwebs $PORT || error     # Install new servers
        echo
    done

    return $retval


}

installnewsubwebs()
{
  port=$1

  retval=0

  echo
  myprompt 'yYnN' "Install new sub/per-user webs now (y/n)" "Y"
  if [ $answer = n ] || [ $answer = N ]
  then
      echo "For details on how to upgrade servers manually, please see"
```

```
        echo "the Server Extension Resource Kit (SERK), located in"
        echo "/usr/local/frontpage/version${VERSION}/serk"
        echo
        return $retval
    fi
    echo


    if [ "$weconfigfile" = "" ]
    then
        until [ "$weconfigfile" != "" ] && [ -f $weconfigfile ]
        do
            port=""
            if [ "$port" = "" ]
            then
                cat <<EOF

You need to specify which server to install the subweb into.
Examples:
        80
        www.virtual.web:80

        where 80 is the port the server is running on.

EOF
                $echo "Which server would you like to install the subweb into:  ${nnl}"
                read port
            fi
            echo
            case $port in
                *:*) weconfigfile="${installdir}/${port}.cnf" ;;
                  *) weconfigfile="${installdir}/we${port}.cnf" ;;
            esac
        done
    fi


    echo
    echo "Using FrontPage Configuration File:  ${weconfigfile}"
    echo

    servertype=`grep -i "^servertype:" $weconfigfile | sed -e 's/servertype://g'`
    configfile=`grep -i "^serverconfig:" $weconfigfile | sed -e '
            s/serverconfig://g
            s/fakeconf.*\///'`
    configfiledir=`dirname $configfile`"/"

    getdocroot $weconfigfile ||
    {
        echo "ERROR:  Unable to get DocumentRoot/UserDir"
        return 1
    }
```

```
services=${docroot}"/_vti_pvt/services.cnf"

if [ ! -f $services ]
then
    echo
    echo "ERROR:  The root web must be installed before sub/per-user webs!"
    echo "Document Root:  ${docroot}"
    $echo "Hit enter to continue${nnl}"
    read continue
    echo
    return $retval
fi

echo
while $echo "Enter the web name (CTRL-D if no more webs): ${nnl}"
     read webname
do
    admin=""
    until [ "$admin" != "" ]
    do
        $echo "FrontPage Administrator's user name:  ${nnl}"
        read admin
    done

    case "$webname" in
        ~*) PERUSER=1
            echo
            echo "Web $webname is a per-user web"
            echo
            webowner=$webname
            ;;
        *) PERUSER=0
            echo
            echo "Web $webname is a subweb"
            echo
            webowner=""
            ;;
    esac

    defwebowner=`$lsg ${docroot}${service} | $awk ' { print $3}'`
    until [ "$webowner" != "" ]
    do
        echo
        $echo "Unix user name of the owner of this new web:[$defwebowner]  ${nnl}"
        read webowner
        if [ "$webowner" = "" ]
        then
            webowner=$defwebowner
        fi
    done
```

```
        getparam Group $configfile
        defgroup=$param
        webgroup=""
        until [ "$webgroup" != "" ]
        do
            echo
            $echo "Unix group of this new web:[$defgroup]  ${nnl}"
            read webgroup
            if [ "$webgroup" = "" ]
            then
                webgroup=$defgroup
            fi
        done

        multihost="."

        if [ "$configfile" = "" ]
        then
            configfile="."
        fi

        if [ "$servertype" = "" ]
        then
            servertype="."
        fi

        installserver $port $multihost $webname $webowner $webgroup $admin
            $configfile $servertype ||
        {
            echo "ERROR:  $webname installation failed."
            $echo "Hit enter to continue${nnl}"
            retval=0
            read continue
        }
        echo
    done

 return $retval
}

installserver()
{
 retval=0

 port="$1"
 multihost="$2"
 webname="$3"
 webowner="$4"
 webgroup="$5"
 admin="$6"
 configfile="$7"
```

```
servertype="$8"

echo
echo "installing server "$webname" on port "$port

if [ "$PERUSER" = 1 ]
then
    user=`echo $webowner | sed -e 's/~//g'`
    echo
    echo "Will chown per-user web to $user as part of install."
    echo "Will chgrp per-user web to $webgroup as part of install."
    chown="-xUser $user -xGroup $webgroup"
else
    if [ "$webowner" != "." ]
    then
        echo
        echo "Will chown web to $webowner as part of install."
        echo "Will chgrp web to $webgroup as part of install."
        chown="-xUser $webowner -xGroup $webgroup"
    else
        chown=""
    fi
fi

if [ "$configfile" != "." ]
then
    config="-s $configfile"
else
    config=""
fi

if [ "$servertype" != "." ]
then
    server="-type $servertype"
else
    server=""
fi

if [ "$webname" != "/" ]
then
    web="-w $webname"
else
    web=""
fi

if [ "$multihost" != "." ]
then
    /usr/local/frontpage/version${VERSION}/bin/fpsrvadm.exe -o install -p $port
        $web $config -u $admin $server $chown -m $multihost || retval=1
else
    /usr/local/frontpage/version${VERSION}/bin/fpsrvadm.exe -o install -p $port
```

```
            $web $config -u $admin $server $chown -m "" || retval=1
    fi

    return $retval

}

getdocroot()
{
  weconfigfile=$1

  servertype=`grep -i "^servertype:" $weconfigfile | sed -e 's/servertype://g'`
  configfile=`grep -i "^serverconfig:" $weconfigfile | sed -e '
             s/serverconfig://g
             s/fakeconf.*\///'`

  echo
  echo "Getting DocumentRoot and UserDir."

  if [ ! -f "$configfile" ]
  then
      echo "$configfile does not exist."
      return 1
  fi

  configfiledir=`dirname $configfile`"/"

  docroot=""

  case $weconfigfile in
      *:*) getvirtualdocroot $weconfigfile $configfile
          ;;
        *) case $servertype in
               *etscape*) getnetscapedocroot $configfile
                  ;;
                      *) getHttpDirective $configfile ResourceConfig $port
                      if [ "$param" != "" ]
                      then
                          if [ "${param}" = "/dev/null" ]
                          then
                              resconffile="${configfile}"
                          else
                              file=`basename $param`
                              resconffile="${configfiledir}${file}"
                          fi
                      else
                          resconffile="${configfiledir}srm.conf"
                      fi

                      if [ ! -f "$resconffile" ]
                      then
```

```
                                echo "ERROR: $resconffile does not exist!"
                                return 1
                        fi

                        echo "Getting DocumentRoot from $resconffile."
                        getHttpRootDirective $resconffile DocumentRoot
                        docroot=$param

                        echo "Getting UserDir from $resconffile."
                        getHttpRootDirective $resconffile UserDir
                        userdir=$param
                        ;;
            esac
            ;;
    esac

    if [ ! -d "${docroot}" ]
    then
        echo "ERROR:  ${docroot} does not exist!"
        return 1
    fi

    if [ "${docroot}" = "" ]
    then
        echo "ERROR:  DocumentRoot not defined!"
        return 1
    fi

    echo
    echo "DocumentRoot: ${docroot}"

    if [ "${userdir}" = "" ]
    then
        echo "WARNING:  UserDir not defined."
    else
        echo "UserDir: ${userdir}"
    fi

    echo

    return 0

}

getHttpDirective()
{
 configfile=$1
 directive=$2
 port=$3

 case $port in
```

```
        *:*) getHttpVirtualDirective $configfile $port $directive ;;
         *) getHttpRootDirective $configfile $directive ;;
    esac

    if [ "$param" = "" ]
    then
        echo "Directive $directive not found."
    else
        echo "Found Directive $directive, value $param."
    fi
}

getMixedCase() {

#
# getMixedCase takes a string and converts it to a regular expression which
# matches all possible case combinations.
#
# String = [Ss][Tt][Rr][Ii][Nn][Gg]
#

mc_string=`echo $1 | $awk "
                BEGIN {
                    newstring = \"\";
                    oldstring = \"$1\";

                    }

                    $functions

                    {

                    strlen = length(oldstring);

                    for ( i = 1; i <= strlen; ++i ) {
                        char = substr(oldstring, i, 1)
                        newstring = newstring \"[\" toupper(char) tolower(char)
                            \"]\";
                    };
                    print newstring}"`


}

getHttpRootDirective()
{
 configfile=$1
 directive=$2

 getMixedCase $directive
```

```
param=`cat $configfile | $awk "
            /^[^#]* *< *[Vv][Ii][Rr][Tt][Uu][Aa][Ll][Hh][Oo][Ss][Tt]/,/^[^#]* *<
               *\/[Vv][Ii][Rr][Tt][Uu][Aa][Ll][Hh][Oo][Ss][Tt]/ { next }
            /^[^#]* *${mc_string}[ $TAB]/  { print \\\$2 }"`

 return 0

}

getHttpVirtualDirective()
{
 configfile=$1
 port=$2
 directive=$3

 virtweb=`echo  $port | sed -e 's/:[0-9]*.$//'`
 virtweb=`basename $virtweb`

 getMixedCase $directive

 param=`cat $configfile | $awk "
                     BEGIN    { value = \"\"; j=0 }
                              { x=0; y=0; server=\"\"; virtname=\"\" }

                     /^[^#]* *<
*[Vv][Ii][Rr][Tt][Uu][Aa][Ll][Hh][Oo][Ss][Tt][ $TAB]/ {
                          virtname = \\\$2; y=1; j++
                     }

                     /^[^#]*[Ss][Ee][Rr][Vv][Ee][Rr][Nn][Aa][Mm][Ee][ $TAB]/  {
                          server = \\\$2; y=2
                     }

                     /^[^#]* *${mc_string}[ $TAB]/  {
                          arg = \\\$2; y=3
                     }


                     {
                          if (y == 1) { gsub(/>/,\"\",virtname); VIRTNAMES[j]
                             = virtname }
                          if (y == 2) { SERVERNAMES[j] = server }
                          if (y == 3) { ARRAY[j] = arg }
                     }

                 END {
                     for ( i =1; i <= j; i++ ) {
                          if (SERVERNAMES[i] == \"$virtweb\" ||
VIRTNAMES[i] == \"$virtweb\" ) {
                               print ARRAY[i]
```

```
                                        }
                                    }
                            } "`

    if [ "$param" = "" ]
    then
        getHttpRootDirective $configfile $directive
    fi

}


getnetscapedocroot()
{
 configfile=$1

 resourcefile=`echo $configfile | sed -e 's/magnus\.conf/obj.conf/'`

 echo
 echo "Getting DocumentRoot from ${resourcefile}."

 exec 4<&0
 exec <$resourcefile

 while read line
 do
      uc_line=`echo $line | tr [a-z] [A-Z]`
      case $uc_line in
          *DOCUMENT-ROOT*) docroot=`echo $line | sed -e '
                                  s/\"//g
                                  s/.* [Rr][Oo][Oo][Tt]= *//
                                  s/ .*//'`
                          ;;
                *SUBDIR*) userdir=`echo $line | sed -e '
                                  s/\"//g
                                  s/.* [Ss][Uu][Bb][Dd][Ii][Rr]= *//
                                  s/ .*//'`
                      ;;
                \<CLIENT*) while read line
                          do
                              uc_line=`echo $line | tr [a-z] [A-Z]`
                              case $uc_line in
                                  \</CLIENT\>) break
                                              ;;
                              esac
                          done
                          ;;
      esac
 done
 exec <&4
```

```
}

getvirtualdocroot()
{

 weconfigfile=$1
 configfile=$2

 virtweb=`echo  $weconfigfile | sed -e '
          s/:/:/
          tmulti
          s/.cnf$//
          s/.*[^0-9]//
          q
          :multi
          s/:[0-9]*.cnf$//'`
 virtweb=`basename $virtweb`

 case $configfile in
      *magnus*) n=0
                resourcefile=`echo $configfile | sed -e
's/magnus\.conf/obj.conf/'`
                exec 4<&0
                exec <$resourcefile
                echo
                echo "Looking for Client block of $resourcefile..."

                while read line
                do
                    uc_line=`echo $line | tr [a-z] [A-Z]`
                    case $uc_line in
                        *URLHOST*) virtname=`echo $line | sed -e '
                                    s/\"//g
                                    s/ *<.*= *//
                                    s/ *>.*//'`

                                if [ "$virtweb" = "$virtname" ]
                                then
                                    echo "Found Client block.  Getting
Document-Root and Subdir..."

                                    while read line
                                    do
                                        uc_line=`echo $line | tr [a-z] [A-
Z]`

                                        case $uc_line in
                                            *DOCUMENT-ROOT*) docroot=`echo
                                                $line | sed -e '
                                                    s/\"//g
                                                    s/.*
[Rr][)o][Oo][Tt]= *//

                                                    s/ .*//'`
                                                ;;
```

```
                                                    *SUBDIR*) userdir=`echo
                                                $line | sed -e '
                                                     s/\"//g
                                                     s/.*

[Ss][Uu][Bb][Dd][Ii][Rr]= *//

                                                     s/ .*//'`
                                                    ;;
                                        \</CLIENT\>) break
                                                    ;;
                            esac
                        done
                    fi
                    ;;
            esac
        done
        exec <&4

        if [ "$docroot" = "" ]
        then
            docroot=`grep -i NameTrans $resourcefile | grep -i $virtweb |
                sed -e "
                            s/\"//g
                            s/.*[Rr][Oo][Oo][Tt]= *//
                            s/ .*//"`
        fi


        ;;
    *) getHttpVirtualDirective $configfile $port DocumentRoot
       docroot=$param

       if [ "$docroot" = "" ]
       then
           echo "VirtualHost block does not contain DocumentRoot
               directive."
           getHttpDirective $configfile ResourceConfig $port
           if [ "$param" != "" ]
           then
               if [ "${param}" = "/dev/null" ]
               then
                   resconffile="${configfile}"
               else
                   file=`basename $param`
                   resconffile="${configfiledir}${file}"
               fi
           else
               resconffile="${configfiledir}srm.conf"
           fi
           echo "Getting DocumentRoot from $resconffile."
           getparam DocumentRoot $resconffile
           docroot=$param
       fi
```

```
                    getHttpVirtualDirective $configfile $port UserDir
                    userdir=$param

                    if [ "$userdir" = "" ]
                    then
                        echo "VirtualHost block does not contain UserDir directive."
                        getHttpDirective $configfile ResourceConfig $port
                        if [ "$param" != "" ]
                        then
                            if [ "${param}" = "/dev/null" ]
                            then
                                resconffile="${configfile}"
                            else
                                file=`basename $param`
                                resconffile="${configfiledir}${file}"
                            fi
                        else
                            resconffile="${configfiledir}srm.conf"
                        fi
                        echo "Getting UserDir from $resconffile."
                        getparam UserDir $resconffile
                        userdir=$param
                    fi
                    ;;
 esac

}

error()
{
 #
 # Print an error message and exit the program
 #

 echo
 echo "Exiting due to an error!  Please fix the error and try again."
 echo

 exit 1
}

getparam() {
#
# gets the value of parameters from the config file
#
    param=`egrep -i "^[ $TAB]*$1[ $TAB]" $2 | $awk '{print $2}'` || return 1
    return 0;
}
#
# This is the main part of the shell script.
#
```

```
initialize
step1
step2
step3
#
# Run the external permissions script.
#
/usr/local/frontpage/version${VERSION}/set_default_perms.sh

echo
echo "Installation completed!  Exiting..."

exit 0
```

The fp_install.sh script is the same used for other Web servers besides Apache. In addition, the installation script will execute other scripts that are included in the FrontPage Extensions package.

The next step is to start the installation script. Note that you should already have a backup of the Web server's data and any other important information before installing the software. If you have a test server available, you may want to practice the installation process to make sure everything comes out the way you expect it to. Before you begin to install, make sure you are logged on as root (the script will check for that) and you have, or know, the following information:

fp40.linux.tar location. The installation process needs to know the location of the FrontPage tar file. In our example the location is /usr/local/ fp2000/.

httpd.conf location. This is needed to indicate where to add the FrontPage extensions. In our example the complete path of httpd.conf is /usr/local/ apache/conf/httpd.conf.

FrontPage author/administrator's name and password. This name and password is used by a FrontPage client when an attempt is made to publish using the FrontPage Extensions. For our example, the Web developer's account name is webdev.

User. This is the name of the user account that owns the content area of the Web server. This is the same name specified in the httpd.conf file. In our example the user name is apache.

Group. This is the name of the group account that owns the content area of the Web server. This is the same name specified in the httpd.conf file. In our example the group name is apache.

httpd location. The installation process needs to know the location of the Apache binary. In our example the complete path and name is /usr/local/apache/bin/httpd.

One final preparation step involves a modification of the httpd.conf file. Look for the area under Section 2 that looks similar to the following example:

```
#
# This should be changed to whatever you set DocumentRoot to.
#
<Directory "/usr/local/apache/htdocs">

#
# This may also be "None", "All", or any combination of "Indexes",
# "Includes", "FollowSymLinks", "ExecCGI", or "MultiViews".
#
# Note that "MultiViews" must be named *explicitly* --- "Options All"
# doesn't give it to you.
#
    Options Indexes FollowSymLinks MultiViews

#
# This controls which options the .htaccess files in directories can
# override. Can also be "All", or any combination of "Options", "FileInfo",
# "AuthConfig", and "Limit"
#
    AllowOverride None

#
# Controls who can get stuff from this server.
#
    Order allow,deny
    Allow from all
</Directory>
```

The <Directory "/usr/local/apache/htdocs"> entry may be different for your environment depending on the location of your Web server's content directory (DocumentRoot).

Change the line that says:

```
AllowOverride None
```

to

```
AllowOverride All
```

This is necessary for the FrontPage extensions to install properly.

Once you have gathered the information and made the change to the httpd.conf file, go ahead and run the installation script by executing at a command prompt:

```
./fp_install.sh
```

Some information about the script is displayed on the screen along with the reminder that you should have a current backup. The first question displayed is:

```
Are you satisfied with your backup of the system (y/n) [N]?
```

The item between the brackets, [N], indicates the default answer when you press the enter key without any other characters. If you choose the default, or enter n, the installation process stops. Enter y when you are ready to proceed with the installation.

The next query asks where you would like to install the FrontPage Extensions.

```
FrontPage Extensions directory [/usr/local/frontpage/]:
```

Either accept the default location or enter the complete directory path. For our example, we will accept the default path. The next step looks for the location of the FrontPage Extensions tar file in the /usr/local/fp2000/ frontpage/version4.0/ directory.

```
Which directory is the file located in (X to cancel)?
```

In our example, the tar file resides at /usr/local/fp2000/, so we will enter the correct path. The installation script then extracts the tar file to /usr/local/frontpage/. The next process checks if there are any existing Web servers with previous versions of the FrontPage extensions that need to be upgraded. Since this is our first time installing on the Web server we need to install a root web.

```
Do you want to install a root web (y/n) [Y]?
```

For our example we will choose the default. This root web specification informs the installation script where the Apache server and files are located. At the prompt:

```
Server config filename:
```

Enter the complete path and name of the Apache httpd.conf file. For our example, we will enter:

```
/usr/local/apache/conf/httpd.conf
```

The next item is to specify the name of the FrontPage Administrator account. This is the name of the user who will be using FrontPage to author the Web pages.

```
FrontPage Administrator's user name:
```

In our example, we will use our webdev account. The next query is to provide the name of the Linux account that owns the Web content which is the name of the User account specified in the httpd.conf file. The installation prompt will include the name of the User discovered in the httpd.conf file. In our example, the User name is apache.

```
Unix user name of the owner of this new web:[apache]
```

If your system has a different User name specified in httpd.conf, the name between the square brackets will be different. In our example, apache is correct so we will accept the default and continue. The next prompt requests the name of the Group specified in the httpd.conf file. The installation script will display the name of the Group entry it read in the httpd.conf file.

```
Unix group of this new web:[apache]
```

As with the User name, the name between the brackets will reflect your environment. In our example, apache is correct so we will accept the default and continue. The next query asks for the type of Web server running on the Linux system.

```
1.  ncsa
2.  apache
3.  apache-fp
4.  netscape-fastrack
5.  netscape-enterprise
6.  stronghold
What type of Server is this:
```

For our example, we will choose 2 for apache. The apache-fp (3) entry is used if you are upgrading Apache that has an earlier version of the FrontPage extensions. The next item is to indicate the password for the FrontPage author account you specified earlier in the script. The prompt will include the name of the account.

```
Password for user "webdev":
```

In our example, we used webdev as the account name. If you have specified a different name, then the name you used will be displayed between the quotes. You will be prompted to enter the password twice for confirmation. The next query requests the local character encoding the Linux system is using.

```
1.  LATIN1 (ISO 8859-1)
2.  LATIN2 (ISO-8859-2)
3.  EUCJP (Japanese EUC)
4.  EUCKR (Korean EUC)
What local character encoding does your system support: [1]
```

Choice 1 (Latin1) refers to English and we will choose that for our example. The next question prompts for the default language.

```
1.  English
2.  French
3.  German
4.  Italian
5.  Japanese
6.  Spanish
What should the default language be: [1]
```

For our example, we will choose English as the default language. The next query asks if you want to install new sub-webs or per-user webs. Per-user webs are used for environments that support user webs and directories. For example, if the environment supports ~username, such as http://myweb .ouraymountainwater.com/~leeann. If you choose not to install this option now, you can install sub-web and per-user web support in the future by running the change_server.sh script or by using the fpsrvadm utility.

```
Install new sub/per-user webs now (y/n) [Y]?
```

In our example, we are not supporting these so we will enter n for no. The next question applies to Web servers that host multiple Web sites or virtual hosting.

```
Do you want to install Virtual Webs (y/n) [Y]
```

Our example public Web server for the Ouray Mountain Water company is not hosting multiple sites so we will choose n for no. When all is done you will see:

```
Installation completed!  Exiting….
```

You can easily perform a quick check to see if the FrontPage Extensions are doing their work. Open the FrontPage application and attempt to access a Web page on the Web server. In FrontPage's Open Web dialog box, enter either the IP address or the name of your Web server in the area labeled Folder name:. The first clue that the extensions are working is the appearance of the Web developer's account and password request window. Enter the name and password of the Web author you specified in the FrontPage Extensions installation process. If there is a Web page in the DocumentRoot directory that matches the name of the file or files listed in the DirectoryIndex specification in the httpd.conf file, the default page will load into FrontPage.

Publishing Your Web Content

Now that the Web servers are all setup and configured to accept Web content, the next step is publishing the Web pages to the Web servers. If your environment consists of a mixture of Linux and Windows systems and/or the Web developers use a variety of tools, you may need to implement several publishing methods. In this section we cover the process of publishing the Web content from the Web developer's systems to the Web servers.

Publishing Web content can be divided into two types. The first involves Web content to a Web server that has no Web content at all. For first time publications, you need to make sure that all the Web content, files, and folders, are placed on the Web server and at the proper places. The second publication type involves updating existing Web site content with new material. When updating Web content, you need to keep in mind whether all the Web content will be replaced or just some of the files.

Publishing for the First Time

There are several methods available for publishing the Web pages created by the Web developers to the Web servers. In the previous chapter we covered the procedures necessary to prepare the Apache Web server for publication of the Web content. In this section, we address the publication process of the different methods from the Web developer's perspective.

Copy and Paste

One way to add new Web content to a Web server involves a simple copy and paste. Once the permissions are in place to allow modification of the Web content directory by the Web developer(s), the next step is educating the Web authors on the process. Windows systems, with their graphical interface, provide an easy mechanism to copy entire directories and their contents to another location. One item to keep in mind is to make sure the Web site contents are placed in the proper location—that is the DocumentRoot directory. As an example, Ouray Mountain Water's Production Web server, a Windows 2000 system, is using the following location for the Web content (DocumentRoot):

```
G:\content\htdocs\
```

The Web developers, either on the same or another machine, have placed the developed Web pages and files into the directory:

```
C:\My Document\My Webs\Production Web\
```

To copy the Web content, the Web developer selects all the needed files and folders in the Production Web folder and pastes a copy to the DocumentRoot location. If the developer copies and pastes the Production Web folder to the htdocs folder, the Web content will not appear when accessed with a browser. Within a browser window, the Web site would look something like Figure 6.1.

The reason for this failure is the Web content is now located at:

```
G:\content\htdocs\Production Web\
```

In this situation, the Web developer needs to copy the contents of the Production Web folder instead of the folder itself.

Windows systems also support a command window interface, and files and directories can be copied from a command line. Using the same example directory structure as before, the following command would copy all the contents of the Production Web directory (folder) to the htdocs directory:

```
xcopy c:\My Documents\My Webs\Production Web g:\content\htdocs\ /s
```

Note that the syntax of the command works from any place with our example file system. If the command window's prompt was currently at the Production

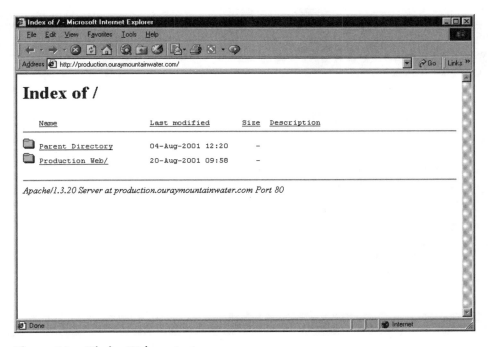

Figure 6.1 Missing Web content.

Web directory (folder), the path to the Production Web folder does not need to be specified and thus, the command would be shorter. The /s option copies all the Production Web folder's subfolders and the contents to the destination.

Sometimes using the command line in Windows involves a lot of typing because of the length of the folders and filenames. Commands that are executed at a command line can be automated through the use of a batch file. To make the batch file easy to use, place a shortcut to the batch file on the Web developer's desktop. When the Web developer needs to copy their files to the Web content directory, all they need to do is run or double-click on the shortcut.

Instead of using Window's long file names and folder names, you can also use the short names of the resources. Short names are the 8dot3 names where the maximum number of characters to the left of the dot is eight and the maximum number of characters to the right of the dot is three—thus, 8dot3. To determine the short names on a Windows 2000 system, execute the following in a command window:

```
dir /x
```

Note that other Windows versions may show the short names without the need for additional parameters with the dir command. Using our sample file system as an example, the dir /x command executed at the root level of the local hard drive, C:, reveals the following output:

```
Volume in drive C has no label.
 Volume Serial Number is 0730-1507

 Directory of C:\

01/30/2001  04:35p                      0               CONFIG.SYS
01/24/2001  04:00p    <DIR>                             FOUND.000
04/23/1999  10:22p               93,890                 COMMAND.COM
01/30/2001  05:03p                9,396                 NETLOG.TXT
01/30/2001  05:07p    <DIR>         MYDOCU~1            My Documents
01/30/2001  05:22p    <DIR>                             NOVELL
01/24/2001  04:09p    <DIR>         PROGRA~1            Program Files
01/30/2001  04:35p                   56                 AUTOEXEC.BAT
01/24/2001  04:03p    <DIR>                             WINNT
05/04/2001  02:34p                  967 COMMAND.PIF     command.PIF
01/24/2001  04:08p    <DIR>         DOCUME~1            Documents and Settings
01/30/2001  05:11p                  728 CONFIG.BAK      config.bak
01/30/2001  05:04p                  146 AUTOEXEC.BAK    autoexec.bak
07/09/2001  07:23a                   75                 NBIHW.CFG
07/03/2001  03:20p               32,143                 SCANDISK.LOG
03/01/2001  07:53a               31,088                 RCVFAX.TRC
02/05/2001  03:16p    <DIR>         W98APPS             W98Apps
03/01/2001  07:53a               30,338                 RCVFAX.LOG
03/17/2001  12:35p    <DIR>         MOC                 moc
01/24/2001  07:29p    <DIR>         MYMUSI~1            My Music
07/02/2001  06:40p               15,324 WINZIP.LOG      winzip.log
05/04/2001  12:02p                  235                 SETUPXLG.TXT
04/05/2001  11:52a                    0 FFASTUNT.FFL    ffastunT.ffl
04/05/2001  11:59a                    0 FFASTUNT.FFX    ffastunT.ffx
              22 File(s)      250,053 bytes

              16 Dir(s)    921,579,520 bytes free
```

Notice, for example, the short name for My Documents is MYDOCU~1. Navigating to the My Documents directory, the dir /x command at that point reveals:

```
Volume in drive C has no label.
 Volume Serial Number is 0730-1507

 Directory of C:\My Documents

01/30/2001  05:07p    <DIR>                             .
01/30/2001  05:07p    <DIR>                             ..
01/30/2001  09:20p    <DIR>         MYPICT~1            My Pictures
```

```
04/06/2001  04:09p                   185 SFU-TS.REG      Sfu-ts.reg
06/26/2001  08:22p      <DIR>            MYEBOO~1         My eBooks
07/09/2001  07:08a                   384 OLDEXC~1.LNK    Old Excel Documents.lnk
07/09/2001  07:29a      <DIR>            MYWEBS~1         My Webs
              2 File(s)              569 bytes
              5 Dir(s)       920,653,824 bytes free
```

In this example, the short name for the My Webs folder is MYWEBS~1. Performing another dir /x command in the My Webs directory results in:

```
Volume in drive C has no label.
 Volume Serial Number is 0730-1507

 Directory of C:\My Documents\My Webs

07/09/2001  07:29a      <DIR>                            .
07/09/2001  07:29a      <DIR>                            ..
07/09/2001  07:48a      <DIR>            PRODUC~1         Production Web
              0 File(s)                0 bytes
              3 Dir(s)       920,563,712 bytes free
```

In the above sample output, the Production Web 8dot3 name is PRODUC~1. Using the short names for the folders, the xcopy command would be:

```
xcopy c:\mydocu~1\mywebs~1\produc~1 g:\htdocs /s
```

If batch files will be created to copy the Web content, the short names for files and directories can be used in place of long names.

Network environments that implement Microsoft networking protocols include methods to copy files from one machine to another. Depending on the nature of the user's accounts, the Web developer may need to logon to the Web server in addition to their own system. Microsoft networks that use domains or Active Directory to manage user accounts and resources may not require the Web developer to authenticate to the Web server. Whether one or multiple logons are necessary, make sure the Web developer knows how to get to the Web server's content directory.

The Windows environment can be customized to make it easier for the Web developer to find the Web server's content directory. If the Web developer is comfortable with drive letters, a drive letter can be mapped to the DocumentRoot directory on the Web server. Map drives can be created through Windows Explorer, the net command at a command prompt, or in a logon script. Once the mapped drive is created, the Web developer navigates to the drive letter the same way they access the hard drive on their own system. Shortcuts to the Web content directory on the Web server can also be used. The shortcuts can either use a mapped drive letter or the name of the server and share name.

Once the Web developer has access to the DocumentRoot directory, they can copy and paste the information from their system to the server. As we mentioned earlier in this section, make sure the Web developer's files are placed in the DocumentRoot directory and not in a sub folder. You can also use the command line to copy files from one machine to another. The syntax is essentially the same as the example we used previously. Make sure to use either a mapped drive letter or include the machine and share name. In addition, file copy batch files and/or shortcuts referring to network resources can be setup on the Web developer's system to assist in automating the file transfer process.

Linux environments support command line and graphical interface solutions for copying files and directories. If the Web developer is working on the same machine as the Web server, the developed content can be copied to the DocumentRoot directory within the graphical environment. Linux GUI solutions, such as kde and GNOME, include file manager tools that support copy and paste functions to transfer data from one location to another. In addition, files can be copied from a command line, or shell, interface from either within the graphical environment or from another session. As an example, the Web developer for the Ouray Mountain Water's Employee Web site is saving the pages she has developed in her home directory, /home/leeann/. The Web developer needs to copy the files she has developed from her home directory to the Web server's content directory, /usr/local/contents/htdocs/. The Linux cp command line utility is used to copy and paste files and directories. For example, using our example scenario file system, the syntax of the cp command would be:

```
cp /home/leeann/employeeweb/* /usr/local/content/htdocs -R
```

The –R option recursively copies all the files and directories below the location specified. Again, we are assuming that the Web developer has the proper permissions to place a copy of the developed files into the Web server's content directory. Since the Web developer will be using the cp command frequently, a script (batch) file is created. With a script, the next time the Web developer needs to transfer files, she simply runs the script. In addition, if the X Window system is in use, you can place a shortcut to the script on the Web developer's desktop.

FTP

The File Transfer Protocol (FTP) is one of the oldest and most common protocols used on networks of all sizes. FTP was designed to provide fast file transfer between two networked and communicating devices. Many companies and organizations have FTP servers for access to files from a variety of computers and operating systems. Almost any operating system you can think of that uses IP also supports FTP. This wide availability of FTP means that a variety of operating systems and hardware can access FTP services and/or provide FTP services. FTP user applications are used to transfer files to and from an FTP server. These end-user applications can be used between the same or different operating systems and hardware. For example, the Web developer's machine may be a Windows 2000 Professional system and the Web server is a Linux system. Or, the Web developer's machine is a Macintosh and the Web servers are Linux and Windows 2000 systems. Between these example combinations, FTP can be used to transfer files from the Web developer's machine to the Web server. This flexibility makes FTP a popular method for publishing Web pages from the Web developer's system to the Web server. Some Web authoring tools include FTP in the software and make it very easy to publish the Web content. If the Web authoring software does not include FTP, there are a lot of FTP software packages available that make it easy to transfer files. Also, most operating systems include a command line oriented FTP. One item to keep in mind when using FTP is case sensitivity. On Linux systems and other UNIX based or similar operating systems, the names of files, directories, accounts, and passwords are case sensitive. Make sure you know the proper case of the source and destination locations. Even one incorrect case letter can make an entire operation fail. On Windows systems, the case of files, directories, and account names is not important, but in most Windows operating systems passwords are case sensitive.

One common application used on Windows platforms to transfer files to an FTP server is WS_FTP32. This graphical application presents an Explorer like interface of the local file system and remote machine's file system. Another nice feature of this tool is the ability to save connection details that can be reloaded to reconnect at another time. Figure 6.2 shows an example of a WS_FTP32 connection or session information.

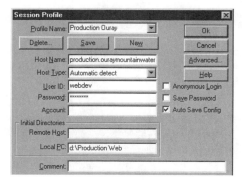

Figure 6.2   WS_FTP32 connection information.

In the example, Figure 6.2, the Host Name field represents the identity of the remote system by using either the DNS name or IP number. The User ID and Password areas specify the account and password on the Web server for the Web developer. The Local PC field allows you to indicate the directory on the local Web developer's machine that is referenced when the FTP connection is established. For example, this directory would be the location on the Web developer's machine where the developed Web pages are stored. By giving a meaningful name to the connection information in the Profile Name field, the Web developer can choose the name of the session without the need to remember all the connection details. Figure 6.3 is an example of a display the Web developer would see when the connection was successfully established.

The left pane of the WS_FTP32 window displays the contents of the local directory (Local System) on the Web developer's machine. For example:

```
C:\My Documents\My Webs\Production Web
```

The right area displays the contents of the directory on the Web server (Remote System), for example:

```
/usr/content/htdocs
```

To transfer files from the Web developer's machine to the server, the Web developer selects the files in the local directory on the left and clicks on the right

Figure 6.3 WS_FTP32 connected session example.

arrow. The bottom pane of the window displays feedback on the progress and status of the file transfers. When all is done, the Close button ends the FTP session and disconnects the Web developer from the Web server. You can obtain information about WS_FTP32 from www.csra.net/SOFTWARE/ftptelnet.htm.

Linux systems that have the X Window system installed often have a graphical FTP application present. If there is not one installed on the system, you can download a graphical FTP application from the Internet or from the Linux distribution CDs. One common graphical FTP user application for Linux is gFTP. In this section, we use gFTP as an example. Figure 6.4 shows the gFTP application window.

At the top of the gFTP screen are four areas of information. The Host section indicates the DNS or IP address of the destination server, for example, the Web server. The User and Pass fields are for the Web developer's account and password on the Web server. The Port number indicates the port the FTP server on the Web server is listening on for activity. If this field is left blank, the gFTP application will use the default FTP port number of 21. Unless the Web server is using a different port number, 21 should work just fine. When the information is entered, the button with the two computers icon to the left of the destination address establishes the connection. When the FTP connection is completed, the left pane displays the Web developer's local machine's file system. The right pane of the gFTP window shows the file system on the Web server and the bottom pane relays status information of the current process. To transfer files, the Web developer navigates in the left pane to the directory on

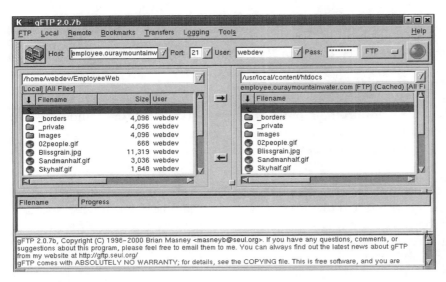

Figure 6.4 gFTP application.

their local system where the Web pages are saved. The Web developer selects the files they want to transfer and then clicks on the right arrow button to start the process. As each file and/or directory is transferred, the status is displayed in the lower pane of the gFTP window. When the file transfer is completed, close the FTP session by clicking on the button with the two computers.

Sometimes it is not easy for users to remember the information needed to make an FTP connection. Once connected to the FTP server, you can save the connection information in gFTP as a Bookmark. Then, the next time the Web developer needs to use gFTP to transfer files, they choose the appropriate Bookmark and all the connection details are recalled.

Linux, Windows, and most operating systems provide a command line FTP application. Fortunately, most vendors support the standard FTP commands, so once you are familiar with the command line FTP in one operating system, you can use the same commands in other operating systems. To start the FTP command line interface on a Linux or Windows system, type ftp at a command prompt. You can also specify the destination address or IP number. For example, to connect to the Employee Web server for Ouray Mountain Water, the syntax would be:

```
ftp employee.ouraymountainwater.com
```

The FTP user application establishes the connection and the prompt in the command window is replaced with the ftp> prompt. To get a list of the available commands, type a question mark (?) at the ftp prompt. To find more information about a particular command, type help followed by the command. You can also start the FTP application without specifying a destination name or address. The open command is used to create a connection to another system within the FTP application. For example, to connect to the Ouray Mountain Water public Web server, the open command would be:

```
open www.ouraymountainwater.com
```

Once the connection to the remote system is established, the remote system will prompt for the account name and password. For our examples this would be the Web developer's account name and password on the Web server.

The FTP prompt does not reflect the directory on the remote system that the FTP session is connected to. Use the pwd command to determine the location the ftp prompt is pointing to on the Web server. To change to a different location on the remote system, use the cd command. For example, to change to the /usr/local/content/htdocs/ directory on the Ouray Mountain Water public Linux Web server, the syntax would be:

```
cd /usr/content/htdocs
```

The previous example will work no matter what directory the FTP application is currently in because the complete path is specified in the cd command. To verify the cd command and the current directory location, use the pwd command.

To change to a directory on the local file system, for example, on the Web developer's system, the lcd command is used. To change to the local directory on a Windows system, such as G:\My Documents\My Web\Public Web, the syntax would be:

```
lcd c:\"My Documents"\"My Webs"\"Public Web"
```

If the directory names contain spaces, the names must be surrounded by quotations. The short name for Windows directories can also be used. Using the same example directory structure, the lcd command syntax with short names would be:

```
lcd c:\mydocu~1\mywebs~1\public~1
```

On a Linux system, if the Web developer's directory is /home/leeann/publicweb, the syntax of the lcd command would be:

```
lcd /home/leeann/publicweb
```

The mput command is used to transfer multiple files from the local directory to the remote system's destination directory. Wildcards can be used to transfer several files at one time. For example, to copy all the files from the local Web developer's directory to the Web server, the syntax would be:

```
mput *
```

The asterisk (*) indicates that every file found in the local directory will be transferred to the remote system's directory. In addition, other wildcard characters, such as ?, are supported. If there are any directories that need to be transferred, the directories must exist on the remote system first. The command line FTP utilities do not provide a means to transfer directories. To transfer the contents of the subdirectories, navigate to each corresponding subdirectory on the local and remote file systems. At each subdirectory level use the mput command to transfer the subdirectory's files.

Most command line FTP applications use an interactive mode for certain operations. Interactive mode requires user input to acknowledge the process. If interactive mode is enabled and you are transferring ten files from the local to the remote system, you will be prompted to answer Y or N for each file selected to be transferred. If you do not want the interactive mode, you can turn this off at the time the FTP connection is established or from within the FTP session. To turn off the interactive mode after the connection is established, execute the prompt command at the ftp prompt. The prompt command is a toggle so if interactive is on, one instance of prompt turns off interactive mode. If interactive mode is off, issuing the prompt command again will turn interactive mode on. Ever time the prompt command is executed, the system echoes back the current state of the interactive mode. The second way interactive mode is turned off is at the time the FTP session is established. By adding a –i with the ftp command, interactive mode is turned off. Interactive mode can be turned on later while in the ftp session by using the prompt command.

Once the files have been transferred between the two systems, the FTP session needs to be closed. To close the FTP connection and the FTP command line application, one of the following commands can be used. Some environments support all, while others only support some of these commands:

```
bye
exit
quit
```

If you want to close the FTP session but keep the FTP command line application open, one or both of the following commands will work:

```
close
disconnect
```

Some Web authoring programs incorporate FTP in the application as a method for publishing Web pages to the Web server. One program that supports FTP within the application is FrontPage, which we use as an example in this section. We cover the steps for publishing the Web pages developed in FrontPage for the Ouray Mountain Water's Production Web server. The Production Web server is a Windows 2000 Server Apache system running Microsoft's IIS FTP Server. Using FTP within FrontPage does not require the FrontPage Extensions on the Web server, and the Production Web server does not have the FrontPage Extensions installed. In the FrontPage application, choose Publish Web from the File menu. This action displays the Publish Page window for specifying the destination and other publication settings. Figure 6.5 is an example of the Publish Web window.

The Specify area at the top of the Publish Web window indicates the destination Web server's name or IP address. For example, to indicate the Production Web server, you would use the address:

```
ftp://production.ouraymountainwater.com
```

Figure 6.5 FrontPage's Publish Web window.

Make sure you specify ftp and not http in the address. If you use http, the application will look for the FrontPage Extensions on the server. In our example here, you would receive an error message because the Production Web server does not have the FrontPage Extensions installed.

There are other settings available in the Publish Web window. If they are not visible, click on the Options button. In the expanded Publish Web window, choose the Publish add pages, overwriting any already on the destination: option. This will ensure that all the files and folders for the Production Web site are transferred. To begin transferring files, click on the Publish button. The Name and Password Required dialog box appears when an attempt is made to modify the Web content on the Web server. The Web developer enters their Web server's account name and password in the appropriate fields. At the end of the file transfer process, a finished dialog box appears and presents the option to view the published Web content.

HTTP

Some applications use the HTTP PUT command to publish Web content from the application to the Web server. As we covered in Chapter 5, the Apache Web server does not natively support the HTTP PUT command. However, by adding a module to the Apache binary, mod_put, or through the use of Web scripting languages, Apache can support the HTTP PUT command. For this section, the Employee Web server for the Ouray Mountain Water company has the mod_put module compiled in the Apache binary running on the server. The Web developer(s) for the Employee Web server are using Netscape Composer and will be publishing to the Web server from the application. Netscape Composer uses the HTTP PUT command to publish to the Web server.

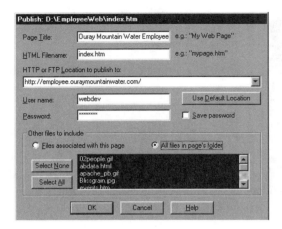

Figure 6.6   Netscape Composer's Publish window.

To start transferring files from Netscape Composer, choose Publish from the File menu. The Publish window contains several items to configure and/or set. Figure 6.6 shows an example of the Publish window for transferring the developed Web pages to the Employee Web server.

The contents of the Page Title and the HTML Filename fields are determined by the Web developer. In the HTTP or FTP Location to publish to field, enter in http:// followed by the name or IP number of the Web server. When http:// is used in front of the address, Netscape will attempt to use the HTTP PUT command to transfer the files to the Web server. Netscape also supports FTP and by using ftp:// in the destination address, Netscape will use FTP instead of HTTP to transfer the files. If Apache running on the destination Web server does not have the ability to accept the HTTP PUT command, you can use FTP to copy files from Netscape Composer to the Web server. The bottom section of the Publish window allows you to specify which files are to be transferred. So that all the content is sent to the Web server, the Files associated with this page option should be selected. The Web developer enters their Web server account name and password in the User name and Password fields. When all the information is entered, the OK button begins the transfer of the files to the Web server. If the Web developer neglects to enter the account name and password in the Publish window, Netscape will prompt for the account name and password when an attempt is made to transfer files.

FrontPage supports both FTP and HTTP to transfer files from within the application to the Web server. To use HTTP to publish from FrontPage, the recipient Web server must have the Apache FrontPage Extensions installed and running. Once the Extensions are in place and configured, you can use HTTP from

FrontPage to publish to the Web server. In the Specify section of FrontPage's Publish Web window, enter http:// followed by the Web server's name or IP address. For example,

```
http://employee.ouraymountainwater.com
```

When http is specified, FrontPage first checks for the presence of the FrontPage Extensions on the destination server. If the Extensions are identified, the publishing process will prompt for an account and password that has the proper permissions to modify the Web server content from FrontPage.

Testing the Published Web Site

Once the Web content has been transferred to the Web server, it is a good idea to access the Web site and make sure everything functions as expected. If the Web server supports a graphical interface, you can launch a browser on the server and enter in the name of the Web server. However, it is probably more realistic to access the new Web site from another machine and if possible, with different browsers.

Another item to keep in mind is to make sure the Web browser used to access the new Web site is not displaying cached pages. Most browsers allow you to specify the amount of memory and/or disk space used to cache Web pages. This feature provides a faster browsing experience for users but can be interfering when used to test the content of a Web site. Some browsers allow you to set the memory and disk space cache amounts to zero. When set to zero, every time the Web site is accessed from a browser, the page's contents come from the server and not from cache. Some browsers also support the option to always get the page from the source when a Web site is accessed. With this feature turned on, the response may be slower but you know that every "hit" on the Web site gets the page from the server and not from disk or memory cache.

Once you are comfortable that the Web browsers used to test the new Web site are always getting the content from the server, the next step is to make sure all the features of the Web site function as expected. For testing, it is best to use a tester that is unfamiliar with the development of the Web site. The Ouray Mountain Water company has set up several computers with Web browsers in the employee break area at the Ouray location and has asked the employees to play with the new Web sites. Each of the three developed Web sites supports the ability to email from the Web pages, and the testers are encouraged to use email for feedback. As a result of the employees' participation, the development of the Web sites continues. Once the Web developers have implemented all the suggested changes, the new Web content will need to be placed on the Web servers and tested again.

Updating the Web Site Content

Updating the content of the Web server is similar to publishing the content for the first time. For each of the possible publishing methods, it is important that the correct new content is placed on the Web server. Some authoring tools provide the ability to upload only pages that have been changed, or the option to upload all the Web content. The Web developers may need to be educated within the appropriate method to make sure the proper files are transferred and replaced. As always, make sure a backup of the current Web site is available before replacing any files in case you need to revert back to the previous version.

CHAPTER

7

Monitoring and
Optimizing Apache

An important aspect of keeping your Web servers well oiled is monitoring their performance and making adjustments as necessary. Shortly after you release a Web server for use, it is recommended that you gather baseline information on your servers' performance and activities. By studying the baseline information you learn the capabilities of your Web servers and may also discover the need to optimize one or all of your Web servers for better performance. Furthermore, knowing what your Web servers can handle today helps determine what may or may not need to change when your Web servers encounter increases in activity and growth. In this chapter, we take a look at techniques for monitoring the performance of the Apache Web server and methods of optimizing Apache.

Baseline information for server systems is collected during times of normal activity. Sometimes normal activity is hard to define, but it is the time during the days and weeks when people are accessing and using the Web server for everyday needs. You want to make sure you pick time frames that are good representatives of normal activity for your network and servers. These time frames may encompass one or multiple days and different time frames throughout the day(s). Let's take as an example, the Ouray Water Mountain company's public Web server, which is accessible to anybody on the Internet. First we try to determine when people are most likely to use the public Web server. In the case of the Ouray

Water Mountain's public Web server, the company's business is within the United States and at locations in different states. At the initial release of the Ouray Mountain Water company's public Web site, we can predict that the majority of Web site visits will be from within the United States. Because of the different geographical locations, we need to account for the different time zones. Thus, a good time to collect data during normal activity is Monday through Friday from 7:00 A.M. Eastern time through 6:00 P.M. Pacific time. Also, in the past the Ouray Mountain Water company has had an increased number of inquiries during holidays and in the summer. Gather statistics during these time frames so that you have data for periods of heavier activity. In addition to normal and heavy times, you should also collect data during the predicted off-peak times to make sure they indeed are off-peak periods. If you take into account all the suggestions mentioned here for gathering data, they boil down to monitoring 24 hours for several days in a row and during periods of expected activity increase.

By gathering all this information and documenting the time frames, you will develop a good profile of the Web server's performance. This type of information is very helpful for predicting the impact of growth on the current Web server's configuration. For example, if your Web server is receiving 5000 hits per day and the CPU and memory usage have reached their limits, then you know that your Web server would not be able to handle any increases in activity. On the other hand, if at 5000 hits per day, your Web server is only using 10 percent of its resources, then it could easily handle a double or even triple increase in the number of hits per day without adversely affecting the performance of the Web server.

There are two main areas to monitor, Apache and the server system running the Web service. In this chapter we cover methods and tools for monitoring Linux, Windows 2000, and Apache. In addition, we address areas to consider for optimization of Linux, Windows 2000, and Apache. Keep in mind that if the server system running Apache is not performing well, any attempt to tweak Apache is not going to help matters. The foundation must first function well and reliably before you begin adding services and expecting them to perform well.

Monitoring Linux

Linux contains several utilities that are useful for determining the state of operating system affairs. In this section we discuss the various tools and utilities that are included with most Linux distributions for gathering information about the operating systems and its activities. If the utility is not currently installed on your Linux system, you can install the tool from either your installation CDs or from various locations on the Internet.

Processes

It is important to be aware of the types of applications and services running at any given time on the Linux server. In addition to what is running, the amount of CPU usage of these processes is important. For example, if suddenly the responsiveness of the Web server drops noticeably and you find out that another application or service is using most of the processor's resources, you may want to stop the other event or schedule it for another time. To gather information about which Linux processes are currently running and their resource consumption, use the top and/or ps utilities. The top utility provides a continuous look at processor activity in real time while the ps command is a snapshot of the processes running at the time the command is issued.

The output of the top command displays a listing of the most CPU-intensive tasks on the system. The tool also provides an interactive interface for manipulating processes. For example, let's take a look at the result of the top command on the Ouray Mountain Water Employee Web server when a user accessed the main page from their browser:

```
 9:08am  up  9:45,  1 user,  load average: 0.07, 0.04, 0.00
45 processes: 44 sleeping, 1 running, 0 zombie, 0 stopped
CPU states:  0.1% user,  0.2% system,  0.0% nice, 99.5% idle
Mem:    46180K av,    43852K used,    2328K free,      0K shrd,   18132K buff
Swap:  133016K av,      40K used,  132976K free                   6980K cached

  PID USER      PRI  NI  SIZE  RSS SHARE STAT %CPU %MEM   TIME COMMAND
 1320 mhoag      14   0   992  992   800 R     8.1  2.1  0:00 top
  797 webadmin   10   0  1112 1112   980 S     1.8  2.4  0:00 httpd
  796 webadmin    9   0  1136 1136   996 S     0.9  2.4  0:00 httpd
    1 root        8   0   512  512   448 S     0.0  1.1  0:04 init
    2 root        9   0     0    0     0 SW    0.0  0.0  0:00 keventd
    3 root        9   0     0    0     0 SW    0.0  0.0  0:00 kapm-idled
    4 root        9   0     0    0     0 SW    0.0  0.0  0:01 kswapd
    5 root        9   0     0    0     0 SW    0.0  0.0  0:00 kreclaimd
    6 root        9   0     0    0     0 SW    0.0  0.0  0:00 bdflush
    7 root        9   0     0    0     0 SW    0.0  0.0  0:00 kupdated
    8 root       -1 -20     0    0     0 SW<   0.0  0.0  0:00 mdrecoveryd
  483 root        9   0   572  572   476 S     0.0  1.2  0:00 syslogd
  488 root        9   0  1084 1084   440 S     0.0  2.3  0:02 klogd
  502 rpc         9   0   544  544   460 S     0.0  1.1  0:00 portmap
  517 rpcuser     9   0   740  740   636 S     0.0  1.6  0:00 rpc.statd
  601 root        8   0   424  424   360 S     0.0  0.9  0:00 apmd
  650 root        9   0   608  608   508 S     0.0  1.3  0:00 automount
  662 daemon      9   0   480  480   408 S     0.0  1.0  0:00 atd
  677 root        9   0  1000  996   816 S     0.0  2.1  0:02 sshd
  697 root        9   0   940  912   740 S     0.0  1.9  0:00 xinetd
  709 root        9   0   416  416   348 S     0.0  0.9  0:00 gpm
  721 root        9   0   644  644   572 S     0.0  1.3  0:00 crond
  757 xfs         9   0  3300 3300   872 S     0.0  7.1  0:01 xfs
```

794	root	9	0	996	996	904	S	0.0	2.1	0:00 httpd
795	root	9	0	428	428	356	S	0.0	0.9	0:00 rotatelogs
798	webadmin	9	0	1136	1136	996	S	0.0	2.4	0:00 httpd
799	webadmin	9	0	1136	1136	996	S	0.0	2.4	0:00 httpd
800	webadmin	9	0	1112	1112	980	S	0.0	2.4	0:00 httpd
803	root	9	0	432	432	368	S	0.0	0.9	0:00 mingetty
804	root	9	0	432	432	368	S	0.0	0.9	0:00 mingetty
805	root	9	0	432	432	368	S	0.0	0.9	0:00 mingetty
806	root	9	0	432	432	368	S	0.0	0.9	0:00 mingetty
807	root	9	0	432	432	368	S	0.0	0.9	0:00 mingetty
860	root	9	0	432	432	368	S	0.0	0.9	0:00 mingetty
1245	root	9	0	812	812	676	S	0.0	1.7	0:00 in.telnetd
1246	root	9	0	1196	1196	960	S	0.0	2.5	0:00 login
1247	mhoag	9	0	1276	1276	988	S	0.0	2.7	0:00 bash
1278	webadmin	9	0	1168	1168	1036	S	0.0	2.5	0:00 httpd
1279	webadmin	9	0	1184	1184	1044	S	0.0	2.5	0:00 httpd
1280	webadmin	9	0	1184	1184	1044	S	0.0	2.5	0:00 httpd
1297	root	9	0	684	684	608	S	0.0	1.4	0:00 crond
1298	root	9	0	888	888	752	S	0.0	1.9	0:00 run-parts
1308	root	9	0	552	552	464	S	0.0	1.1	0:00 awk
1309	root	9	0	852	852	736	S	0.0	1.8	0:00 sa1
1311	root	9	0	492	492	428	S	0.0	1.0	0:00 sadc

The first five lines of the output from the top command displays the following information:

Uptime. This line displays the time the system has been up and the three load averages for the system. The load averages are the average number of processes ready to run during the last 1, 5, and 15 minutes.

Processes. The total number of processes running at the time of the last update. This is also broken down into the number of tasks which are running, sleeping, stopped, or undead (zombies).

CPU states. Shows the percentage of CPU time in user mode, system mode, niced tasks, and idle. (Niced tasks are processes whose priority level has been changed. The top command only displays processes whose nice value is negative which means their priority has been increased.) Time spent in niced tasks will also be counted in system and user time, so the total may be more than 100 percent.

Mem. This entry displays statistics on memory usage, including total available memory, free memory, used memory, shared memory, and memory used for buffers.

Swap. Statistics on swap space, including total swap space, available swap space, and used swap space are indicated on this line. The information following Swap and Mem is the same as the output of the free command.

The column headers from left to right in the top output are as follows:

PID. The process ID of the task.

USER. The user name of the task's owner.

PRI. The priority of the task.

NI. The nice value of the task. Negative nice values are higher priority.

SIZE. The size in kilobytes of the task's code plus data plus stack space.

RSS. The total amount of physical memory in kilobytes used by the task.

SHARE. The amount of shared memory used by the task.

STAT. The state of the task. The state is either S for sleeping, D for uninterruptible sleep, R for running, Z for zombies, or T for stopped or traced.

%CPU. The task's share of the CPU time since the last screen update, expressed as a percentage of total CPU time per processor.

%MEM. The task's share of the physical memory.

TIME. Total CPU time the task has used since it started. If cumulative mode is on, this also includes the CPU time used by the process's children which have been destroyed.

COMMAND. The task's command name. It is truncated if it is too long to be displayed on one line. Tasks in memory will have a full command line, but swapped-out tasks will only have the name of the program in parentheses for example, (getty).

Looking at our sample top output, there are no processes running that are taking a lot of resources. However, if you suspect that some event is consuming an unusual amount of resources, the top command may help you find the culprit. The top application can also be used to sort the tasks by CPU usage, memory usage, and runtime, and it supports other options such as setting the refresh rate. However, keep in mind that the top command itself uses resources. You want to make sure the top command is not using too many resources and impacting the server's performance!

The ps command gives a snap shot of the current processes running when the command was issued. Executing ps without any parameters simply lists the processes initiated by the account which issued the ps command. To view details of all the processes on the system started by Linux and any other user, use the ps command with the –auxw or –eauxw options. For example, the sample listing below is from the Ouray Mountain Water's Employee Linux Apache Web server when the ps-auxw command was executed:

```
USER        PID %CPU %MEM   VSZ  RSS TTY      STAT START    TIME COMMAND
root          1  1.7  1.1  1340  512 ?        S     23:22   0:04 init [3]
root          2  0.0  0.0     0    0 ?        SW    23:22   0:00 [keventd]
root          3  0.0  0.0     0    0 ?        SW    23:22   0:00 [kapm-idled]
root          4  0.0  0.0     0    0 ?        SW    23:22   0:00 [kswapd]
```

```
root          5  0.0  0.0     0    0 ?       SW   23:22   0:00 [kreclaimd]
root          6  0.0  0.0     0    0 ?       SW   23:22   0:00 [bdflush]
root          7  0.0  0.0     0    0 ?       SW   23:22   0:00 [kupdated]
root          8  0.0  0.0     0    0 ?       SW<  23:22   0:00 [mdrecoveryd]
root        483  0.2  1.2  1400  584 ?       S    23:23   0:00 syslogd -m 0
root        488  1.1  2.3  2000 1084 ?       S    23:23   0:02 klogd -2
rpc         502  0.0  1.2  1484  568 ?       S    23:23   0:00 portmap
rpcuser     517  0.0  1.6  1536  756 ?       S    23:23   0:00 rpc.statd
root        601  0.0  1.0  1324  476 ?       S    23:23   0:00 /usr/sbin/apmd -p
     10 -w 5 -W -P /etc/sysconfig/apm-scripts/apmscript
root        650  0.0  1.3  1452  616 ?       S    23:23   0:00
     /usr/sbin/automount --timeout 60 /misc file /etc/auto.misc
daemon      662  0.0  1.1  1372  540 ?       S    23:23   0:00 /usr/sbin/atd
root        677  1.7  2.3  2560 1080 ?       S    23:24   0:02 /usr/sbin/sshd
root        697  0.0  2.0  2204  948 ?       S    23:24   0:00 xinetd -stayalive
     -reuse -pidfile /var/run/xinetd.pid
root        709  0.0  1.0  1368  472 ?       S    23:24   0:00 gpm -t ps/2 -m
     /dev/mouse
root        721  0.0  1.4  1524  652 ?       S    23:24   0:00 crond
xfs         757  0.9  7.1  4584 3300 ?       S    23:24   0:01 xfs -droppriv
     -daemon
root        794  0.0  2.1  2316 1000 ?       S    23:24   0:00
     /usr/local/apache/bin/httpd
root        795  0.0  0.7  1688  360 ?       S    23:24   0:00
     /usr/local/apache/bin/rotatelogs /usr/local/apache/logs/employee-acce
webadmin    796  0.0  2.3  2468 1068 ?       S    23:24   0:00
     /usr/local/apache/bin/httpd
webadmin    797  0.0  2.3  2468 1068 ?       S    23:24   0:00
     /usr/local/apache/bin/httpd
webadmin    798  0.0  2.3  2468 1068 ?       S    23:24   0:00
     /usr/local/apache/bin/httpd
webadmin    799  0.0  2.3  2468 1068 ?       S    23:24   0:00
     /usr/local/apache/bin/httpd
webadmin    800  0.0  2.3  2468 1068 ?       S    23:24   0:00
     /usr/local/apache/bin/httpd
root        802  0.1  2.3  2268 1072 tty1    S    23:24   0:00 login -- root
root        803  0.0  0.9  1312  432 tty2    S    23:24   0:00 /sbin/mingetty tty2
root        804  0.0  0.9  1312  432 tty3    S    23:24   0:00 /sbin/mingetty tty3
root        805  0.0  0.9  1312  432 tty4    S    23:24   0:00 /sbin/mingetty tty4
root        806  0.0  0.9  1312  432 tty5    S    23:24   0:00 /sbin/mingetty tty5
root        807  0.0  0.9  1312  432 tty6    S    23:24   0:00 /sbin/mingetty tty6
root        810  0.7  2.8  2368 1332 tty1    S    23:25   0:00 -bash
root        848  0.0  1.7  2716  820 tty1    R    23:26   0:00 ps -auxw
```

The %CPU and %MEM values indicate the amount of CPU resources and memory the listed processes are using. All of the processes in this example are consuming very little processing power and memory because at the time this sample was taken, the server was essentially idle and had just been restarted. Using ps with the –eauxw gives slightly more information as displayed in the following example:

```
USER       PID %CPU %MEM   VSZ  RSS TTY      STAT START   TIME COMMAND
root         1  1.5  1.1  1340  512 ?        S    23:22   0:04 init [3]   HOME=/
     TERM=linux BOOT_IMAGE=linux BOOT_FILE=/boot/vmlinuz-
root         2  0.0  0.0     0    0 ?        SW   23:22   0:00 [keventd]
root         3  0.0  0.0     0    0 ?        SW   23:22   0:00 [kapm-idled]
root         4  0.0  0.0     0    0 ?        SW   23:22   0:00 [kswapd]
root         5  0.0  0.0     0    0 ?        SW   23:22   0:00 [kreclaimd]
root         6  0.0  0.0     0    0 ?        SW   23:22   0:00 [bdflush]
root         7  0.0  0.0     0    0 ?        SW   23:22   0:00 [kupdated]
root         8  0.0  0.0     0    0 ?        SW<  23:22   0:00 [mdrecoveryd]
root       483  0.2  1.2  1400  584 ?        S    23:23   0:00 syslogd -m 0
     PWD=/ BOOT_FILE=/boot/vmlinuz-2.4.2-2 HOSTNAME=employee.
root       488  1.0  2.3  2000 1084 ?        S    23:23   0:02 klogd -2 PWD=/
     BOOT_FILE=/boot/vmlinuz-2.4.2-2 HOSTNAME=employee.oura
rpc        502  0.0  1.2  1484  568 ?        S    23:23   0:00 portmap PWD=/
     BOOT_FILE=/boot/vmlinuz-2.4.2-2 HOSTNAME=employee.ouray
rpcuser    517  0.0  1.6  1536  756 ?        S    23:23   0:00 rpc.statd PWD=/
     BOOT_FILE=/boot/vmlinuz-2.4.2-2 HOSTNAME=employee.our
root       601  0.0  1.0  1324  476 ?        S    23:23   0:00 /usr/sbin/apmd -p
     10 -w 5 -W -P /etc/sysconfig/apm-scripts/apmscript
root       650  0.0  1.3  1452  616 ?        S    23:23   0:00
/usr/sbin/automount --timeout 60 /misc file /etc/auto.misc PWD=/ BOOT
daemon     662  0.0  1.1  1372  540 ?        S    23:23   0:00 /usr/sbin/atd
     PWD=/ BOOT_FILE=/boot/vmlinuz-2.4.2-2 HOSTNAME=employee
root       677  1.5  2.3  2560 1080 ?        S    23:24   0:02 /usr/sbin/sshd
     PWD=/ BOOT_FILE=/boot/vmlinuz-2.4.2-2 HOSTNAME=employe
root       697  0.0  2.0  2204  948 ?        S    23:24   0:00 xinetd -stayalive
     -reuse -pidfile /var/run/xinetd.pid PWD=/ BOOT_FILE
root       709  0.0  1.0  1368  472 ?        S    23:24   0:00 gpm -t ps/2 -m
     /dev/mouse PWD=/ BOOT_FILE=/boot/vmlinuz-2.4.2-2 HOSTN
root       721  0.0  1.4  1524  652 ?        S    23:24   0:00 crond PWD=/
     BOOT_FILE=/boot/vmlinuz-2.4.2-2 HOSTNAME=employee.ouraymo
xfs        757  0.8  7.1  4584 3300 ?        S    23:24   0:01 xfs -droppriv -
daemon PWD=/usr/share/fonts/ja/TrueType BOOT_FILE=/boo
root       794  0.0  2.1  2316 1000 ?        S    23:24   0:00
     /usr/local/apache/bin/httpd PWD=/ BOOT_FILE=/boot/vmlinuz-2.4.2-2 HOS
root       795  0.0  0.7  1688  360 ?        S    23:24   0:00
     /usr/local/apache/bin/rotatelogs /usr/local/apache/logs/employee-acce
webadmin   796  0.0  2.3  2468 1068 ?        S    23:24   0:00
     /usr/local/apache/bin/httpd PWD=/ BOOT_FILE=/boot/vmlinuz-2.4.2-2 HOS
webadmin   797  0.0  2.3  2468 1068 ?        S    23:24   0:00
     /usr/local/apache/bin/httpd PWD=/ BOOT_FILE=/boot/vmlinuz-2.4.2-2 HOS
webadmin   798  0.0  2.3  2468 1068 ?        S    23:24   0:00
     /usr/local/apache/bin/httpd PWD=/ BOOT_FILE=/boot/vmlinuz-2.4.2-2 HOS
webadmin   799  0.0  2.3  2468 1068 ?        S    23:24   0:00
     /usr/local/apache/bin/httpd PWD=/ BOOT_FILE=/boot/vmlinuz-2.4.2-2 HOS
webadmin   800  0.0  2.3  2468 1068 ?        S    23:24   0:00
     /usr/local/apache/bin/httpd PWD=/ BOOT_FILE=/boot/vmlinuz-2.4.2-2 HOS
root       802  0.1  2.3  2268 1072 tty1     S    23:24   0:00 login -- root
root       803  0.0  0.9  1312  432 tty2     S    23:24   0:00 /sbin/mingetty
     tty2 HOME=/ TERM=linux BOOT_IMAGE=linux BOOT_FILE=/boo
```

```
root        804  0.0  0.9  1312  432 tty3      S    23:24    0:00 /sbin/mingetty
      tty3 HOME=/ TERM=linux BOOT_IMAGE=linux BOOT_FILE=/boo
root        805  0.0  0.9  1312  432 tty4      S    23:24    0:00 /sbin/mingetty
      tty4 HOME=/ TERM=linux BOOT_IMAGE=linux BOOT_FILE=/boo
root        806  0.0  0.9  1312  432 tty5      S    23:24    0:00 /sbin/mingetty
      tty5 HOME=/ TERM=linux BOOT_IMAGE=linux BOOT_FILE=/boo
root        807  0.0  0.9  1312  432 tty6      S    23:24    0:00 /sbin/mingetty
      tty6 HOME=/ TERM=linux BOOT_IMAGE=linux BOOT_FILE=/boo
root        810  0.5  2.8  2368 1332 tty1      S    23:25    0:00 -bash HOME=/root
      PATH=/usr/local/sbin:/usr/local/bin:/sbin:/bin:/usr/
root        849  0.0  1.7  2716  820 tty1      R    23:27    0:00 ps -eauxw PWD=/
      HOSTNAME=employee.ouraymountainwater.com QTDIR=/usr/l
```

In this example, the –e option with ps added to the information the IP number or name of the host initiating the process. The ps command is a useful utility for displaying the resource consumption by the different resources, but it is only a snap shot of the information. If you need continuous data, you may need to use the top utility.

There are other Linux commands that display some of the same information reported by the top and ps commands. These are useful if you need to look at just one parameter without the need to look at a number of different factors. If you want to track processes started by one of the running processes, use the pstree utility. For example, to display any httpd processes started by the first httpd process when the Apache server was loaded, use pstree with the PID of the first httpd process. If the PID of the initial httpd process is 794, then the syntax of pstree is:

```
pstree 794 -pl
```

The p and l options display all the child process and in a long format. Running pstree for the initial httpd process on the Ouray Mountain Water company's Employee Web server generated the following information:

```
httpd(794)-+-httpd(796)
           |-httpd(797)
           |-httpd(798)
           |-httpd(799)
           |-httpd(800)
           |-httpd(1278)
           |-httpd(1279)
           |-httpd(1280)
           `-rotatelogs(795)
```

In this example we get the expected five spawned httpd processes plus a few more for active Web browser connections to the server. If the pstree output showed many more httpd processes than expected, then you would need to determine why so many processes were being created. However, keep in mind, by knowing the type of activity and load your Web server is currently under may not mean there is a problem with too many httpd processes.

To determine how long the Linux system has been running with some processor usage information, use the uptime tool. The uptime utility gives a one line display of the current time, how long the system has been running, how many users are currently logged on, and the system load averages for the past 1, 5, and 15 minutes. Running uptime on the Ouray Mountain Water's Employee Web server reported the following information:

```
1:55pm  up 14:33,  1 user,  load average: 0.00, 0.00, 0.00
```

Memory

The free command displays the total amount of free and used physical and swap memory currently in use by the system. It also displays the shared memory and buffers used by the kernel. Using free with the –m option will display the information as megabytes. The default setting is to display the results in kilobytes. Issuing the free –m command on Ouray Mountain Water's Employee server reports the following:

	total	used	free	shared	buffers	cached
Mem:	45	41	3	0	15	7
-/+ buffers/cache:	17	27				
Swap:	129	0	129			

Notice that nearly all the physical memory is in use, which does not necessarily mean that there is a problem. However, we should keep an eye on memory usage. If the system starts using more and more swap space, then adding more physical memory might be helpful.

The vmstat utility displays a summary of what is going on in the Linux system's memory. In contrast to some of the other commands, vmstat gives a much more complete picture of the system's memory. You can use vmstat without any options to capture a single instance of the state of the memory. To gather data over time, use the time delay and count options with vmstat. For example, if you wish to gather information every second for ten times in a row, the syntax for vmstat would be:

```
vmstat 1 10
```

Issuing vmstat 1 10 on the Ouray Mountain Water company's Employee Web server while two remote systems were requesting the main page as fast as the users could hit the refresh button revealed the following results:

procs			memory				swap			io		system				cpu
r	b	w	swpd	free	buff	cache	si	so	bi	bo	in	cs	us	sy	id
1	0	0	40	4160	24248	5832	0	0	0	0	105	8	0	0	100
0	0	0	40	4152	24248	5832	0	0	0	0	118	25	3	4	93
0	0	0	40	4152	24248	5832	0	0	0	0	120	36	7	3	91
0	0	0	40	4148	24248	5836	0	0	0	0	119	44	8	2	90
0	0	0	40	4148	24248	5836	0	0	0	2	136	46	7	2	91
0	0	0	40	4148	24248	5836	0	0	0	0	165	75	6	6	89
0	0	0	40	4148	24248	5836	0	0	0	0	164	120	12	6	82
0	0	0	40	4144	24248	5840	0	0	0	0	179	95	6	6	87
0	0	0	40	4144	24248	5840	0	0	0	0	177	109	9	4	87
0	0	0	40	4140	24248	5844	0	0	0	0	164	120	7	6	87
0	0	0	40	4140	24248	5844	0	0	0	0	194	108	9	5	86
0	0	0	40	4140	24248	5844	0	0	0	0	174	73	4	6	91
0	0	0	40	4140	24248	5844	0	0	0	0	148	56	7	5	88
0	0	0	40	4136	24248	5848	0	0	0	0	147	132	13	6	82
0	0	0	40	4136	24248	5848	0	0	0	0	178	95	8	5	88
0	0	0	40	4136	24248	5848	0	0	0	0	186	111	8	8	83
0	0	0	40	4132	24248	5852	0	0	0	0	193	111	9	7	83
0	0	0	40	4132	24248	5852	0	0	0	0	130	27	3	5	93
0	0	0	40	4132	24248	5852	0	0	0	0	106	9	4	1	95
0	0	0	40	4132	24248	5852	0	0	0	0	107	7	5	0	95

The information in the columns reading from left to right is:

PROCS

r   Processes waiting for run time

b   Processes in uninterruptable sleep

w   Processes swapped out but otherwise runnable

MEMORY

swpd   Amount of swapped or virtual memory used in kilobytes

free   Amount of memory not in use in kilobytes

buff   Amount of memory used for buffers in kilobytes

SWAP

si   Amount of the memory swapped in from disk expressed as kilobytes per second

so   The memory swapped to disk reported as kilobytes per second

IO

bi   Number of blocks sent to a block device expressed as blocks per second

bo   The number of blocks received from a block device reported as blocks per second

SYSTEM

in   The number of interrupts per second, this value includes those involving the clock

cs   The number of context switches per second

CPU

us	The percentage of CPU usage for user times
sy	The percentage of CPU usage for system times
id	The percentage of CPU idle time

The vmstat utility is useful for tracking memory pattern usages. For example, if a process were consuming more memory than expected, the vmstat command would help determine what areas of memory management were being heavily used by the process.

Events

Linux comes with a nice utility to capture various system messages and events. It is called the System Logger Deamon (syslogd) and it usually runs by default on most Linux distributions. The outputs of syslogd are usually placed in the /var/log/ directory. In addition, there is a configuration file for syslogd that determines what is logged and where the different log files are placed. The configuration file is called syslog.conf and it is typically found in the /etc directory. As an example, the syslog.conf file for Ouray Water Mountain's Employee Web server is listed below:

```
# Log all kernel messages to the console.
# Logging much else clutters up the screen.
#kern.*                                             /dev/console

# Log anything (except mail) of level info or higher.
# Don't log private authentication messages!
*.info;mail.none;news.none;authpriv.none;cron.none
/var/log/messages

# The authpriv file has restricted access.
authpriv.*                                          /var/log/secure

# Log all the mail messages in one place.
mail.*                                              /var/log/maillog


# Log cron stuff
cron.*                                              /var/log/cron

# Everybody gets emergency messages, plus log them on another
# machine.
*.emerg                                                  *

# Save mail and news errors of level err and higher in a
# special file.
uucp,news.crit                                  /var/log/spooler
```

```
# Save boot messages also to boot.log
local7.*                                        /var/log/boot.log

#
# INN
#
news.=crit                                      /var/log/news/news.crit
news.=err                                       /var/log/news/news.err
news.notice                                     /var/log/news/news.notice
```

The structure of the entries, or rules, in syslog.conf indicates what is logged, at what level it is logged, and where the log file is placed. Every rule consists of two fields, a selector field and an action field. One or more spaces or tabs separate these two fields. The selector field itself consists of two parts, a facility and a priority, separated by a period (.). Lines starting with a hash mark (#) and empty lines are ignored. The generic structure of a syslog.conf rule is:

facility.priority   action

where facility is either the application or event generating the message. Priority allows you to specify at what type of condition the item is logged and action indicates what to do with the logged event. In most cases, action refers to the location of the log file so the events can be captured and observed at another time.

The facility specifies the system that produced the message. The facility is one of the following keywords: auth, auth priv, cron, daemon, kern, lpr, mail, news, syslog, user, uucp, and local0 through local7. The priority defines the severity of the message and is one of the following keywords, in ascending order: debug, info, notice, warning, err, crit, alert, emerg. An asterisk (*) stands for all facilities or all priorities, depending on where it is used (before or after the period). The keyword none stands for no priority of the given facility. You can specify multiple facilities with the same priority pattern in one statement using the comma (,) operator. You can also define as many facilities as you want. However, only the facility portion from a multiple facility statement is taken and the priority part is ignored. Multiple selectors may be specified for a single action using the semicolon (;) separator. Note that each selector in the selector field is capable of overwriting any preceding ones. Utilizing this type of behavior allows you to exclude some priorities from the pattern. Let's take a look at some of the rules in our sample syslog.conf file and determine what is being logged and what action(s) are specified. For example:

```
# Log all the mail messages in one place.
mail.*                                          /var/log/maillog
```

In this example, messages of any priority level generated by the mail system are recorded in the maillog file which is located in the /var/log directory. Analyzing another syslog.conf rule example:

```
# Log anything (except mail) of level info or higher.
# Don't log private authentication messages!
*.info;mail.none;news.none;authpriv.none;cron.none
/var/log/messages
```

reveals that messages of info priority from all applications or facilities except mail, news, authpriv, and cron are recorded in the messages file which is located in the /var/log directory. However, let's take a look at the relative position of these two rules in the syslog.conf file. For example:

```
# Log anything (except mail) of level info or higher.
# Don't log private authentication messages!
*.info;mail.none;news.none;authpriv.none;cron.none
/var/log/messages


...

# Log all the mail messages in one place.
mail.*                                          /var/log/maillog
```

Even though the first rule says to not log mail messages, the second rule results in mail messages being logged since the second rule follows the first rule in the syslog.conf file.

Using the capabilities of syslogd and the configuration file allows you to capture messages of specified priority levels so you can analyze the information for possible problems or general information. For example, if you suspected another service on the server was causing problems, you might be able to capture messages generated by the situation into a file.

Who Has Been Using My System?

The last command is used to determine the users who have been logging into the system. The results of last shows who has logged in, from where, the date, and how long they were logged in. Using last with the –a option will display the hostname or number of the connection in the last column. The –x option will also include any system shutdowns and reboots. Below is an example of a portion of the results from the last –ax command issued on the Ouray Mountain Water's Employee Web server:

```
mhoag     pts/0     Thu Jul 26 22:05    still logged in    172.16.3.220
root      tty1      Thu Jul 26 20:21    still logged in
```

```
mhoag      pts/0         Thu Jul 26 15:39 - 20:20  (04:41)    172.16.3.220
mhoag      pts/0         Thu Jul 26 10:21 - 15:17  (04:56)    172.16.3.220
mhoag      pts/0         Wed Jul 25 14:20 - 15:56  (01:35)    172.16.3.200
mhoag      pts/0         Wed Jul 25 09:09 - 14:19  (05:09)    172.16.3.200
runlevel   (to lvl 3)    Wed Jul 25 07:07 - 22:12  (1+15:05)  2.4.2-2
reboot     system boot   Wed Jul 25 07:07           (1+15:05)  2.4.2-2
shutdown   system down   Sat Jul 21 20:34 - 22:12  (5+01:38)  2.4.2-2
runlevel   (to lvl 6)    Sat Jul 21 20:34 - 20:34  (00:00)    2.4.2-2
webadmin   ftpd1150      Sat Jul 21 16:42 - 16:42  (00:00)    172.16.3.80
webadmin   ftpd1144      Sat Jul 21 16:34 - 16:35  (00:00)    172.16.3.80
webadmin   ftpd1122      Sat Jul 21 16:25 - 16:26  (00:00)    172.16.3.80
webadmin   ftpd1106      Sat Jul 21 16:23 - 16:23  (00:00)    172.16.3.80
webdev     ftpd1075      Sat Jul 21 16:19 - 16:19  (00:00)    172.16.3.80
webdev     ftpd1061      Sat Jul 21 16:14 - 16:15  (00:00)    172.16.3.80
webdev     ftpd1038      Sat Jul 21 16:05 - 16:06  (00:00)    172.16.3.80
webdev     ftpd1003      Sat Jul 21 15:59 - 15:59  (00:00)    172.16.3.80
mhoag      pts/0         Sat Jul 21 15:54 - 18:57  (03:02)    172.16.3.80
```

Looking at the results of our sample last command output, notice that the system was down for a period of four days. While this may not be unusual for a Web server undergoing testing and development, this would not be good for a released Web server. Also, notice the users webadmin and webdev connected to the system for a short period of time through the FTP service on the Linux server. In this example, this activity is okay and actually reflects the times when the Web developer was publishing to the Web server using FTP as the means to transfer the data. Looking and analyzing the results of the last command can help determine the duration and type of activities performed by users logging into the Linux system. If the Web server was experiencing some performance problems, investigating the last command may help you to determine if an activity of a logged-in user was impacting the performance of the server.

Storage Space

Another important area to monitor is the amount of free disk remaining. For Web sites that are adding a lot of content that is rich in graphics and multimedia, the amount of space consumed by the Web site may become quite high. In addition, for Web sites that support publication of pages by users, such as sub Webs, the monitoring of free disk space may become a frequent event. On Linux systems, the df utility reports the amount of disk space that is used and is available. Issuing the df command without any options produces results that are not the easiest to read. If you use the –h option, for human readable, the information is displayed in megabytes and/or gigabytes. In addition, the –T option will display the file system type of the file system checked. If your Linux directories are spread across multiple partitions, you can receive information about all partitions at one time or a specific partition. By adding the path of a directory on a partition, you will receive information about that partition. Instead of a directory you can also use the name of the device, such as /dev/hdc2.

As an example, we issued the df –hT command on Ouray Mountain Water's Employee Linux Web server and received the following information:

```
Filesystem    Type    Size  Used Avail Use% Mounted on
/dev/hdc1     ext2    1.9G  1.6G  278M  86% /
/dev/hda2     ext2     30M  3.5M   25M  12% /boot
```

The root (/) partition on the Employee Web server contains the Web content and there is 278Mb of disk space free. In this case this is not a problem because the amount of Web content for the Employee Web server is fairly small and is not expected to grow much.

Network

Another area to look at is the network statistics for the Linux server. The netstat utility displays network connections, routing tables, interface statistics, masquerade connections, and multicast memberships. By default, netstat displays a list of open sockets. If an address family or families is/are not specified, then the active sockets of all configured address families are reported. To view the active connections for http, use the following form of netstat:

```
netstat -t
```

The –t option displays just the network activity for TCP connections and since HTTP runs over TCP, you will be able to view the HTTP network status. Issuing netstat –t on Ouray Mountain Water's Employee Web server results in the following example:

```
Active Internet connections (w/o servers)
Proto Recv-Q Send-Q Local Address          Foreign Address       State
tcp        0      2 employee.ouraymo:telnet 172.16.3.220:1355    ESTABLISHED
tcp        0      0 employee.ouraymoun:http 172.16.3.220:1461    FIN_WAIT2
tcp        0      0 employee.ouraymoun:http 172.16.3.220:1460    FIN_WAIT2
tcp        0      0 employee.ouraymoun:http 172.16.3.220:1463    FIN_WAIT2
tcp        0      0 employee.ouraymoun:http 172.16.3.220:1462    FIN_WAIT2
tcp        0      0 employee.ouraymoun:http 172.16.3.220:1466    ESTABLISHED
tcp        0      0 employee.ouraymoun:http 172.16.3.12:1107     ESTABLISHED
```

From the information on our sample netstat output, there are two systems currently communicating with the Web server using HTTP. In addition, there is one connection using telnet, which is another protocol that uses TCP. If you wish to view the status for client and server TCP connections issue netstat –ta where –a lists both server and client information. Issuing netstat –ta on the same Ouray Mountain Water Employee server results in the following:

```
Active Internet connections (servers and established)
Proto Recv-Q Send-Q Local Address          Foreign Address        State
tcp      0      0 *:1024                   *:*                    LISTEN
tcp      0      0 *:rsync                  *:*                    LISTEN
tcp      0      0 *:sunrpc                 *:*                    LISTEN
tcp      0      0 *:http                   *:*                    LISTEN
tcp      0      0 *:ftp                    *:*                    LISTEN
tcp      0      0 *:ssh                    *:*                    LISTEN
tcp      0      0 *:telnet                 *:*                    LISTEN
tcp      0      2 employee.ouraymo:telnet 172.16.3.220:1355      ESTABLISHED
tcp      0      0 employee.ouraymoun:http 172.16.3.220:1487      FIN_WAIT2
tcp      0      0 employee.ouraymoun:http 172.16.3.220:1486      FIN_WAIT2
tcp      0      0 employee.ouraymo:telnet 172.16.3.220:1355      ESTABLISHED
tcp      0      0 employee.ouraymoun:http 172.16.3.12:1115       ESTABLISHED
tcp      0      0 employee.ouraymoun:http 172.16.3.220:1487      FIN_WAIT2
```

The different states listed in the netstat output are:

ESTABLISHED. The listed socket has an established connection.

SYN_SENT. The socket is actively attempting to establish a connection.

SYN_RECV. A connection request has been received from the network.

FIN_WAIT1. The socket is closed, and the connection is shutting down.

FIN_WAIT2. Connection is closed, and the socket is waiting for a shutdown from the remote end.

TIME_WAIT. The socket is waiting after a close to handle packets still in the network.

CLOSED. The listed socket is not being used.

CLOSE_WAIT. The remote end has shut down and the system is waiting for the socket to close.

LAST_ACK. The remote end has shut down, the socket is closed and now waiting for an acknowledgement.

LISTEN. The socket is listening for incoming connections. These sockets are not included in the output unless you specify the listening (-l) or all (-a) option.

CLOSING. Both sockets on the sender and receiver are shut down but all the data has not been sent.

UNKNOWN. The state of the socket is unknown.

Issuing the netstat command as in our examples produces a snap shot of the information at the time the command was issued. If you want a continuous display of information, include the –c option in the netstat command.

If you need to observe the network traffic traveling between your Web server and the systems accessing the Web sites then a network or protocol analyzer is needed. There are a number available for Linux that range from command line output to GUI displays. For Ethernet based Web servers, the Ethereal application is a well known and fairly complete packet capture and display program. Ethereal is open source and is available from www.ethereal.com.

Monitoring Windows 2000 Server

Windows 2000 Server includes tools to assist in monitoring the performance and activities of the system. Some of these are included when you install Windows 2000 Server and others are available from the Windows 2000 Server Resource Kit. Portions of the Microsoft Resource Kits for the different operating systems and services are available from www.microsoft.com/windows 2000/techinfo/reskit/default.asp. To go directly to the tools available for download, check out www.microsoft.com/windows2000/techinfo/reskit/tools/default.asp. However, to get access to all the information and tools, you will need to purchase the Windows 2000 Server Resource Kit. Another good source of information and tools about Microsoft products is TechNet. This is a subscription based product but portions of TechNet are available on Microsoft's Web site at www.microsoft.com/technet. In this section, we will cover some of the tools native to the system and from the Resource Kit that are helpful in monitoring Windows 2000.

Performance

Windows 2000 Server includes a tool that allows you to monitor and observe many different aspects of the operating system. The tool is called Performance and it is accessible by default from the Administrative Tools menu under the Programs menu. When you first open the utility, no information is presented because first you must specify what you wish to monitor. With System Monitor selected in the left pane, click on the + button in the right pane to begin adding counters. There are many categories to choose from that allow you to decide exactly what you want to monitor.

For example, to monitor processor activities, choose Processor from the Performance object listing and then in the Select counters from list options choose %Processor Time. Click on the Add button to add the selected counter. To monitor memory usage, select Memory from the Performance object list and Pages/sec from the Select counters from list options. You might want to also add Available Mbytes as a counter for memory usage. The Network Interface option under Performance object allows you to choose which network card or cards to monitor. From the Select counters from list options choose Bytes Total/sec. For a Web server you may also want to track Bytes Received/sec and

Bytes sent/sec so you can see how much is coming in and going out. If you suspect there might be problems with the packets arriving at the Web server, you may also want to monitor some of the error parameters such as Packets Received Errors. To determine the frequency and usage of Windows 2000 virtual memory, choose Paging File as a Performance object and %Usage as the counter. To watch the activity levels of the physical storage systems, choose PhysicalDisk as the Performance object and counters such as % Disk Time. To determine how busy the server is, choose Server from the Performance object selections and Bytes Total/sec from the Select counters from list choices.

To observe a specific process usage of system resources, choose Process from the Performance object categories. When that is selected you can choose counters such as %Processor Time and the actual process to monitor from the Select instances from list choices. Apache processes are available from the instances list so you can select and add these to determine how much processor time Apache is using.

Once you have made all your counter choices, Performance begins displaying the results in real time. Each counter displays the results graphically as a different color. To determine which counter is which on the graph, double click on the line in question and the associated counter is selected in the bottom pane of the window.

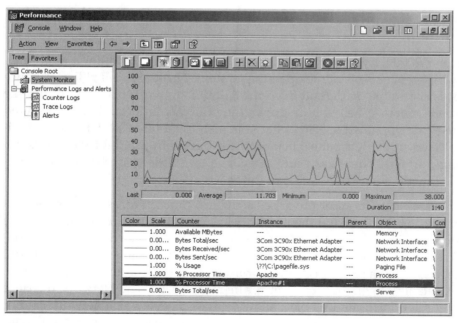

Figure 7.1   Performance and Apache Processes.

You can also get different views of the data by clicking on the view buttons on the panel above the real-time display. There are three views available: Chart, Histogram, and Report.

The Windows 2000 Resource Kit includes Performance Monitor 4 which is essentially the same as the Performance tool included with Windows 2000 except Performance Monitor 4 is a separate application and is not an MMC (Microsoft Management Console) component.

Another item you can use to observe memory and processor usage is the Windows Task Manager. Probably the quickest way to access this tool is to double click on an empty area on the taskbar at the bottom of the screen. You can also secondary mouse click on the taskbar and choose Task Manager from the list of available choices. Also, in the Windows Security window, clicking on the Task Manager button displays the Task Manager and dismisses the Windows Security window. The Task Manager contains a Processes tab that lists all the running processes on the system. This display is dynamic and you can sort the list in ascending or descending order by the name of the process, the CPU Time, or by any of the column headings by clicking on the header name. Figure 7.2 shows an example of the Task Manager where the information has been sorted by CPU Time.

The Task Manager's Performance tab displays a graphical representation of the CPU and memory usage over time. The tool also provides the ability to perform other tasks such as ending a process or changing the priority level.

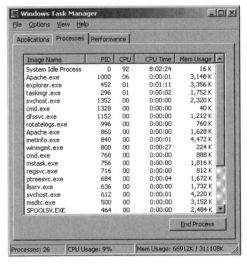

Figure 7.2   Windows 2000 Task Manager.

The Windows 2000 Performance tool gives you the ability to monitor lots of different events within one utility. To observe a smaller subset or a category, some of the tools on the Resource Kit and utilities included with Windows 2000 can be used. In the remaining portion of this section on Monitoring Windows 2000 Server, we take a look at some of these tools.

Processes

One of the tools in the Resource Kit, called Process Tree, allows you to determine the process PIDs running on the local or remote systems. Executing ptree without any arguments displays all the process. For example, running ptree on Ouray Mountain Water's Production Web server results in the following information:

```
[System Process] (0)
    System (8)
        smss.exe (152)
            csrss.exe (180)
            winlogon.exe (200)
                lsass.exe (240)
                services.exe (228)
                    Apache.exe (600)
                        Apache.exe (684)
                            cmd.exe (840)
                                rotatelogs.exe (856)
                    dfssvc.exe (1140)
                    inetinfo.exe (1112)
                    llssrv.exe (644)
                    msdtc.exe (496)
                    msiexec.exe (868)
                    mstask.exe (700)
                    ptreesvc.exe (1388)
                    regsvc.exe (748)
                    SPOOLSV.EXE (456)
                    svchost.exe (1212)
                    svchost.exe (620)
                    svchost.exe (416)
                        dllhost.exe (1436)
                        dllhost.exe (328)
                        MDM.EXE (480)
                    winmgmt.exe (796)
explorer.exe (1224)
    cmd.exe (1164)
        ptree.exe (1512)
    IEXPLORE.EXE (284)
        hh.exe (1548)
    mspaint.exe (1328)
```

You can also use ptree to destroy or kill a process and all of its subprocesses.

Another related tool is Process List by User (pulist) which displays all the processes running on the system. The tool will also list the PID and the username associated with each process. Executing pulist on the Production Web server revealed the following information:

```
Process            PID   User
Idle               0
System             8
smss.exe           152   NT AUTHORITY\SYSTEM
csrss.exe          180   NT AUTHORITY\SYSTEM
winlogon.exe       200   NT AUTHORITY\SYSTEM
services.exe       228   NT AUTHORITY\SYSTEM
lsass.exe          240   NT AUTHORITY\SYSTEM
svchost.exe        416   NT AUTHORITY\SYSTEM
SPOOLSV.EXE        456   NT AUTHORITY\SYSTEM
msdtc.exe          496   NT AUTHORITY\SYSTEM
Apache.exe         600   NT AUTHORITY\SYSTEM
svchost.exe        620   NT AUTHORITY\SYSTEM
llssrv.exe         644   NT AUTHORITY\SYSTEM
regsvc.exe         748   NT AUTHORITY\SYSTEM
mstask.exe         700   NT AUTHORITY\SYSTEM
Apache.exe         684   NT AUTHORITY\SYSTEM
winmgmt.exe        796   NT AUTHORITY\SYSTEM
cmd.exe            840   NT AUTHORITY\SYSTEM
rotatelogs.exe     856   NT AUTHORITY\SYSTEM
inetinfo.exe       1112  NT AUTHORITY\SYSTEM
dfssvc.exe         1140  NT AUTHORITY\SYSTEM
explorer.exe       1224  PRODUCTION\Administrator
svchost.exe        1212  NT AUTHORITY\SYSTEM
mspaint.exe        1328  PRODUCTION\Administrator
IEXPLORE.EXE       284   PRODUCTION\Administrator
MDM.EXE            480   PRODUCTION\Administrator
cmd.exe            1164  PRODUCTION\Administrator
msiexec.exe        868   NT AUTHORITY\SYSTEM
ptreesvc.exe       1388  NT AUTHORITY\SYSTEM
dllhost.exe        1436  NT AUTHORITY\SYSTEM
cmd.exe            1660  PRODUCTION\Administrator
pulist.exe         1496  PRODUCTION\Administrator
```

The Process List by User tool is also available for download from Microsoft's Web site.

CPU Usage by Process (qslice.exe) is a graphical tool that dynamically displays the CPU usage of each running process on the system. Running qslice on the Production Web server for Ouray Mountain Water while a user was repeatedly requesting the main page produced the information displayed in Figure 7.3.

The CPU Usage by Process tool is also available from Microsoft's Web site.

QuickSlice
PID Image Name
% Process CPU Usage
0 SystemProcess
8 system
98 smss.exe
b4 csrss.exe
c8 winlogon.exe
e4 services.exe
f0 lsass.exe
svchost.exe
spoolsv.exe
msdtc.exe
apache.exe
svchost.exe
llssrv.exe
regsvc.exe
mstask.exe
apache.exe
winmgmt.exe
cmd.exe

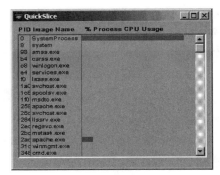

Figure 7.3 CPU Usage by Process tool display.

The Time-Ordered Processes (top) tool contained in the Resource Kit lists the processes in order based on their CPU usage. The information is continuously updated and does not show all the running processes—just those using the CPU at the time the data sample was collected. Figure 7.4 is an example of the Windows 2000 top tool display for the Ouray Mountain Water's Production Web server.

A subset of the processes running on a system is the services. You can obtain information about the status of the services from the Services tool in the Administrative Tools menu under the Programs menu. The different services are listed alphabetically by default and you can quickly tell if a service is running or not. Figure 7.5 shows a portion of the Services window for Ouray Mountain Water's Production server.

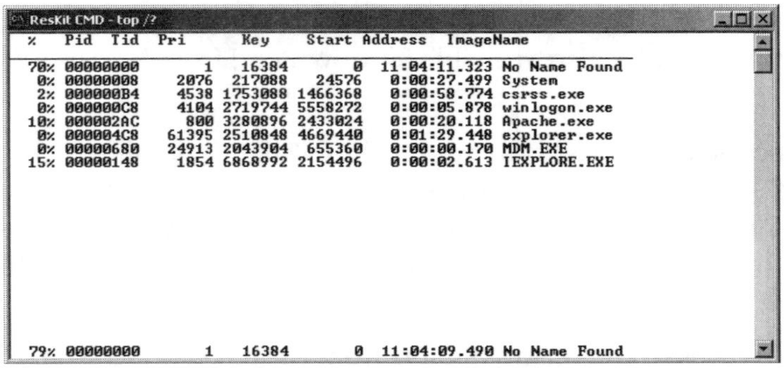

ResKit CMD - top /?
% Pid Tid Pri Key Start Address ImageName
70% 00000000 1 16384 0 11:04:11.323 No Name Found
0% 00000008 2076 217088 24576 0:00:27.499 System
2% 000000B4 4538 1753088 1466368 0:00:58.774 csrss.exe
0% 000000C8 4104 2719744 5558272 0:00:05.878 winlogon.exe
10% 000002AC 800 3280896 2433024 0:00:20.118 Apache.exe
0% 000004C8 61395 2510848 4669440 0:01:29.448 explorer.exe
0% 00000680 24913 2043904 655360 0:00:00.170 MDM.EXE
15% 00000148 1854 6868992 2154496 0:00:02.613 IEXPLORE.EXE
79% 00000000 1 16384 0 11:04:09.490 No Name Found

Figure 7.4 Windows 2000 top tool output.

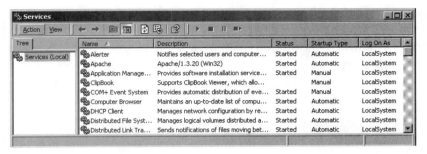

Figure 7.5 Services Administrative Tool.

To obtain detailed information about a service, double click on the service listed in the right pane. For example, the Properties window for the Apache service running on the Production server is shown in Figure 7.6.

The service Properties window allows you to stop and start services, specify the account the service runs under, indicate what to do when and if the service fails, and any dependencies the service may have. Each of these main category items can be accessed and set through the appropriate tab in the service's Properties window.

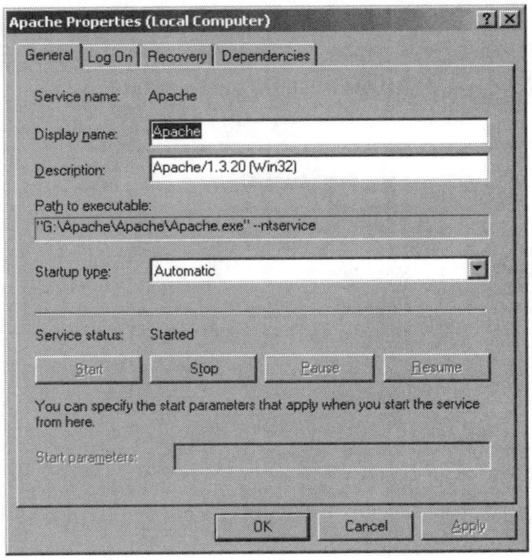

Figure 7.6 Apache service Properties window.

There is also a command line utility in the Resource Kit that permits you to show the status of services on the local or remote system. The Service List (sclist.exe) tool supports a –r option to display just the running services and a –s parameter to list any services that are stopped. Executing sclist on Ouray Mountain Water's Production server resulted in the following information:

```
-------------------------------------------
- Service list for Local Machine
-------------------------------------------
running      Alerter                 Alerter
running      Apache                  Apache
running      AppMgmt                 Application Management
running      Browser                 Computer Browser
stopped      cisvc                   Indexing Service
stopped      ClipSrv                 ClipBook
running      Dfs                     Distributed File System
running      Dhcp                    DHCP Client
stopped      dmadmin                 Logical Disk Manager
        Administrative Service
running      dmserver                Logical Disk Manager
running      Dnscache                DNS Client
running      Eventlog                Event Log
running      EventSystem             COM+ Event System
stopped      Fax                     Fax Service
running      IISADMIN                IIS Admin Service
stopped      IsmServ                 Intersite Messaging
stopped      kdc                     Kerberos Key Distribution Center
running      lanmanserver            Server
running      lanmanworkstation       Workstation
running      LicenseService          License Logging Service
running      LmHosts                 TCP/IP NetBIOS Helper Service
running      Messenger               Messenger
stopped      mnmsrvc                 NetMeeting Remote Desktop Sharing
running      MSDTC                   Distributed Transaction
        Coordinator
running      MSFTPSVC                FTP Publishing Service
running      MSIServer               Windows Installer
stopped      NetDDE                  Network DDE
stopped      NetDDEdsdm              Network DDE DSDM
stopped      Netlogon                Net Logon
running      Netman                  Network Connections
stopped      NtFrs                   File Replication
stopped      NtLmSsp                 NT LM Security Support Provider
running      NtmsSvc                 Removable Storage
running      PlugPlay                Plug and Play
running      PolicyAgent             IPSEC Policy Agent
running      ProtectedStorage        Protected Storage
stopped      RasAuto                 Remote Access Auto Connection
        Manager
stopped      RasMan                  Remote Access Connection Manager
```

```
stopped      RemoteAccess                      Routing and Remote Access
running      RemoteRegistry                    Remote Registry Service
stopped      RpcLocator                        Remote Procedure Call (RPC)
      Locator
running      RpcSs                             Remote Procedure Call (RPC)
stopped      RSVP                              QoS RSVP
running      SamSs                             Security Accounts Manager
stopped      SCardDrv                          Smart Card Helper
stopped      SCardSvr                          Smart Card
running      Schedule                          Task Scheduler
running      seclogon                          RunAs Service
running      SENS                              System Event Notification
stopped      SharedAccess                      Internet Connection Sharing
running      Spooler                           Print Spooler
stopped      SysmonLog                         Performance Logs and Alerts
running      TapiSrv                           Telephony
stopped      TermService                       Terminal Services
stopped      TlntSvr                           Telnet
stopped      TrkSvr                            Distributed Link Tracking Server
running      TrkWks                            Distributed Link Tracking Client
stopped      UPS                               Uninterruptible Power Supply
stopped      UtilMan                           Utility Manager
stopped      Visual Studio Analyzer RPC bridge Visual Studio Analyzer RPC
      bridge
stopped      W32Time                           Windows Time
running      WinMgmt                           Windows Management
      Instrumentation
running      Wmi                               Windows Management
      Instrumentation Driver Extensions
running      Ptreesvc                          Process Tree Service
```

Another tool in the Resource Kit for working with services is Service Controller Tool (sc). This command utility has many options including the ability to start and stop services and to query the status of a service. Some sc command options that are useful for gaining information about a service are query, queryex, and qc. The query parameter reports the status of the service. For example, executing the following on Ouray Mountain Water's Production server:

```
sc query apache
```

results in the following information:

```
SERVICE_NAME: apache
        TYPE               : 10  WIN32_OWN_PROCESS
        STATE              : 4   RUNNING
                                 (STOPPABLE,NOT_PAUSABLE,ACCEPTS_SHUTDOWN)
        WIN32_EXIT_CODE    : 0 (0x0)
        SERVICE_EXIT_CODE  : 0 (0x0)
        CHECKPOINT         : 0x0
        WAIT_HINT          : 0x0
```

Using the queryex parameter displays extended status information about the service specified. The output of the following command:

```
sc queryex apache
```

reveals the following data:

```
SERVICE_NAME: apache
        TYPE              : 10  WIN32_OWN_PROCESS
        STATE             : 4   RUNNING
                                (STOPPABLE,NOT_PAUSABLE,ACCEPTS_SHUTDOWN)
        WIN32_EXIT_CODE   : 0 (0x0)
        SERVICE_EXIT_CODE : 0 (0x0)
        CHECKPOINT        : 0x0
        WAIT_HINT         : 0x0
        PID               : 600
        FLAGS             :
```

The qc option for the Service Controller Tool performs a query on the configuration for the specified service. Executing the following on the Ouray Mountain Water company's Production Web server:

```
sc qc apache
```

produced the following results:

```
[SC] GetServiceConfig SUCCESS

SERVICE_NAME: apache
        TYPE              : 10  WIN32_OWN_PROCESS
        START_TYPE        : 2   AUTO_START
        ERROR_CONTROL     : 1   NORMAL
        BINARY_PATH_NAME  : "G:\Apache\Apache\Apache.exe" --ntservice
        LOAD_ORDER_GROUP  :
        TAG               : 0
        DISPLAY_NAME      : Apache
        DEPENDENCIES      : Tcpip
                          : Afd
        SERVICE_START_NAME : LocalSystem
```

Each of these sc command options displays different information, which can be useful for determining the status of the service and its condition.

The Service Monitoring Tool (srvmon) contained in the Windows 2000 Resource Kit permits you to monitor for changes in the state of services. This tool includes a configuration wizard for specifying the service or services to monitor. Figure 7.7 shows an example of the service selection window of the Service Monitor Configuration Wizard.

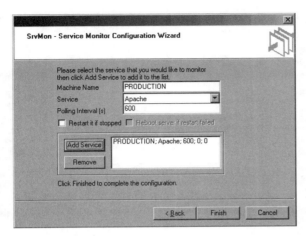

Figure 7.7   Service selection of the Service Monitor Configuration Wizard.

The configuration wizard for the Service Monitor Tool is designed to work with Microsoft's Exchange email system to send messages when a state change is detected by the monitoring tool.

Events

Windows 2000 comes with an Event Viewer tool that allows you to take a look at certain types of events that occur on the system. The default location to access Event Viewer is from the Administration Tools menu, which is under the Programs menu. There are three types of event logs handled by the Event Viewer. The Application Log will trap application-oriented events if the application has been coded to work with the Event Viewer logs. The Security Log is used to monitor changes in security policies and permissions. This log will only trap events if security logging is enabled and configured on the system. The last log, System Log, traps messages that are generated by events in the operating system and dependent services. This is a good place to look if you are experiencing troubles with a Windows 2000 service or embedded application. The Event Viewer can also be accessed from within some of the other tools under the Administration Tools menu.

The Windows 2000 Resource Kit includes the Up Time (uptime) tool which displays information such as basic system information and how long the system has been running. The /a option with uptime displays all of the information the utility supports. Executing the following on the Ouray Mountain Water Production Web server:

```
uptime /a
```

revealed the following information:

```
Uptime Report for: \\PRODUCTION


Current OS: Microsoft Windows 2000 Uniprocessor Free.
Time Zone: Central Daylight Time


System Events as of 7/29/2001 9:10:32 AM:

Date:        Time:          Event:              Comment:
----------   -----------    ------------------  ----------------------------------
 7/28/2001  11:44:37 PM    Shutdown
 7/28/2001  11:46:42 PM    Boot                 Prior downtime:0d 0h:2m:5s


Current System Uptime: 0 day(s), 9 hour(s), 24 minute(s), 46 second(s)



--------------------------------------------------------------------------------


Since 7/28/2001:

          System Availability: 99.6319%
                 Total Uptime: 0d 9h:23m:50s
               Total Downtime: 0d 0h:2m:5s
                Total Reboots: 1
    Mean Time Between Reboots: 0.39 days
            Total Bluescreens: 0
    Total Application Failures: 0
```

The Server Information (srvinfo) tool in the Resource Kit displays information such as the services, disk space, IP address, and so on. Using the Server Information tool on the Production Web server displayed the following information:

```
Server Name: PRODUCTION
Security: Users
NT Type:  NT Member Server - Terminal Server
Version: 5.0
Build: 2195
Current Type: Uniprocessor Free
Product Name: Microsoft Windows 2000
Registered Owner: Production Web Server
Registered Organization: Ouray Mountain Water
ProductID: XXXXX-XXX-XXXXXXX-XXXXX
Original Install Date: Wed Jun 13 07:47:00 2001
Domain: Error 2
PDC: Error 2453
IP Address: 172.16.3.12
CPU[0]: x86 Family 5 Model 4 Stepping 3: 199 MHz
Hotfixes:
```

```
    [Q147222]:
Drive:          [FileSys]  [ Size ]  [ Free ]   [ Used ]
  C$    NTFS       2749       1466       1283
  G$    NTFS        249        204         45
Services:
  [Running]  Alerter
  [Running]  Apache
  [Running]  Application Management
  [Running]  Computer Browser
  [Stopped]  Indexing Service
  [Stopped]  ClipBook
  [Running]  Distributed File System
  [Running]  DHCP Client
  [Stopped]  Logical Disk Manager Administrative Service
  [Running]  Logical Disk Manager
  [Running]  DNS Client
  [Running]  Event Log
  [Running]  COM+ Event System
  [Stopped]  Fax Service
  [Running]  IIS Admin Service
  [Stopped]  Intersite Messaging
  [Stopped]  Kerberos Key Distribution Center
  [Running]  Server
  [Running]  Workstation
  [Running]  License Logging Service
  [Running]  TCP/IP NetBIOS Helper Service
  [Running]  Messenger
  [Stopped]  NetMeeting Remote Desktop Sharing
  [Running]  Distributed Transaction Coordinator
  [Running]  FTP Publishing Service
  [Running]  Windows Installer
  [Stopped]  Network DDE
  [Stopped]  Network DDE DSDM
  [Stopped]  Net Logon
  [Running]  Network Connections
  [Stopped]  File Replication
  [Stopped]  NT LM Security Support Provider
  [Running]  Removable Storage
  [Running]  Plug and Play
  [Running]  IPSEC Policy Agent
  [Running]  Protected Storage
  [Stopped]  Remote Access Auto Connection Manager
  [Stopped]  Remote Access Connection Manager
  [Stopped]  Routing and Remote Access
  [Running]  Remote Registry Service
  [Stopped]  Remote Procedure Call (RPC) Locator
  [Running]  Remote Procedure Call (RPC)
  [Stopped]  QoS RSVP
  [Running]  Security Accounts Manager
  [Stopped]  Smart Card Helper
```

```
       [Stopped]   Smart Card
       [Running]   Task Scheduler
       [Running]   RunAs Service
       [Running]   System Event Notification
       [Stopped]   Internet Connection Sharing
       [Running]   Print Spooler
       [Stopped]   Performance Logs and Alerts
       [Running]   Telephony
       [Stopped]   Terminal Services
       [Stopped]   Telnet
       [Stopped]   Distributed Link Tracking Server
       [Running]   Distributed Link Tracking Client
       [Stopped]   Uninterruptible Power Supply
       [Stopped]   Utility Manager
       [Stopped]   Visual Studio Analyzer RPC bridge
       [Stopped]   Windows Time
       [Running]   Windows Management Instrumentation
       [Running]   Windows Management Instrumentation Driver Extensions
       [Running]   Process Tree Service
Network Card [0]:
System Up Time: 0 Days, 9 Hr, 31 Min, 13 Sec
```

Storage Systems

Keeping track of the amount of disk space consumed by the Web content and related files may be an ongoing activity. If the Web site supports the ability for users to publish their own pages, such as sub Webs, and/or the Web content contains a lot of multimedia data, it is important to make sure sufficient disk space is present. To determine the size of a directory and/or how much overall disk space is used and available, you can use Windows Explorer. To collect the information, navigate to the directory or drive letter you wish to investigate. Choosing Properties from the File menu or from the secondary mouse button menu presents the Properties window. For example, the Properties window for Ouray Mountain Water company's Windows 2000 Apache Web server hosting the Production server displays the information in Figure 7.8.

In our example, there is 203 MB free space, which, for the role of this Web server, is not a concern. The Production Web server is essentially a front end to a database that contains all the information the users would be accessing. In this case, the content of the database is stored on another drive letter/partition so both systems' disk space usage does not cramp each other's. Opening the Properties window on the Web server's content directory, htdocs in this example, reveals different information as shown in Figure 7.9.

In this example, we only see the amount of disk space consumed by the selected directory and nothing about overall disk space usage.

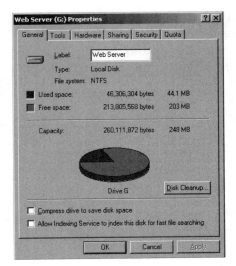

Figure 7.8   Windows 2000 drive letter Properties window.

The dir command line utility can also be used to gather some information about disk space. The results of the dir command displays the amount of disk space free and the size of files. It does not present size information about directories. To view the information about all the files, including hidden files, in a directory and all subdirectories and files, use the following syntax:

```
dir <path> /a /s
```

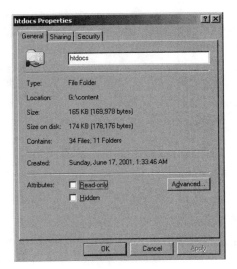

Figure 7.9   Windows 2000 directory Properties window.

where <path> is the directory to begin the information listing. If the command prompt is at the directory you wish to investigate, the <path> specification is not required. Executing the dir command with the /a and /s options on the content directory of Ouray Mountain Water's Production server revealed the following information:

```
Volume in drive G is Web Server
 Volume Serial Number is 343C-635A

Directory of G:\content\htdocs

07/21/2001  09:02p    <DIR>          .
07/21/2001  09:02p    <DIR>          ..
07/21/2001  06:56p    <DIR>          images
07/21/2001  08:59p           4,792  index.html
07/21/2001  07:05p    <DIR>          manufacturing
07/21/2001  08:59p           3,785  omwprivate.htm
07/21/2001  06:56p    <DIR>          warehouse
07/21/2001  08:32p    <DIR>          _borders
07/21/2001  06:56p    <DIR>          _derived
07/21/2001  06:56p    <DIR>          _private
              2 File(s)          8,577 bytes

Directory of G:\content\htdocs\images

07/21/2001  06:56p    <DIR>          .
07/21/2001  06:56p    <DIR>          ..
07/21/2001  08:59p             668  02PEOPLE.GIF
07/21/2001  08:59p           1,024  05SKY.GIF
07/21/2001  08:59p           1,386  39BOR.GIF
07/21/2001  08:59p           2,557  Barbedwire.gif
07/21/2001  08:59p          11,319  Blissgrain.jpg
07/21/2001  08:59p             666  Border2.gif
07/21/2001  08:59p           2,497  hosted5.gif
07/21/2001  08:59p             549  loginbutton.gif
07/21/2001  08:59p             322  logo.gif
07/21/2001  08:59p          82,128  Pastel.gif
07/21/2001  08:59p           9,404  RT Clip Art.gif
07/21/2001  08:59p           1,357  Sandman.gif
07/21/2001  08:59p           3,036  Sandmanhalf.gif
07/21/2001  08:59p           1,648  Skyhalf.gif
07/21/2001  08:59p             926  smallnew.gif
07/21/2001  08:59p           8,489  Sun.gif
07/21/2001  08:59p           1,375  Sun3rd.gif
07/21/2001  08:59p             973  Sunbullet.gif
07/21/2001  08:59p           1,061  Sunfacebullet.gif
07/21/2001  08:59p           2,502  Sunhalf.gif
07/21/2001  08:59p           6,808  Sunhorntrans2.gif
             21 File(s)        140,695  bytes
```

```
Directory of G:\content\htdocs\manufacturing

07/21/2001  07:05p    <DIR>          .
07/21/2001  07:05p    <DIR>          ..
07/21/2001  06:56p    <DIR>          images
07/21/2001  08:59p            2,546 index.html
07/21/2001  08:59p            1,648 Skyhalf.gif
07/21/2001  06:56p    <DIR>          _borders
07/21/2001  06:56p    <DIR>          _private
             2 File(s)         4,194 bytes

Directory of G:\content\htdocs\manufacturing\images

07/21/2001  06:56p    <DIR>          .
07/21/2001  06:56p    <DIR>          ..
07/21/2001  08:59p              668 02people.gif
07/21/2001  08:59p           11,319 Blissgrain.jpg
             2 File(s)        11,987 bytes

Directory of G:\content\htdocs\manufacturing\_borders

07/21/2001  06:56p    <DIR>          .
07/21/2001  06:56p    <DIR>          ..
07/21/2001  08:59p              356 bottom.htm
             1 File(s)           356 bytes

Directory of G:\content\htdocs\manufacturing\_private

07/21/2001  06:56p    <DIR>          .
07/21/2001  06:56p    <DIR>          ..
             0 File(s)             0 bytes

Directory of G:\content\htdocs\warehouse

07/21/2001  06:56p    <DIR>          .
07/21/2001  06:56p    <DIR>          ..
07/21/2001  06:56p    <DIR>          images
07/21/2001  08:59p              415 index.html
07/21/2001  06:56p    <DIR>          _private
             1 File(s)           415 bytes

Directory of G:\content\htdocs\warehouse\images

07/21/2001  06:56p    <DIR>          .
07/21/2001  06:56p    <DIR>          ..
             0 File(s)             0 bytes

Directory of G:\content\htdocs\warehouse\_private

07/21/2001  06:56p    <DIR>          .
07/21/2001  06:56p    <DIR>          ..
```

```
           0 File(s)                0 bytes

Directory of G:\content\htdocs\_borders

07/21/2001  08:32p     <DIR>          .
07/21/2001  08:32p     <DIR>          ..
07/21/2001  08:59p             1,099 bottom.htm
07/21/2001  08:59p               423 left.htm
07/21/2001  08:59p               658 top.htm
           3 File(s)           2,180 bytes

Directory of G:\content\htdocs\_derived

07/21/2001  06:56p     <DIR>          .
07/21/2001  06:56p     <DIR>          ..
07/21/2001  08:59p             1,574 nortbots.htm
           1 File(s)           1,574 bytes

Directory of G:\content\htdocs\_private

07/21/2001  06:56p     <DIR>          .
07/21/2001  06:56p     <DIR>          ..
07/21/2001  08:59p                 0 form_results.txt
           1 File(s)               0 bytes

   Total Files Listed:
          34 File(s)       169,978 bytes
          35 Dir(s)    213,805,568 bytes free
```

Information about the different storage devices on the Windows 2000 system can also be viewed from the Computer Management utility available from the Administrative Tools menu, which is accessed from the Programs menu. In the Computer Management console window, select the Storage category and then within that area choose Disk Management. The initial view displays all the storage devices the tool can find and information about each device. Figure 7.10 displays the information presented in the Computer Management tool for Ouray Mountain Water's Production Web server.

When the drive/partition you wish to investigate is selected and the corresponding Properties window is opened, the display shows the same information as in Figure 7.8, which was gathered from Explorer. However, the Disk Management tool allows you to perform other actions such as creating or deleting partitions and defragmentation.

The Windows 2000 Resource Kit contains several tools for gathering information about the storage systems on the server. The Directory Disk Usage (diruse) tool displays information such as directory size values. The /s option with diruse will include subdirectory information in addition to the directory or location specified. The /m option displays the size information in megabytes.

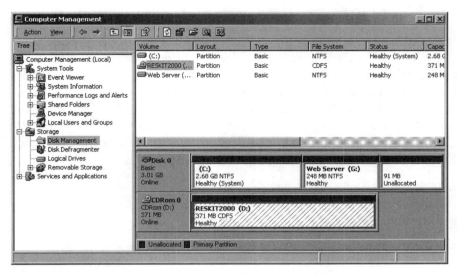

Figure 7.10   Computer Management Disk Management information.

Executing the diruse command on the Web content directory of Ouray Mountain Water's Production server with the /m and /s options:

```
diruse /s /m G:\content\htdocs
```

revealed the following information:

```
Size (mb)  Files  Directory
     0.01     2   G:\CONTENT\HTDOCS
     0.13    21   G:\CONTENT\HTDOCS\images
     0.00     2   G:\CONTENT\HTDOCS\manufacturing
     0.01     2   G:\CONTENT\HTDOCS\manufacturing\images
     0.00     1   G:\CONTENT\HTDOCS\manufacturing\_borders
     0.00     0   G:\CONTENT\HTDOCS\manufacturing\_private
     0.00     1   G:\CONTENT\HTDOCS\warehouse
     0.00     0   G:\CONTENT\HTDOCS\warehouse\images
     0.00     0   G:\CONTENT\HTDOCS\warehouse\_private
     0.00     3   G:\CONTENT\HTDOCS\_borders
     0.00     1   G:\CONTENT\HTDOCS\_derived
     0.00     1   G:\CONTENT\HTDOCS\_private
     0.16    34   SUB-TOTAL: G:\CONTENT\HTDOCS

     0.16    34   TOTAL: G:\CONTENT\HTDOCS
```

The Directory Disk Usage tool is also available from Microsoft's Web site.

If you need to determine the amount of disk space consumed by user files, then take a look at the Disk Use (diskuse) tool included in the Resource Kit. The tool supports the ability to find files owned by a specific user or for all users. For example, we want to determine how much disk space is used by files owned by the Web Developer for Ouray Mountain Water company's Production server. The name of the account used by the developer to publish the content to the Web server is webdev and the location of the Web content is on G:\content\htdocs. With this information, the syntax of the diskuse command is:

```
diskuse G:\content\htdocs /s /u:webdev
```

This command produced the following information:

```
DiskUse                    Version 1.3

Scanning Path g:\content\htdocs\............
Resolving Names.
Sorting.



User: PRODUCTION\WebDev
Space Used: 169978
```

The Disk Use tool is also available from Microsoft's Web site.

Disk Manager Diagnostics (dmdiag) in the Resource Kit is a command line tool that displays data about the storage systems on the server. This tool gives extensive information which you will probably never need unless you are working at the device level with the storage systems. The Disk Manager Diagnostics tool is also available from Microsoft's Web site.

Network

Windows 2000 comes with a tool to observe and capture network traffic into and out of the server system. The version that is delivered with Windows 2000 only supports the viewing of network traffic that is local to the machine. Another version of Network Monitor that is delivered with Microsoft's SMS (Systems Management Server) product can observe and capture any traffic that goes by as long as the network card driver supports promiscuous mode—that is, the ability to see all traffic on the media whether it's for me or not.

Network Monitor's default access location is in the Administrative Tools menu under the Programs menu. When you first open up the application, a multi-paned window is presented that contains no data content. To begin capturing data for analysis, choose Start under the Capture menu or click on the right arrow button on the tool bar. A window similar to Figure 7.11 appears which updates dynamically as the data is captured.

When you have enough packets captured for your analysis, you can display a summary of the information as in Figure 7.12.

You can also go into more detail of the actual packets captured and of each packet. For example, the packets captured on Ouray Mountain Water's Production server while a user was accessing the Web site reveals Figure 7.13.

You can also specify what types of packets to capture by selecting Filter from the Capture menu. In the Filter window you can choose what type of packets to collect, for example just IP and/or just TCP traffic, and from which types of addresses.

In addition to the tools provided by Microsoft, there are many commercial, freeware, and shareware network monitors available. One that is free and open source for Ethernet based Web servers is Ethereal. In contrast to the Network Monitor included with Windows 2000, Ethereal will capture all packets it sees whether they are destined for the machine Ethereal is running on or not. Figure 7.14 is an example of a packet captured by Ethereal while a user was browsing the Web site on Ouray Mountain Water's Production server.

Ethereal is available from www.ethereal.com.

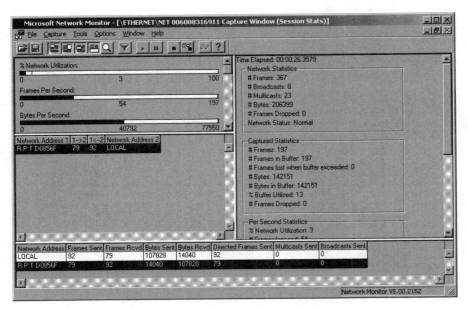

Figure 7.11   Network Monitor actively capturing packets.

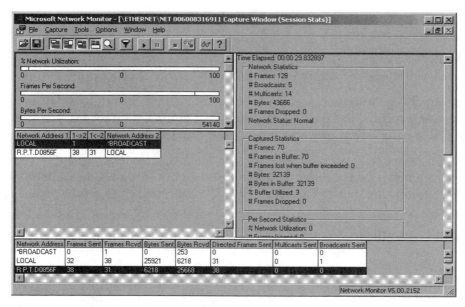

Figure 7.12 Network Monitor captured packets summary.

Windows 2000 includes a command line utility called netstat that takes a snapshot of the state of the different ports on the system when the command is executed. Executing netstat without any parameters captures a single instance of open ports. To collect data over a period of time append a time interval in

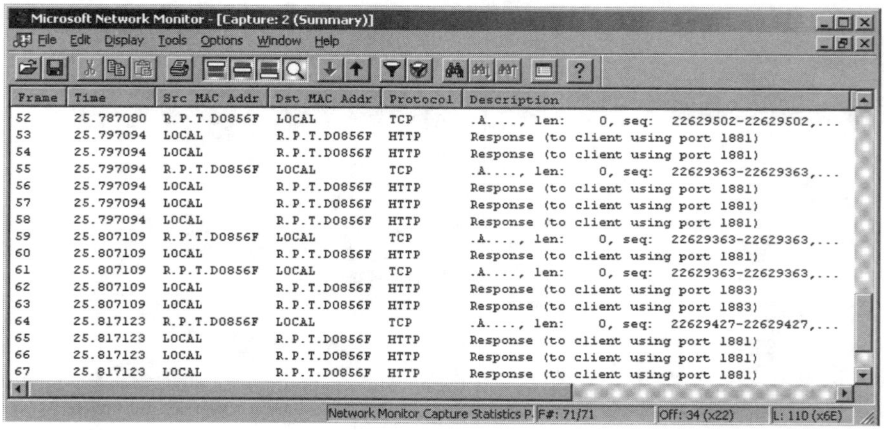

Figure 7.13 Network Monitor captured packets listing.

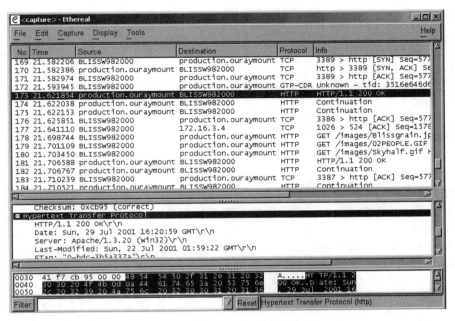

Figure 7.14   Ethereal for Windows 2000 sample capture.

seconds at the end of the command. To observe the activity on all ports whether active or not, use the –a option. For example, to capture the status of all ports every five seconds, use the following syntax for netstat:

```
netstat –a 5
```

The command executed on the Ouray Mountain Water company's Production server revealed the following information (only one time slice of data is presented):

```
Active Connections

    Proto   Local Address          Foreign Address           State
    TCP     production:ftp          production.ouraymountainwater.com:0   LISTENING
    TCP     production:http         production.ouraymountainwater.com:0   LISTENING
    TCP     production:epmap        production.ouraymountainwater.com:0   LISTENING
    TCP     production:microsoft-ds production.ouraymountainwater.com:0   LISTENING
    TCP     production:1025         production.ouraymountainwater.com:0   LISTENING
    TCP     production:1026         production.ouraymountainwater.com:0   LISTENING
    TCP     production:1028         production.ouraymountainwater.com:0   LISTENING
    TCP     production:1029         production.ouraymountainwater.com:0   LISTENING
    TCP     production:3372         production.ouraymountainwater.com:0   LISTENING
```

```
TCP     production:http          BLISSW982000:2529       ESTABLISHED
TCP     production:http          BLISSW982000:2555       ESTABLISHED
TCP     production:netbios-ssn   production.ouraymountainwater.com:0  LISTENING
UDP     production:epmap         *:*
UDP     production:microsoft-ds  *:*
UDP     production:1027          *:*
UDP     production:3456          *:*
UDP     production:netbios-ns    *:*
UDP     production:netbios-dgm   *:*
UDP     production:isakmp        *:*
```

Apache Logs

One of the items at your disposal for determining the usage and activities of your Apache Web server are the Apache log files. Apache has fairly extensive logging capabilities that permit you to monitor users' activities on your Web sites and any errors the Web server encounters.

One of the log files generated by Apache maintains a record of every request made to the Web server. The log file is found in the default directory, logs, under the apache directory. On Linux the name of the file is access_log and on Windows 2000 it is named access.log. The name and location of the access log file is defined by the CustomLog directive in the httpd.conf file. On Linux, the default specification for the access_log file location and name is:

```
#
# The location and format of the access logfile (Common Logfile Format).
# If you do not define any access logfiles within a <VirtualHost>
# container, they will be logged here.  Contrariwise, if you *do*
# define per-<VirtualHost> access logfiles, transactions will be
# logged therein and *not* in this file.
#
CustomLog /usr/local/apache/logs/access_log common
```

On a Windows 2000 system, the default location and name of the access.log file in the httpd.conf file is:

```
#
# The location and format of the access logfile (Common Logfile Format).
# If you do not define any access logfiles within a <VirtualHost>
# container, they will be logged here.  Contrariwise, if you *do*
# define per-<VirtualHost> access logfiles, transactions will be
# logged therein and *not* in this file.
#
CustomLog logs/access.log common
```

Below is an example extracted from the access.log file on Ouray Mountain Water's Windows 2000 Production Apache Web server:

```
172.16.3.80 - - [21/Jul/2001:16:23:25 -0500] "GET / HTTP/1.0" 200 541
172.16.3.80 - - [21/Jul/2001:16:28:26 -0500] "GET / HTTP/1.0" 200 1005
172.16.3.80 - - [21/Jul/2001:16:28:26 -0500] "GET /icons/folder.gif HTTP/1.0"
    200 225
172.16.3.80 - - [21/Jul/2001:16:28:26 -0500] "GET /icons/text.gif HTTP/1.0" 200 229
172.16.3.80 - - [21/Jul/2001:16:31:30 -0500] "GET / HTTP/1.0" 200 3086
172.16.3.80 - - [21/Jul/2001:16:31:30 -0500] "GET /images/Sandmanhalf.gif
    HTTP/1.0" 200 3036
172.16.3.80 - - [21/Jul/2001:16:31:30 -0500] "GET /images/Blissgrain.jpg
    HTTP/1.0" 200 11319
172.16.3.80 - - [21/Jul/2001:16:31:30 -0500] "GET /images/Skyhalf.gif HTTP/1.0"
    200 1648
172.16.3.80 - - [21/Jul/2001:16:31:30 -0500] "GET /images/02people.gif HTTP/1.0"
    404 301
172.16.3.80 - - [21/Jul/2001:16:35:15 -0500] "GET / HTTP/1.0" 200 3086
172.16.3.80 - - [21/Jul/2001:16:35:15 -0500] "GET /images/Blissgrain.jpg
    HTTP/1.0" 200 11319
172.16.3.80 - - [21/Jul/2001:16:35:15 -0500] "GET /images/02people.gif HTTP/1.0"
    404 301
172.16.3.80 - - [21/Jul/2001:16:42:38 -0500] "GET / HTTP/1.0" 200 3086
172.16.3.80 - - [21/Jul/2001:16:42:38 -0500] "GET /images/Blissgrain.jpg
    HTTP/1.0" 200 11319
172.16.3.80 - - [21/Jul/2001:16:42:38 -0500] "GET /images/02people.gif HTTP/1.0"
    200 668
172.16.3.12 - - [21/Jul/2001:19:00:05 -0500] "GET / HTTP/1.1" 200 3086
172.16.3.12 - - [21/Jul/2001:19:00:06 -0500] "GET /images/Blissgrain.jpg
    HTTP/1.1" 200 11319
172.16.3.12 - - [21/Jul/2001:19:00:06 -0500] "GET /images/02people.gif HTTP/1.1"
    200 668
172.16.3.12 - - [21/Jul/2001:19:00:06 -0500] "GET /images/Skyhalf.gif HTTP/1.1"
    200 1648
172.16.3.12 - - [21/Jul/2001:19:00:06 -0500] "GET /images/Sandmanhalf.gif
    HTTP/1.1" 200 3036
```

The access log file is in the CLF (Common Log Format) format. Each line entry contains fields and if any of the field values are empty a dash is used as a place holder for the field's value. The fields used in the CLF format (read from left to right) are:

host This value is the IP address or name of the system making the request.

ident The identity of the machine making the request.

authuser If user authentication is required by the location the user is attempting to access, the authuser field contains the name of the login account.

date The date and time of the request. The format is YY/MM/DD :HH:MM:SS OFFSET where OFFSET is the numbers of hours the local time is different than GMT time.

request The content of the request.

status The three digit HTTP code indicating the status of the request.

bytes The size of the response sent back to the requester from the server. This value does not include the size of any headers in the response.

The Apache logging capabilities also allow you to customize the log reports. The ServerSignature parameter in httpd.conf can be used to include the name of the Web server and the version of the Web server in the log file.

```
Optionally add a line containing the server version and virtual host
# name to server-generated pages (error documents, FTP directory listings,
# mod_status and mod_info output etc., but not CGI generated documents).
# Set to "EMail" to also include a mailto: link to the ServerAdmin.
# Set to one of:  On | Off | EMail
#
ServerSignature On
```

If you want the name of the requesting device instead of the IP address for the host field in the log file, the HostnameLookups directive needs to be set to On in the httpd.conf file.

```
# HostnameLookups: Log the names of clients or just their IP addresses
# e.g., www.apache.org (on) or 204.62.129.132 (off).
# The default is off because it'd be overall better for the net if people
# had to knowingly turn this feature on, since enabling it means that
# each client request will result in AT LEAST one lookup request to the
# nameserver.
#
HostnameLookups Off
```

The default setting for HostnameLookups is Off primarily because setting the directive to On will impact the performance of the Web server. When HostnameLookups is enabled, more time is needed to lookup the name of the requesting system which slows down the behavior of the Web server. If you need to know the name of the system making the request it is better to do an analysis of the log file after it is created. The log file can be post-processed so the IP address is replaced with the corresponding name of the system.

The Identification Protocol (ident or Ident Protocol RFC 1413) is used on TCP connections to determine the identity of the system or user. The server runs an ident daemon service which listens for TCP connections on the TCP port number 113. When a TCP connection to the server is established, the server reads the data which includes specifics on the connection's requests.

Based on the information collected, the server may then either shut the connection down or it may continue to read and/or respond to multiple requests. In order to have the ident information entered in the access log ident field, the server running Apache must have the ident service running. The second requirement is that the IdentityCheck directive in the httpd.conf file must be set to On. The default for IdentityCheck is Off and it is highly recommended that this be left Off especially for Internet Web servers. If IdentityCheck is enabled, each request to the Web server may add up to an additional 30-second latency to the normal response time. In addition to the time delay, there is no guarantee that the information gathered by the ident service is trustworthy. The information can be any content the requester decides to choose and thus the requester can say anything they want to. If you decide to experiment with the ident protocol, enable the IdentityCheck directive on a test server that has limited and controlled access to the network.

The authuser field is filled in if the location the user is attempting to access requires a successful login. When the user logs in, the account name is placed in the authuser field. For typical Web browsing activities where the user is navigating through Web pages and no authentication is required, this field is empty. However, for actions that require login, the authuser field will indicate the name of the account used for the request.

The date field is essentially a timestamp for the request. This information is very useful when you are analyzing the Web server's activities during different time frames.

The items between the quotation marks specify the nature of the request to the Web server. The request field indicates the type of request, the file accessed, the protocol, and the version of the protocol used.

The next field in the log line entry is the status of the request. These status numbers are three-digits and reflect items such as successes and failures. Here is a listing of some of the HTTP status numbers:

200 = request was successful

302 = a redirection occurred

4xx = client errors

- 401 = authorization is denied
- 403 = forbidden
- 404 = not found
- 5xx = server errors

As an example, let's analyze the following entry:

```
172.16.3.200 - webdev [08/Jul/2001:18:34:53 -0500] "PUT /index.html HTTP/1.0" 200 39
```

The host is 172.16.3.200, which is the IP address of the machine making the request to the Web server. In this example there is no entry for ident so a dash is added as a placeholder. Following the ident field is the authuser entry. In our example, webdev is the name of the account used to make the request to the Web server. The remaining text in the example is the request value field. The contents of the request value field indicate the file index.html was copied (PUT) to the Web server's document root directory. The status of 200 lets us know the request was successful and the size of the response was 39 bytes.

The default format for Apache log files is CLF and most log analysis tools work with log files in the CLF format. However, Apache log files can be customized for different formats depending on the information and style you wish. The specification of the format for the Apache log files is defined in the httpd.conf file. The first example is from the httpd.conf file on a Linux system.

```
#
# The following directives define some format nicknames for use with
# a CustomLog directive (see below).
#
LogFormat "%h %l %u %t \"%r\" %>s %b \"%{Referer}i\" \"%{User-Agent}i\"" combined
LogFormat "%h %l %u %t \"%r\" %>s %b" common
LogFormat "%{Referer}i -> %U" referer
LogFormat "%{User-agent}i" agent


#
# The location and format of the access logfile (Common Logfile Format).
# If you do not define any access logfiles within a <VirtualHost>
# container, they will be logged here.  Contrariwise, if you *do*
# define per-<VirtualHost> access logfiles, transactions will be
# logged therein and *not* in this file.
#
CustomLog /usr/local/apache/logs/access_log common
```

The example below is from an httpd.conf file on a Windows 2000 system:

```
#
# The following directives define some format nicknames for use with
# a CustomLog directive (see below).
#
LogFormat "%h %l %u %t \"%r\" %>s %b \"%{Referer}i\" \"%{User-Agent}i\"" combined
LogFormat "%h %l %u %t \"%r\" %>s %b" common
LogFormat "%{Referer}i -> %U" referer
LogFormat "%{User-agent}i" agent


#
# The location and format of the access logfile (Common Logfile Format).
# If you do not define any access logfiles within a <VirtualHost>
# container, they will be logged here.  Contrariwise, if you *do*
# define per-<VirtualHost> access logfiles, transactions will be
```

```
# logged therein and *not* in this file.
#
CustomLog logs/access.log common
```

The default format for the access log file is specified with the CustomLog entry which indicates to use the format called common which has been defined previously. Let's examine the LogFormat entry that defines the structure of the common format style.

```
LogFormat "%h %l %u %t \"%r\" %>s %b" common
```

Each of the single letter variables, or tokens, refers to a field in the log file entry.

h = host

l = ident

u = authuser

t = date

r = request

s = status

b = bytes

The other LogFormat entries in the httpd.conf file define three other formats for log files. The LogFormat called combined includes two additional items in the log file entries. These are the referrer header, which is the name of the referring URL, and the user-agent header, which is also known as the browser field, and indicates the user's browser type. Below is the combined LogFormat as defined in the httpd.conf file:

```
LogFormat "%h %l %u %t \"%r\" %>s %b \"%{Referer}i\" \"%{User-Agent}i\"" combined
```

Table 7.1 lists the additional variables you can use to specify the fields in the log file.

In addition to the access log file, Apache also generates an error log file which records such events as any internal server errors and missing files. The default location of the error log file is the Apache logs directory. On Linux, the name of the error log file is error_log and on Windows it is called error.log. The location and name of the error log file can be changed by modifying the ErrorLog directive in the httpd.conf file. Below is an example of the default specification of the error log file on a Linux system:

```
#
# ErrorLog: The location of the error log file.
# If you do not specify an ErrorLog directive within a <VirtualHost>
```

Table 7.1   Log File Field Variables

VARIABLE	DESCRIPTION
a	Remote system's IP address
A	Local system's IP address
B	Number of bytes sent in the response—this does not include the number of bytes in the headers
b	Number of bytes sent in the response—this does not include the number of bytes in the headers—the b variable is for CLF formats and if the response is 0 bytes a dash(-) instead of a zero (0) will be placed in the log file
{var}e	Display the value of the environment variable called var
f	Name of the file
h	IP address or name of the remote system making the request to the server
H	Protocol used by the remote system making the request to the server
{name}i	Display the contents of the name's header lines in the request
I	Name of the requester if the ident protocol service is running on the server
m	The method used in the request
{note}n	Display the contents of the note from an Apache module
{data}o	Display the contents of the data's header lines contained in the response from the server
p	Canonical port of the server responding to the request
q	Display the query string if it exists
r	Display the first line of the incoming request
s	Display the status of the original request—to see the last request made by a connection use the format of %>s
{format}t	Display time in the format specified by {format}
T	Display the time in seconds used to respond to the request
u	Remote user's name
U	Path of the URL requested by the system making the request to the server
v	Canonical name of the device making the request
V	Name of the server specified by the UseCanonicalName parameter

```
# container, error messages relating to that virtual host will be
# logged here.  If you *do* define an error logfile for a <VirtualHost>
# container, that host's errors will be logged there and not here.
#
ErrorLog /usr/local/apache/logs/error_log
```

The default setting for the name and location of the error log file defined in the httpd.conf file on a Windows 2000 system is:

```
#
# ErrorLog: The location of the error log file.
# If you do not specify an ErrorLog directive within a <VirtualHost>
# container, error messages relating to that virtual host will be
# logged here.  If you *do* define an error logfile for a <VirtualHost>
# container, that host's errors will be logged there and not here.
#
ErrorLog logs/error.log
```

When the Apache service is stopped, started, or restarted on a Linux system, the event is recorded in the error_log file. For example, when the Apache service is started, a line similar to the following is added to the error_log file.

```
[Thu Jul 26 10:27:24 2001] [notice] Apache/1.3.20 (Unix) configured - resuming
    normal operations
```

When the service is stopped, a message similar to the following is added to the error_log file:

```
[Thu Jul 26 10:27:18 2001] [notice] caught SIGTERM, shutting down
```

On a Linux system, if the graceful parameter is used with the apachectl command, the following information is placed on the error_log file:

```
[Wed Jul 25 14:28:32 2001] [notice] SIGUSR1 received.  Doing graceful restart
[Wed Jul 25 14:28:32 2001] [notice] Apache/1.3.20 (Unix) configured - resuming
    normal operations
```

The type of information included in the error log file is determined by the LogLevel directive in the httpd.conf file.

```
#
# LogLevel: Control the number of messages logged to the error_log.
# Possible values include: debug, info, notice, warn, error, crit,
# alert, emerg.
#
LogLevel warn
```

The default setting in the httpd.conf file is warn for the LogLevel directive.

On Windows 2000, the error.log file does not contain information about the stopping and/or starting of the Apache Web server when the LogLevel is set to warn. To view information about the Apache service starting, the LogLevel needs to be set to info. With LogLevel set to info, the error.log file will contain entries for each time the service is started. Below is an example of the entries reflecting that the Apache service was started:

```
[Thu Jul 26 13:33:47 2001] [info] Parent: Created child process 952
[Thu Jul 26 13:33:47 2001] [info] Parent: Duplicating socket 220 and sending it
to child process 952
[Thu Jul 26 13:33:47 2001] [info] BytesRead = 372 WSAProtocolInfo = 2006620
```

When the service is stopped with LogLevel set to info, the error.log file will contain information similar to the following:

```
[Thu Jul 26 13:33:44 2001] [info] master_main: Shutdown event signaled. Shutting
the server down.
[Thu Jul 26 13:33:44 2001] [info] removed PID file
g:/apache/apache/logs/httpd.pid (pid=1040)
```

The different levels and definitions for LogLevel in order of decreasing significance are listed below. These definitions are taken directly from the Apache Software Foundation's Web site, http://httpd.apache.org/docs/mod/core.html:

LEVEL	DESCRIPTION	EXAMPLE
emerg	Emergencies - system is unusable.	"Child cannot open lock file. Exiting"
alert	Action must be taken immediately.	"getpwuid: couldn't determine user name from uid"
crit	Critical Conditions.	"socket: Failed to get a socket, exiting child"
error	Error conditions.	"Premature end of script headers"
warn	Warning conditions.	"child process 1234 did not exit, sending another SIGHUP"
notice	Normal but significant condition.	"httpd: caught SIGBUS, attempting to dump core in ..."
info	Informational.	"Server seems busy, (you may need to increase StartServers, or Min/MaxSpare-Servers)..."
debug	Debug-level messages	"Opening config file ..."

Whatever level is specified, any messages that correspond to any higher levels are also entered into the error log file. For example, if LogLevel is set to error then any error, crit, alert, and emerg messages are entered into the error log file. It is recommended that the LogLevel be set to at least crit to catch any messages that are significant to the operation of Apache.

As time goes on, the size of the log files may become quite large and/or you may want to save the contents across multiple files. In the bin directory under the apache directory is a tool called rotatelogs. This utility gives you the ability to specify the interval at which a new log file is created. The rotatelogs tool works in conjunction with the TransferLog directive in the httpd.conf file. To use the rotatelogs utility for a Linux based Apache Web server, add the item in bold to the httpd.conf file:

```
#
# The location and format of the access logfile (Common Logfile Format).
# If you do not define any access logfiles within a <VirtualHost>
# container, they will be logged here.  Contrariwise, if you *do*
# define per-<VirtualHost> access logfiles, transactions will be
# logged therein and *not* in this file.
#
# CustomLog /usr/local/apache/logs/access_log common
```

TransferLog "|/usr/local/apache/bin/rotatelogs /usr/local/apache/logs/employee-access_log 86400"

On a Windows 2000 Apache server, add the line in bold to the httpd .conf file.

```
#
# The location and format of the access logfile (Common Logfile Format).
# If you do not define any access logfiles within a <VirtualHost>
# container, they will be logged here.  Contrariwise, if you *do*
# define per-<VirtualHost> access logfiles, transactions will be
# logged therein and *not* in this file.
#
# CustomLog logs/access.log common
```

TransferLog "|G:/apache/apache/bin/rotatelogs G:/apache/apache/logs/prod-access_log 86400"

The parameters for TransferLog are first, the location of the rotatelogs utility. The location on the Linux system is the default location of the bin directory. On the Windows 2000 system, the default location is relative to the drive letter and name of the directory where you installed Apache. The second parameter for TransferLog is the location and name of the log file. In both examples, we are using the default location of the Apache logs directory. For the name of the files, we choose to include a reference to the name of the server so we can tell which log files are from which systems. For example, the Linux TransferLog example is from the Ouray Mountain Water Employee server so we placed employee at the beginning of the file name. For the Windows 2000 example, which is from Ouray Mountain Water's Production server, we placed prod at the beginning of the file name. Since these are access log information, we decided to leave the name access_log in the file name so we can distinguish these log files from other types of log files. The final parameter for the TransferLog directive is the time frame for when a new log file is generated. This value is in seconds and for our examples we used 86400 seconds, which translates to 24 hours. So, once every twenty-four hours a new log file is created in the Apache logs directory. To keep the log files separate, a time reference value is placed automatically at the end of the log file. For example,

```
employee-access_log.099610560
```

Note that the ability to create rolling log files natively within Apache is only applicable to the access log files.

Analyzing the Apache Log Files

The log files generated by Apache are standard text files that can be read by any text file editor. However, over the course of time, you may find it more difficult to find information or trends due to the quantity of information. There are several tools available that are specifically designed to help make it easier to work with log files. In this section we will discuss some of these log files analysis tools.

Logresolve

The logresolve tool, which is included with Apache, is not a log analysis tool but a utility to process the log files to resolve IP numbers to names. Depending on the length of the log file and responsiveness of the DNS server(s), it may take a long time to process the log file. The logresolve utility is located in the bin directory and requires the location and name of the log file and the name and destination of a file within which to place the results. For example, on the Ouray Mountain Water company's Production Windows 2000 Apache Web server, the logresolve command executed at the bin directory would be:

```
logresolve <G:\apache\apache\logs\access.log>
G:\apache\apache\logs\resolvedaccess.log
```

The item within the <> is the full path to the location of the log file you wish to process. The second parameter is the full path and the name of the file you wish the processed results to go to. As an example of the results of logresolve, take a look at the following information:

```
BLISSW982000 - - [26/Jul/2001:10:03:44 -0700] "GET /index.html HTTP/1.1" 304 -
BLISSW982000 - - [26/Jul/2001:10:03:44 -0700] "GET /images/Blissgrain.jpg
    HTTP/1.1" 304 -
BLISSW982000 - - [26/Jul/2001:10:03:44 -0700] "GET /images/02PEOPLE.GIF
    HTTP/1.1" 304 -
BLISSW982000 - - [26/Jul/2001:10:03:44 -0700] "GET /images/Skyhalf.gif HTTP/1.1"
    304 -
```

```
BLISSW982000 - - [26/Jul/2001:10:03:44 -0700] "GET /images/loginbutton.gif
   HTTP/1.1" 304 -
BLISSW982000 - - [26/Jul/2001:10:03:44 -0700] "GET /images/Sandmanhalf.gif
   HTTP/1.1" 304 -
BLISSW982000 - - [26/Jul/2001:10:05:12 -0700] "GET /index.html HTTP/1.1" 304 -
BLISSW982000 - - [26/Jul/2001:10:05:12 -0700] "GET /images/Blissgrain.jpg
   HTTP/1.1" 304 -
BLISSW982000 - - [26/Jul/2001:10:05:12 -0700] "GET /images/Skyhalf.gif HTTP/1.1"
   304 -
BLISSW982000 - - [26/Jul/2001:10:05:12 -0700] "GET /images/02PEOPLE.GIF
   HTTP/1.1" 304 -
BLISSW982000 - - [26/Jul/2001:10:05:12 -0700] "GET /images/loginbutton.gif
   HTTP/1.1" 304 -
BLISSW982000 - - [26/Jul/2001:10:05:12 -0700] "GET /images/Sandmanhalf.gif
   HTTP/1.1" 304 -
```

The above data came from the following information in the access.log Windows 2000 Apache file on the Ouray Mountain Water Production server:

```
172.16.3.220 - - [26/Jul/2001:10:03:44 -0700] "GET /index.html HTTP/1.1" 304 -
172.16.3.220 - - [26/Jul/2001:10:03:44 -0700] "GET /images/Blissgrain.jpg
   HTTP/1.1" 304 -
172.16.3.220 - - [26/Jul/2001:10:03:44 -0700] "GET /images/02PEOPLE.GIF
   HTTP/1.1" 304 -
172.16.3.220 - - [26/Jul/2001:10:03:44 -0700] "GET /images/Skyhalf.gif HTTP/1.1"
   304 -
172.16.3.220 - - [26/Jul/2001:10:03:44 -0700] "GET /images/loginbutton.gif
   HTTP/1.1" 304 -
172.16.3.220 - - [26/Jul/2001:10:03:44 -0700] "GET /images/Sandmanhalf.gif
   HTTP/1.1" 304 -
172.16.3.220 - - [26/Jul/2001:10:05:12 -0700] "GET /index.html HTTP/1.1" 304 -
172.16.3.220 - - [26/Jul/2001:10:05:12 -0700] "GET /images/Blissgrain.jpg
   HTTP/1.1" 304 -
172.16.3.220 - - [26/Jul/2001:10:05:12 -0700] "GET /images/Skyhalf.gif HTTP/1.1"
   304 -
172.16.3.220 - - [26/Jul/2001:10:05:12 -0700] "GET /images/02PEOPLE.GIF
   HTTP/1.1" 304 -
172.16.3.220 - - [26/Jul/2001:10:05:12 -0700] "GET /images/loginbutton.gif
   HTTP/1.1" 304 -
172.16.3.220 - - [26/Jul/2001:10:05:12 -0700] "GET /images/Sandmanhalf.gif
   HTTP/1.1" 304 -
```

The format for logresolve is the same on Linux with the paths and filenames using the proper Linux naming conventions. For example, to run the logresolve utility on Ouray Mountain Water company's Employee Linux Apache Web server, the syntax would be:

```
logresolve </usr/local/apache/logs/access_log>
/usr/local/apache/logs/resolvedaccess_log
```

Analog

Analog is a program that analyses log files from Web servers. Analog is available for both Linux and Windows in addition to many other operating systems, http://analog.sourceforge.net/. Analog is designed to be fast and to produce attractive statistics. Analog shows you the usage patterns on your Web server. Some of its features include:

- Ultra-fast
- Scalable
- Highly configurable
- Reports in 37 languages
- Works on any operating system
- Free software

There is also an add-on program for Analog that presents the results in a graphical format. It is called Report Magic and it is freeware available from www.reportmagic.org.

Summary

Summary is a Web server log analysis software available from www.summary .net and it is available for Linux and Windows platforms. The software is reasonably priced and you can download a 30-day trial version.

Webalizer

This tool is available from www.mrunix.net/webalizer/ and is available for Linux but not Windows. According to the information on the Webalizer Web site:

The Webalizer is a fast, free Web server log file analysis program. It produces highly detailed, easily configurable usage reports in HTML format, for viewing with a standard Web browser.

FEATURES

Is written in C to be extremely fast and highly portable. On a 200Mhz Pentium machine, over 10,000 records can be processed in one second, with a 40-Megabyte file taking roughly 15 seconds (over 150,000 records).

Supports standard Common Logfile Format server logs. In addition, several variations of the Combined Logfile Format are supported, allowing statistics to be generated for referring sites and browser types as well. Now also has native support for **wu-ftpd xferlog** FTP and **squid** log formats as well.

Generated reports can be configured from the command line, or by use of one or more configuration files. Detailed information on configuration options can be found in the README file, supplied with all distributions.

Supports multiple languages. Currently, Catalan, Chinese (traditional and simplified), Croatian, Czech, Danish, Dutch, English, Estonian, Finnish, French, Galician, German, Greek, Hungarian, Icelandic, Indonesian, Italian, Japanese, Korean, Latvian, Malay, Norwegian, Polish, Portuguese (Portugal and Brazil), Romanian, Russian, Serbian, Slovak, Slovene, Spanish, Swedish, Turkish, and Ukrainian are available.

Unlimited log file sizes and partial logs are supported. This allows logs to be rotated as often as needed, and eliminates the need to keep huge monthly files on the system.

Distributed under the GNU General Public License, complete source code is available, as well as binary distributions for some of the more popular platforms. Please read the Copyright notices for additional information.

Wusage

Wusage is a Web server log analyzer and is available for Linux and Windows, and many UNIX platforms. Features include an ISP mode with support for automatic log rotation and generation for many virtual domains. Individual virtual domain holders can log in and edit their own settings in a controlled environment. Wusage is available from www.boutell.com/wusage and it is shareware.

When to Analyze the Apache Log Files

Now that you have set up the Apache environment to generate log files with the name, location, and format you wish, the question then becomes, When do I look at them? The type of information you are looking for will help to determine the frequency of log analysis. Factors that come into play include the nature of the Web site's information. Does the Web site contain sensitive or private information? If it does, you will want to look at the log files at least once a day, if not more, to make sure there are no unauthorized access attempts (or successes) to the Web site. Also note that unauthorized attempts may not be just a one time event. The individual attempting to gain access may try several times for short periods of time, over a long period, and/or at random intervals. In this situation, it is important to track trends and/or events over the course of several days and/or weeks. For this type of analysis, some of the log analysis tools we mentioned earlier in this chapter may be of assistance. If your Web site does not contain sensitive information and does not contain time dependent information or data, then checking the log files once or a few times a week may be sufficient. In the early stages of your new Web sites and servers, check the log files often and then, using the information you have collected, determine what is an appropriate log analysis interval.

Monitoring Apache

Apache includes a module called mod_status that provides information about the Web server. When the module is enabled in Apache the information it collects is viewed with a browser. The mod_status module is compiled by default into the version of Apache for Linux. It is not included by default into the Apache binary for Windows but it can be enabled as a DSO with the httpd.conf file. To use mod_status on Windows 2000 systems running Apache, look for the following information in the httpd.conf file:

```
#
# Dynamic Shared Object (DSO) Support
#
# To be able to use the functionality of a module which was built as a DSO you
# have to place corresponding `LoadModule' lines at this location so the
# directives contained in it are actually available _before_ they are used.
# Please read the file README.DSO in the Apache 1.3 distribution for more
# details about the DSO mechanism and run `apache -l' for the list of already
# built-in (statically linked and thus always available) modules in your Apache
# binary.
#
# Note: The order in which modules are loaded is important.  Don't change
# the order below without expert advice.
#
#LoadModule anon_auth_module modules/mod_auth_anon.so
#LoadModule dbm_auth_module modules/mod_auth_dbm.so
#LoadModule digest_auth_module modules/mod_auth_digest.so
#LoadModule cern_meta_module modules/mod_cern_meta.so
#LoadModule digest_module modules/mod_digest.so
#LoadModule expires_module modules/mod_expires.so
#LoadModule headers_module modules/mod_headers.so
#LoadModule proxy_module modules/mod_proxy.so
#LoadModule rewrite_module modules/mod_rewrite.so
#LoadModule speling_module modules/mod_speling.so
#LoadModule info_module modules/mod_info.so
#LoadModule status_module modules/mod_status.so
#LoadModule usertrack_module modules/mod_usertrack.so
```

The pound sign or hash mark (#) at the beginning of the line indicates that the item is not loaded. To enable the mod_status module, remove the # sign at the beginning of the appropriate line and save the file. In the example above, the appropriate line is the second to last item in the list. Once the change to the httpd.conf file is made, the Apache service on the Windows 2000 system will need to be restarted. This can be done from the Services tool in the Administration Tools menu, the net command, or by selecting Restart from the Control Apache Server menu which is found under the Apache httpd Server menu. Once the service has been restarted, then you can access the information collected by the mod_status module.

To observe the information produced by mod_status, add the file name server-status at the end of the URL of the Web server. For example, to view the server status page for Ouray Mountain Water company's Employee Web server, the address is:

```
http://employee.ouraymountainwater.com/server-status
```

The data collected by mod_status on the Employee Web server is shown in Figure 7.15.

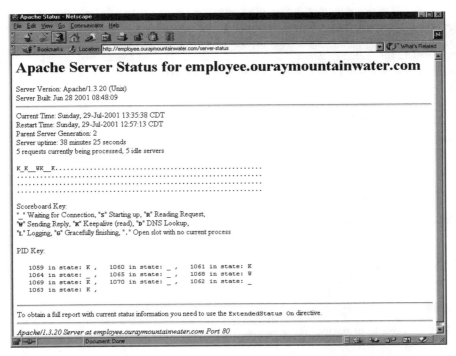

Figure 7.15   Example of a mod_status server status page for Apache on Linux.

Once mod_status is enabled in a Windows 2000 system, you access the information through the same syntax; that is, URL of the Web server plus server-status. For example, to view the server status page for Ouray Mountain Water's Windows 2000 Production Apache Web server, the address is:

```
http://production.ouraymountainwater.com/server-status
```

The data collected by mod_status on the Production Web server is shown in Figures 7.16 and 7.17.

The details presented include:

- The time the server was started/restarted and its running time
- The current hosts and requests being processed
- The number of children (Web server child process) serving requests
- The number of idle children
- The status of each child

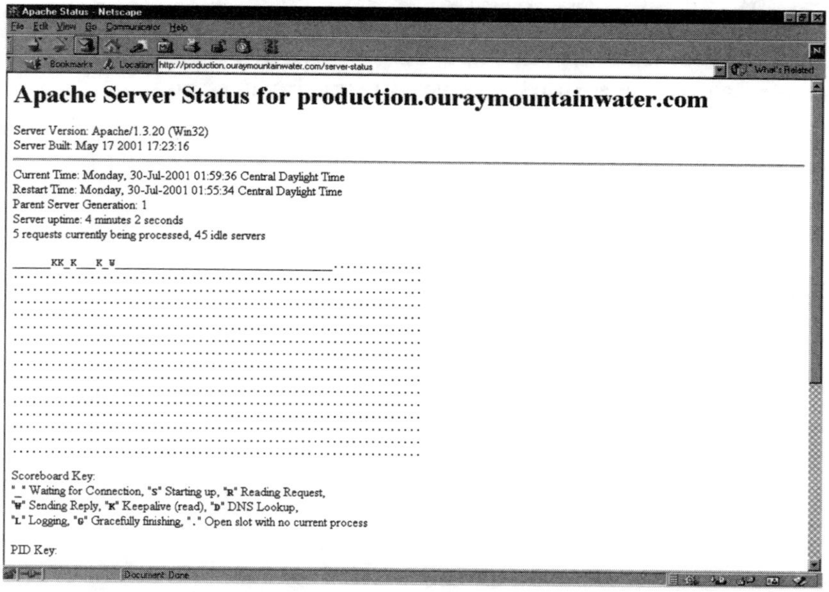

Figure 7.16 Example of a mod_status server status page for Apache on Windows 2000, part 1.

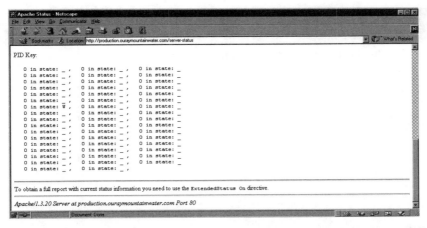

Figure 7.17 Example of a mod_status server status page for Apache on Windows 2000, part 2.

You can collect more information by enabling the ExtendedStatus directive in the httpd.conf file. By default ExtendedStatus is not enabled. To activate the directive, look for the following in the httpd.conf file:

```
#
# ExtendedStatus controls whether Apache will generate "full" status
# information (ExtendedStatus On) or just basic information (ExtendedStatus
# Off) when the "server-status" handler is called. The default is Off.
#
#ExtendedStatus On
```

Remove the pound sign (#) in front of the ExtendedStatus On line and save the changes to the httpd.conf file. This change is the same for the httpd.conf file on a Linux or Windows 2000 Apache system. To activate the extended features of the server status page, the Web service will need to be restarted. To access the extended information, use the same address we discussed previously for viewing the server-status page. Figures 7.18 and 7.19 illustrate the extended status information for Ouray Mountain Water's Employee Linux Apache Web server.

Figures 7.20 through 7.23 display the extended information gathered from Ouray Mountain Water's Windows 2000 Apache Web server called Production.

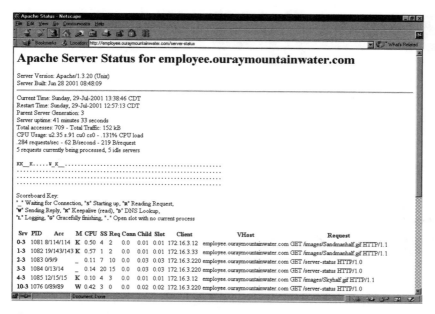

Figure 7.18 Sample extended server status page for Apache on Linux, part 1.

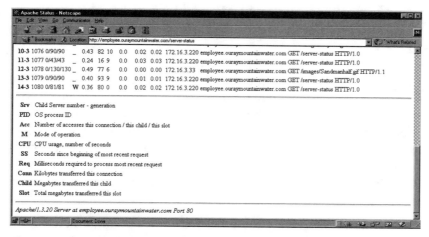

Figure 7.19 Sample extended server status page for Apache on Linux, part 2.

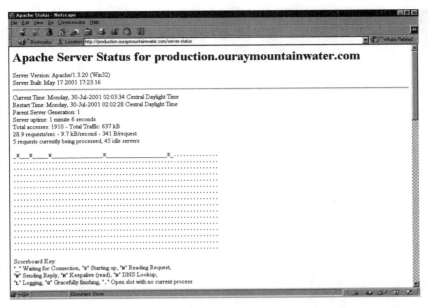

Figure 7.20   Sample extended server status page for Apache on Windows 2000, part 1.

Srv	PID	Acc	M	SS	Req	Conn	Child	Slot	Client	VHost	Request
0-0	0	0/3/3	_	3	0	0.0	0.02	0.02	172.16.3.220	(unavailable)	GET /server-status HTTP/1.0
1-0	0	2/60/60	K	1	0	0.0	0.00	0.00	172.16.3.33	(unavailable)	GET /images/loginbutton.gif HTTP/1.1
2-0	0	0/2/2	_	3	0	0.0	0.01	0.01	172.16.3.220	(unavailable)	GET /server-status HTTP/1.0
3-0	0	0/95/95	_	11	0	0.0	0.00	0.01	172.16.3.12	(unavailable)	GET /images/Blissgrain.jpg HTTP/1.1
4-0	0	0/9/9	_	3	0	0.0	0.01	0.01	172.16.3.12	(unavailable)	GET / HTTP/1.1
5-0	0	6/35/35	K	0	0	0.0	0.01	0.01	172.16.3.12	(unavailable)	GET /images/Skyhalf.gif HTTP/1.1
6-0	0	0/38/38	_	2	0	0.0	0.02	0.02	172.16.3.220	(unavailable)	GET /server-status HTTP/1.0
7-0	0	0/21/21	_	1	0	0.0	0.02	0.02	172.16.3.220	(unavailable)	GET /server-status HTTP/1.0
8-0	0	0/102/102	_	6	0	0.0	0.01	0.01	172.16.3.220	(unavailable)	GET /server-status HTTP/1.0
9-0	0	0/102/102	_	6	0	0.0	0.01	0.01	172.16.3.220	(unavailable)	GET /server-status HTTP/1.0
10-0	0	0/3/3	_	11	0	0.0	0.02	0.02	172.16.3.220	(unavailable)	GET /server-status HTTP/1.0
11-0	0	0/2/2	W	0	0	0.0	0.01	0.01	172.16.3.220	(unavailable)	GET /server-status HTTP/1.0
12-0	0	0/44/44	_	10	0	0.0	0.00	0.00	172.16.3.12	(unavailable)	GET / HTTP/1.1
13-0	0	0/82/82	_	7	0	0.0	0.01	0.01	172.16.3.12	(unavailable)	GET /images/Sandmanhalf.gif HTTP/1.1
14-0	0	0/10/10	_	10	0	0.0	0.01	0.01	172.16.3.220	(unavailable)	GET /server-status HTTP/1.0
15-0	0	0/2/2	_	10	0	0.0	0.02	0.02	172.16.3.220	(unavailable)	GET /server-status HTTP/1.0
16-0	0	0/1/1	_	11	0	0.0	0.01	0.01	172.16.3.220	(unavailable)	GET /server-status HTTP/1.0
17-0	0	0/32/32	_	8	0	0.0	0.01	0.01	172.16.3.220	(unavailable)	GET /server-status HTTP/1.0
18-0	0	0/132/132	_	4	0	0.0	0.00	0.00	172.16.3.12	(unavailable)	GET /images/Blissgrain.jpg HTTP/1.1
19-0	0	0/9/9	_	10	0	0.0	0.01	0.01	172.16.3.33	(unavailable)	GET /images/Sandmanhalf.gif HTTP/1.1
20-0	0	0/4/4	_	8	0	0.0	0.02	0.02	172.16.3.220	(unavailable)	GET /server-status HTTP/1.0
21-0	0	0/2/2	_	9	0	0.0	0.02	0.02	172.16.3.220	(unavailable)	GET /server-status HTTP/1.0
22-0	0	0/4/4	_	9	0	0.0	0.01	0.01	172.16.3.220	(unavailable)	GET /server-status HTTP/1.0
23-0	0	0/101/101	_	8	0	0.0	0.00	0.00	172.16.3.33	(unavailable)	GET / HTTP/1.1
24-0	0	0/81/81	_	10	0	0.0	0.00	0.00	172.16.3.33	(unavailable)	GET /images/Sandmanhalf.gif HTTP/1.1
25-0	0	0/2/2	_	8	0	0.0	0.02	0.02	172.16.3.220	(unavailable)	GET /server-status HTTP/1.0

Figure 7.21   Sample extended server status page for Apache on Windows 2000, part 2.

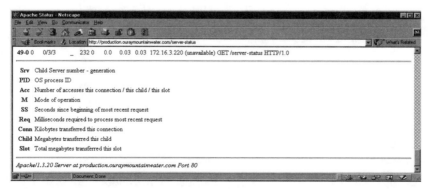

Figure 7.22 Sample extended server status page for Apache on Windows 2000, part 3.

The extended status option displays additional information such as:

- The number of requests that child has performed and the total number of bytes served by the child
- The total number of accesses and byte count delivered
- Average values for the number of requests per second, the number of bytes served per second and the average number of bytes per request

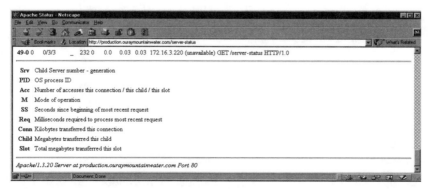

Figure 7.23 Sample extended server status page for Apache on Windows 2000, part 4.

- The current percentage CPU used by each child and the total used by Apache

The version of Apache for Linux also gives you the ability to display the information produced by mod_status at a command line. In order for this to function, the mod_status module must be enabled in Apache. In addition, the Linux system needs to have a text based Web browser available so the information can be properly displayed. A common text-based Web browser for Linux is Lynx and it is found on many Linux distributions. If your system does not have Lynx available, you can install it from your Linux installation CDs or from the Internet. The information presented can be the extended status data if the ExtendedStatus directive is enabled or regular status if the directive is not activated. To collect the information, the apachectl controlling script is used with the appropriate options. For example, to gather the regular, non-extended information, use the syntax:

```
apacehctl status
```

Executing this on Ouray Mountain Water's Employee Linux Apache Web server generated the following information:

```
Apache Server Status for employee.ouraymountainwater.com

    Server Version: Apache/1.3.20 (Unix)
    Server Built: Jun 28 2001 08:48:09
    _____

    Current Time: Sunday, 29-Jul-2001 15:43:10 CDT
    Restart Time: Sunday, 29-Jul-2001 12:57:13 CDT
    Parent Server Generation: 4
    Server uptime: 2 hours 45 minutes 57 seconds
    5 requests currently being processed, 4 idle servers
K___.K_KKW.................................................
...........................................................
...........................................................
...........................................................

    Scoreboard Key:
    "_" Waiting for Connection, "S" Starting up, "R" Reading Request,
    "W" Sending Reply, "K" Keepalive (read), "D" DNS Lookup,
    "L" Logging,  "G" Gracefully finishing, "." Open slot with no current
    process
```

The apachectl script also supports a fullstatus option that gives a little more information even when the ExtendedStatus directive is not enabled. For example, executing apachectl fullstatus on the Employee Web server revealed the following information:

```
Apache Server Status for employee.ouraymountainwater.com

    Server Version: Apache/1.3.20 (Unix)
    Server Built: Jun 28 2001 08:48:09
    _____


    Current Time: Sunday, 29-Jul-2001 15:44:04 CDT
    Restart Time: Sunday, 29-Jul-2001 12:57:13 CDT
    Parent Server Generation: 4
    Server uptime: 2 hours 46 minutes 51 seconds
    5 requests currently being processed, 4 idle servers
__KK.WK__K.......................................................
.................................................................
.................................................................
.................................................................

    Scoreboard Key:
    "_" Waiting for Connection, "S" Starting up, "R" Reading Request,
    "W" Sending Reply, "K" Keepalive (read), "D" DNS Lookup,
    "L"  Logging,  "G" Gracefully finishing, "." Open slot with no current
    process

    PID Key:
    1189 in state: _ ,   1190 in state: _ ,   1193 in state: K
    1194 in state: K ,   1145 in state: W ,   1146 in state: K
    1147 in state: _ ,   1148 in state: _ ,   1149 in state: K
    _____


    To  obtain  a  full report with current status information you need to
    use the ExtendedStatus On directive.
    _____


    Apache/1.3.20 Server at employee.ouraymountainwater.com Port 80
```

When the ExtendedStatus directive is enabled, executing apachectl status on the Employee Web server generated the following data:

```
Apache Server Status for employee.ouraymountainwater.com

    Server Version: Apache/1.3.20 (Unix)
    Server Built: Jun 28 2001 08:48:09
    _____


    Current Time: Sunday, 29-Jul-2001 15:46:24 CDT
    Restart Time: Sunday, 29-Jul-2001 12:57:13 CDT
    Parent Server Generation: 5
    Server uptime: 2 hours 49 minutes 11 seconds
    Total accesses: 904 - Total Traffic: 227 kB
    CPU Usage: u1.38 s.56 cu0 cs0 - .0191% CPU load
    .0891 requests/sec - 22 B/second - 257 B/request
```

```
   5 requests currently being processed, 3 idle servers
KW_.K.....K__K.................................................
...............................................................
...............................................................
...............................................................

   Scoreboard Key:
   "_" Waiting for Connection, "S" Starting up, "R" Reading Request,
   "W" Sending Reply, "K" Keepalive (read), "D" DNS Lookup,
   "L"  Logging,  "G" Gracefully finishing, "." Open slot with no current
   process
```

This produces slightly more information than status even when the Extended-Status directive is not enabled. However, executing apachectl fullstatus when ExtendedStatus is activated, generates more information. For example, the output of fullstatus with the ExtendedStatus directive activated on the Employee Web server revealed the following data:

```
Apache Server Status for employee.ouraymountainwater.com

   Server Version: Apache/1.3.20 (Unix)
   Server Built: Jun 28 2001 08:48:09
   _____

   Current Time: Sunday, 29-Jul-2001 15:46:48 CDT
   Restart Time: Sunday, 29-Jul-2001 12:57:13 CDT
   Parent Server Generation: 5
   Server uptime: 2 hours 49 minutes 35 seconds
   Total accesses: 1099 - Total Traffic: 231 kB
   CPU Usage: u1.26 s.52 cu0 cs0 - .0175% CPU load
   .108 requests/sec - 23 B/second - 215 B/request
   5 requests currently being processed, 4 idle servers
____W.....KKKK.................................................
...............................................................
...............................................................
...............................................................

   Scoreboard Key:
   "_" Waiting for Connection, "S" Starting up, "R" Reading Request,
   "W" Sending Reply, "K" Keepalive (read), "D" DNS Lookup,
   "L"  Logging,  "G" Gracefully finishing, "." Open slot with no current
   process

   Srv PID Acc M CPU SS Req Conn Child Slot Client VHost Request
   0-5   1251   0/52/168   _   0.23   1   2   0.0   0.00   0.01   172.16.3.12
   employee.ouraymountainwater.com GET /images/Sandmanhalf.gif HTTP/1.1
   1-5   1252   0/5/168    _   0.03   3   2   0.0   0.00   0.02   172.16.3.12
   employee.ouraymountainwater.com GET /images/Sandmanhalf.gif HTTP/1.1
   2-5   1253   0/5/16     _   0.04   3   2   0.0   0.00   0.03   172.16.3.12
   employee.ouraymountainwater.com GET /images/02people.gif HTTP/1.1
```

```
3-5   1260  0/33/49   _  0.15   1   2  0.0  0.00  0.04  172.16.3.12
employee.ouraymountainwater.com GET /images/Skyhalf.gif HTTP/1.1
4-5   1246  0/72/72   W  0.21  22   0  0.0  0.02  0.02  127.0.0.1
employee.ouraymountainwater.com GET /server-status HTTP/1.0
10-5  1247  4/150/150 K  0.22   0   2  0.0  0.03  0.03  172.16.3.12
employee.ouraymountainwater.com GET /images/Skyhalf.gif HTTP/1.1
11-5  1248  32/97/97  K  0.27   0   2  0.0  0.03  0.03  172.16.3.33
employee.ouraymountainwater.com GET /images/Skyhalf.gif HTTP/1.1
12-5  1249  33/184/184 K 0.16   0   2  0.0  0.01  0.01  172.16.3.33
employee.ouraymountainwater.com GET /images/Sandmanhalf.gif HTTP/1.1
13-5  1250  6/112/112 K  0.09   0   2  0.0  0.02  0.02  172.16.3.12
employee.ouraymountainwater.com GET /images/Sandmanhalf.gif HTTP/1.1
14-3   - 0/83/83 . 0.38 7603 9 0.0 0.02 0.02 172.16.3.220 (unavailable)
GET /server-status HTTP/1.0
```

```
Srv   Child Server number - generation
PID   OS process ID
Acc   Number of accesses this connection / this child / this slot
  M   Mode of operation
CPU   CPU usage, number of seconds
 SS   Seconds since beginning of most recent request
 Req  Milliseconds required to process most recent request
Conn  Kilobytes transferred this connection
Child Megabytes transferred this child
Slot  Total megabytes transferred this slot
```

```
Apache/1.3.20 Server at employee.ouraymountainwater.com Port 80
```

Note that the information generated by apachectl at the command line is the same information visible from a graphical Web browser.

The Apache package comes equipped with a benchmarking tool that runs on Linux systems. The tool is located in the default location of /usr/local/apache/bin and it is called ab for ApacheBench. The idea behind this tool is to determine the capacity level of the Web server. The options for ab include items such as the number of requests, including concurrent requests, for a period of time. For example, let's say you wanted to test the capability of the Ouray Mountain Water Employee Web server for handling 100 requests (-n) with 10 requests occurring simultaneously (-c) each time. The syntax for ab would be:

```
ab -n 100 -c 10 employee.ouraymountainwater.com/
```

This command results in the following information:

```
This is ApacheBench, Version 1.3c <$Revision: 1.45 $> apache-1.3
```

```
Copyright (c) 1996 Adam Twiss, Zeus Technology Ltd, http://www.zeustech.net/
Copyright (c) 1998-2000 The Apache Group, http://www.apache.org/

Benchmarking employee.ouraymountainwater.com (be patient)...

Server Software:        Apache/1.3.20
Server Hostname:        employee.ouraymountainwater.com
Server Port:            80

Document Path:          /
Document Length:        3086 bytes

Concurrency Level:      10
Time taken for tests:   0.873 seconds
Complete requests:      100
Failed requests:        0
Total transferred:      333400 bytes
HTML transferred:       308600 bytes
Requests per second:    114.55
Transfer rate:          381.90 kb/s received

Connnection Times (ms)
             min   avg   max
Connect:      15    37    55
Processing:   63    46    31
Total:        78    83    86
```

You can also specify a time period and the benchmark tool will automatically set the number of requests to 50000. For example, let's test the Employee Web server for 30 seconds (-t) and see what happens. The syntax of the ab command is:

```
ab -t 30 employee.ouraymountainwater.com/
```

The result of the ab command with the time option reveals the following information:

```
This is ApacheBench, Version 1.3c <$Revision: 1.45 $> apache-1.3
Copyright (c) 1996 Adam Twiss, Zeus Technology Ltd, http://www.zeustech.net/
Copyright (c) 1998-2000 The Apache Group, http://www.apache.org/

Benchmarking employee.ouraymountainwater.com (be patient)...

Server Software:        Apache/1.3.20
Server Hostname:        employee.ouraymountainwater.com
Server Port:            80

Document Path:          /
Document Length:        3086 bytes
```

```
Concurrency Level:       1
Time taken for tests:    30.008 seconds
Complete requests:       3358
Failed requests:         0
Total transferred:       11195572 bytes
HTML transferred:        10362788 bytes
Requests per second:     111.90
Transfer rate:           373.09 kb/s received


Connnection Times (ms)
              min    avg    max
Connect:        1      1      4
Processing:     6      6     14
Total:          7      7     18
```

Now let's check for the same time period but add 500 simultaneous requests. In this case, the ab syntax is:

```
ab -t 30 -c 500 employee.ouraymountainwater.com/
```

The information from this ab command reveals the following data:

```
This is ApacheBench, Version 1.3c <$Revision: 1.45 $> apache-1.3
Copyright (c) 1996 Adam Twiss, Zeus Technology Ltd, http://www.zeustech.net/
Copyright (c) 1998-2000 The Apache Group, http://www.apache.org/


Benchmarking employee.ouraymountainwater.com (be patient)...

Server Software:         Apache/1.3.20
Server Hostname:         employee.ouraymountainwater.com
Server Port:             80

Document Path:           /
Document Length:         3086 bytes

Concurrency Level:       500
Time taken for tests:    30.978 seconds
Complete requests:       3002
Failed requests:         0
Total transferred:       10508768 bytes
HTML transferred:        9727072 bytes
Requests per second:     96.91
Transfer rate:           339.23 kb/s received

Connnection Times (ms)
              min    avg    max
Connect:        7    754  21398
Processing:   379   1988   3502
Total:        386   2742  24900
```

You can also add the –w option to the ab command to output the data in html format. Thus, you can redirect the output to an html file and view the information from a browser. For example, the ab command syntax to generate an html file for the same testing conditions as above is:

```
ab -t 30 -c 500 -w employee.ouraymountainwater.com/ > ¬
/usr/local/content/htdocs/abdata.html
```

The information generated results in a Web page that looks similar to Figure 7.24.

NOTE Make sure the name of the system or IP number you use in the ab command has a trailing forward slash at the end. If this is missing you will see help about using ab rather than the results you expect.

From the data collected from the ab utility, it appears that the capacity of the Web server is around 90 pages per second with up to 500 simultaneous requests. Those values are quite acceptable for the Employee Web server since the only users accessing the system are employees of the Ouray Mountain Water company. FYI: For the ApacheBench results used in this section, the

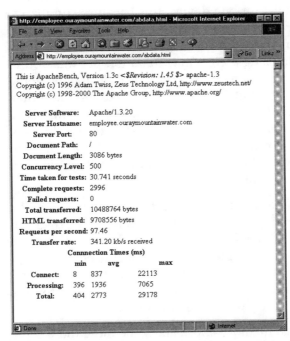

Figure 7.24 Results of the ab command viewed in a Web Browser.

Employee Web server is running on a P90 machine with 48MB of RAM! At this stage in the development cycle, the Employee server is running on a test system. The released version of the Employee server will be housed on a newer, more powerful machine. However, even on a 90MHz machine, Apache running on Linux doesn't do too badly!

Optimizing Apache

Now that you have used some of the methods described here to gather information about your Web server, and determined that you may need to do some optimizing, what are some of things you can tweak? There are two main areas to address when it comes to possible optimization: Apache and the server system running the Web service. In this section we cover software based optimization areas since we are assuming the hardware you are using is sufficient for the operating system and services. After all, if the hardware is lacking, nothing on the software side can overcome hardware limitations!

For server systems of any operating system, one area to help improve performance is to run a bare bones environment. By this we mean, do not load services, drivers, and/or applications for items that are not used. For example, having a driver loaded for a device that is not used occupies some memory and uses some processor resources to maintain its presence in the operating system. While this may seem trivial for one device, this becomes cumulative when more and more devices are loaded and not used. A good place to start with just the necessities is when you are installing Linux and/or Windows 2000. For both environments, choosing a custom installation permits you to choose exactly what you want installed. It may take a little longer going through all the options and choices, but it may actually take less time than going back later and removing all the stuff that is not needed. Also, installing fewer items reduces the chances of a negative interaction between different services, drivers, and/or applications. However, if it turns out you forgot to include something when your were installing the operating system, you can always go back and add the component at another time.

On Linux environments you can further trim down the core elements of the core operating system by recompiling the Linux kernel. Many of the distributions install a Linux kernel that contains support for lots of different hardware that may not be on your system. For example, you will probably not need support for PCMCIA or sound on a Linux server. Use the lsmod command to find out what modules are loaded and use that information as a guideline for any changes you want to make when recompiling the Linux kernel.

Servers, in general, like physical memory and usually the more there is the happier they are. Because a Web server is constantly sending out the same information to the same or different users simultaneously, it is much more efficient to keep the Web pages in the server's memory instead of retrieving the files from the disk. To determine how much memory is needed, use some of the techniques we mentioned earlier in this chapter to find out how much memory the operating system and Apache are using when users are not accessing the Web content. Then add up the file sizes of the Web content. This gives you a rough idea of how much memory space the Web content occupies when the pages are loaded. If there is not enough physical memory to hold the operating system, Apache, and the Web content, then your system may begin to use more virtual memory or swap space. Monitor the virtual memory and swap space usage of the Web server and if necessary, add more physical memory. On Linux systems, if your system does need to use swap space, place the swap space on a separate drive or partition different from the location of the Web content.

Servers are meant to run the service(s) they are assigned for and are not meant to be local desktop operating systems. For example, on Linux systems, there is no need to keep the X Window system loaded when it is not being used by anybody or any application. On Windows 2000 systems, the graphical environment is always there, but there are some things you can do to reduce resource usage by the GUI. One item that really impacts processor performance is screen savers. Some of these take over 50 percent of the available processor time when they are running! There is no need to use a screen saver at all on a server system—just turn the monitor off! In addition to freeing up the processor by not running a screen saver, you also save on electricity and generate less heat! Another item that uses up resources on a Windows 2000 system is sound and/or multimedia. Sound is not necessary for a Windows 2000 server running Apache so turn off the alert sounds through the Control Panels. Some server Administrators remove the drivers for sound and other multimedia devices on Windows 2000 servers since these are not necessary.

On Windows 2000 another item to consider for improving performance is disabling the Indexing Service from indexing the information on the disks. Apache does not use the information collected by the Indexing Service since Apache contains its own indexing capabilities. To turn off this feature, open the Properties window for a drive letter/partition and remove the checkbox next to the item Allow Indexing Service to index this disk for fast file searching. When you choose Apply or OK a Confirm Attribute Changes window appears asking if you want to disable indexing for the root of the selected drive or for all subfolders and files. Since we don't need this service for any of the files, choose the option to apply the changes to the drive and all subfolders and files. Depending on the size of the drive and the number of files and folders, this process may take awhile.

Over the course of time, if the disks on the Windows 2000 system are performing a lot of writing, the contents of the disk may become fragmented. A fragmented disk means the contents of files are spread all over the disk in segments instead of occupying contiguous areas on the disk. Accessing a fragmented drive requires the disk drives to work "harder" and can impact the speed of retrieving files. To check if a drive is fragmented, choose the Computer Management tool from the Administrative Tools menu. In the left pane of the tool, select Disk Defragmenter and in the right pane choose the drive letter of the disk you want to check. On the bottom area of the window, click on the Analyze button and the tool will begin checking the disk and will display the results in graphical form in the middle of the screen. Once the analysis is finished, an Analysis Complete window appears. In this window you can choose View Report which displays the information in text so you can see if the drive is fragmented. If you decide the drive or drives need defragmenting you can start the process within the Computer Management tool.

NOTE Before beginning a defragmentation, make sure you have a reliable backup of the data on the drives. In addition, the defragmentation process may take quite a long period of time so it should be scheduled when the system is not in use. On Linux systems, defragmentation is not an issue because of the method in which files are stored on the partitions.

Apache itself can be trimmed down and optimized to improve performance. Probably the best way is to look at the modules included in the Apache binary. The pre-compiled Apache binary, or one that is compiled with the default setup, may contain modules that you don't need. By evaluating what type of content your Web server will be hosting, you may be able to eliminate some modules. For example, if our Web site does not support user directories, you can exclude mod_userdir. If all of the Web content directories have index files, you can eliminate using the mod_autoindex module. If your Web site does not contain imagemaps, consider removing the use of the mod_imap module. Similarly, if you are not using any asis files, the mod_asis module can be excluded. In addition, you may not want some of the monitoring capabilities, such as mod_status, included. However, if you wish to keep mod_status, then consider not enabling the ExtendedStatus directive. The ExtendedStatus directive is not enabled by default in the httpd.conf file. In any case, if you decide to not include a module, you will need to make the appropriate changes to the source code files and recompile Apache.

Another important Apache on Linux performance issue is making sure the Web server is running as a standalone and that it was not started by a system process. You can run Apache as either a daemon (standalone) or it can be started by the system process inetd. The daemon or standalone choice is highly recommended. If you choose to use inetd, then each time a request comes into the Web server a new copy of the Web server is launched. This introduces a lot of overhead in the system when creating and closing down the application. The way Apache is running is configured with the ServerType directive in the httpd.conf file.

```
#
# ServerType is either inetd, or standalone.  Inetd mode is only supported on
# Unix platforms.
#
ServerType standalone
```

The default setting in the httpd.conf file for ServerType is standalone.

When Apache on Linux starts up it creates a Web server pool with a minimum number of httpd processes. When users begin accessing the Web server, additional processes are created in the pool as needed to handle multiple simultaneous requests. When the upper limit of the pool size is reached, additional processes are still created but they are terminated after servicing one request. Thus, the Apache Web server pool's size is based on the current system load instead of fixed upper and lower limits. The specifications for the Apache Web server pool are controlled by directives in the httpd.conf file.

```
#
# Server-pool size regulation.  Rather than making you guess how many
# server processes you need, Apache dynamically adapts to the load it
# sees --- that is, it tries to maintain enough server processes to
# handle the current load, plus a few spare servers to handle transient
# load spikes (e.g., multiple simultaneous requests from a single
# Netscape browser).
#
# It does this by periodically checking how many servers are waiting
# for a request.  If there are fewer than MinSpareServers, it creates
# a new spare.  If there are more than MaxSpareServers, some of the
# spares die off.  The default values are probably OK for most sites.
#
MinSpareServers 5
MaxSpareServers 10


#
# Number of servers to start initially --- should be a reasonable ballpark
# figure.
#
StartServers 5
```

The Linux Apache Web server will initially start the number of servers specified by the StartServers directive. Then the Apache server checks the status of the processes in the server pool every few seconds. If the number of idle servers falls below the value set by MinSpareServers, extra servers are created at the rate of one per second. If the number of idle servers exceeds the value set by MaxSpareServers, the extra servers are removed. The default settings for these directives indicate that the Apache server starts five servers, makes sure that there are always at least five idle servers, and does not let the number of idle servers exceed ten.

Another directive related to the server pool is the MaxRequestPerChild setting. This value specifies the maximum number of requests a child process can service. When this value is reached, the process is removed and a new one is created to handle the requests. This directive was created in case of a problem with a corrupted server process or a memory leak from a new or untested module. With this directive, the process will essentially destroy itself as it processes more requests. Thus, a process cannot go haywire and bring down the system. This directive is set in the httpd.conf file:

```
#
# MaxRequestsPerChild: the number of requests each child process is
# allowed to process before the child dies.  The child will exit so
# as to avoid problems after prolonged use when Apache (and maybe the
# libraries it uses) leak memory or other resources.  On most systems, this
# isn't really needed, but a few (such as Solaris) do have notable leaks
# in the libraries. For these platforms, set to something like 10000
# or so; a setting of 0 means unlimited.
#
# NOTE: This value does not include keepalive requests after the initial
#       request per connection. For example, if a child process handles
#       an initial request and 10 subsequent "keptalive" requests, it
#       would only count as 1 request towards this limit.
#
MaxRequestsPerChild 0
```

The default setting for MaxRequestPerChild is 0, which means there is no limit set. There are no memory leaks in Linux so leaving the value at zero will not create problems. If you are testing a new module and are not sure if there may be coding problems, you may want to set the MaxRequestPerChild to something like 100 or 200.

Windows 2000 Apache servers handle items a little differently than Linux. For example, let's look at the appropriate section of the httpd.conf file:

```
#
# Apache on Win32 always creates one child process to handle requests.  If it
# dies, another child process is created automatically.  Within the child
# process multiple threads handle incoming requests.  The next two
# directives control the behaviour of the threads and processes.
#
```

```
#
# MaxRequestsPerChild: the number of requests each child process is
# allowed to process before the child dies.  The child will exit so
# as to avoid problems after prolonged use when Apache (and maybe the
# libraries it uses) leak memory or other resources.  On most systems, this
# isn't really needed, but a few (such as Solaris) do have notable leaks
# in the libraries.  For Win32, set this value to zero (unlimited)
# unless advised otherwise.
#
# NOTE: This value does not include keepalive requests after the initial
#       request per connection. For example, if a child process handles
#       an initial request and 10 subsequent "keptalive" requests, it
#       would only count as 1 request towards this limit.
#
MaxRequestsPerChild 0


#
# Number of concurrent threads (i.e., requests) the server will allow.
# Set this value according to the responsiveness of the server (more
# requests active at once means they're all handled more slowly) and
# the amount of system resources you'll allow the server to consume.
#
ThreadsPerChild 50
```

On Windows 2000 there is not a pool of Web server processes but instead one process is created. However, you can set the number of simultaneous requests that the process can handle. This is specified with the ThreadsPer-Child directive and the default setting is 50. If you increase this value, make sure the change does not impact the performance of the Web server.

On Linux systems running Apache, the MaxClients directive in the httpd.conf file allows you to specify the maximum number of simultaneous connections to the Web server.

```
#
# Limit on total number of servers running, i.e., limit on the number
# of clients who can simultaneously connect --- if this limit is ever
# reached, clients will be LOCKED OUT, so it should NOT BE SET TOO LOW.
# It is intended mainly as a brake to keep a runaway server from taking
# the system with it as it spirals down...
#
MaxClients 150
```

On Windows 2000 Apache servers, similar settings are controlled by the ThreadsPerChild directive.

```
#
# Number of concurrent threads (i.e., requests) the server will allow.
```

```
# Set this value according to the responsiveness of the server (more
# requests active at once means they're all handled more slowly) and
# the amount of system resources you'll allow the server to consume.
#
ThreadsPerChild 50
```

The Apache directive, DirectoryIndex, in the httpd.conf file allows you to specify the file to look for and load when a user accesses a directory when a file name is not specified. For example, www.ouraymountainwater.com instead of www.ouraymountainwater.com/index.html. If possible, use only one default file name throughout the Web content directories and then explicitly specify the file name with the DirectoryIndex directive. If you do have more than one file name used in different directories, place the multiple file names with the DirectoryIndex directive in the order they are most used. For example, if most of the content directories use index.html and some use default.html, place index.html first in the list.

```
#
# DirectoryIndex: Name of the file or files to use as a pre-written HTML
# directory index.  Separate multiple entries with spaces.
#
<IfModule mod_dir.c>
    DirectoryIndex index.html default.html
</IfModule>
```

Avoid using a wildcard type lookup for the name of the default Web page. For example,

```
#
# DirectoryIndex: Name of the file or files to use as a pre-written HTML
# directory index.  Separate multiple entries with spaces.
#
<IfModule mod_dir.c>
    DirectoryIndex index
</IfModule>
```

will check for any file in the directory that begins with index. If, for example, the files are named index.html in some directories and index.htm at other locations, use the following format instead:

```
#
# DirectoryIndex: Name of the file or files to use as a pre-written HTML
# directory index.  Separate multiple entries with spaces.
#
<IfModule mod_dir.c>
    DirectoryIndex index.html index.htm
</IfModule>
```

Apache supports the DSO or Dynamic Shared Object architecture, which allows modules to be loaded at runtime instead of contained in the complied binary. This style allows a great deal of flexibility for loading and unloading modules and for testing new components without the need to recompile the binary. The DSO support in Apache is handled by the mod_so module. Overall, DSO does not impact the performance of Apache once the service is started and is running. However, DSO does slow down the initial loading of Apache. In Apache versions prior to 1.3, the mod_so module was not stable and reliable. Therefore, if you plan on using DSO, make sure you are using a version of Apache that is 1.3 or higher. The mod_so module is not compiled by default into the Linux Apache binary but it is included by default in the apache.exe for Windows.

Apache includes the ability to generate logs so you can observe who is accessing the Web server, what they are requesting, and errors. To help improve performance, only log what is necessary for your environment. For example, consider lowering the LogLevel in the httpd.conf file from warn to crit. Another option available for log files is the HostnameLookups directive. This directive places the name of the system accessing the Web server instead of the IP address. However, when HostameLookups is On in the httpd.conf file, the Web server will slow down because for every request, a DNS lookup is initiated. If you need to know the name of the systems accessing the Web server, it is much better for performance reasons to process the log file for DNS lookups after it is collected.

The Apache httpd.conf file also includes the ability to specify different access levels and permissions with the Allow and Deny directives and .htaccess files. Whenever possible, use IP numbers to refer to systems instead of names. When names are used, a DNS lookup is initiated and a reverse name lookup is also generated to prevent spoofing of names. Adding DNS requests on top of everything else that is going on decreases the performance of the Web server. Also, the levels in the directory structure where Allow and Deny are used impacts the performance of the request. In general, use Deny at the root of the directory and then use Allow where necessary lower in the directory structure. This design reduces the checking of access permissions for all the requests coming into the server. Another related factor is to consider limiting the use of .htaccess files. When these are used, the server has to access the file for each request. The use of .htaccess files and Allow and Deny are covered in Chapter 8, "Backup and Security."

After you have finished testing your Apache setup and are ready to go live, make sure the Apache binary you are running is not a debug version. An application that is compiled as a debug version allows the programmer to interact with the running program within the development environment. This permits tracking and tracing of problems and viewing the state of actions and variables.

However, debug versions of applications run slower because of the added overhead of the debugging features so you will want to make sure the final Apache binary is not a debug version.

One final area to touch upon is maintenance of your Linux and/or Apache Web servers. For both operating systems, you should regularly check for updates or patches for the operating system and Apache. Make sure the Web servers have *all* the necessary security patches installed and configured properly for both the operating system and any services. And one final note, documentation. It is important that you keep a record or log of hardware and software details including configuration files and settings. In addition, a change log for both hardware and software is necessary. This information should be readily available in the event there is a failure or problem and you need to look something up. Keeping the information in both electronic and paper form is recommended because if the computer system storing the documentation suddenly fails....

CHAPTER

8

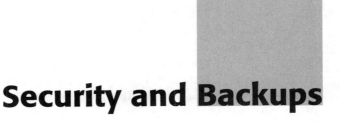

Security and Backups

Once the Apache Web server software is installed, configured, and optimized for best performance, it is imperative to secure the Web content information. It is also important to backup the system so that in case something gets lost, you can quickly recover and get back on line. In this section we take a look at some aspects of securing Apache on both Linux and Windows 2000 systems. At the end of the chapter we address some solutions for backing up the Apache system and data.

Securing Apache

Securing Apache involves the server operating system and the Apache service. If the server system is not secure then it's going to make it much harder, if not impossible, to properly secure the Apache Web service. Linux and Windows 2000 Server security systems are different in many ways but in others they are the same. For example, both systems have users, passwords, and groups to control access to the system and what users can do in the system. Both systems provide a means to set access permissions on files and directories. And finally, both environments have mechanisms to control remote access and activities in the systems. The big differences are in how each system implements these major concepts. While it is outside the scope of this chapter to cover Linux and Windows 2000 Server security, we will address some of the areas to keep in mind concerning the Apache service and the Web server content. No matter what operating systems you are using, you should always be aware of any security issues pertaining to operating systems and the services. A good place to keep abreast of these topics is the SANS Institute, www.sans.org. In addition to all the security related material SANS has online, you can subscribe to an email service that informs you of the security happenings of the week. Also, if there is a destructive event or condition developing, as with the Red Code problem, you will receive an email immediately. Apache on Linux has a long-standing reputation of reliability and good security but it is not invulnerable and there are patches available for any found security holes. It is very important to apply these if they are applicable to the versions of Linux and Apache you are using. Since Apache on Windows 2000, and other Windows platforms, is relatively new, there is very little history developed about any Windows specific Apache security problems. For information about security issues that pertain to the Windows operating system, you can check out the SANS Institute information or Microsoft's security information at www.microsoft.com/security/default.asp.

To protect the Web content, you need to be able to secure the content directories and files from unauthorized access. There are two areas involved in file access, local and remote. If the Web servers support user accounts and allow users to log into the systems from either a local or remote access, the directories and files need to be secured through the server's operating system methods. On Linux Apache Web servers, make sure the proper users are the appropriate owners of the Web content files and other files on the system. In addition, set the file permissions so the necessary users have the rights they need to do their work, but not too many rights. For example, the Web developers who are putting files into the Web server's content directories will need the ability to create and modify files in the document root directory. Similarly, other users on the system who are not Web developers do not need the same permissions the Web developer has on the Web content directory. The same concepts apply to Windows 2000 Server systems. Make sure the Web server and the Web content are on NTFS partitions so the files can be properly secured for both local and remote access.

Here are some suggested access permissions for different user types in the Apache file system:

Web User. Read access to the Web content and, if any scripts are executed on the server side, the Execute permission may be necessary.

Web Developer. Read, Write, and Execute permissions on the document root directory and all subdirectories and files below the Web content directory. They do not need access to the log files, configuration files, or other Apache utilities.

Web Administrator. Read, Write and Execute permissions on the configuration files and the Web content. For the log files and Apache utilities, the Read and Execute permissions are needed.

You can control access to Web content directories and files with Apache in the httpd.conf file through the use of the Allow, Deny, and Order directives. The specifications are defined in the httpd.conf file and can be defined for locations, directories, and files. Within these areas you can control access by IP address, the hostname, or other items in the content of the request. The Allow and Deny directives are used to set the type of access, while the Order specification determines the order in which Allow and Deny are applied. That is, are the Allow rules applied first and then the Deny rules, or are the Deny settings applied first followed by the Allow settings? In most cases, the recommended order is Deny first followed by Allow. This order specifies that everything is set to Deny and permits you to turn on access to only the areas you want. If the order is reversed so that Allow occurs first, then access is permitted to all and you have to go back in and specify denies at multiple levels. Also, the order of Allow followed by Deny opens the possibility of missing an area to deny which could result in unauthorized access to the area. In most cases, the default order is Deny followed by Allow. Let's take a look at some examples of Order, Allow, and Deny at work.

```
#
# This should be changed to whatever you set DocumentRoot to.
#
<Directory "/usr/local/apache/htdocs">

#
# This may also be "None", "All", or any combination of "Indexes",
# "Includes", "FollowSymLinks", "ExecCGI", or "MultiViews".
#
# Note that "MultiViews" must be named *explicitly* --- "Options All"
# doesn't give it to you.
#
    Options Indexes FollowSymLinks MultiViews

#
# This controls which options the .htaccess files in directories can
# override. Can also be "All", or any combination of "Options", "FileInfo",
# "AuthConfig", and "Limit"
#
    AllowOverride None

#
# Controls who can get stuff from this server.
#
    Order allow,deny
```

```
    Allow from all
</Directory>
```

The line beginning with <Directory specifies the location the settings that follow apply to until the next </Directory> line is encountered. In this example, we are looking at the specifications for the Web server's document root directory. The Order statement near the end of the example indicates that Allow is applied first and any Denies would reverse any Allows for the indicated categories. The second to last line:

```
    Allow from all
```

means that anybody is allowed access to the document root directory. In this example, these specifications make sense for the Web server's root directory because users accessing the Web server with their browsers must be able to access the Web pages. If the Allow from all is changed to Deny from all and a user attempts to access the Web site, they will receive something similar to Figure 8.1.

You can also apply restrictions to a specific user or host and/or for a specific service or function. The Ouray Mountain Water's Employee Linux Apache server supports the HTTP PUT command so the Web developers can publish from applications that use HTTP PUT, such as Netscape. To support this type of feature you use a combination of httpd.conf settings and htpasswd files. As an example, let's take a look at what was done in the Employee Web server's httpd.conf file to permit the Web developer to copy files using HTTP PUT to the server. Before any modifications were done, the httpd.conf file section pertaining to securing the Web server's document root directory was as follows:

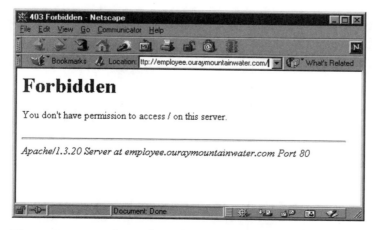

Figure 8.1   Deny from all result in a user's browser.

```
#
# Each directory to which Apache has access, can be configured with respect
# to which services and features are allowed and/or disabled in that
# directory (and its subdirectories).
#
# First, we configure the "default" to be a very restrictive set of
# permissions.
#
<Directory />
    Options FollowSymLinks
    AllowOverride None
</Directory>


#
# Note that from this point forward you must specifically allow
# particular features to be enabled - so if something's not working as
# you might expect, make sure that you have specifically enabled it
# below.
#


#
# This should be changed to whatever you set DocumentRoot to.
#
<Directory "/usr/local/apache/htdocs">


#
# This may also be "None", "All", or any combination of "Indexes",
# "Includes", "FollowSymLinks", "ExecCGI", or "MultiViews".
#
# Note that "MultiViews" must be named *explicitly* --- "Options All"
# doesn't give it to you.
#
    Options Indexes FollowSymLinks MultiViews


#
# This controls which options the .htaccess files in directories can
# override. Can also be "All", or any combination of "Options", "FileInfo",
# "AuthConfig", and "Limit"
#
    AllowOverride None


#
# Controls who can get stuff from this server.
#
    Order allow,deny
    Allow from all
</Directory>
```

The AllowOverride None directive setting prevents the use of files or other methods to override any settings in the Web server's content directory and lower. With that set, for any place we want to apply different settings, we must assign those at the necessary location. In the case of the HTTP PUT, the necessary access settings need to be set at the document root directory. However, we don't everybody being able to publish, just the Web developer. We also want to restrict the usage of one option, HTTP PUT, but not other available functions supported by the Web server. To meet these criteria, the AllowOverride is set to Limit and we define the details of the Limit. In the listing below, the items in bold were those changed or added to the httpd.conf file to support the use of HTTP PUT by the Web developer.

```
#
# This controls which options the .htaccess files in directories can
# override. Can also be "All", or any combination of "Options", "FileInfo",
# "AuthConfig", and "Limit"
#
    AllowOverride Limit


#
# Controls who can get stuff from this server.
#
    Order allow,deny
    Allow from all
    EnablePUT On
    <Limit PUT>
      AuthType Basic
      AuthName "Web Publishing"
      AuthUserFile /usr/local/apache/webpasswd
      require valid-user
    </Limit>
</Directory>
```

The EnablePUT statement turns on the acceptance of HTTP PUT commands by Apache. The items enclosed by the Limit statements restrict who can use the PUT command. When an attempt is made to use PUT, the

```
require valid-user
```

statement directs Apache to look in the /usr/local/apache/webpasswd file:

```
AuthUserFile /usr/local/apache/webpasswd
```

and check if the user attempting access is listed. If the user is not in the list they cannot use the PUT command.

The webpasswd file of permitted users is generated by one of the utilities included with Apache, htpasswd. The htpasswd application is usually located in the same directory as httpd. This first usage of the htpasswd utility creates the file and adds one user to the authorized list. For our examples, bob is the account for one of the Web developers and webpasswd is the name of the PUT permission list we will use. You can use a name other than webpasswd for the name of the file. In our example, at a command prompt in the Apache bin directory, execute the following:

```
./htpasswd --c webpasswd bob
```

At the New password prompt enter the password for bob. Note that this does not have to be the same password used by bob to log into Linux. You will be asked to verify the password again at the Re-type new password prompt. To add another Web developer to an existing PUT permission list, use the htpasswd command again but without the –c (create file) option. For example, to add leeann to the webpasswd file, the syntax would be:

```
./htpasswd webpasswd leeann
```

Again, you will be prompted to enter and verify the password for the user you are adding to the PUT permission list. By the way, the passwords are stored in the PUT permission list file in an encrypted format.

```
leeann:bgbsI02AIPby.
webadmin:oWuAPFSWftRXw
bob:2d/Il4iztxUtk
```

Once you have added all the Web developers to the file, you need to put the file in the location you specified in the httpd.conf file. Notice in the example above we did not place the webpasswd file at the same location as the Web content. This was done for security reasons. If the Web developers have permissions to read and write the contents of the Web content directory and the PUT permission list is at the same location, the file could be accidentally, or intentionally, modified. In our example, the Web developers do not have access to the /usr/local/apache/ directory. For additional security you can hide the htpasswd generated file by placing a period at the beginning of the name. Once you have made the appropriate changes to the httpd.conf file, you will need to restart the Apache Web server.

Note that you can also place the directives permitting the use of the HTTP PUT command in an .htaccess file in the document root directory. However, using .htaccess files slows down the performance of the Web server because of the added overhead of accessing and reading the .htaccess file for each request to the directory by users browsing the Web server.

Another item to keep in mind is that any of the methods that implement a password mechanism send the password across the network media as clear text. However, if you implement SSL, the password information is not sent as clear text.

Apache, like most Web servers, supports the use of symbolic links, which are essentially pointers to another file or directory. The support for this feature is configured in the httpd.conf file. For example, let's examine a portion of the httpd.conf file from the Ouray Mountain Water company's Employee Apache Linux server:

```
#
# Each directory to which Apache has access, can be configured with respect
# to which services and features are allowed and/or disabled in that
# directory (and its subdirectories).
#
# First, we configure the "default" to be a very restrictive set of
# permissions.
#
<Directory />
    Options FollowSymLinks
    AllowOverride None
</Directory>

#
# Note that from this point forward you must specifically allow
# particular features to be enabled - so if something's not working as
# you might expect, make sure that you have specifically enabled it
# below.
#
```

Notice that, by default, Apache is configured to follow symbolic links. The FollowSymLinks option tells Apache to go to the location referenced in the link regardless of who the owner of the linked location is. Thus, a link could traverse out of the Web content directory structure into someplace else in the file system. To make sure that the link only follows to a location that is owned by the same user as the link itself, consider changing the Options line to (in bold):

```
<Directory />
    Options FollowSymLinksIfOwnerMatch
    AllowOverride None
</Directory>
```

If your Web site is supporting links, using FollowSymLinksIfOwnerMatch is a better choice from a security perspective.

A very important security issue is the name of the user and group the Web server runs as. The following example of the Ouray Mountain Water's Employee server's httpd.conf file defines the name of the accounts under which the Web server runs:

```
#
# If you wish httpd to run as a different user or group, you must run
```

```
# httpd as root initially and it will switch.
#
# User/Group: The name (or #number) of the user/group to run httpd as.
#  . On SCO (ODT 3) use "User nouser" and "Group nogroup".
#  . On HPUX you may not be able to use shared memory as nobody, and the
#    suggested workaround is to create a user www and use that user.
#  NOTE that some kernels refuse to setgid(Group) or semctl(IPC_SET)
#  when the value of (unsigned)Group is above 60000;
#  don't use Group nobody on these systems!
#
User webadmin
Group webadmin
```

You should *never* run the server as nobody which is sometimes the default setting for user and group in the httpd.conf file. There are other processes running on the Linux system that use nobody and if you ever need to track events or security issues by user account, it is literally impossible to distinguish the Apache activities from the other nobody processes. Another issue related to the Apache user and group discussion is the owner of the Apache files and directories. It is a good idea to make sure that the files and directories in the Apache directory hierarchy are not owned by root. It is a better practice to set the owner of the Apache files to be the same as the name of the user and group specified in the httpd.conf file.

A potential security issue on Web servers is the use of CGI and SSI scripts and programs. Before allowing a newly added CGI or SSI program to execute on the Web server, you should check to make sure it is doing what it is supposed to do and nothing more. A bad CGI or SSI program could modify, change, and/or remove stuff from the system. In addition, you should control who can put CGI and SSI programs on the system and place them initially in a safe location so they can be checked before release.

In order for a CGI or SSI program to run, the owner of the program usually has to be the same as the user the Apache server runs under. This can also lead to problems because if a misbehaved CGI or SSI program gets out-of-hand, it could potentially harm anything owned by the same user. Because of this possibility, Apache can be configured to support suEXEC, which allows you to run CGI and SSI programs under a different user. Configuring and implementing suEXEC is for administrators who are very experienced in all aspects of the local operating system and Apache security. Because of this level of required experience, and the potential for a misconfigured suEXEC environment introducing additional security problems and holes, suEXEC is not part of the default installation for Apache. For more information on suEXEC, take a look at the suexec.html file included in the Apache documentation. You can also access the information at the Apache Software Foundation's Web site at http://httpd.apache.org/docs/suexec.html.

Backing Up

You are probably already aware of the importance of maintaining a reliable backup of the information on your servers and other critical elements. Maybe, unfortunately, you discovered the hard way the effects of a lack of good backup. Things failed and then there was…nothing. Also, users, and perhaps yourself, accidentally delete files and then need them back. With a backup system in place, the deleted files can be restored. If your environment doesn't already have a backup solution, then *now* is the time to create one.

> **NOTE** Linux and Windows 2000 Server systems both support the use of software and hardware RAID systems. RAID provides real-time online availability of data in the event of hardware failure, but RAID is not a substitute for data backup. If your servers and attached peripherals are destroyed by water or fire, the RAID system will not help since they would also have been destroyed by the same incident. Maintaining current backups that are stored at a location physically different than the servers provides a means to retrieve your data in the event of a disaster. Some government agencies and companies define data backup guidelines that dictate storage locations and rules, such as a minimum distance from the original and/or conditions under which the backup media is stored.

The purpose of backing up data is to maintain a recent copy of the data that is stored at another location that is physically different from the original data. In the event there is a loss of the original information, the information can be restored by the data stored on the backup media. A critical aspect of a good backup solution is performing data backups at regular intervals and verifying the quality of the backup. Most backup solutions are scheduled to perform the backup once every twenty-four hours during a time when there is little to no activity and/or usage of the data.

There are different types of backup media that can be used to store data. One of the most common choices is 4mm and 8mm digital audio tape (DAT). This solution is relatively cheap and has high capacity. On the other hand, tapes are slow because of the sequential nature of storing and retrieving data. Other solutions provide faster storage and retrieval times but are more expensive. These options include CD-R (compact disk recordable) and DVD-R (DVD recordable), which allow you to write once to the CD and read any number of times. For environments that backup large quantities of data every day, a jukebox that automatically changes and houses multiple tapes, CDs, or DVDs may be the best solution. Whatever backup media you decide to use, tapes, CD-R and DVD-R systems are supported by both Linux and Windows 2000 Server.

The backup types are usually divided into three categories—full, differential, and incremental. Some software packages may use slightly different terms, but the definitions are pretty much the same. Backup solutions typically revolve around a weekly cycle so that the start of a new backup begins on one of the days of the week. For example, the Ouray Mountain Water company's backup operation begins Sunday morning at 2:00 A.M. A full backup means the entire contents of the selected device are backed up at each time interval. For example, a full backup of the Ouray Mountain Water's public Web server begins at 2:00 and all the specified directories and files are copied to the backup media. An incremental backup begins with a full backup performed at the first designated time of the cycle. Then, at each backup time, the data that has changed since the last backup in the cycle is copied to the backup media. Thus, throughout the one-week cycle, the data is backed up in increments. A differential backup also begins with a full backup at the first scheduled time in the cycle. On each subsequent day, the data that has changed since the last full backup is copied to the backup media. Thus, as the week goes on, the data backed up includes the current day's changes and any previous days' file changes since the full backup at the beginning of the week.

The format in which the backed up data is stored on the backup media is usually some type of encoded format. To save space, many backup solutions offer the option of backing up the data in a compressed format. In addition, some backup program vendors incorporate their own proprietary format for data storage. Because of the file format techniques used to backup the data, you will need access to the backup software to be able to retrieve the information. Some backup solutions use formats that can be read by other programs and some do not. Investigate the details of the vendors supported file formats to determine which choices are available and best fit your needs.

In the remainder of this section we introduce the basics of backups for Linux and Windows 2000 Servers. The backup tools and solutions we cover are native to each operating system. There are quite a number of other solutions available for Linux and Windows 2000 that cover a wide range of capabilities and prices, from $0.00 on up!

Linux

Linux has long used the tar and cpio tools to backup data. The tar, or tape archival, utility was originally written to save data to tape, thus, the name of the utility. However, tar can be used to backup data to a file, which can be saved to any storage system you prefer. The file that tar creates is called a tarfile, or tarball, and the names usually end with .tar so it is easy to identify the file type. There are many options supported by the tar command, the majority of which you will probably never encounter. The idea behind tar is the ability to group together a collection of files and directories so they can be restored later to their original state. That is, the directory structure, dates, and attributes of the files and directories are retained. Since tar just groups together the files into a single file, the size of the tarfile is around the same size as all the original files. To reduce the size of the tarfile, the tar utility also has the ability to save files in a compressed format. As an example, let's step through the process of using tar to backup Ouray Mountain Water's public Web server content. The Web site's content is located at /usr/local/content/htdocs and the resulting tarfile will be located at /var/local/tarfiles. The syntax of the tar command to backup our example is:

```
tar --vzcf /var/local/tarfiles/web.tar.gz /usr/local/content/htdocs
```

The –v option specifies a verbose output as the files are archived and –z compresses the files. If you are backing up a lot of files and directories, you may not want to use the –v option. The –c option means to create a file and the –f followed by a file name indicates the name of the tarfile. You have the ability to compress the tarfile by including the -z or -Z option. The -z choice will use gzip to reduce file sizes and the -Z option will use compress to compact the information. Compress does not compact the data as much as gzip does and most current uses of tar use the gzip method. The standard file name extension for files compacted with compress is .Z and with gzip the extension .gz is typically used. In our example, if we used –Z in the tar command instead of -z, web.tar.Z would have been the name of our backup file.

The tar utility is also used to decompress a tarfile. The syntax is basically the same with an additional option, -x, for extract. When you extract a tarfile with the tar command, the files will be extracted at the location where the tarfile is created. If you have specified the complete pathname of the directory to backup in the tar command to create the archive, the files and subdirectories will be extracted using the same paths from your current location. For example, if the tar file is copied to the directory /var/local/tarfiles/restored and the tar command to extract the files is executed from the /var/local/tarfiles/restored directory, the location of the extracted files and all subdirectories would be:

```
/var/local/tarfiles/restored/usr/local/content/htdocs
```

If you didn't specify the full path in the original tar command to create the archive, then the extracted location would be:

```
/var/local/tarfiles/restored/htdocs
```

In addition to creating and extracting tar files, the tar command can be used to examine the contents of a tar file. For example, to list the contents of our example tar file, web.tar.gz, the syntax is:

```
tar -tzf web.tar.gz
```

Executing this command on Ouray Water Mountain's public Web server resulted in the following information:

```
usr/local/content/htdocs/
usr/local/content/htdocs/_vti_pvt/
usr/local/content/htdocs/_vti_pvt/frontpg.lck
usr/local/content/htdocs/_vti_pvt/service.lck
usr/local/content/htdocs/_vti_pvt/service.cnf
usr/local/content/htdocs/_vti_pvt/.htaccess
usr/local/content/htdocs/_vti_pvt/service.pwd
usr/local/content/htdocs/_vti_pvt/service.grp
usr/local/content/htdocs/_vti_pvt/bots.cnf
usr/local/content/htdocs/_vti_pvt/services.cnf
usr/local/content/htdocs/_vti_pvt/botinfs.cnf
usr/local/content/htdocs/_vti_pvt/doctodep.btr
usr/local/content/htdocs/_vti_pvt/deptodoc.btr
usr/local/content/htdocs/_vti_pvt/linkinfo.cnf
usr/local/content/htdocs/_vti_pvt/writeto.cnf
usr/local/content/htdocs/_vti_pvt/structure.cnf
usr/local/content/htdocs/_vti_pvt/access.cnf
usr/local/content/htdocs/_vti_pvt/svcacl.cnf
usr/local/content/htdocs/_vti_pvt/_vti_cnf/
usr/local/content/htdocs/_vti_pvt/_vti_cnf/_x_todo.htm
usr/local/content/htdocs/_vti_pvt/_x_todo.htm
usr/local/content/htdocs/Animas Mist.htm
usr/local/content/htdocs/.htaccess
usr/local/content/htdocs/_vti_log/
usr/local/content/htdocs/_vti_log/.htaccess
usr/local/content/htdocs/_private/
usr/local/content/htdocs/_private/.htaccess
usr/local/content/htdocs/_private/_vti_cnf/
usr/local/content/htdocs/_private/_vti_cnf/inforeq.htm
usr/local/content/htdocs/_private/_vti_cnf/inforeq.txt
usr/local/content/htdocs/_private/inforeq.htm
usr/local/content/htdocs/_private/inforeq.txt
usr/local/content/htdocs/_vti_txt/
usr/local/content/htdocs/_vti_txt/.htaccess
usr/local/content/htdocs/_vti_cnf/
usr/local/content/htdocs/_vti_cnf/.htaccess
usr/local/content/htdocs/_vti_cnf/Animas Mist.htm
usr/local/content/htdocs/_vti_cnf/index.html
usr/local/content/htdocs/_vti_cnf/products.htm
usr/local/content/htdocs/_vti_cnf/news.htm
usr/local/content/htdocs/_vti_cnf/Mountain Morning Mineral.htm
usr/local/content/htdocs/_vti_cnf/Ouray Mountain Spring.htm
usr/local/content/htdocs/_vti_cnf/Red Mountain Berry.htm
usr/local/content/htdocs/_vti_cnf/Uncompahgre Drinking.htm
usr/local/content/htdocs/_vti_cnf/feedback.htm
usr/local/content/htdocs/_vti_cnf/local_information.htm
```

```
usr/local/content/htdocs/_vti_cnf/toc.htm
usr/local/content/htdocs/_vti_bin/
usr/local/content/htdocs/_vti_bin/_vti_adm/
usr/local/content/htdocs/_vti_bin/_vti_adm/.htaccess
usr/local/content/htdocs/_vti_bin/_vti_aut/
usr/local/content/htdocs/_vti_bin/_vti_aut/.htaccess
usr/local/content/htdocs/_vti_bin/fpcount.exe
usr/local/content/htdocs/_vti_bin/.htaccess
usr/local/content/htdocs/images/
usr/local/content/htdocs/images/_vti_cnf/
usr/local/content/htdocs/images/_vti_cnf/Sunfacebullet.gif
usr/local/content/htdocs/images/_vti_cnf/02PEOPLE.GIF
usr/local/content/htdocs/images/_vti_cnf/05SKY.GIF
usr/local/content/htdocs/images/_vti_cnf/39BOR.GIF
usr/local/content/htdocs/images/_vti_cnf/Barbedwire.gif
usr/local/content/htdocs/images/_vti_cnf/Blissgrain.jpg
usr/local/content/htdocs/images/_vti_cnf/Border2.gif
usr/local/content/htdocs/images/_vti_cnf/Pastel.gif
usr/local/content/htdocs/images/_vti_cnf/RT Clip Art.gif
usr/local/content/htdocs/images/_vti_cnf/Sandman.gif
usr/local/content/htdocs/images/_vti_cnf/Sandmanhalf.gif
usr/local/content/htdocs/images/_vti_cnf/Skyhalf.gif
usr/local/content/htdocs/images/_vti_cnf/Sun.gif
usr/local/content/htdocs/images/_vti_cnf/Sun3rd.gif
usr/local/content/htdocs/images/_vti_cnf/Sunbullet.gif
usr/local/content/htdocs/images/_vti_cnf/smallnew.gif
usr/local/content/htdocs/images/_vti_cnf/Sunhalf.gif
usr/local/content/htdocs/images/_vti_cnf/hosted5.gif
usr/local/content/htdocs/images/_vti_cnf/Sunhorntrans2.gif
usr/local/content/htdocs/images/_vti_cnf/logo.gif
usr/local/content/htdocs/images/02PEOPLE.GIF
usr/local/content/htdocs/images/05SKY.GIF
usr/local/content/htdocs/images/39BOR.GIF
usr/local/content/htdocs/images/Barbedwire.gif
usr/local/content/htdocs/images/Blissgrain.jpg
usr/local/content/htdocs/images/Border2.gif
usr/local/content/htdocs/images/Pastel.gif
usr/local/content/htdocs/images/RT Clip Art.gif
usr/local/content/htdocs/images/Sandman.gif
usr/local/content/htdocs/images/Sandmanhalf.gif
usr/local/content/htdocs/images/Skyhalf.gif
usr/local/content/htdocs/images/Sun3rd.gif
usr/local/content/htdocs/images/Sun.gif
usr/local/content/htdocs/images/Sunfacebullet.gif
usr/local/content/htdocs/images/Sunbullet.gif
usr/local/content/htdocs/images/smallnew.gif
usr/local/content/htdocs/images/Sunhalf.gif
usr/local/content/htdocs/images/hosted5.gif
usr/local/content/htdocs/images/Sunhorntrans2.gif
usr/local/content/htdocs/images/logo.gif
usr/local/content/htdocs/_vti_inf.html
```

```
usr/local/content/htdocs/Mountain Morning Mineral.htm
usr/local/content/htdocs/_borders/
usr/local/content/htdocs/_borders/_vti_cnf/
usr/local/content/htdocs/_borders/_vti_cnf/bottom.htm
usr/local/content/htdocs/_borders/_vti_cnf/left.htm
usr/local/content/htdocs/_borders/_vti_cnf/top.htm
usr/local/content/htdocs/_borders/bottom.htm
usr/local/content/htdocs/_borders/left.htm
usr/local/content/htdocs/_borders/top.htm
usr/local/content/htdocs/Ouray Mountain Spring.htm
usr/local/content/htdocs/Red Mountain Berry.htm
usr/local/content/htdocs/Uncompahgre Drinking.htm
usr/local/content/htdocs/feedback.htm
usr/local/content/htdocs/local_information.htm
usr/local/content/htdocs/news.htm
usr/local/content/htdocs/products.htm
usr/local/content/htdocs/toc.htm
usr/local/content/htdocs/index.html
```

Notice that the entire path of each file is retained so that if you need to restore a file or files you know the locations. Also, since the original file was compressed using gzip, you need to include, when extracting, the option for the compression method used. If you omit the appropriate compression option, you will receive a message similar to the following:

```
tar: This does not look like a tar archive
tar: Skipping to next header
tar: 470 garbage bytes ignored at end of archive
tar: Error exit delayed from previous errors
```

If the wrong compression option is used, for example –Z instead of –z, you will receive a message similar to the following:

```
stdin: not in compressed format
tar: Child returned status 1
tar: Error exit delayed from previous errors
```

However, if the file has been compressed with the –Z option, you can use either –Z or –z to list the contents of the tarfile.

Other options supported by the tar utility include: append files to an existing archive, don't overwrite older files, remove file(s) from an archive, and update, which only appends files that are newer than the archive's files.

The cpio utility can also be used to create backups of data. The command structure is different than tar in that cpio is fed a list of files to backup. To create the list, you can use the ls or find command and then redirect (pipe) the information to the cpio utility. If the directory you are backing up contains subdirectories and files, you will want to use the find command with cpio to retain the directory structure and files. For example, to use cpio on Ouray Mountain Water's public Web server Web content location, execute the following:

```
find /usr/local/content/htdocs --depth -print | cpio --ov >
/var/local/cpiofiles/web.cpio
```

If the command prompt is at the /usr/local/content/htdocs directory, the syntax to use cpio is:

```
find . --depth -print | cpio --ov > /var/local/cpiofiles/web.cpio
```

The –o indicates output and the –v is for verbose so you receive feedback as cpio executes the command. If you are doing a large number of files you may want to suppress the feedback. In this case, omit the v from the options.

To extract the files, navigate to the location of the original source directory of the files contained in the archive. To extract the files using our example web.cpio file, the syntax is:

```
cpio --idv < /var/local/cpiofiles/web.cpio
```

The –i option indicates to extract the files and the –d creates directories as needed. If the directory you are extracting files to already contains files and directories of the same names, the matching files and directories will not be extracted. If you include –r in the options, when a name conflict arises, you will be prompted to rename the file that will be extracted. The cpio utility also has the ability to copy files into and out of a tar or cpio archive file.

Both of these tools are command line utilities and can be set to execute "automatically" through the use of cron. The cron utility is a scheduling tool for specifying at what time(s) and frequencies commands or scripts are executed. The tool uses a crontab file to indicate when a scheduled action is to take place. The default location for the system-wide crontab file is in the /etc directory. You can also support user specific crontab files through the use of the crontab utility. The syntax of the crontab file can be a bit cryptic. The format consists of 6 columns of information where each column is separated by some non-numeric ASCII character, such as a space. The crontab file columns definitions and the order across the line are:

```
min hr dom mnth dow command
```

The definitions for each item are:

min Minute

hr Hour based on a 24 hour clock

dom (day of the month) This may be numeric or a three-letter abbreviation

mnth (month) This may be numeric or a three-letter abbreviation

dow (day of the week) This may be numeric or a three-letter abbreviation

command The command to be executed; this can also be a script which is useful when you need to execute multiple commands

To specify time intervals, commas can be used for specific instances and dashes indicate ranges. If you want to specify, for example, each month, use an asterisk (*) in the mnth location. For example, to execute the tar command to backup the Web content every Monday at 2:00am, the entry in the crontab file would be:

```
0 2 * * mon tar --vzcf /var/local/tarfiles/web.tar.gz /usr/local/content/htdocs
```

Windows 2000 Server

Windows 2000 Server comes equipped with its own backup solution called Backup. The default location to gain access to the utility is Programs | Accessories | System Tools | Backup. When you open the tool, the initial screen presents four areas that are accessed with the tabs at the top of the window (see Figure 8.2).

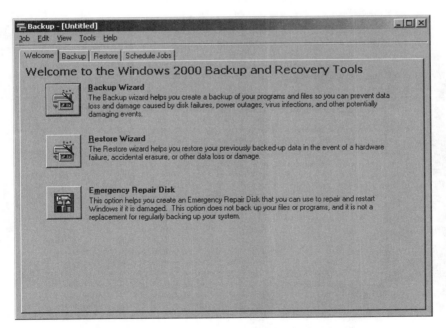

Figure 8.2 Windows 2000 Server Backup initial screen.

The Welcome section contains Wizards to get you started on setting up a backup configuration or performing a restoration. The last option in this section is the creation of the Emergency Repair Disk. To start configuring a backup environment, select the Backup Wizard button. The Wizard then steps you through the process of setting up the backup conditions. Figure 8.3 illustrates the first screen in the Backup Wizard tool.

To continue, click on the Next button. The Backup Wizard presents three options for the information that you want to backup. These are shown in Figure 8.4.

As an example, the Web content of Ouray Mountain Water's Production Windows 2000 Apache server will be backed up using the Windows 2000 Server Backup software. In this case, we chose the option Back up selected files, drives, or network data. Once you have made your selection, click on Next to continue. In the Items to Back Up window, navigate to the Web server's content directory in the left pane and place a checkmark next to the document root directory. For example, G:\content\htdocs (see Figure 8.5).

You can also select more than one directory and location if you prefer. When you have finished making your choices, click on the Next button to advance to the next stage. The Where to Store the Backup window appears and allows you to chose the location of the backup file. In our example, we will be saving the information to a file. In the Backup media or file name field, enter the name of the destination file. You can also use the Browse button to navigate to a loca-

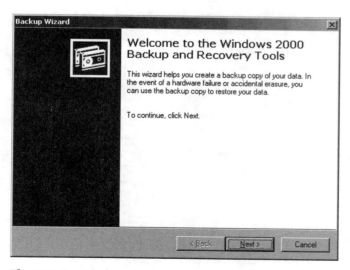

Figure 8.3   Windows 2000 Server Backup Wizard tool.

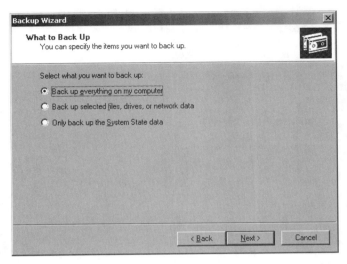

Figure 8.4   Windows 2000 Server Backup Wizard content selection.

tion. As an example, the backup file will be created in G:\webbackup and the name of the file is ProductionWeb08012001 (see Figure 8.6).

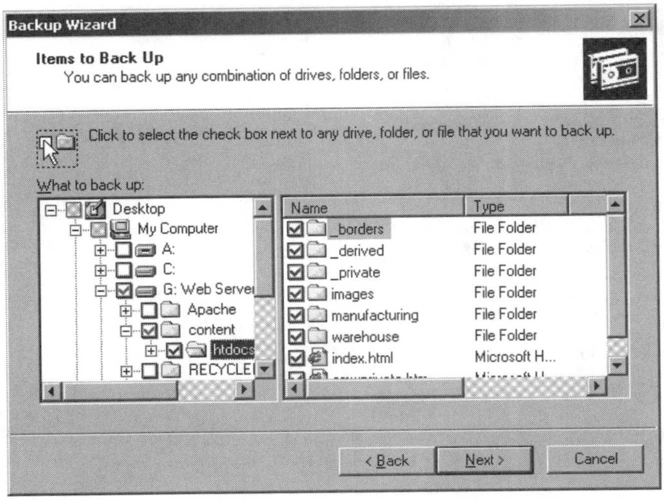

Figure 8.5   Windows 2000 Server Backup, Items to Back Up selection window.

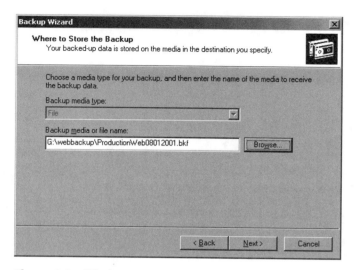

Figure 8.6   Windows 2000 Server Backup, Where to Store the Backup selection window.

When you have completed your destination location, click on the Next button to continue. A confirmation window appears that lists the items you have selected and configured (see Figure 8.7).

The Advanced tab displays the Backup Type area of the Options window where you can specify items such as the type of backup—Normal, Differential, and Incremental (see Figure 8.8).

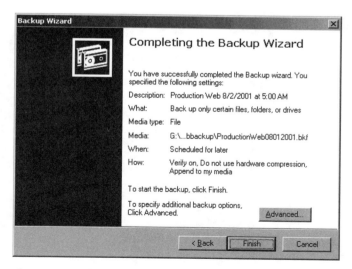

Figure 8.7   Windows 2000 Server Backup, confirmation window.

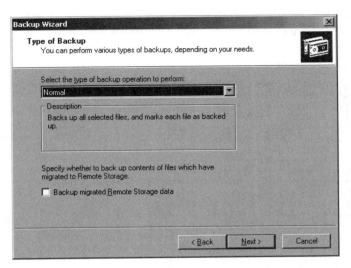

Figure 8.8 Windows 2000 Server Backup, backup type options.

When you have finished making your selections, choose Next to continue. The How to Back Up window allows you to specify data verification after the backup and hardware compression if the backup device supports compression. In our example, we chose Verify Data after backup to ensure the integrity of the backup. When you have made your choices, click on the Next button. The Media Options window is for specifying whether to append data to the backup media or to replace the data. In our example, we chose to Append this backup to the media (see Figure 8.9).

When you have made your selections, click the Next button. The Backup Label window allows you to specify the name of the backup label and media label. You can accept the defaults or edit the information to match your environment (see Figure 8.10).

When you have made your choices, click Next to continue. In the When to Back Up window you can choose to backup the data now or later. For our example, we chose Later so we can specify a time. When you specify Later, you need to supply an account name and password that has permission to perform backups. The Set Schedule button displays the Schedule Job window (see Figure 8.11).

In the Schedule Job window you can specify the time and frequency of the backup starts. When you have finished making the schedule settings, click OK to continue and then click on Next in the When to Back Up window. At the Completing the Backup Wizard window (see Figure 8.12), click on Finish when you are ready.

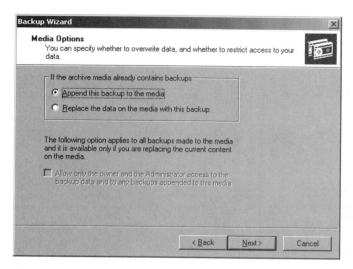

Figure 8.9   Windows 2000 Server Backup, Media Options window.

During and at the completion of the backup, a Backup Progress window appears so you can see the amount of time involved and/or any errors. Figure 8.13 shows the completed Backup Progress window for the Ouray Mountain Water's Production Web server's Web content.

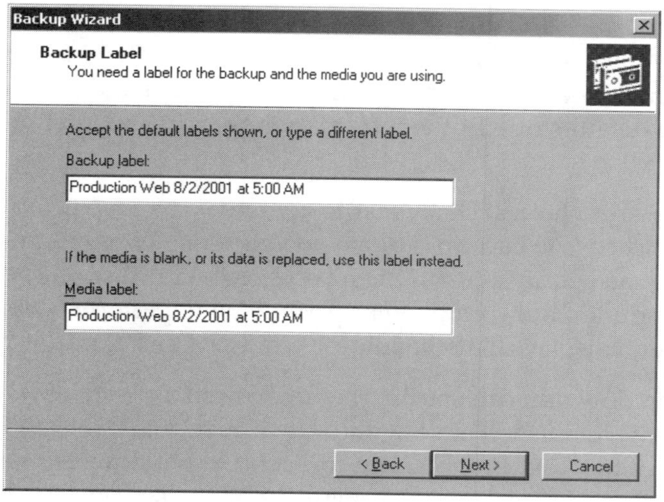

Figure 8.10   Windows 2000 Server Backup, Backup Label window.

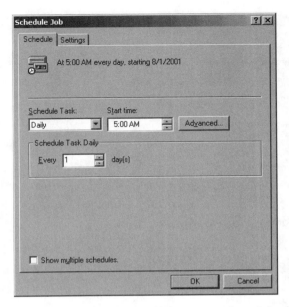

Figure 8.11   Windows 2000 Server Backup, Schedule Job window.

When the session is completed, click on the Report button to display the backup session's details in Notepad:

```
Backup Status
Operation: Backup
```

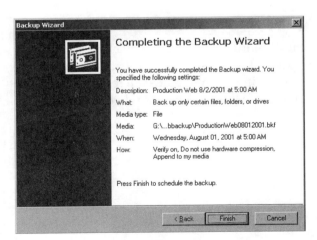

Figure 8.12   Windows 2000 Server Backup, Completing the Backup Wizard window.

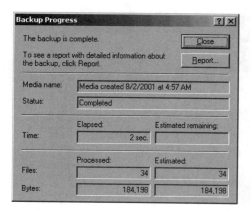

Figure 8.13 Windows 2000 Server Backup, Progress window.

```
Active backup destination: File
Media name: "Media created 8/2/2001 at 4:57 AM"

Backup of "G: Web Server"
Backup set #1 on media #1
Backup description: "Set created 8/2/2001 at 4:58 AM"
Backup Type: Normal

Backup started on 8/2/2001 at 4:58 AM.
Backup completed on 8/2/2001 at 4:58 AM.
Directories: 14
Files: 34
Bytes: 184,198
Time:  2 seconds


----------------------
```

The Restore process using the Windows 2000 Server Backup program is
essentially the same as setting up a backup session except that you specify the
backup media source and the location in which to place the restored files. You
can also specify details such as to replace files or not, and whether to restore to
an alternate location.

CHAPTER

9

Troubleshooting

Troubleshooting is a combination of technical expertise, experimentation, and luck. There are usually two approaches to a problem, forward chaining and backward chaining. To demonstrate these two styles, we examine a problem where a user is unable to print to a network printer. In this example, the operating systems on the network use print queues (directories) to store the print files, and print servers to handle the delivery of the print files to the printers. In a forward chaining approach, troubleshooting begins at the location of the problem and then follows the process, in order, to the last step. In our problem print example, the process begins at the user's system because that is where the problem originates. The first step is to determine if the problem resides at the user's workstation. For example, we begin by asking questions such as the following:

- Can any other workstation on the same network segment print?
- Can the user print from another application?
- Is the print file arriving at the network queue?

If the answer to the first two questions is yes and the last question's answer is no, there is a good chance the problem resides at the user's workstation.

However, if the answers are no to the first two and yes to the last, then the problem is probably not the workstation.

The next step in the network printing process is to ask print queue related questions such as:

- Are there print files in the print queue?
- Is there sufficient disk space remaining to store the print files?
- Are there any errors on the print server that refer to the print queue?

If the answer to the first two questions is yes and the last is no, then there is a good chance the problem is not at the print queue, but in the remaining steps of the process. In a reverse chain process you begin analysis at the last portion of the process. For our printing problem example, reverse chain troubleshooting would begin at the printer because that is the final item involved in network printing. It doesn't matter which approach you take as long as each part of the process is addressed and in some logical order. Also, documentation is extremely important when troubleshooting. After all, if you have spent several hours fixing a problem, you probably don't want to spend another several hours at another time fixing the same problem. Good documentation will not get rid of troubleshooting but it will help guide you when you encounter the same or similar problem in the future.

In this section, we address some of the different areas that can cause problems. In the first portion we take a look at some areas to think about when troubleshooting. We then cover some sample problem scenarios and discuss the symptoms, the problem(s) that caused the condition, and the solution(s) used to resolve the problem. While it is impossible to cover all the problem areas that can affect Linux, Windows 2000, and Apache, we hope that by addressing some of the common areas we will reduce the number of headaches.

There are many areas in a network that can experience problems and their effects range from minor annoyances to major problems that impact many users and/or your clients. In general, you can divide problems dealing with network services into two major areas:

Hardware. Any hardware component that is involved in the network and services can create trouble spots. These include items such as the network cabling, connection devices (e.g., switches and routers), WAN connection portals, hard drives, network cards, power supplies, and so on.

Software. Any piece of software on any of the systems and hardware involved can generate problems. This includes all the software pieces that make the operating systems, the network client software, the protocols, the different services software, and so on.

Now that we have essentially said that anything could be a problem, will you be spending your days (and nights) constantly chasing problems or should you go crawl under a rock and hide? Things don't have to be quite that drastic, especially if you have the environment's documentation and the backups up-to-date. In addition, if the systems' hardware is current, the likelihood of massive hardware failures should be minimal. Of course, there is no guarantee that new hardware won't fail but the probability is less when the systems have not accumulated years of use.

Once you have determined there is a problem, what resources are available to help assist you in troubleshooting? An immediate source is the documentation about your environment. Reviewing information noted before about related problems or recent changes in the network may lead you to the solution immediately or help to reduce the number of possible sources. Beyond your own documentation, there are numerous resources available on the Internet and in bookstores covering details of operating systems and networks. Similarly, there is a lot of information available from vendor's Web sites and other generic information technology Web sites where you may find assistance in your troubleshooting tasks. In addition, a lot of vendors now deliver the documentation in electronic format.

There is an official Apache bug Web site at which you can search the bug database by keywords and other criteria. The Web site address is http://bugs .apache.org. Here are some other useful Web sites about Apache and related issues:

- www.apacheweek.com
- www.devshed.com
- www.oreillynet.com/cs/user/forum/cs_disc/234

The majority of the topics addressed in these Web sites are aimed at Apache running on Linux, but some of the information applies to both platforms. Also, when searching for information about Apache on Windows 2000, include Windows NT or just Windows in your search criteria. Since Apache can run on different versions of Windows, you may be narrowing your search too much by specifying Windows 2000.

One final sanity note. When you are in the middle of a crisis, make sure you can quickly access the information you need. You may find it useful to print out some of the information on paper in case you are not able to access the information electronically while in the middle of a troubleshooting session.

Tools and Techniques

In this section we address a collection of tools and areas to be aware of when troubleshooting Apache. They are presented in no particular order and do not cover all the possible combinations of problems and solutions.

Troubleshooting with Browsers

Depending on the nature of the problem, you may find it necessary to verify that the Web browser is retrieving the files from the Web server. Browser's typically use cache to store Web pages so that the next time the user goes to the Web site, the content can be retrieved from stored cache. This improves the response time to the user but can get in the way when troubleshooting. Most browsers allow you to specify to get the page from the server every time you access the page and/or set the cache to 0. When these options are set, and you access one of your Web servers, then you know the pages are coming from the Web server.

httpd.conf

There are several areas in the httpd.conf file that can create problems if not configured properly. Before making changes to a current working httpd.conf file, it is a good idea to have a backup of the working version. Then, if necessary, you can switch back to the working copy if the current changes are not functioning properly. In this section, we address some of the areas in the httpd.conf file that will create problems if not configured properly.

Listen

This directive allows you to specify a port and/or specific IP address to bind Apache with.

```
#
# Listen: Allows you to bind Apache to specific IP addresses and/or
# ports, in addition to the default. See also the <VirtualHost>
# directive.
#
#Listen 3000
#Listen 12.34.56.78:80
```

If the Listen port is not set properly, the browser will return a message similar to Figure 9.1.

If the Listen IP address does not match one of the IP addresses on the system, then the Apache service will not start. If a valid IP address is entered but is not for the same network segment servicing the workstations, then the users will not be able to browse the Web server.

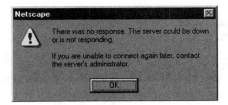

Figure 9.1   Browser response to an incorrect Listen address or port number.

Port

This is the standard port used by Web browsers to access the contents of a Web server. If you change this port value, the users will need to know how to access the Web server with a different port. The relevant Port section in the httpd.conf file for a Windows 2000 Apache server is:

```
#
# Port: The port to which the standalone server listens.  Certain firewall
# products must be configured before Apache can listen to a specific port.
# Other running httpd servers will also interfere with this port.  Disable
# all firewall, security, and other services if you encounter problems.
# To help diagnose problems use the Windows NT command NETSTAT -a
#
Port 80
```

On a Linux Apache server the appropriate section in the httpd.conf file reveals:

```
#
# Port: The port to which the standalone server listens. For
# portS < 1023, you will need httpd to be run as root initially.
#
Port 80
```

For example, if the port number for the Production Web server were changed to 65530, then the URL or address would be:

```
http://production.ouraymountainwater.com:65530
```

If the port is not specified, the user will receive an error message in their browser similar to Figure 9.1.

User and Group (Linux)

Make sure the name of the user and group specified in the httpd.conf correctly matches the names of the user and group account you have set up for Apache.

```
#
# If you wish httpd to run as a different user or group, you must run
# httpd as root initially and it will switch.
#
# User/Group: The name (or #number) of the user/group to run httpd as.
#  . On SCO (ODT 3) use "User nouser" and "Group nogroup".
#  . On HPUX you may not be able to use shared memory as nobody, and the
#    suggested workaround is to create a user www and use that user.
#  NOTE that some kernels refuse to setgid(Group) or semctl(IPC_SET)
#  when the value of (unsigned)Group is above 60000;
#  don't use Group nobody on these systems!
#
User webadmin
Group webadmin
```

In addition, verify that the user and group defined in the httpd.conf file are the owners of the Apache directories and files. If the ownership of the files does not match up with the settings in the httpd.conf file, the Web server may have trouble reading and/or accessing some of its files.

ServerName

The complete DNS name specified in the httpd.conf file must be the same name defined in the various DNS servers that service the network. If these do not match, users will not be able to browse the server by using a name.

```
#
# ServerName allows you to set a host name which is sent back to clients for
# your server if it's different than the one the program would get (i.e., use
# "www" instead of the host's real name).
#
# Note: You cannot just invent host names and hope they work. The name you
# define here must be a valid DNS name for your host. If you don't understand
# this, ask your network administrator.
# If your host doesn't have a registered DNS name, enter its IP address here.
# You will have to access it by its address (e.g., http://123.45.67.89/)
# anyway, and this will make redirections work in a sensible way.
#
# 127.0.0.1 is the TCP/IP local loop-back address, often named localhost. Your
# machine always knows itself by this address. If you use Apache strictly for
# LOCAl testing and development, you may use 127.0.0.1 as the server name.
#
ServerName employee.ouraymountainwater.com
```

When Apache is first installed on your system, there may be a default name entered for the name of the server and/or the ServerName entry in the httpd.conf file may be commented out. In addition, if the Web server will have a presence on the Internet, the name of the domain must be registered.

DocumentRoot

The DocumentRoot directive specifies the root directory of the Web content. It is recommended that you use a complete name for the directory path and not a path relative to the Apache server's root directory. For example, the DocumentRoot definition for the Ouray Mountain Water Employee Linux Apache server is:

```
#
# DocumentRoot: The directory out of which you will serve your
# documents. By default, all requests are taken from this directory, but
# symbolic links and aliases may be used to point to other locations.
#
DocumentRoot "/usr/local/content/htdocs"
```

For the company's Windows 2000 Production Apache Web server, the DocumentRoot directive is:

```
#
# DocumentRoot: The directory out of which you will serve your
# documents. By default, all requests are taken from this directory, but
# symbolic links and aliases may be used to point to other locations.
#
DocumentRoot "G:/content/htdocs"
```

If the DocumentRoot setting does not correspond to the actual location of the Web content, users will not be able to access any information on the Web servers from their browsers.

HostnameLookups

If the performance of delivering pages to the user's Web browsers is very slow and there are no apparent hardware or network traffic issues, make sure the HostNameLookups setting in the httpd.conf is Off. For example, the HostnameLookup section in the httpd.conf file is:

```
#
# HostnameLookups: Log the names of clients or just their IP addresses
# e.g., www.apache.org (on) or 204.62.129.132 (off).
# The default is off because it'd be overall better for the net if people
# had to knowingly turn this feature on, since enabling it means that
# each client request will result in AT LEAST one lookup request to the
# nameserver.
#
HostnameLookups Off
```

When the HostnameLookups is set to On, a lot of time is added to each request because the Apache server issues a DNS name resolution request for each IP address accessing the Web server. It is better to turn this off and collect the IP addresses in the log files. You can then process the log files later for IP address to name resolution queries without adding all the overhead of each request to the Web server.

LogLevel

If you need to log Web server access information, set the log level so that only the messages important to your analysis are captured. If you set the log level to high and log a lot of unneeded events, more time is used to write the logged information to the log files. Accessing files and the hard drive more frequently will slow down the performance of the Web server.

```
#
# LogLevel: Control the number of messages logged to the error_log.
# Possible values include: debug, info, notice, warn, error, crit,
# alert, emerg.
#
LogLevel warn
```

If you don't need to log access information at all then disable logging to improve performance.

DSO Support

If you are using the DSO functionality in Apache, the order in which the modules are loaded is very important. For example, take a look at the DSO section of the httpd.conf file from a Windows 2000 Apache server:

```
# Dynamic Shared Object (DSO) Support
#
# To be able to use the functionality of a module which was built as a DSO you
# have to place corresponding `LoadModule' lines at this location so the
# directives contained in it are actually available _before_ they are used.
# Please read the file README.DSO in the Apache 1.3 distribution for more
# details about the DSO mechanism and run `apache -l' for the list of already
# built-in (statically linked and thus always available) modules in your Apache
# binary.
#
# Note: The order in which modules are loaded is important.  Don't change
# the order below without expert advice.
#
#LoadModule anon_auth_module modules/mod_auth_anon.so
#LoadModule dbm_auth_module modules/mod_auth_dbm.so
#LoadModule digest_auth_module modules/mod_auth_digest.so
#LoadModule cern_meta_module modules/mod_cern_meta.so
#LoadModule digest_module modules/mod_digest.so
#LoadModule expires_module modules/mod_expires.so
#LoadModule headers_module modules/mod_headers.so
#LoadModule proxy_module modules/mod_proxy.so
```

```
#LoadModule rewrite_module modules/mod_rewrite.so
#LoadModule speling_module modules/mod_speling.so
#LoadModule info_module modules/mod_info.so
#LoadModule status_module modules/mod_status.so
#LoadModule usertrack_module modules/mod_usertrack.so
```

By default, these are commented out, but if you wish to use more than one, make sure you retain the proper order. For more information about DSO, consult the dso.html file that is included with the Apache documentation.

Checking the httpd.conf File

You can check the httpd.conf file for syntax errors on Linux and Windows 2000 systems to help narrow down a problem area. On Linux systems, execute the following at Apache's bin directory:

```
./apachectl configtest
```

If the syntax of the httpd.conf file is okay, you will see the following message:

```
Syntax OK
```

If there is a problem with the httpd.conf file, you will receive feedback similar to the following:

```
Syntax error on line 276 of /usr/local/apache/conf/httpd.conf:
ServerName takes one argument, The hostname of the server
```

In this example, a space was accidentally inserted in the definition of the ServerName directive.

On a Windows 2000 system, you can check the integrity of the httpd.conf file by selecting Test Configuration from the Programs | Apache httpd Server | Configure Apache Server menu. When there are no problems, the Test Configuration menu option displays the feedback in Figure 9.2.

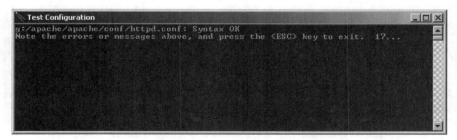

Figure 9.2   Test Configuration satisfactory report.

Figure 9.3   Test Configuration unsatisfactory report.

When an error occurs, such as the error mentioned above, where a space was inserted in the ServerName settings, the test reveals the feedback displayed in Figure 9.3.

Time

Some elements in the HTTP protocol conversations between Web servers and clients are expressed as the time of day. Therefore, it is important that the Web servers reflect the proper time for the time zone they are running in. Linux and Windows 2000 Servers can be configured to synchronize or get their time from an external time source. The NTP (Network Time Protocol) is part of the TCP/IP suite and both Linux and Windows 2000 can use NTP time. If you already have a time synchronization solution in place for the other services and servers on your network, consider adding your Web servers to the same solution. Configuring the environment so that the services and/or servers reference the same time information is the best solution. However, keep in mind that configuring time synchronization does take some planning and testing.

A good starting source for information about NTP can be found at www.eecis.udel.edu/~ntp. For Windows 2000 Server specific information, check out www.windows2000faq.com/Articles/Index.cfm?ArticleID=14943. For Linux systems, the configuration and setup information is included with the NTP package that is available from www.eecis.udel.edu/~ntp. Some Linux distributions include NTP and you may want to check the installation CDs to determine if NTP is included in the package.

For the remainder of this chapter we examine some problem scenarios, techniques used to track down problems, and the solutions to problems.

A Sampler of Troubles

The Ouray Mountain Water company has finished setting up and installing three Web servers—www.ouraymountainwater.com, employee.ouraymountainater .com, and production.ouraymountainwater.com. The Web development team is now ready to release the Web servers so the employees can test them and provide feedback. The company's Web solution development team has documented each system's hardware and software inventory. The Apache services have been configured, and, for some systems, additional components have been installed and setup. The servers have been through benchmark tests and, where needed, have been optimized. The team has gone through and secured the operating system and Apache files and from all counts, the servers are ready to meet the public. The Web solution's team has set up several workstations in the employees' break and lunch room area at the company's headquarters in Colorado. Their plan is to leave the test workstations in place for a week and then place additional workstations at the other facilities in California and Pennsylvania. Adding the remote test workstations will allow the team to evaluate the systems for both local and remote access. Any problems and/or suggestions the employees encounter while testing the systems are sent to the team as email or internal memos.

The two-week testing period has been completed and during that timeframe, the team encountered several problems which they had to troubleshoot and solve. In addition, there were good suggestions for changes to the Web design and many requested features. Those have been forwarded to the Web developers. Even though the testing environment will not catch all the potential problems and issues, there were quite a number of items discovered and fixed.

Problem 1

One of the workstations in the employees' break and lunch area at the Colorado facility cannot access any of the Web servers. All of the other test workstations at the Colorado location can access the Web servers and have no problems to report.

> **Troubleshooting.** First, we check the obvious stuff. Is the workstation turned on and are all the cables and connections snugly attached? This may seem silly, but if the network cable attached to the back of the system is not inserted all the way, then nothing on the network will be accessible. Also, check and see if anything has been physically moved since the last time users were able to access the Web servers. Sometimes components become loose during physical motion or when other items in the vicinity have been moved. For example, did the cleaning crew accidentally move something while vacuuming? After you have checked all the physical items and are sure everything is connected properly, check to determine if the workstation can access the Web servers. In our sample problem with the workstation, the

system still cannot access the Web servers even after checking all the hardware items.

The next step is to take a look at network communications. Instead of using an application, like a Web browser, to test communications, we begin at a lower level. The reason we choose this procedure is to make sure none of the extra things going on in an application will interfere with the testing. Often, the simplest approach is the best method. Probably one of the quickest ways to check communications with another device on the network is through the use of ping. PING (Packet Internetwork Groper) is actually a protocol and its most common usage is to check if one networked system can be seen by another networked device. The ability to use PING is usually bundled with most TCP/IP protocol suites as an application called ping. The PING protocol uses a series of ICMP (Internet Control Message Protocol) echo messages to determine if the remote system is available and the amount of time it took for the echo to return to the sending station. Most implementations of PING support several options that are used with the ping command. For example, the available options for the ping command on a Linux system are:

```
Usage: ping [-LRUbdfnqrvV] [-c count] [-i interval] [-w wait]
        [-p pattern] [-s packetsize] [-t ttl] [-I interface address]
        [ -T timestamp option ] [ -Q tos ] host
```

To get more details about the options, read the man pages for the ping utility.

On a Windows 2000 Server, the ping.exe options are:

```
Usage: ping [-t] [-a] [-n count] [-l size] [-f] [-i TTL] [-v TOS]
        [-r count] [-s count] [[-j host-list] | [-k host-list]]
        [-w timeout] destination-list

Options:
    -t              Ping the specified host until stopped.
                    To see statistics and continue - type Control-Break;
                    To stop - type Control-C.
    -a              Resolve addresses to hostnames.
    -n count        Number of echo requests to send.
    -l size         Send buffer size.
    -f              Set Don't Fragment flag in packet.
    -i TTL          Time To Live.
    -v TOS          Type Of Service.
    -r count        Record route for count hops.
    -s count        Timestamp for count hops.
    -j host-list    Loose source route along host-list.
    -k host-list    Strict source route along host-list.
    -w timeout      Timeout in milliseconds to wait for each reply.
```

Notice that the supported options for ping on both platforms are very similar, if not identical, in some cases. The ping command uses either the IP address or the DNS name of the destination device you wish to check. It is recommended that you use the IP address instead of the DNS name because if the DNS service has a problem, you have introduced another layer of complexity in the troubleshooting process. Another address you can use ping to test against is the loopback address (127.0.0.1 or DNS name) of the machine you are issuing the ping command from. This allows you to test the integrity of the TCP/IP protocol stack on the system. If any element of the TCP/IP stack on the machine has a problem, then any service or application that is dependent on TCP/IP will have problems.

On one of the Ouray Mountain Water test workstations, the first way the ping command is used is to make sure the TCP/IP stack on the workstation is okay. The workstation is a Windows 98 SE system and the ping command syntax for checking the TCP/IP stack is:

```
ping 127.0.0.1
```

Notice, we specify the loopback IP address and not the name of the machine. As we mentioned above, we want to keep things simple so we use the IP address instead of the machine's DNS name. In addition, in the Ouray Mountain's DNS server system, the names of workstations are not included in the DNS database. Thus, if we used the name of the test workstation in the ping command, we would receive an error anyway which would further complicate troubleshooting matters. The results of using ping with the loopback IP address on the problem workstation results in the following information:

```
Pinging 127.0.0.1 with 32 bytes of data:

Reply from 127.0.0.1: bytes=32 time<10ms TTL=128
Reply from 127.0.0.1: bytes=32 time<10ms TTL=128
Reply from 127.0.0.1: bytes=32 time<10ms TTL=128
Reply from 127.0.0.1: bytes=32 time<10ms TTL=128

Ping statistics for 127.0.0.1:
    Packets: Sent = 4, Received = 4, Lost = 0 (0% loss),
Approximate round trip times in milli-seconds:
    Minimum = 0ms, Maximum =  0ms, Average =  0ms
```

The ping results indicate no errors so the TCP/IP protocol stack is functioning properly on the system. The next check is to ping one of the Web servers' IP addresses. Issuing the ping command with the Production Web server's IP address reveals the following information:

```
Pinging 172.16.3.12 with 32 bytes of data:

Destination host unreachable.
```

```
Destination host unreachable.
Destination host unreachable.
Destination host unreachable.

Ping statistics for 172.16.3.12:
    Packets: Sent = 4, Received = 0, Lost = 4 (100% loss),
Approximate round trip times in milli-seconds:
    Minimum = 0ms, Maximum =  0ms, Average =  0ms
```

This information indicates that something dealing with TCP/IP on the workstation is probably not configured correctly. The next step would be to check the IP settings on the workstation. The results of the ipconfig command with the /all option executed on the problem workstation reveals the following information:

```
0 Ethernet adapter :

        Description . . . . . . . . : FEM656B Ethernet Adapter
        Physical Address. . . . . . : 00-10-5A-93-3F-0F
        DHCP Enabled. . . . . . . . : No
        IP Address. . . . . . . . . : 172.16.3.200
        Subnet Mask . . . . . . . . : 255.255.255.254
        Default Gateway . . . . . . : 172.16.3.1
        Primary WINS Server . . . . :
        Secondary WINS Server . . . :
        Lease Obtained. . . . . . . :
        Lease Expires . . . . . . . :
```

Solution. When we analyze the information revealed by the ipconfig command to the TCP/IP settings of other devices on the same network segment, one of the values is incorrect. The network or subnet mask of the network segment is 255.255.255.0 and the problem workstation's subnet mask is 255.255.255.254. To fix the problem, the subnet mask of the workstation was changed to 255.255.255.0 and the machine was rebooted. The workstation was able to successfully browse the Web servers when the subnet address was corrected.

Problem 2

The test workstations at the California location are unable to browse the Production Web server (production.ouraymountainwater.com) located at the Ouray location. The test workstations at the Pennsylvania and Ouray locations can browse the Production Web server at the Ouray location. All the test systems at both locations can access other locations on the Internet with no problem. Note that the Production Web server is a private Intranet Web server and is not accessible from an Internet location.

Troubleshooting. In this scenario there are several machines affected so we need to take a look at issues that can affect multiple machines. Since all the machines are in the same area, we'll take a look at physical items that all the systems share. Because all the machines have been moved to a new location, a new hub was placed near the machines so they could connect to the network. But, since the machines can access the Internet, the problem is probably not physical. The next step would be the analysis of the software components that allow the systems to communicate with each other. The fact that the systems can access the Internet indicates that the TCP/IP stack is functioning properly. In addition, since the systems at the other locations can access the Production Web server, the problem does not reside at the Web server. First, we need to determine if the problem workstations can communicate with the Production server at a simple level. Again, the ping utility is our troubleshooting tool. First, we ping the IP address, 172.16.3.12, of the Production Web server, and the following information is returned:

```
Pinging 172.16.3.12 with 32 bytes of data:

Reply from 172.16.3.12: bytes=32 time=1ms TTL=128
Reply from 172.16.3.12: bytes=32 time<10ms TTL=128
Reply from 172.16.3.12: bytes=32 time<10ms TTL=128
Reply from 172.16.3.12: bytes=32 time<10ms TTL=128

Ping statistics for 172.16.3.12:
    Packets: Sent = 4, Received = 4, Lost = 0 (0% loss),
Approximate round trip times in milli-seconds:
    Minimum = 0ms, Maximum =  1ms, Average =  0ms
```

With this information, we know that the Production Web server is accessible from the workstations at the California location. The next step is to test again with ping but this time with the name of the Production Web server. The following command is executed at several of the test workstations:

```
ping production.ouraymountainwater.com
```

The ping test reveals the following information:

```
Unknown host production.ouraymountainwater.com.
```

Solution. The results of the two ping tests reveal that the DNS name of the server cannot be resolved. When the team checked the configuration of the DNS server at the California location they found that a record for the Production server had not been added to the DNS database. The administrator added a new DNS record for the Production Web server and restarted the DNS service for the California location. Performing a verification check with the ping command returned the following data:

```
Pinging production.ouraymountainwater.com [172.16.3.12] with 32 bytes of data:

Reply from 172.16.3.12: bytes=32 time=1ms TTL=128
Reply from 172.16.3.12: bytes=32 time<10ms TTL=128
Reply from 172.16.3.12: bytes=32 time<10ms TTL=128
Reply from 172.16.3.12: bytes=32 time<10ms TTL=128

Ping statistics for 172.16.3.12:
    Packets: Sent = 4, Received = 4, Lost = 0 (0% loss),
Approximate round trip times in milli-seconds:
    Minimum = 0ms, Maximum =  1ms, Average =  0ms
```

The workstations at the California site can now successfully browse the Production Web server by using the name of the server, http://production .ouraymountainwater.com.

Problem 3

The Web development team has done some reconfiguration on the Production Web server to allow for more disk space. The team anticipates that more disk space may be needed for the Production database and has made some file system adjustments. When the team then attempts to start the Apache service on the Production Web server through the Services tool, they receive the error message displayed in Figure 9.4.

> **Troubleshooting.** The message shown in Figure 9.4 states that the service did not start but does not indicate the cause. The team then decides to try starting the service from the Apache menus under the Programs menu. When the attempt is made to start the Apache service from the Apache Start menu option, the message shown in Figure 9.5 appears.
>
> The message in the dialog box shown in Figure 9.5 is more informative than the first message (Figure 9.4). The information displayed indicates the ApacheCore.dll file cannot be found at the locations listed in the dialog box. The recent configuration changes on the Production Web server are probably the cause of the problem.

Figure 9.4   Apache start error message on Windows 2000 Server.

Figure 9.5   Apache start error message on Windows 2000 Server.

> **NOTE**   On a Linux Apache server, the following message would appear for
> the same situation:

```
./apachectl graceful: configuration broken, ignoring restart
./apachectl graceful: (run 'apachectl configtest' for details)
```

and executing apachectl configtest results in the following information:

```
./apachectl: /usr/local/apache/bin/httpd: No such file or directory
```

Solution. The team used the Windows 2000 Server Search feature in Explorer to locate the ApacheCore.dll file and found it in the G:\apache directory. The administrator moved the file back to the proper place, G:\apache\apache, and then attempted to start the Apache service. This resulted in another error, which is covered next.

Problem 4

When the administrator attempted to start the Apache service using the Services tool application on the Windows 2000 Server Production Web server, the message in Figure 9.6 appeared.

Troubleshooting. The message in Figure 9.6 is not very specific about the nature of the error, so the team attempts to start the service from the Apache menus. When the attempt is made to start Apache from the Apache Start menu, the following window displayed in Figure 9.7 appears.

Figure 9.6   Apache start error message on Windows 2000 Server.

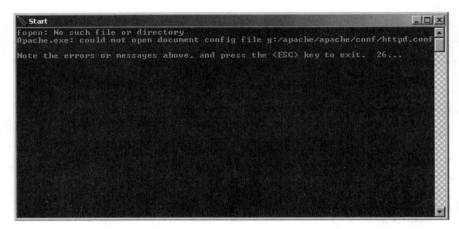

Figure 9.7 Apache start error message on Windows 2000 Server.

The information received in Figure 9.7 is much more informative about the cause of the problem. In this case, the httpd.conf file cannot be located. The recent configuration changes on the Production Web server are probably the cause of the problem.

NOTE On a Linux Apache Web server, the following message is reported when the same situation is present:

```
./apachectl graceful: configuration broken, ignoring restart
./apachectl graceful: (run 'apachectl configtest' for details)
```

and executing apachectl config test reveals the following information:

```
fopen: No such file or directory
httpd: could not open document config file /usr/local/apache/conf/httpd.conf
```

Solution. The team used the Windows 2000 Server Search feature in Explorer to locate the httpd.conf file and discovered it in the G:\apache\ directory. The administrator moved the httpd.conf file back to the proper place, G:\apache\apache\conf, and then attempted to start the Apache service. The Apache service started properly and no messages were displayed.

Problem 5

After the administrator successfully started the Apache service on the Production server, the team decided to check to make sure a user could access the Web site. When an attempt was made to browse the Production Web server, the message in Figure 9.8 was displayed in the browser's window.

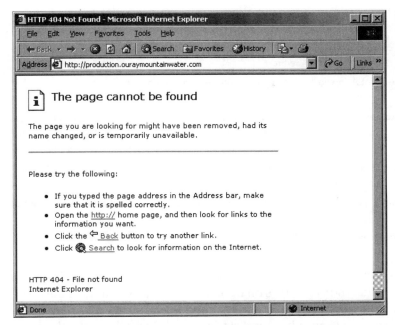

Figure 9.8   Browser message when attempting to access an Apache Web Server.

Troubleshooting. The message displayed in the browser window is very informative. The information clearly states that the content cannot be located. Also, the bottom of the browser window displays an HTTP 404 error message. Depending on the type of HTTP error message, the browser may or may not display the error code number.

The first digit in the HTTP code indicates the code category:

1xx	Informational	Displays information about status, such as switching protocols
2xx	Successful	The request sent by the client was successfully received, understood and accepted
3xx	Redirection	Further action is needed and the browser may or may not require user intervention
4xx	Client Error	It appears the client is in error based on the server's perspective
5xx	Server Error	The server detects it has an error or it cannot respond to the request

Under each of these categories are HTTP codes for different items. Some of the common error codes are listed here:

401	Unauthorized	Some type of authentication is needed, such as a user name and password

403	Forbidden	The Web server understood the request but access is not allowed
404	Not Found	The browser cannot locate the document specified in the request
405	Method Not Allowed	Often this results when an attempt is made to run a script that is not permitted
406	Not Acceptable	Information sent to the browser by the server cannot be understood. For example, the server is sending Flash content to the browser but the browser does not have the proper plugin
500	Internal Server Error	The Web server experienced an error and is unable to fulfill the request
501	Not Implemented	The Web server accepted the request but is not capable of fulfilling the request
503	Service Unavailable	The Web server is overloaded and cannot accept or fulfill any requests

The HTTP code reported by the browser in our problem scenario is 404 which implies that the problem is on the client side. To determine if the problem is specific to one machine or not, the team attempts to browse the Production Web server from other workstations and they all receive the same 404 error. Thus, even though it appears to be a client error, it may not be a problem with the client machine but the file the browser is attempting to access. On the Production Web server, the Web content is located at G:\content\htdocs and the files the Web server will look for and load when the document root directory is accessed are defined in the httpd.conf file. The pertinent section in the httpd.conf file for the Production Web server is:

```
#
# DirectoryIndex: Name of the file or files to use as a pre-written HTML
# directory index.  Separate multiple entries with spaces.
#
<IfModule mod_dir.c>
    DirectoryIndex index.htm index.html home.html
</IfModule>
```

If one of the three specified files is not there, or the name does match what is defined in the httpd.conf file, browsers will not be able to access the Web site. When the administrators search for the location of the files, they find an index.html file but it is not located in the document root directory, G:\content\htdocs.

Solution. On closer examination of the Web server, the Web development team discovered the entire Web content directory was not located at the directory specified in the httpd.conf file. When the content directory was moved back to the proper location, the workstations were able to successfully browse the Production Web server.

CHAPTER 10

Apache Add-Ons

There are many things you can add to Apache to provide more features and functions. Because the very nature of Apache is modular and open source, anyone can create and add their own stuff to Apache. However, if you are not into programming and coding, there are a number of add-ons for Apache available on the Internet and, in some cases, on the Linux installation CDs. In this chapter, we cover some of the additional components that are often found on Apache Web servers.

The first three add-ons we address together as a group because their combination enables features that greatly enhance Apache Web servers, especially for eCommerce and heavily used Web sites. Together, these three add-on products, MySQL, PHP, and SSL, permit Apache to handle secure data transfers between user and server, manipulate and/or retrieve queried information from databases, and present the information in customized formats for users of the Web site. SSL provides the information security, MySQL supplies database support, and PHP allows dynamic creation and manipulation of Web page content. In addition to MySQL, PHP, and SSL, we cover two more Apache add-ons separately. For some Web sites and servers it is desirable to use proxy services for performance and security. One solution is to set up Apache proxy servers and we cover this topic near the end of the chapter. Another add-on that is potentially useful for large Web development projects is WebDAV. At the end of this chapter we discuss how to add WebDAV support to Apache.

Each of the add-ons discussed in this chapter could themselves take up another book or two and involve a good deal of learning and time investment for new Web administrators. The goal of this chapter is to get you going on these products, installing them, and performing the minimal configuration to get them running. If you are new to any of these technologies, it is highly recommended that you experiment on a test system because, if components and settings are not configured properly, the server and/or you network could become compromised. The add-ons covered in this chapter are available for both Linux and Windows. All of the installation and compilation examples used in this chapter are performed on Linux systems running RedHat 7.1 and Apache 1.3.20. For other Linux and Unix based platforms, some of the commands and settings may need to be adjusted to fit your environment. For platform specific compilation, installation, and configuration procedures, refer to the individual product's documentation.

MySQL

MySQL is open source software for creating and working with SQL databases. Some Linux distributions include a copy of MySQL which may or may not be installed on your system. To obtain the latest version of MySQL for Linux or Windows, go to www.mysql.com. If you want to incorporate MySQL with Apache or other products, make sure you download the source code and not just the binary package.

To begin the installation process for the Linux version of MySQL, place the MySQL tarfile in an appropriate location in your directory structure. As an example in this section, we placed the tarfile in the /usr/local/download directory. The tar command is used to extract the necessary files from the MySQL tarfile. For the example used in this section, the file mysql-3.23.40.tar.gz is used. To extract the files, execute the following at a command prompt:

```
tar -xzf mysql-3.23.40.tar.gz
```

A subdirectory of the same name, minus the .tar.gz portion, is created at the same location as the tarfile. This directory, for example, mysql-3.23.40, contains all of the components necessary to build and install MySQL. Before you begin the installation process, the necessary MySQL user and group must be created. To perform this task, execute the following commands at a command prompt:

```
groupadd mysql
useradd -g mysql mysql
```

Navigate to the directory that contains the extracted files from the MySQL tarfile and execute the following command:

```
./configure --prefix=/usr/local/mysql
```

The prefix parameter specifies where MySQL will be installed. To start the process of building the MySQL binary, execute the following at the command prompt:

```
make
```

Note that running make for MySQL may take a long time depending on your system's hardware. When the make step is completed, the next task is to install the MySQL files in the /usr/local/mysql directory. Execute the following at the command line to install MySQL:

```
make install
```

To create the MySQL grant tables, execute the following command:

```
scripts/mysql_install_db
```

Some of the directories that are part of MySQL need to have the proper ownerships assigned. Execute the following commands to set the correct owners:

```
chown -R root /usr/local/mysql
chown -R mysql /usr/local/mysql/var
chgrp -R mysql /usr/local/mysql
```

To create the configuration file MySQL uses, execute the following command:

```
cp support-files/my-medium.cnf /etc/my.cnf
```

To load and initialize the MySQL application, execute the following command:

```
/usr/local/mysql/bin/safe_mysqld --user=mysql &
```

The MySQL installation and setup process creates two SQL databases. The mysql database is used to store all database privileges. The test database is used to test MySQL and contains entry privileges for the user who ran mysql_install_db and for root. These entries initially have no passwords but passwords can be assigned. To test and make sure MySQL is running properly and can locate the databases, navigate to the /usr/local/mysql/bin and execute the following command:

```
./mysqladmin version
```

The information displayed on the screen will be similar to the following example:

```
Ver 8.21 Distrib 3.23.40, for pc-linux-gnu on i586
Copyright (C) 2000 MySQL AB & MySQL Finland AB & TCX DataKonsult AB
This software comes with ABSOLUTELY NO WARRANTY. This is free software,
and you are welcome to modify and redistribute it under the GPL license

Server version          3.23.40-log
Protocol version        10
Connection              Localhost via UNIX socket
UNIX socket             /tmp/mysql.sock
Uptime:                 1 min 28 sec

Threads: 1  Questions: 2  Slow queries: 0  Opens: 6  Flush tables: 1  Open
tables: 0 Queries per second avg: 0.023
```

To verify the variables that are known to MySQL, execute the following from the /usr/local/mysql/bin directory:

```
./mysqladmin variables
```

The generated variable listing will be similar to the following:

```
+----------------------------+--------------------------------------------
---------------------------------------------------------------------------
----------------------------+
| Variable_name              | Value
|
+----------------------------+--------------------------------------------
---------------------------------------------------------------------------
----------------------------+
| ansi_mode                  | OFF
|
| back_log                   | 50
|
| basedir                    | /usr/local/mysql/
|
| binlog_cache_size          | 32768
|
| character_set              | latin1
|
| character_sets             | latin1 dec8 dos german1 hp8 koi8_ru latin2
swe7 usa7 cp1251 danish hebrew win1251 estonia hungarian koi8_ukr win1251ukr
greek win1250 croat cp1257 latin5 |
| concurrent_insert          | ON
|
| connect_timeout            | 5
|
```

datadir	/usr/local/mysql/var/
delay_key_write	ON
delayed_insert_limit	100
delayed_insert_timeout	300
delayed_queue_size	1000
flush	OFF
flush_time	0
have_bdb	NO
have_gemini	NO
have_innodb	NO
have_isam	YES
have_raid	NO
have_ssl	NO
init_file	
interactive_timeout	28800
join_buffer_size	131072
key_buffer_size	16773120
language	/usr/local/mysql/share/mysql/english/
large_files_support	ON
locked_in_memory	OFF
log	OFF
log_update	OFF
log_bin	ON
log_slave_updates	OFF
long_query_time	10

low_priority_updates		OFF
lower_case_table_names		0
max_allowed_packet		1047552
max_binlog_cache_size		4294967295
max_binlog_size		1073741824
max_connections		100
max_connect_errors		10
max_delayed_threads		20
max_heap_table_size		16777216
max_join_size		4294967295
max_sort_length		1024
max_user_connections		0
max_tmp_tables		32
max_write_lock_count		4294967295
myisam_recover_options		OFF
myisam_max_extra_sort_file_size		256
myisam_max_sort_file_size		2047
myisam_sort_buffer_size		8388608
net_buffer_length		7168
net_read_timeout		30
net_retry_count		10
net_write_timeout		60
open_files_limit		0
pid_file		/usr/local/mysql/var/apache2.pid
port		3306
protocol_version		10

```
| record_buffer                  | 131072
|
| query_buffer_size              | 0
|
| safe_show_database             | OFF
|
| server_id                      | 1
|
| slave_net_timeout              | 3600
|
| skip_locking                   | ON
|
| skip_networking                | OFF
|
| skip_show_database             | OFF
|
| slow_launch_time               | 2
|
| socket                         | /tmp/mysql.sock
|
| sort_buffer                    | 524280
|
| table_cache                    | 64
|
| table_type                     | MYISAM
|
| thread_cache_size              | 0
|
| thread_stack                   | 65536
|
| transaction_isolation          | READ-COMMITTED
|
| timezone                       | CDT
|
| tmp_table_size                 | 33554432
|
| tmpdir                         | /tmp/
|
| version                        | 3.23.40-log
|
| wait_timeout                   | 28800
|
+--------------------------------+-------------------------------------------
--------------------------------------------------------------------------
------------------------------+
```

It is a good idea to verify that you can shutdown and restart the MySQL service. To shutdown the service, execute the following command:

```
./mysqladmin -u root shutdown
```

To restart the service, use the following command:

```
./safe_mysqld --log &
```

To verify the presence of the databases, make sure MySQL is running and execute the following from the /usr/local/mysql/bin directory:

```
./mysqlshow
```

The results of the command should be like the following example:

```
+-----------+
| Databases |
+-----------+
| mysql     |
| test      |
+-----------+
```

To check the information in the MySQL database, use the following command:

```
./mysqlshow mysql
```

The results you receive should be similar to the following:

```
Database: mysql
+--------------+
|    Tables    |
+--------------+
| columns_priv |
| db           |
| func         |
| host         |
| tables_priv  |
| user         |
+--------------+
```

That is as far as we will go into SQL at this point because SQL is a whole other topic of its own!

PHP

PHP is a scripting language that is typically used to enhance Web pages to present, for example, information customized to the user browsing the page. The structure of PHP is similar to C and includes many features like database access, handling CGI requests, and image creation and manipulation. PHP is implemented on Apache as an add-on module, mod_php. When a user's browser requests a PHP-enabled page, the module acts on the document and makes changes to it before the Web server sends the results back to the user. Information about PHP and where to download the software is available at www.php.net.

PHP includes many extensions for working with other services and information on your system. For example, you can integrate PHP with MySQL, XML, and so on. In general, if you want PHP to work with one of the supported extensions in your environment, make sure the services and products are installed and configured before setting up PHP. As an example, we will compile and setup PHP to integrate with Apache 1.3.20 and MySQL. If you have performed the steps in the MySQL section of this chapter, then you are set to continue to add PHP with MySQL support. Before you begin the process of building PHP, Apache 1.3.20 must be preconfigured so PHP knows where everything is in the Apache source hierarchy. If Apache 1.3.20 source directory is not already present on your system, extract the Apache 1.3.20 tarfile. Navigate to the location of the extracted Apache files and execute the following at a command prompt:

```
./configure --prefix=/usr/local/apache
```

The prefix parameter indicates where Apache will be installed on the system. The next step is to start the PHP build process. Place the downloaded PHP tarfile in an appropriate location in your directory hierarchy and execute the following at a command prompt:

```
tar -xzf php-4.0.6.tar.gz
```

For the PHP setup example we are using in this section, the following directories are used:

`/usr/local/mysql`	Location of the installed and configured MySQL product
`/var/local/download/apache_1.3.20`	Location of the extracted files from the Apache 1.3.20 tarfile
`/var/local/download/php-4.0.6`	Location of the extracted files from the PHP 4 tarfile

Navigate to the directory that contains the extracted files from the PHP tarfile and execute the following at the command line:

```
./configure --with-mysql=/usr/local/mysql --with- ¬
apache=/var/local/download/apache_1.3.20 --enable-track-vars
```

The two with parameters indicate that PHP will be used together with MySQL and Apache. The next step is to compile the PHP binary. Execute the following at the command prompt:

```
make
```

The make process may take some time depending on your system's hardware and speed. When the binary build process is finished, the next step is to install the PHP software. Execute the following at the command prompt to install PHP:

```
make install
```

SSL

SSL or Secure Sockets Layer protocol provides the ability to transport data in a secure form across a network that may or may not be secure. The protocol provides its features in a client server type environment to prevent eavesdropping, tampering, or message forgery. SSL was originally developed by Netscape and is now managed by the IETF (Internet Engineering Task Force) organization. IETF renamed SSL to TSL or Transport Layer Security but you will still see both terms used and they essentially refer to the same protocol. TSL is defined in RFC 2246 which is available at www.ietf.org/rfc/rfc2246 .txt?number=2246. The key features of the TSL protocol are summarized below:

The connection is private. Cryptography is used for data encryption and the keys are generated uniquely for each connection and are based on a secret negotiated by another protocol.

The connection is reliable. Message transport includes a message integrity check.

The peer's identity can be authenticated using public key cryptography. This authentication can be made optional, but is generally required for at least one of the peers.

The negotiation of a shared secret is secure. This allows the negotiated secret to be unavailable to eavesdroppers.

The negotiation is reliable. If an attacker attempts to modify the negotiation communication between the peers, the action is detected by the peers.

One nice advantage of the TLS protocol is that it is application protocol independent. This allows higher level protocols to layer on top of the TLS Protocol transparently. An example of where SSL or TSL is used is in transporting credit card information and other sensitive data between the user and the servers across the non-secured Internet.

HTTP data transfers that are protected with SSL use port 443 instead of the standard non-secure HTTP port 80. In addition, you have to specify the protocol in the URL. For example, https://humanresources.ouraymountainwater .com. Notice the use of https instead of http.

There are two ways in which SSL can be implemented in Apache. One method is Apache-SSL, which is a secure Web server based on Apache, and SSLeay/OpenSSL. Information about Apache-SSL is available from www .apache-ssl.org. The second method is to use the mod_ssl module which is also based on OpenSSL. The mod_ssl module and information about the module is available from www.modssl.org. By the way, even though Apache-SSL and mod_ssl sound similar, they are not the same thing! To setup either implementation of SSL, the openssl-0.9.5a or higher component is needed. The OpenSSL module can be obtained from www.openssl.org. In this section we concentrate on the mod_ssl module.

To begin the build process of the mod_ssl module for Apache, OpenSSL must first be installed and setup. The compilation environment also needs access to the Apache 1.3.20 source files. If these are not already present on your system, extract the Apache 1.3 tarfile and make a notation of the location of the extracted files. For the example in this section, the following directories are used:

`/var/local/download/apache_1.3.20`	Location of the extracted files from the Apache 1.3.20 tarfile
`/var/local/download/openssl-0.9.6b`	Location of the extracted files from the OpenSSL tarfile
`/var/local/download/mod_ssl-2.0.4-1.3.20`	Location of the extracted files from the mod_ssl tarfile

Place the OpenSSL tarfile in an appropriate location in your directory hierarchy and extract the contents with the tar command. The default installation destination directory for OpenSSL is /usr/local/ssl directory. As an example in this section, the openssl-0.9.6b.tar.gz file is used and is located in the /var/local/download directory. To extract the files, execute the following at the /var/local/download command prompt:

```
tar -xzf openssl-0.9.6b.tar.gz
```

The extracted files will be placed in a directory where the name is the same as the tarfile without the .tar.gz extension. The next step is to start the process by running the config script. To perform this task, execute the following at a command prompt that is pointing to the contents of the extracted tarfile (for example, /var/local/download/openssl-0.9.6b):

```
./config
```

Depending on the hardware capabilities of the Linux system, the config phase of building OpenSSL may take a long time. When configure is completed, the next step is to make the OpenSSL binary. Execute the following at the command prompt:

```
make
```

The OpenSSL build environment includes a test tool that is run before you install the binary. To run the OpenSSL test, execute the following at the command prompt:

```
make test
```

The test may take several minutes to complete and the status of the test process is echoed on the screen. When the test is completed, execute the following to install the OpenSLL binary:

```
make install
```

The next step in the process is to configure the mod_ssl source environment so it knows the appropriate location of the Apache source files. Navigate to the directory that contains the downloaded mod_ssl tarfile and perform the following to extract the files:

```
tar -xzf mod_ssl-2.0.4-1.3.20.tar.gz
```

The tar command will extract the files to a directory that has the same name as the tarfile without the .tar.gz portion. Change to the extracted mod_ssl files directory to begin the build process. The first task is to run the configure script and specify the location of the Apache source files. Based on the example we are using in this section, the syntax for configure is:

```
./configure --with-apache=/var/local/download/apache_1.3.20
```

This process will add the appropriate references to the Apache source files so when Apache is compiled, all the necessary SSL elements will be included.

Compiling Apache with MySQL, PHP, and SSL Support

Now that all the individual pieces are compiled, installed, and/or configured, the next step is to compile Apache. Navigate to the directory that contains the

Apache source code. For the example in this section the directory is /var/local/download/apache_1.3.20. The configure command is used to start the process but with a number of options specified to include the additional elements. To begin, execute the following at a command prompt—note that this is a long command:

```
./configure --enable-module=ssl --activate-module=src/modules/php4/libphp4.a ┐
    --prefix=/usr/local/apache
```

The enable and activate parameters tell the environment to include mod_ssl and mod_php. When the configure step is completed, the next task is to create the Apache binary. At the command prompt, execute the following:

```
make
```

When make is completed, you should see the following at the end of the process:

```
+---------------------------------------------------------------+
| Before you install the package you should now prepare the SSL |
| certificate system by running the 'make certificate' command. |
| For different situations the following variants are provided: |
|                                                               |
| % make certificate TYPE=dummy     (dummy self-signed Snake Oil cert) |
| % make certificate TYPE=test      (test cert signed by Snake Oil CA) |
| % make certificate TYPE=custom    (custom cert signed by own CA) |
| % make certificate TYPE=existing (existing cert) |
|         CRT=/path/to/your.crt [KEY=/path/to/your.key] |
|                                                               |
| Use TYPE=dummy    when you're a  vendor package maintainer, |
| the TYPE=test     when you're an admin but want to do tests only, |
| the TYPE=custom   when you're an admin willing to run a real server |
| and TYPE=existing when you're an admin who ugrades a server. |
| (The default is TYPE=test)                                    |
|                                                               |
| Additionally add ALGO=RSA (default) or ALGO=DSA to select     |
| the signature algorithm used for the generated certificate.   |
|                                                               |
| Use 'make certificate VIEW=1' to display the generated data.  |
|                                                               |
| Thanks for using Apache & mod_ssl       Ralf S. Engelschall   |
|                                         rse@engelschall.com   |
|                                         www.engelschall.com   |
+---------------------------------------------------------------+
```

The next step is to create a certificate before installing Apache 1.3.20. There are four types of certificates available:

Dummyself Signed certificate that is used if you are the vendor of a software package.

Testself Signed certificate used for a test environment.

Custom This type of certificate is used for a production server.

Existing This certificate type is used for servers that are being upgraded.

If you don't specify the type of certificate, the default type is a test certificate. As an example, we will create a custom certificate. To perform this task, execute the following at the command prompt:

```
make certificate TYPE=custom
```

The process will prompt you to choose if you want the certificate to use RSA or DSA. The default is RSA and we will use that choice in our example. There are several prompts that follow for entering information about your environment. This data is included in the certificates the system will create.

```
1. Country name (2 letter code)
2. State or Province Name (full name)
3. Locality Name (eg, city)
4. Organization Name (eg, company)
5. Organization Unit Name (eg, section)
6. Common Name (eg, CA name)
7. Email address (eg, name@FQDN)
8. Certificate Validity (days)
Certificate Version (1 or 3) [default=3]
Encrypt the private key now?
Enter PEM pass phrase:
```

You will pass through these steps twice to create client side and server side certificates. At the end of the certificate setup process you will see the phrase on the screen:

```
Congratulations that you established your server with real certificates.
```

The last step is to install Apache. Execute the following at a command prompt:

```
make install
```

At the end of the install process you will see completion information along with some instructions:

```
+--------------------------------------------------------+
| You now have successfully built and installed the      |
| Apache 1.3 HTTP server. To verify that Apache actually |
| works correctly you now should first check the         |
| (initially created or preserved) configuration files   |
|                                                        |
|    /usr/local/apache/conf/httpd.conf                   |
|                                                        |
| and then you should be able to immediately fire up     |
| Apache the first time by running:                      |
|                                                        |
|    /usr/local/apache/bin/apachectl start               |
|                                                        |
| Or when you want to run it with SSL enabled use:       |
|                                                        |
|    /usr/local/apache/bin/apachectl startssl            |
|                                                        |
| Thanks for using Apache.        The Apache Group       |
|                                 http://www.apache.org/ |
+--------------------------------------------------------+
```

When the make install process is done, a copy of the php.ini-dist file needs to be placed in the /usr/local/lib directory and named php.ini. To accomplish this task, navigate to the directory that contains the extracted files from the PHP tarfile and execute the following at the command prompt:

```
cp php.ini-dist /usr/local/lib/php.ini
```

The php.ini file is used to control PHP. It must be called php.ini and located in the same place as the PHP working directory.

Before you start the Apache Web server, edit the httpd.conf file to set the proper ServerName directive. In addition, to enable basic usage of PHP, locate the following line in the httpd.conf file and remove the # (pound) sign at the beginning of the line so the line looks like the following:

```
AddType application/x-httpd-php .php
```

To start the Apache service, navigate to the /usr/local/apache/bin directory and execute the following:

```
./apachectl start
```

Once the service is started, open up your browser and access the default Web page on the server. The test page you should see will be similar to Figure 10.1.

To check the functionality of the SSL portion, you will need to stop the Web server with the command:

```
./apachectl stop
```

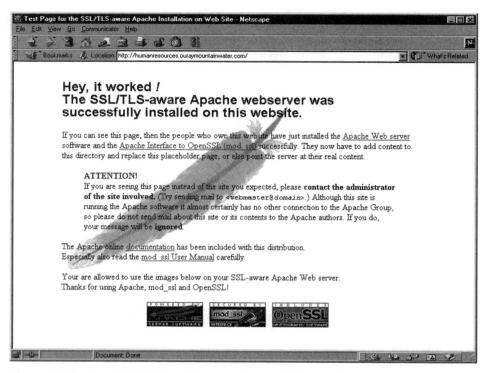

Figure 10.1   Sample Test Page from an SSL enabled Apache Server using the mod_ssl module.

and restart the service with SSL support. To activate SSL with Apache, enter the following at the command prompt:

```
./apachectl startssl
```

A prompt will appear asking you to enter the pass phrase that you defined when creating the certificate. When that information is successfully entered and accepted, the Apache service is started. To verify Apache with SSL functionality, access the Web server using https in the URL or address. For example,

```
https://humanresources.ouraymountainwater.com
```

Depending on the browser you are using, you will receive prompts to accept the certificate. Figures 10.2 through 10.6 show examples of the new certificate windows that appear in Netscape.

Figure 10.2   Netscape New Certificate prompt, 1 of 5.

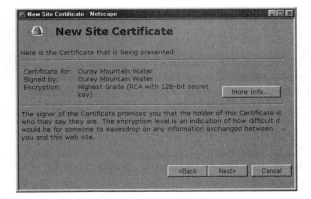

Figure 10.3   Netscape New Certificate prompt, 2 of 5.

Figure 10.4   Netscape New Certificate prompt, 3 of 5.

Figure 10.5 Netscape New Certificate prompt, 4 of 5.

Figure 10.7 is an example of the new certificate window that appears in Internet Explorer when a secure site is first accessed.

When you have completed the steps to accept the new certificate, the browser will display the default Apache Web server page. Figure 10.8 is an example of the Web server's test page.

The contents of the test page are identical to the example in Figure 10.1 but notice the lock icon shown in the toolbar and at the lower left corner is in the locked state. This indicates that the transmission of the information between the browser and the Web server is secure. The display of the Web pages in the browser may be a little slower on an SSL connection. This reason for the slower transmission is because the information going back and forth is being

Figure 10.6 Netscape New Certificate prompt, 5 of 5.

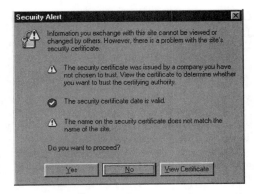

Figure 10.7   Internet Explorer New Certificate prompt.

encrypted and decrypted, and signed but that is okay because you want the information transmitted in a form that cannot be understood by unauthorized parties.

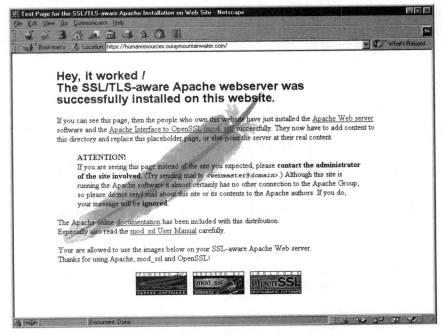

Figure 10.8   Apache Test Page for an SSL enabled Web Server.

To test the functionality of PHP, create an HTML document, such as test.php.html, and include a tag to use the phpinfo function. Below is an example of HTML code that was used to retrieve information about PHP on the PHP enabled Web server:

```
<!doctype html public "-//w3c//dtd html 4.0 transitional//en">
<html>
<head>
   <meta http-equiv="Content-Type" content="text/html; charset=iso-8859-1">
   <meta name="Author" content="Melanie Hoag">
   <meta name="GENERATOR" content="Mozilla/4.75 [en] (Win98; U) [Netscape]">
   <title>PHP Test</title>
</head>
<body>
<?phpinfo()?>
</body>
</html>
```

The key line to retrieve the PHP data is shown in bold in the above example. The rest of the content should be changed and modified to fit your environment. Copy the PHP info HTML document you created to the document root directory on the Web server. To view the information about PHP on the Web server, enter in the name of the PHP info HTML document after the server's name. For example, in this chapter the test server we are using is called humanresources.ouraymountainwater.com and the name of the PHP info HTML document is test.php.html. Using our example information, the syntax of the URL is:

```
http://humanresources.ouraymountainwater.com/test.php
```

The PHP info results displayed in the browser window cover many screens. We have included a few examples below to illustrate the type of information available. The beginning portion of the PHP information for the Human Resources Linux Web server is shown in Figure 10.9.

Information about the MySQL and PHP environment is illustrated in Figure 10.10.

The Apache environment with PHP information is displayed in Figure 10.11.

If Apache has been started with SSL support, the information gathered from phpinfo includes the SSL environment details. An example of a portion of the SSL data is shown in Figure 10.12.

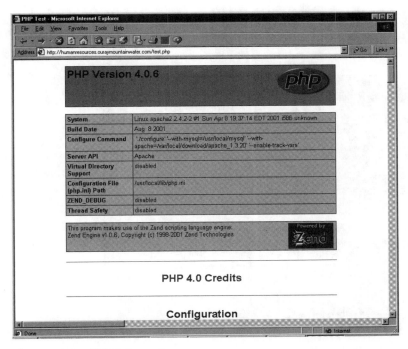

Figure 10.9   PHP information.

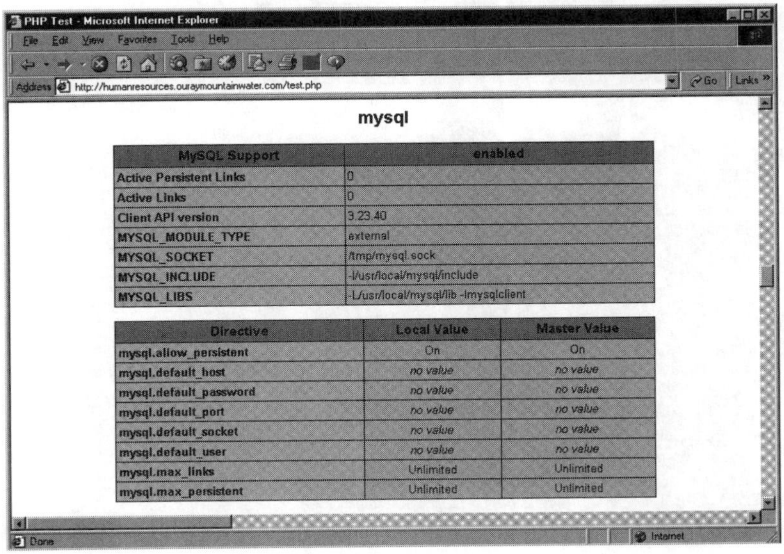

Figure 10.10   MySQL PHP information

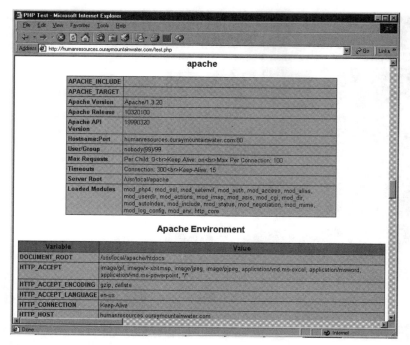

Figure 10.11   Apache PHP information.

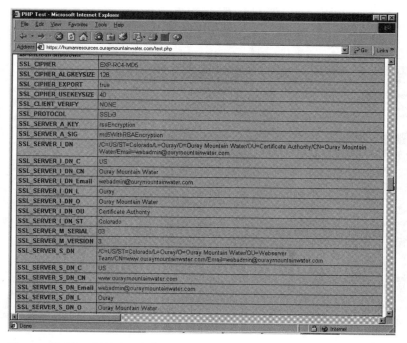

Figure 10.12   PHP SSL information.

Apache Proxy

In this section we address adding a proxy service to Apache. Proxies are services that operate between the Web service and the user and make requests to the Web server on behalf of the user or client. A proxy can help speed up the delivery of Web pages to the user because the proxy will store Web pages in memory. When a request comes into the proxy for a Web page, the proxy will first look to see if the page is in memory and if it is, deliver the page to the user. Serving pages from memory is much faster than accessing the disk for each request and the proxy service will only access the disk if necessary. A proxy service can be a separate server that is physically placed between the Web server and client, or it can run on the same system as the Web server. For security purposes, it is preferred to run the proxy service on a separate server to reduce unauthorized attempted communications with the Web server.

The mod_proxy module is used to add the proxy service to Apache. This module is not usually in the standard set of modules compiled into Apache but is included in the Apache source. To add the mod_proxy module, your will need to recompile Apache. As an example for this section, Apache 1.3.20 and the default /usr/local/apache installation directory are used. The location of the Apache 1.3.20 source files are located in the /var/local/download/apache_1.3.20 directory. To begin the process, navigate to the src directory under the root directory of the Apache source files /var/local/download/apache_1.3.20/src. Edit the Configuration.tmpl file in the Apache src directory and remove the # (pound) sign from the beginning of the AddModule line for libproxy.a. The section should then look like the following example:

```
## Optional Proxy
##
## The proxy module enables the server to act as a proxy for outside
## http and ftp services. It's not as complete as it could be yet.
## NOTE: You do not want this module UNLESS you are running a proxy;
##       it is not needed for normal (origin server) operation.

AddModule modules/proxy/libproxy.a
```

The next few steps involve building and installing the Apache application. Navigate to the root directory of the Apache source files and execute the following:

```
make
```

When make is completed, install Apache by executing the following at the command prompt:

```
make install
```

To verify the mod_proxy module is included in the compiled Apache, execute the following:

```
/usr/local/apache/bin/httpd -l
```

You should see mod_proxy.c in the list of compiled-in modules.

Before using the proxy service, the httpd.conf file must be modified to enable the proxy service. Listed below is the appropriate section of the httpd.conf file before any changes were made to activate the proxy.

```
#
# Proxy Server directives. Uncomment the following lines to
# enable the proxy server:
#
#<IfModule mod_proxy.c>
#    ProxyRequests On

#    <Directory proxy:*>
#        Order deny,allow
#        Deny from all
#        Allow from .your_domain.com
#    </Directory>

    #
    # Enable/disable the handling of HTTP/1.1 "Via:" headers.
    # ("Full" adds the server version; "Block" removes all outgoing Via:
headers)
    # Set to one of: Off | On | Full | Block
    #
#    ProxyVia On

    #
    # To enable the cache as well, edit and uncomment the following lines:
    # (no cacheing without CacheRoot)
    #
#    CacheRoot "/usr/local/apache/proxy"
#    CacheSize 5
#    CacheGcInterval 4
#    CacheMaxExpire 24
#    CacheLastModifiedFactor 0.1
#    CacheDefaultExpire 1
#    NoCache a_domain.com another_domain.edu joes.garage_sale.com

#</IfModule>
# End of proxy directives.
```

Notice that all of the necessary elements are in place but are commented out and are therefore not enabled.

The first item is to activate the proxy service, which is defined by the following directive.

```
ProxyRequests On
```

Enabling the ProxyRequests directive is all that is actually needed to enable the proxy capability. The next item is to specify what directories are proxied and who can use the proxy service. For example, to allow all directories to be included and to allow access only from a specific network, the following settings are used:

```
<Directory proxy:*>
    Order deny,allow
    Deny from all
    Allow from .ouraymountainwater.com
</Directory>
```

For the Allow directive you can include other domains and/or IP addresses. For example, to allow all machines from a specific subnet, 172.16.3.0, the following could be used:

```
Allow from 172.16.3.0/255.255.255.0
```

The Apache proxy can also be configured to use disk cache. Activating Proxy-Requests by itself does not enable caching. If you want to enable caching, then the following directive must be configured:

```
CacheRoot "/usr/local/apache/proxy"
```

Once the directory is specified for the cache, other directives can be set for the caching environment. For example, to set the size of the cache to 10MB, use the following setting for CacheSize:

```
CacheSize 10240
```

The CacheGcInterval directive allows you to specify the frequency to check the size of the files in the cache. If the total is greater than the CacheSize, files will be deleted to bring down the size of the cache. The unit of time for the CacheGC-Interval is in hours and you can specify portions of an hour. For example, to set the CacheGcInterval to check every three and a half hours, the setting is:

```
CacheGcInterval 3.5
```

The CacheMaxExpire directive indicates the amount of time a document can remain in cache before contacting the Web server where the document originated from. The unit of time for the CacheMaxExpire directive is in hours. To set the limit to 24 hours, use the following:

```
CacheMaxExpire 24
```

Documents sent from a Web server can contain an expiration time. However, if one is not supplied with the document, you can use the CacheLast-ModifiedFactor to calculate an expiration time. This directive uses the last modified time information on the document and multiplies that value by the number specified in the directive. For example, if the directive is defined as:

```
CacheLastModifiedFactor 0.1
```

and the last time the document was modified was 20 hours ago, the generated expiration time for the document is 2 hours. However, some documents do not support expiration times so attempting to calculate an expiration time would do no good. In these cases, you can set an expiration time with the Cache-DefaultExpire directive. For example, the following would set the Cache-DefaultExpire time to one hour:

```
CacheDefaultExpire 1
```

Note that the CacheMaxExpire directive does not override the CacheDefaultExpire value.

After making all the necessary changes to the httpd.conf file, the relevant section of the httpd.conf file now looks like the following:

```
#
# Proxy Server directives. Uncomment the following lines to
# enable the proxy server:
#
<IfModule mod_proxy.c>
    ProxyRequests On

    <Directory proxy:*>
        Order deny,allow
        Deny from all
        Allow from .ouraymountainwater.com 172.16.3.0/255.255.255.0
    </Directory>

    #
    # Enable/disable the handling of HTTP/1.1 "Via:" headers.
    # ("Full" adds the server version; "Block" removes all outgoing Via:
headers)
    # Set to one of: Off | On | Full | Block
    #
#    ProxyVia On

    #
    # To enable the cache as well, edit and uncomment the following lines:
    # (no cacheing without CacheRoot)
```

```
           #
           CacheRoot "/usr/local/apache/proxy"
           CacheSize 10240
           CacheGcInterval 3.5
           CacheMaxExpire 24
           CacheLastModifiedFactor 0.1
           CacheDefaultExpire 1
     #     NoCache a_domain.com another_domain.edu joes.garage_sale.com

     </IfModule>
     # End of proxy directives.
```

There are other settings and configuration options that can be used with mod_proxy. A good place to start is the listings and explanations of the mod_proxy directives. This information is available in the Apache documentation contained in your Apache installation or at http://httpd.apache.org/docs/mod/mod_proxy.html.

WebDAV

WebDAV is one of the hot protocols of great interest to the Web development community. On large Web site development projects that contain many participants, such as artists, scripting language coders, page layout teams, and others, it can be difficult keep track of the most current versions of all the files involved. WebDAV, or Web-Based Distributed Authoring and Versioning, provides a means to manage all these components in a Web development environment. WebDAV support can be added to Apache 1.3.x through the mod_dav module that is available from the Internet. The mod_dav module for Linux (and Windows) is available from www.webdav.org/mod_dav. For Apache 2, the WebDAV module is included with the Apache 2 distribution.

In this section, we will briefly cover basic aspects of WebDAV in Apache 1.3.20 on Linux. Before you implement WebDAV in your environment, it is recommended that you understand some of the security implications of this protocol. Since WebDAV allows Web developers to directly copy and manipulate files on the WebDAV enabled server, you need to be cautious of how you configure access to the system. When you enable WebDAV for a directory or a location you should also implement user authentication for access to the information.

To compile the mod_dav module into the Apache binary, you will need access to the Apache source files. For the example in this section, the Apache 1.3.20 source files are located at /var/local/download/apache_1.3.20. The downloaded mod_dav file will need to be placed in a directory in your file system and then extracted. For the example here, the mod_dav file, mod_dav-1.0.2-1.3.6.targz, is located in the /var/local/download directory. To extract the file contents, navigate to the /var/local/download directory and execute the following:

```
tar -xzf mod_dav-1.0.2-1.3.6.tar.gz
```

When that is completed, navigate to the directory created by the tar command, mod_dav-1.0.2-1.3.6. To begin the compilation process, we use configure and specify the location of the Apache source files:

```
./configure --with-apache=/var/local/download/apache_1.3.20
```

When configure is finished, the next step is to build the mod_dav elements by executing the following at the command prompt:

```
make
```

The next task is to install the mod_dav elements so they will be included in the Apache binary. Execute the following at the command prompt:

```
make install
```

After make install completes, which is very fast, the next step is to recompile Apache. Navigate to the directory that contains the Apache source files, /var/local/download/apache_1.3.20, and execute the following:

```
./configure --activate-module=src/modules/dav/libdav.a -- ¬
prefix=/usr/local/apache
```

The next task is to create the Apache binary with mod_dav built in. This is performed by executing the following at the command prompt:

```
make
```

When make is finished, the last step is to install Apache in the destination directory of /usr/local/apache by executing the following:

```
make install
```

To verify that mod_dav is included in the Apache binary, navigate to the /usr/local/apache/bin directory and execute the following:

```
./httpd -l
```

You should see in the list of compiled-in modules an entry for mod_dav.c.

Before mod_dav can be used, there are a few things to add to the httpd.conf file. The first is to activate the WebDAV environment. This can be done for a directory or a location. As an example here, we will turn on WebDAV support for the Web server's document root directory. To do this, add the line in bold to the area in the httpd.conf file that defines the Web content directory:

```
#
# This should be changed to whatever you set DocumentRoot to.
#
<Directory "/usr/local/apache/htdocs">

    DAV On

#
# This may also be "None", "All", or any combination of "Indexes",
# "Includes", "FollowSymLinks", "ExecCGI", or "MultiViews".
#
# Note that "MultiViews" must be named *explicitly* --- "Options All"
# doesn't give it to you.
#
    Options Indexes FollowSymLinks MultiViews

#
# This controls which options the .htaccess files in directories can
# override. Can also be "All", or any combination of "Options", "FileInfo",
# "AuthConfig", and "Limit"
#
    AllowOverride None

#
# Controls who can get stuff from this server.
#
    Order allow,deny
    Allow from all
</Directory>
```

In a portion of the httpd.conf file that is not inside a directory or location definition, add the following lines shown in bold:

```
#
# ServerName allows you to set a host name which is sent back to clients for
# your server if it's different than the one the program would get (i.e., use
# "www" instead of the host's real name).
#
# Note: You cannot just invent host names and hope they work. The name you
# define here must be a valid DNS name for your host. If you don't understand
# this, ask your network administrator.
# If your host doesn't have a registered DNS name, enter its IP address here.
# You will have to access it by its address (e.g., http://123.45.67.89/)
# anyway, and this will make redirections work in a sensible way.
```

```
#
# 127.0.0.1 is the TCP/IP local loop-back address, often named localhost. Your
# machine always knows itself by this address. If you use Apache strictly for
# local testing and development, you may use 127.0.0.1 as the server name.
#
ServerName humanresources.ouraymountainwater.com


DAVLockDB /usr/local/apache/bar/DAVLock


DAVMinTimeout 600


#
# DocumentRoot: The directory out of which you will serve your
# documents. By default, all requests are taken from this directory, but
# symbolic links and aliases may be used to point to other locations.
#
DocumentRoot "/usr/local/apache/htdocs"
```

These two settings specify where in the file system to place the lock file that mod_dav generates and the minimum lifetime in seconds of the lock. There are other directives you may want to explore for mod_dav, such as setting access permissions. The documentation for working with mod_dav is included with the downloaded mod_dav file and is also available online at www.webdav.org/mod_dav/install.html#apache.

Apache 2

Development of the Apache Web server is an ongoing process. The Apache Software Foundation's members and other organizations and people are continuously working on improving Apache, adding new features, and functions. One of the major projects underway is the development of Apache 2, which is in beta at the time of this writing. The most recent version of Apache 2 can be downloaded from http://httpd.apache.org/dist/httpd. It is advised that during the beta and alpha version releases, you test Apache 2 on systems separate from your production Web servers. While there are already a few sites running Apache 2 (www.apache.org, for example), it is best to run the different versions of Apache on different systems. Apache 2 versions are available for both Linux and Windows platforms in addition to other environments. Documentation for Apache 2 is available at http://httpd.apache.org/docs-2.0 and is included on the Apache 2 package you download.

Apache 2 includes many enhancements to the core components and to many of the modules. One of the overall objectives for Apache 2 is scalability on high-end hardware systems to utilize all the possible hardware power. With the increased usage of the Internet, more hardware horsepower is needed on heavily used Web sites and Web farms. Apache 1.3 already performs well under extreme conditions and Apache 2 makes the service even better.

What's New in Apache 2

Several areas of Apache have been enhanced in version 2 to improve performance and to add new features. In Tables 11.1 through 11.3, we summarize some of the areas that have been improved and/or extended.

Table 11.1 Enhancements to the Apache Core

AREA	DESCRIPTION
UNIX Threading	This enhancement only applies to the Linux (and other UNIX derivatives) version of Apache. The threading capability allows Apache to run natively on a multi-processor system and with multiple, simultaneous threads. This feature makes Apache 2 much more scalable on high-end hardware server systems.
New Build Environment	The architecture for compiling Apache under Linux has been reworked so it is similar to other package development environments. Apache 2.0 uses autoconf and libtool to determine which components of Apache are built. This new design is similar to the APACI architecture used for compiling Apache 1.3.
Multiprotocol Support	The underlying infrastructure necessary to support multiple protocols has been added to Apache 2. For example, Apache could be setup to handle HTTP and FTP so that a separate FTP service would not have to be added to the server environment.
Improved Support for non-UNIX Platforms	Apache runs faster and is more reliable on non-Linux and non–UNIX-based platforms such as Windows.
New Apache API	This is probably the biggest area of change, especially for programmers and developers working with the Apache 2 code and/or add-on modules.
IPv6 Support	If your system already has IPv6 supported by the underlying Apache Portable Runtime library, then Apache 2 will receive IPv6 listening sockets by default. Also, some of the directives have been modified to accept the IPv6 addressing methods. These directives include Listen, NameVirtualHost, and <VirtualHost>.
Filtering	Apache modules can be written to include filters on the information going into and out of the different modules that are used by the Web server. For example, a CGI script could be passed through a filter to look for Server Side Include references.

Table 11.2   Enhancements to Existing Apache Modules

MODULE	DESCRIPTION
mod_auth-db	This authentication module includes support for Berkely DB 3.0.
mod_auth_digest	This authentication module contains additional support for caching of session data across processes that are using shared memory.
mod_headers	The main enhancement to this module is improved flexibility. For example, request headers that are used by mod_proxy can be modified and response headers can be set depending on specified conditions.

Other features of Apache will include native support for SSL without the need to modify the Apache core.

One of main goals of the Apache project from the beginning has been modularity and Apache 2 further extends this concept. Apache 2 is bundled with a collection of Multi-Processing Modules (MPM) capable of binding to the available network ports available on the system. Each of these bindings can accept requests and start new processes as necessary. On Windows platforms, this MPM architecture makes Apache more efficient than previous versions because the modules can use native networking features in place of the POSIX layer that is used in Apache 1.3. The MPMs can be customized to fit a variety of environments, such as those that need a lot of scalability or those that need compatibility with older software. The MPMs that you wish to use must be

Table 11.3   New Modules

MODULE	DESCRIPTION
mod_charset_lite	This is an experimental module that allows for character set translation or recoding.
mod_dav	This module adds DAV support to Apache. DAV is the HTTP Distributed Authoring and Versioning specification, and is used to maintain and post Web content in a collaborative environment.
mod_file_cache	This module includes the functionality of the Apache 1.3 mod_nmap_static module plus additional caching abilities.

selected during configuration of the environment before compiling Apache. The available MPMs in Apache 2.0.16BETA are:

CORE PLATFORM	NAME
Linux	mpm_threaded_module
Linux	mpm_perchild_module
Linux	mpm_prefork_module
Windows	mpm_winnt_module

In addition, many of the directives that are in the Apache 1.3 core are now implemented in the MPMs.

Installing Apache 2 on Linux

When you are working with the beta and alpha builds of Apache 2 for Linux, you need to compile and install the Apache software. The process is very similar to compiling and installing Apache 1.3.20, which is covered in Chapter 2, "Installing Linux and Apache." The first step is to place the Apache 2 file you downloaded in a directory on your system, such as /var/local/download. The next step is to decompress the file with gzip. For example, the syntax for gzip for version Apache 2.0.016 beta is:

```
gzip -d httpd-2_0_16-beta.tar.gz
```

Execution of the gzip command results in a tarfile of the same name minus the .gz, for example, httpd-2_0_16-beta.tar. The next step in the process is to extract the contents of the tarfile with the tar command. The syntax to extract the files from httpd-2_0_16-beta.tar is:

```
tar -xvf httpd-2_0_16-beta.tar
```

The tar command creates a directory with the same name as the tarfile minus the –beta.tar portion of the name. The directory contains all the files necessary to compile Apache 2 and the documentation. To begin the process of compilation, change into the httpd-2_0_16-beta directory that contains all the extracted files from the tar command.

The default location to compile Apache 2 is /usr/local/apache2 If this is not the location you want, refer to the Compiling and Installing Apache.htm document that explains how to specify a different installation path. For the example, in this section, we will accept and use the default location /usr/local/

apache. To begin the process, execute the following at a command line in the extracted files directory:

```
./configure
```

The next step is to make the Apache 2 binary. That is initiated by executing the following at the command prompt:

```
make
```

The make step may take several minutes depending on the system's hardware. When make is finished, the last item is to copy the necessary files to the Apache 2 server root directory. This is performed by executing the following at the command prompt:

```
make install
```

Once you have compiled and installed Apache 2, some configuration is necessary to make the server functional. We have included here, as is, the contents of the httpd.conf file immediately following a compilation of Apache 2 on Linux before any modifications are made. By default, the httpd.conf file is located in the /usr/local/apache2/conf directory.

```
#
# Based upon the NCSA server configuration files originally by Rob McCool.
#
# This is the main Apache server configuration file.  It contains the
# configuration directives that give the server its instructions.
# See <URL:http://www.apache.org/docs/> for detailed information about
# the directives.
#
# Do NOT simply read the instructions in here without understanding
# what they do.  They're here only as hints or reminders.  If you are unsure
# consult the online docs. You have been warned.
#
# The configuration directives are grouped into three basic sections:
#  1. Directives that control the operation of the Apache server process as a
#     whole (the 'global environment').
#  2. Directives that define the parameters of the 'main' or 'default' server,
#     which responds to requests that aren't handled by a virtual host.
#     These directives also provide default values for the settings
#     of all virtual hosts.
#  3. Settings for virtual hosts, which allow Web requests to be sent to
#     different IP addresses or hostnames and have them handled by the
#     same Apache server process.
#
# Configuration and logfile names: If the filenames you specify for many
```

```
# of the server's control files begin with "/" (or "drive:/" for Win32), the
# server will use that explicit path.  If the filenames do *not* begin
# with "/", the value of ServerRoot is prepended -- so "logs/foo.log"
# with ServerRoot set to "/usr/local/apache" will be interpreted by the
# server as "/usr/local/apache/logs/foo.log".
#

### Section 1: Global Environment
#
# The directives in this section affect the overall operation of Apache,
# such as the number of concurrent requests it can handle or where it
# can find its configuration files.
#


#
# ServerRoot: The top of the directory tree under which the server's
# configuration, error, and log files are kept.
#
# NOTE!  If you intend to place this on an NFS (or otherwise network)
# mounted filesystem then please read the LockFile documentation
# (available at <URL:http://www.apache.org/docs/mod/core.html#lockfile>);
# you will save yourself a lot of trouble.
#
# Do NOT add a slash at the end of the directory path.
#
ServerRoot "/usr/local/apache2"


#
# The LockFile directive sets the path to the lockfile used when Apache
# is compiled with either USE_FCNTL_SERIALIZED_ACCEPT or
# USE_FLOCK_SERIALIZED_ACCEPT. This directive should normally be left at
# its default value. The main reason for changing it is if the logs
# directory is NFS mounted, since the lockfile MUST BE STORED ON A LOCAL
# DISK. The PID of the main server process is automatically appended to
# the filename.
#
#LockFile logs/accept.lock


#
# PidFile: The file in which the server should record its process
# identification number when it starts.
#
PidFile logs/httpd.pid


#
# ScoreBoardFile: File used to store internal server process information.
# Not all architectures require this.  But if yours does (you'll know because
# this file will be  created when you run Apache) then you *must* ensure that
# no two invocations of Apache share the same scoreboard file.
#
<IfModule !perchild.c>
```

```
ScoreBoardFile logs/apache_runtime_status
</IfModule>

#
# Timeout: The number of seconds before receives and sends time out.
#
Timeout 300

#
# KeepAlive: Whether or not to allow persistent connections (more than
# one request per connection). Set to "Off" to deactivate.
#
KeepAlive On

#
# MaxKeepAliveRequests: The maximum number of requests to allow
# during a persistent connection. Set to 0 to allow an unlimited amount.
# We recommend you leave this number high, for maximum performance.
#
MaxKeepAliveRequests 100

#
# KeepAliveTimeout: Number of seconds to wait for the next request from the
# same client on the same connection.
#
KeepAliveTimeout 15

##
## Server-Pool Size Regulation (MPM specific)
##

# prefork MPM
# StartServers ......... number of server processes to start
# MinSpareServers ...... minimum number of server processes which are kept spare
# MaxSpareServers ...... maximum number of server processes which are kept spare
# MaxClients .......... maximum number of server processes allowed to start
# MaxRequestsPerChild .. maximum number of requests a server process serves
<IfModule prefork.c>
StartServers          5
MinSpareServers       5
MaxSpareServers      10
MaxClients           20
MaxRequestsPerChild   0
</IfModule>

# pthread MPM
# StartServers ......... initial  number of server processes to start
# MaxClients .......... maximum  number of server processes allowed to start
# MinSpareThreads ...... minimum  number of worker threads which are kept spare
# MaxSpareThreads ...... maximum  number of worker threads which are kept spare
# ThreadsPerChild ...... constant number of worker threads in each server process
```

```
# MaxRequestsPerChild .. maximum  number of requests a server process serves
<IfModule threaded.c>
StartServers        3
MaxClients          8
MinSpareThreads     5
MaxSpareThreads    10
ThreadsPerChild    25
MaxRequestsPerChild 0
</IfModule>

# perchild MPM
# NumServers ........... constant number of server processes
# StartThreads ......... initial  number of worker threads in each server
    process
# MinSpareThreads ...... minimum  number of worker threads which are kept spare
# MaxSpareThreads ...... maximum  number of worker threads which are kept spare
# MaxThreadsPerChild ... maximum  number of worker threads in each server process
# MaxRequestsPerChild .. maximum  number of connections per server process (then
    it dies)
<IfModule perchild.c>
NumServers          5
StartThreads        5
MinSpareThreads     5
MaxSpareThreads    10
MaxThreadsPerChild 20
MaxRequestsPerChild 0
</IfModule>

#
# Listen: Allows you to bind Apache to specific IP addresses and/or
# ports, in addition to the default. See also the <VirtualHost>
# directive.
#
#Listen 3000
#Listen 12.34.56.78:80

#
# BindAddress: You can support virtual hosts with this option. This directive
# is used to tell the server which IP address to listen to. It can either
# contain "*", an IP address, or a fully qualified Internet domain name.
# See also the <VirtualHost> and Listen directives.
#
#BindAddress *

#
# Dynamic Shared Object (DSO) Support
#
# To be able to use the functionality of a module which was built as a DSO you
# have to place corresponding `LoadModule' lines at this location so the
# directives contained in it are actually available _before_ they are used.
# Please read the file README.DSO in the Apache 1.3 distribution for more
```

```
# details about the DSO mechanism and run `httpd -l' for the list of already
# built-in (statically linked and thus always available) modules in your httpd
# binary.
#
# Note: The order is which modules are loaded is important.  Don't change
# the order below without expert advice.
#
# Example:
# LoadModule foo_module modules/mod_foo.so

### Section 2: 'Main' server configuration
#
# The directives in this section set up the values used by the 'main'
# server, which responds to any requests that aren't handled by a
# <VirtualHost> definition.  These values also provide defaults for
# any <VirtualHost> containers you may define later in the file.
#
# All of these directives may appear inside <VirtualHost> containers,
# in which case these default settings will be overridden for the
# virtual host being defined.
#


#
# If your ServerType directive (set earlier in the 'Global Environment'
# section) is set to "inetd", the next few directives don't have any
# effect since their settings are defined by the inetd configuration.
# Skip ahead to the ServerAdmin directive.
#


#
# Port: The port to which the standalone server listens. For
# ports < 1023, you will need httpd to be run as root initially.
#
Port 80


#
# If you wish httpd to run as a different user or group, you must run
# httpd as root initially and it will switch.
#
# User/Group: The name (or #number) of the user/group to run httpd as.
#  . On SCO (ODT 3) use "User nouser" and "Group nogroup".
#  . On HPUX you may not be able to use shared memory as nobody, and the
#    suggested workaround is to create a user www and use that user.
#  NOTE that some kernels refuse to setgid(Group) or semctl(IPC_SET)
#  when the value of (unsigned)Group is above 60000;
#  don't use Group #-1 on these systems!
#
User nobody
Group #-1

#
```

```
# ServerAdmin: Your address, where problems with the server should be
# e-mailed.  This address appears on some server-generated pages, such
# as error documents.
#
ServerAdmin you@your.address


#
# ServerName allows you to set a host name which is sent back to clients for
# your server if it's different than the one the program would get (i.e., use
# "www" instead of the host's real name).
#
# Note: You cannot just invent host names and hope they work. The name you
# define here must be a valid DNS name for your host. If you don't understand
# this, ask your network administrator.
# If your host doesn't have a registered DNS name, enter its IP address here.
# You will have to access it by its address (e.g., http://123.45.67.89/)
# anyway, and this will make redirections work in a sensible way.
#
#ServerName new.host.name


#
# DocumentRoot: The directory out of which you will serve your
# documents. By default, all requests are taken from this directory, but
# symbolic links and aliases may be used to point to other locations.
#
DocumentRoot "/usr/local/apache2/htdocs"


#
# Each directory to which Apache has access, can be configured with respect
# to which services and features are allowed and/or disabled in that
# directory (and its subdirectories).
#
# First, we configure the "default" to be a very restrictive set of
# permissions.
#
<Directory />
    Options FollowSymLinks
    AllowOverride None
</Directory>


#
# Note that from this point forward you must specifically allow
# particular features to be enabled - so if something's not working as
# you might expect, make sure that you have specifically enabled it
# below.
#


#
# This should be changed to whatever you set DocumentRoot to.
#
<Directory "/usr/local/apache2/htdocs">
```

```
#
# This may also be "None", "All", or any combination of "Indexes",
# "Includes", "FollowSymLinks", "ExecCGI", or "MultiViews".
#
# Note that "MultiViews" must be named *explicitly* --- "Options All"
# doesn't give it to you.
#
    Options Indexes FollowSymLinks MultiViews


#
# This controls which options the .htaccess files in directories can
# override. Can also be "All", or any combination of "Options", "FileInfo",
# "AuthConfig", and "Limit"
#
    AllowOverride None


#
# Controls who can get stuff from this server.
#
    Order allow,deny
    Allow from all
</Directory>


#
# UserDir: The name of the directory which is appended onto a user's home
# directory if a ~user request is received.
#
UserDir public_html


#
# Control access to UserDir directories.  The following is an example
# for a site where these directories are restricted to read-only.
#
#<Directory /home/*/public_html>
#    AllowOverride FileInfo AuthConfig Limit
#    Options MultiViews Indexes SymLinksIfOwnerMatch IncludesNoExec
#    <Limit GET POST OPTIONS PROPFIND>
#        Order allow,deny
#        Allow from all
#    </Limit>
#    <LimitExcept GET POST OPTIONS PROPFIND>
#        Order deny,allow
#        Deny from all
#    </LimitExcept>
#</Directory>


#
# DirectoryIndex: Name of the file or files to use as a pre-written HTML
# directory index.  Separate multiple entries with spaces.
#
```

```
DirectoryIndex index.html

#
# AccessFileName: The name of the file to look for in each directory
# for access control information.
#
AccessFileName .htaccess

#
# The following lines prevent .htaccess files from being viewed by
# Web clients.  Since .htaccess files often contain authorization
# information, access is disallowed for security reasons.  Comment
# these lines out if you want Web visitors to see the contents of
# .htaccess files.  If you change the AccessFileName directive above,
# be sure to make the corresponding changes here.
#
# Also, folks tend to use names such as .htpasswd for password
# files, so this will protect those as well.
#
<Files ~ "^\.ht">
    Order allow,deny
    Deny from all
</Files>

#
# CacheNegotiatedDocs: By default, Apache sends "Pragma: no-cache" with each
# document that was negotiated on the basis of content. This asks proxy
# servers not to cache the document. Uncommenting the following line disables
# this behavior, and proxies will be allowed to cache the documents.
#
#CacheNegotiatedDocs

#
# UseCanonicalName:  (new for 1.3)  With this setting turned on, whenever
# Apache needs to construct a self-referencing URL (a URL that refers back
# to the server the response is coming from) it will use ServerName and
# Port to form a "canonical" name.  With this setting off, Apache will
# use the hostname:port that the client supplied, when possible.  This
# also affects SERVER_NAME and SERVER_PORT in CGI scripts.
#
UseCanonicalName On

#
# TypesConfig describes where the mime.types file (or equivalent) is
# to be found.
#
TypesConfig conf/mime.types

#
# DefaultType is the default MIME type the server will use for a document
# if it cannot otherwise determine one, such as from filename extensions.
```

```
# If your server contains mostly text or HTML documents, "text/plain" is
# a good value.  If most of your content is binary, such as applications
# or images, you may want to use "application/octet-stream" instead to
# keep browsers from trying to display binary files as though they are
# text.
#
DefaultType text/plain


#
# The mod_mime_magic module allows the server to use various hints from the
# contents of the file itself to determine its type.  The MIMEMagicFile
# directive tells the module where the hint definitions are located.
# mod_mime_magic is not part of the default server (you have to add
# it yourself with a LoadModule [see the DSO paragraph in the 'Global
# Environment' section], or recompile the server and include mod_mime_magic
# as part of the configuration), so it's enclosed in an <IfModule> container.
# This means that the MIMEMagicFile directive will only be processed if the
# module is part of the server.
#
<IfModule mod_mime_magic.c>
    MIMEMagicFile conf/magic
</IfModule>


#
# HostnameLookups: Log the names of clients or just their IP addresses
# e.g., www.apache.org (on) or 204.62.129.132 (off).
# The default is off because it'd be overall better for the net if people
# had to knowingly turn this feature on, since enabling it means that
# each client request will result in AT LEAST one lookup request to the
# nameserver.
#
HostnameLookups Off


#
# ErrorLog: The location of the error log file.
# If you do not specify an ErrorLog directive within a <VirtualHost>
# container, error messages relating to that virtual host will be
# logged here.  If you *do* define an error logfile for a <VirtualHost>
# container, that host's errors will be logged there and not here.
#
ErrorLog logs/error_log


#
# LogLevel: Control the number of messages logged to the error_log.
# Possible values include: debug, info, notice, warn, error, crit,
# alert, emerg.
#
LogLevel warn


#
# The following directives define some format nicknames for use with
```

```
# a CustomLog directive (see below).
#
LogFormat "%h %l %u %t \"%r\" %>s %b \"%{Referer}i\" \"%{User-Agent}i\""
   combined
LogFormat "%h %l %u %t \"%r\" %>s %b" common
LogFormat "%{Referer}i -> %U" referer
LogFormat "%{User-agent}i" agent


#
# The location and format of the access logfile (Common Logfile Format).
# If you do not define any access logfiles within a <VirtualHost>
# container, they will be logged here.  Contrariwise, if you *do*
# define per-<VirtualHost> access logfiles, transactions will be
# logged therein and *not* in this file.
#
CustomLog logs/access_log common


#
# If you would like to have agent and referer logfiles, uncomment the
# following directives.
#
#CustomLog logs/referer_log referer
#CustomLog logs/agent_log agent


#
# If you prefer a single logfile with access, agent, and referer information
# (Combined Logfile Format) you can use the following directive.
#
#CustomLog logs/access_log combined


#
# Optionally add a line containing the server version and virtual host
# name to server-generated pages (error documents, FTP directory listings,
# mod_status and mod_info output etc., but not CGI generated documents).
# Set to "EMail" to also include a mailto: link to the ServerAdmin.
# Set to one of:  On | Off | EMail
#
ServerSignature On


#
# Aliases: Add here as many aliases as you need (with no limit). The format is
# Alias fakename realname
#
# Note that if you include a trailing / on fakename then the server will
# require it to be present in the URL.  So "/icons" isn't aliased in this
# example, only "/icons/"..
#
Alias /icons/ "/usr/local/apache2/icons/"

<Directory "/usr/local/apache2/icons">
    Options Indexes MultiViews
```

```
        AllowOverride None
        Order allow,deny
        Allow from all
</Directory>


#
# ScriptAlias: This controls which directories contain server scripts.
# ScriptAliases are essentially the same as Aliases, except that
# documents in the realname directory are treated as applications and
# run by the server when requested rather than as documents sent to the client.
# The same rules about trailing "/" apply to ScriptAlias directives as to
# Alias.
#
ScriptAlias /cgi-bin/ "/usr/local/apache2/cgi-bin/"

<IfModule mod_cgid.c>
#
# Additional to mod_cgid.c settings, mod_cgid has Scriptsock <path>
# for setting UNIX socket for communicating with cgid.
#
#Scriptsock             logs/cgisock
</IfModule>


#
# "/usr/local/apache2/cgi-bin" should be changed to whatever your ScriptAliased
# CGI directory exists, if you have that configured.
#
<Directory "/usr/local/apache2/cgi-bin">
    AllowOverride None
    Options None
    Order allow,deny
    Allow from all
</Directory>


#
# Redirect allows you to tell clients about documents which used to exist in
# your server's namespace, but do not anymore. This allows you to tell the
# clients where to look for the relocated document.
# Format: Redirect old-URI new-URL
#


#
# Directives controlling the display of server-generated directory listings.
#


# FancyIndexing is whether you want fancy directory indexing or standard.
# VersionSort is whether files containing version numbers should be
# compared in the natural way, so that `apache-1.3.9.tar' is placed before
# `apache-1.3.12.tar'.
IndexOptions FancyIndexing VersionSort
```

```
#
# AddIcon* directives tell the server which icon to show for different
# files or filename extensions.  These are only displayed for
# FancyIndexed directories.
#
AddIconByEncoding (CMP,/icons/compressed.gif) x-compress x-gzip

AddIconByType (TXT,/icons/text.gif) text/*
AddIconByType (IMG,/icons/image2.gif) image/*
AddIconByType (SND,/icons/sound2.gif) audio/*
AddIconByType (VID,/icons/movie.gif) video/*

AddIcon /icons/binary.gif .bin .exe
AddIcon /icons/binhex.gif .hqx
AddIcon /icons/tar.gif .tar
AddIcon /icons/world2.gif .wrl .wrl.gz .vrml .vrm .iv
AddIcon /icons/compressed.gif .Z .z .tgz .gz .zip
AddIcon /icons/a.gif .ps .ai .eps
AddIcon /icons/layout.gif .html .shtml .htm .pdf
AddIcon /icons/text.gif .txt
AddIcon /icons/c.gif .c
AddIcon /icons/p.gif .pl .py
AddIcon /icons/f.gif .for
AddIcon /icons/dvi.gif .dvi
AddIcon /icons/uuencoded.gif .uu
AddIcon /icons/script.gif .conf .sh .shar .csh .ksh .tcl
AddIcon /icons/tex.gif .tex
AddIcon /icons/bomb.gif core

AddIcon /icons/back.gif ..
AddIcon /icons/hand.right.gif README
AddIcon /icons/folder.gif ^^DIRECTORY^^
AddIcon /icons/blank.gif ^^BLANKICON^^

#
# DefaultIcon is which icon to show for files which do not have an icon
# explicitly set.
#
DefaultIcon /icons/unknown.gif

#
# AddDescription allows you to place a short description after a file in
# server-generated indexes.  These are only displayed for FancyIndexed
# directories.
# Format: AddDescription "description" filename
#
#AddDescription "GZIP compressed document" .gz
#AddDescription "tar archive" .tar
#AddDescription "GZIP compressed tar archive" .tgz

#
```

```
# ReadmeName is the name of the README file the server will look for by
# default, and append to directory listings.
#
# HeaderName is the name of a file which should be prepended to
# directory indexes.
#
# The server will first look for name.html and include it if found.
# If name.html doesn't exist, the server will then look for name.txt
# and include it as plaintext if found.
#
ReadmeName README
HeaderName HEADER


#
# IndexIgnore is a set of filenames which directory indexing should ignore
# and not include in the listing.  Shell-style wildcarding is permitted.
#
IndexIgnore .??* *~ *# HEADER* README* RCS CVS *,v *,t


#
# AddEncoding allows you to have certain browsers (Mosaic/X 2.1+) uncompress
# information on the fly. Note: Not all browsers support this.
# Despite the name similarity, the following Add* directives have nothing
# to do with the FancyIndexing customization directives above.
#
AddEncoding x-compress Z
AddEncoding x-gzip gz tgz


#
# DefaultLanguage and AddLanguage allows you to specify the language of
# a document. You can then use content negotiation to give a browser a
# file in a language the user can understand.
#
# Specify a default language. This means that all data
# going out without a specific language tag (see below) will
# be marked with this one. You probably do NOT want to set
# this unless you are sure it is correct for all cases.
#
# * It is generally better to not mark a page as
# * being a certain language than marking it with the wrong
# * language!
#
# DefaultLanguage nl
#
# Note 1: The suffix does not have to be the same as the language
# keyword --- those with documents in Polish (whose net-standard
# language code is pl) may wish to use "AddLanguage pl .po" to
# avoid the ambiguity with the common suffix for perl scripts.
#
# Note 2: The example entries below illustrate that in
# some cases the two character 'Language' abbreviation is not
```

```
# identical to the two character 'Country' code for its country,
# E.g. 'Danmark/dk' versus 'Danish/da'.
#
# Note 3: In the case of 'ltz' we violate the RFC by using a three char
# specifier. There is 'work in progress' to fix this and get
# the reference data for rfc1766 cleaned up.
#
# Danish (da) - Dutch (nl) - English (en) - Estonian (et)
# French (fr) - German (de) - Greek-Modern (el)
# Italian (it) - Norwegian (no) - Korean (kr)
# Portugese (pt) - Luxembourgeois* (ltz)
# Spanish (es) - Swedish (sv) - Catalan (ca) - Czech(cz)
# Polish (pl) - Brazilian Portuguese (pt-br) - Japanese (ja)
# Russian (ru)
#
AddLanguage da .dk
AddLanguage nl .nl
AddLanguage en .en
AddLanguage et .et
AddLanguage fr .fr
AddLanguage de .de
AddLanguage el .el
AddLanguage it .it
AddLanguage ja .ja
AddLanguage pl .po
AddLanguage kr .kr
AddLanguage pt .pt
AddLanguage no .no
AddLanguage pt-br .pt-br
AddLanguage ltz .ltz
AddLanguage ca .ca
AddLanguage es .es
AddLanguage sv .se
AddLanguage cz .cz
AddLanguage ru .ru
AddLanguage tw .tw
AddLanguage zh-tw .tw


# LanguagePriority allows you to give precedence to some languages
# in case of a tie during content negotiation.
#
# Just list the languages in decreasing order of preference. We have
# more or less alphabetized them here. You probably want to change this.
#
LanguagePriority en da nl et fr de el it ja kr no pl pt pt-br ltz ca es sv tw


# Specify a default charset for all pages sent out. This is
# always a good idea and opens the door for future internationalisation
# of your web site, should you ever want it. Specifying it as
# a default does little harm; as the standard dictates that a page
```

```
# is in iso-8859-1 (latin1) unless specified otherwise i.e. you
# are merely stating the obvious. There are also some security
# reasons in browsers, related to javascript and URL parsing
# which encourage you to always set a default char set.
#
AddDefaultCharset       ISO-8859-1


#
# Commonly used filename extensions to character sets. You probably
# want to avoid clashes with the language extensions, unless you
# are good at carefully testing your setup after each change.
# See ftp://ftp.isi.edu/in-notes/iana/assignments/character-sets for
# the official list of charset names and their respective RFCs
#
AddCharset ISO-8859-1  .iso8859-1  .latin1
AddCharset ISO-8859-2  .iso8859-2  .latin2 .cen
AddCharset ISO-8859-3  .iso8859-3  .latin3
AddCharset ISO-8859-4  .iso8859-4  .latin4
AddCharset ISO-8859-5  .iso8859-5  .latin5 .cyr .iso-ru
AddCharset ISO-8859-6  .iso8859-6  .latin6 .arb
AddCharset ISO-8859-7  .iso8859-7  .latin7 .grk
AddCharset ISO-8859-8  .iso8859-8  .latin8 .heb
AddCharset ISO-8859-9  .iso8859-9  .latin9 .trk
AddCharset ISO-2022-JP .iso2022-jp .jis
AddCharset ISO-2022-KR .iso2022-kr .kis
AddCharset ISO-2022-CN .iso2022-cn .cis
AddCharset Big5         .Big5       .big5
# For russian, more than one charset is used (depends on client, mostly):
AddCharset WINDOWS-1251 .cp-1251    .win-1251
AddCharset CP866        .cp866
AddCharset KOI8-r       .koi8-r .koi8-ru
AddCharset KOI8-ru      .koi8-uk .ua
AddCharset ISO-10646-UCS-2 .ucs2
AddCharset ISO-10646-UCS-4 .ucs4
AddCharset UTF-8        .utf8


# The set below does not map to a specific (iso) standard
# but works on a fairly wide range of browsers. Note that
# capitalization actually matters (it should not, but it
# does for some browsers).
#
# See ftp://ftp.isi.edu/in-notes/iana/assignments/character-sets
# for a list of sorts. But browsers support few.
#
AddCharset GB2312       .gb2312 .gb
AddCharset utf-7        .utf7
AddCharset utf-8        .utf8
AddCharset big5              .big5 .b5
AddCharset EUC-TW       .euc-tw
AddCharset EUC-JP       .euc-jp
AddCharset EUC-KR       .euc-kr
```

```
AddCharset shift_jis   .sjis

# AddType allows you to tweak mime.types without actually editing it, or to
# make certain files to be certain types.
#
# For example, the PHP3 module (not part of the Apache distribution - see
# http://www.php.net) will typically use:
#
#AddType application/x-httpd-php3 .php3
#AddType application/x-httpd-php3-source .phps

AddType application/x-tar .tgz

#
# AddHandler allows you to map certain file extensions to "handlers",
# actions unrelated to filetype. These can be either built into the server
# or added with the Action command (see below)
#
# If you want to use server side includes, or CGI outside
# ScriptAliased directories, uncomment the following lines.
#
# To use CGI scripts:
#
#AddHandler cgi-script .cgi

#
# To use server-parsed HTML files
#
#<FilesMatch "\.shtml(\..+)?$">
#    SetOutputFilter INCLUDES
#</FilesMatch>

#
# Uncomment the following line to enable Apache's send-asis HTTP file
# feature
#
#AddHandler send-as-is asis

#
# If you wish to use server-parsed imagemap files, use
#
#AddHandler imap-file map

#
# To enable type maps, you might want to use
#
#AddHandler type-map var

#
# Action lets you define media types that will execute a script whenever
# a matching file is called. This eliminates the need for repeated URL
```

```
# pathnames for oft-used CGI file processors.
# Format: Action media/type /cgi-script/location
# Format: Action handler-name /cgi-script/location
#


#
# MetaDir: specifies the name of the directory in which Apache can find
# meta information files. These files contain additional HTTP headers
# to include when sending the document
#
#MetaDir .web


#
# MetaSuffix: specifies the file name suffix for the file containing the
# meta information.
#
#MetaSuffix .meta


#
# Customizable error response (Apache style)
#  these come in three flavors
#
#    1) plain text
#ErrorDocument 500 "The server made a boo boo."
#
#    2) local redirects
#ErrorDocument 404 /missing.html
# to redirect to local URL /missing.html
#ErrorDocument 404 "/cgi-bin/missing_handlder.pl"
#    i.e. any string which starts with a '/' and has
#    no spaces.
# N.B.: You can redirect to a script or a document using server-side-includes.
#
#    3) external redirects
#ErrorDocument 402 http://some.other_server.com/subscription_info.html
#    i.e. any string whichis a valid  URL.
# N.B.: Many of the environment variables associated with the original
# request will *not* be available to such a script.
#
#    4) borderline case
#ErrorDocument 402 "http://some.other_server.com/info.html is the place to look"
#    treated as case '1' as it has spaces and thus is not a valid URL
#
# The following directives modify normal HTTP response behavior.
# The first directive disables keepalive for Netscape 2.x and browsers that
# spoof it. There are known problems with these browser implementations.
# The second directive is for Microsoft Internet Explorer 4.0b2
# which has a broken HTTP/1.1 implementation and does not properly
# support keepalive when it is used on 301 or 302 (redirect) responses.
#
BrowserMatch "Mozilla/2" nokeepalive
```

```
BrowserMatch "MSIE 4\.0b2;" nokeepalive downgrade-1.0 force-response-1.0


#
# The following directive disables HTTP/1.1 responses to browsers which
# are in violation of the HTTP/1.0 spec by not being able to grok a
# basic 1.1 response.
#
BrowserMatch "RealPlayer 4\.0" force-response-1.0
BrowserMatch "Java/1\.0" force-response-1.0
BrowserMatch "JDK/1\.0" force-response-1.0


#
# Allow server status reports, with the URL of http://servername/server-status
# Change the ".your_domain.com" to match your domain to enable.
#
#<Location /server-status>
#    SetHandler server-status
#    Order deny,allow
#    Deny from all
#    Allow from .your_domain.com
#</Location>


#
# Allow remote server configuration reports, with the URL of
#  http://servername/server-info (requires that mod_info.c be loaded).
# Change the ".your_domain.com" to match your domain to enable.
#
#<Location /server-info>
#    SetHandler server-info
#    Order deny,allow
#    Deny from all
#    Allow from .your_domain.com
#</Location>


#
# There have been reports of people trying to abuse an old bug from pre-1.1
# days.  This bug involved a CGI script distributed as a part of Apache.
# By uncommenting these lines you can redirect these attacks to a logging
# script on phf.apache.org.  Or, you can record them yourself, using the script
# support/phf_abuse_log.cgi.
#
#<Location /cgi-bin/phf*>
#    Deny from all
#    ErrorDocument 403 http://phf.apache.org/phf_abuse_log.cgi
#</Location>


#
# Proxy Server directives. Uncomment the following lines to
# enable the proxy server:
#
#<IfModule mod_proxy.c>
```

```
#ProxyRequests On
#
#<Directory proxy:*>
#    Order deny,allow
#    Deny from all
#    Allow from .your_domain.com
#</Directory>

#
# Enable/disable the handling of HTTP/1.1 "Via:" headers.
# ("Full" adds the server version; "Block" removes all outgoing Via: headers)
# Set to one of: Off | On | Full | Block
#
#ProxyVia On

#
# To enable the cache as well, edit and uncomment the following lines:
# (no cacheing without CacheRoot)
#
#CacheRoot "/usr/local/apache2/proxy"
#CacheSize 5
#CacheGcInterval 4
#CacheMaxExpire 24
#CacheLastModifiedFactor 0.1
#CacheDefaultExpire 1
#NoCache a_domain.com another_domain.edu joes.garage_sale.com

#</IfModule>
# End of proxy directives.

### Section 3: Virtual Hosts
#
# VirtualHost: If you want to maintain multiple domains/hostnames on your
# machine you can setup VirtualHost containers for them. Most configurations
# use only name-based virtual hosts so the server doesn't need to worry about
# IP addresses. This is indicated by the asterisks in the directives below.
#
# Please see the documentation at <URL:http://www.apache.org/docs/vhosts/>
# for further details before you try to setup virtual hosts.
#
# You may use the command line option '-S' to verify your virtual host
# configuration.

#
# Use name-based virtual hosting.
#
#NameVirtualHost *

#
# VirtualHost example:
# Almost any Apache directive may go into a VirtualHost container.
```

```
# The first VirtualHost section is used for requests without a known
# server name.
#
#<VirtualHost *>
#    ServerAdmin webmaster@dummy-host.example.com
#    DocumentRoot /www/docs/dummy-host.example.com
#    ServerName dummy-host.example.com
#    ErrorLog logs/dummy-host.example.com-error_log
#    CustomLog logs/dummy-host.example.com-access_log common
#</VirtualHost>
```

The minimum necessary change to the httpd.conf file so other systems can access the Apache 2 server is to set the ServerName directive. Once you have made the necessary changes to the httpd.conf file, the Apache service needs to be started. Navigate to the Apache bin directory—default is /usr/local/apache2/bin—and execute the following:

```
./apachectl graceful
```

If all works well, the results of apachectl should indicate the Web service was successfully started.

Installing Apache 2 on Windows 2000

Microsoft Visual C++ 5.0 or higher is needed to compile Apache 2 for Windows platforms. To begin the build process, copy the Apache 2 file you downloaded to a directory on your hard drive. The Apache 2 file is delivered in a compressed format so you will need WinZip, or some other appropriate utility that can decompress .zip files. Also, you will need to download awk.exe, which is used to modify some of the files during the build process. The awk.exe utility is available from http://cm.bell-labs.com/cm/cs/who/bwk/awk95.exe. After you have downloaded the awk95.exe file, rename it to awk.exe and place it where the development environment can find it. For example, place it in the same directory as the nmake.exe application.

To begin the Apache 2 compilation process, execute the following at the command prompt pointing to the extracted files from the Apache 2 .zip file:

```
nmake /f Makefile.win _apacher
```

NOTE   If your Microsoft Visual C++ environment is not configured to run from the command line, run the vcvars32.bat script. For example, for Microsoft Visual C++ 6.0, the file is located at:

```
C:\Program Files\Microsoft Visual Studio\VC98\Bin\vcvars32.bat
```

The next step in the process is to install the Apache 2 files in the Web server's root directory. The default is the apache2 directory, which is directly below the root of the drive letter you are running the installation and build process from. At a command prompt pointing to the same location as the extracted files, execute the following:

```
nmake /f Makefile.win installr
```

When this process is completed, Apache needs to be installed as a service. In the development stages of Apache 2, there may not be an MSI file so Apache cannot be installed through the Microsoft Windows Installer application interface. To install Apache as a service, navigate to the directory that contains the apache.exe file and execute the following from the command line:

```
apache -k install -n "Apache"
```

The name inside the quotations is what you prefer to call the service—it does not have to be Apache. If you do not specify a name, the default name apache will be used.

Before you start the Apache 2 service, the ServerName directive in the httpd.conf file needs to be set so others can access the Web server from other systems. Below is the httpd.conf file that was created immediately after Apache 2 was compiled on Windows 2000 and before any modifications were made. The Apache 2 httpd.conf file for the Windows platform is very similar to the Apache 2 httpd.conf file for Linux, but there are some differences.

```
#
# Based upon the NCSA server configuration files originally by Rob McCool.
#
# This is the main Apache server configuration file.  It contains the
# configuration directives that give the server its instructions.
# See <URL:http://www.apache.org/docs/> for detailed information about
# the directives.
#
# Do NOT simply read the instructions in here without understanding
# what they do.  They're here only as hints or reminders.  If you are unsure
# consult the online docs. You have been warned.
#
# The configuration directives are grouped into three basic sections:
#  1. Directives that control the operation of the Apache server process as a
#     whole (the 'global environment').
#  2. Directives that define the parameters of the 'main' or 'default' server,
#     which responds to requests that aren't handled by a virtual host.
#     These directives also provide default values for the settings
#     of all virtual hosts.
#  3. Settings for virtual hosts, which allow Web requests to be sent to
#     different IP addresses or hostnames and have them handled by the
```

```
#      same Apache server process.
#
# Configuration and logfile names: If the filenames you specify for many
# of the server's control files begin with "/" (or "drive:/" for Win32), the
# server will use that explicit path.  If the filenames do *not* begin
# with "/", the value of ServerRoot is prepended -- so "logs/foo.log"
# with ServerRoot set to "/usr/local/apache" will be interpreted by the
# server as "/usr/local/apache/logs/foo.log".
#
# NOTE: Where filenames are specified, you must use forward slashes
# instead of backslashes (e.g., "c:/apache" instead of "c:\apache").
# If a drive letter is omitted, the drive on which Apache.exe is located
# will be used by default.  It is recommended that you always supply
# an explicit drive letter in absolute paths, however, to avoid
# confusion.
#


### Section 1: Global Environment
#
# The directives in this section affect the overall operation of Apache,
# such as the number of concurrent requests it can handle or where it
# can find its configuration files.
#


#
# ServerRoot: The top of the directory tree under which the server's
# configuration, error, and log files are kept.
#
# Do NOT add a slash at the end of the directory path.
#
ServerRoot "/Apache2.0"


#
# PidFile: The file in which the server should record its process
# identification number when it starts.
#
PidFile logs/httpd.pid


#
# ScoreBoardFile: File used to store internal server process information.
# Not all architectures require this.  But if yours does (you'll know because
# this file will be  created when you run Apache) then you *must* ensure that
# no two invocations of Apache share the same scoreboard file.
#
#ScoreBoardFile logs/apache_status


#
# Timeout: The number of seconds before receives and sends time out.
#
Timeout 300
```

```
#
# KeepAlive: Whether or not to allow persistent connections (more than
# one request per connection). Set to "Off" to deactivate.
#
KeepAlive On


#
# MaxKeepAliveRequests: The maximum number of requests to allow
# during a persistent connection. Set to 0 to allow an unlimited amount.
# We reccomend you leave this number high, for maximum performance.
#
MaxKeepAliveRequests 100


#
# KeepAliveTimeout: Number of seconds to wait for the next request from the
# same client on the same connection.
#
KeepAliveTimeout 15


#
# Apache on Win32 always creates one child process to handle requests.  If it
# dies, another child process is created automatically.  Within the child
# process multiple threads handle incoming requests.  The next two
# directives control the behaviour of the threads and processes.
#


#
# MaxRequestsPerChild: the number of requests each child process is
# allowed to process before the child dies.  The child will exit so
# as to avoid problems after prolonged use when Apache (and maybe the
# libraries it uses) leak memory or other resources.  On most systems, this
# isn't really needed, but a few (such as Solaris) do have notable leaks
# in the libraries.  For Win32, set this value to zero (unlimited)
# unless advised otherwise.
#
MaxRequestsPerChild 0


#
# Number of concurrent threads (i.e., requests) the server will allow.
# Set this value according to the responsiveness of the server (more
# requests active at once means they're all handled more slowly) and
# the amount of system resources you'll allow the server to consume.
#
ThreadsPerChild 250


#
# Listen: Allows you to bind Apache to specific IP addresses and/or
# ports, in addition to the default. See also the <VirtualHost>
# directive.
#
#Listen 3000
```

```
#Listen 12.34.56.78:80

#
# BindAddress: You can support virtual hosts with this option. This directive
# is used to tell the server which IP address to listen to. It can either
# contain "*", an IP address, or a fully qualified Internet domain name.
# See also the <VirtualHost> and Listen directives.
#
#BindAddress *

#
# Dynamic Shared Object (DSO) Support
#
# To be able to use the functionality of a module which was built as a DSO you
# have to place corresponding `LoadModule' lines at this location so the
# directives contained in it are actually available _before_ they are used.
# Please read the file README.DSO in the Apache 1.3 distribution for more
# details about the DSO mechanism and run `apache -l' for the list of already
# built-in (statically linked and thus always available) modules in your Apache
# binary.
#
# Note: The order in which modules are loaded is important.  Don't change
# the order below without expert advice.
#
#LoadModule auth_anon_module modules/mod_auth_anon.so
#LoadModule auth_dbm_module modules/mod_auth_dbm.so
#LoadModule auth_digest_module modules/mod_auth_digest.so
#LoadModule cern_meta_module modules/mod_cern_meta.so
#LoadModule dav_module modules/mod_dav.so
#LoadModule dav_fs_module modules/mod_dav_fs.so
#LoadModule expires_module modules/mod_expires.so
#LoadModule file_cache_module modules/mod_file_cache.so
#LoadModule headers_module modules/mod_headers.so
#LoadModule info_module modules/mod_info.so
#LoadModule proxy_module modules/mod_proxy.so
#LoadModule rewrite_module modules/mod_rewrite.so
#LoadModule speling_module modules/mod_speling.so
#LoadModule status_module modules/mod_status.so
#LoadModule usertrack_module modules/mod_usertrack.so

### Section 2: 'Main' server configuration
#
# The directives in this section set up the values used by the 'main'
# server, which responds to any requests that aren't handled by a
# <VirtualHost> definition.  These values also provide defaults for
# any <VirtualHost> containers you may define later in the file.
#
# All of these directives may appear inside <VirtualHost> containers,
# in which case these default settings will be overridden for the
# virtual host being defined.
#
```

```
#
# If your ServerType directive (set earlier in the 'Global Environment'
# section) is set to "inetd", the next few directives don't have any
# effect since their settings are defined by the inetd configuration.
# Skip ahead to the ServerAdmin directive.
#


#
# Port: The port to which the standalone server listens.
#
Port 80

#
# ServerAdmin: Your address, where problems with the server should be
# e-mailed.  This address appears on some server-generated pages, such
# as error documents.  e.g. admin@your-domain.com
#
#ServerAdmin @@ServerAdmin@@

#
# ServerName allows you to set a host name which is sent back to clients for
# your server if it's different than the one the program would get (i.e., use
# "www" instead of the host's real name).
#
# 127.0.0.1 is the TCP/IP local loop-back address. Your machine
# always knows itself by this address. If you machine is connected to
# a network, you should change this to be your machine's name
#
# Note: You cannot just invent host names and hope they work. The name you
# define here must be a valid DNS name for your host. If you don't understand
# this, ask your network administrator.
# If your host doesn't have a registered DNS name, enter its IP address here.
# You will have to access it by its address (e.g., http://123.45.67.89/)
# anyway, and this will make redirections work in a sensible way.
#
#ServerName @@ServerName@@

#
# DocumentRoot: The directory out of which you will serve your
# documents. By default, all requests are taken from this directory, but
# symbolic links and aliases may be used to point to other locations.
#
DocumentRoot "/Apache2.0/htdocs"

#
# Each directory to which Apache has access, can be configured with respect
# to which services and features are allowed and/or disabled in that
# directory (and its subdirectories).
#
# First, we configure the "default" to be a very restrictive set of
```

```
# permissions.
#
<Directory />
    Options FollowSymLinks
    AllowOverride None
</Directory>


#
# Note that from this point forward you must specifically allow
# particular features to be enabled - so if something's not working as
# you might expect, make sure that you have specifically enabled it
# below.
#


#
# This should be changed to whatever you set DocumentRoot to.
#
<Directory "/Apache2.0/htdocs">


#
# This may also be "None", "All", or any combination of "Indexes",
# "Includes", "FollowSymLinks", "ExecCGI", or "MultiViews".
#
# Note that "MultiViews" must be named *explicitly* --- "Options All"
# doesn't give it to you.
#
    Options Indexes FollowSymLinks MultiViews


#
# This controls which options the .htaccess files in directories can
# override. Can also be "All", or any combination of "Options", "FileInfo",
# "AuthConfig", and "Limit"
#
    AllowOverride None


#
# Controls who can get stuff from this server.
#
    Order allow,deny
    Allow from all
</Directory>


#
# UserDir: The name of the directory which is appended onto a user's home
# directory if a ~user request is received.
#
# Under Win32, we do not currently try to determine the home directory of
# a Windows login, so a format such as that below needs to be used.  See
# the UserDir documentation for details.
#
UserDir "/Apache2.0/users/"
```

```
#
# DirectoryIndex: Name of the file or files to use as a pre-written HTML
# directory index.  Separate multiple entries with spaces.
#
DirectoryIndex index.html


#
# AccessFileName: The name of the file to look for in each directory
# for access control information.
#
AccessFileName .htaccess


#
# The following lines prevent .htaccess files from being viewed by
# Web clients.  Since .htaccess files often contain authorization
# information, access is disallowed for security reasons.  Comment
# these lines out if you want Web visitors to see the contents of
# .htaccess files.  If you change the AccessFileName directive above,
# be sure to make the corresponding changes here.
#
<Files .htaccess>
    Order allow,deny
    Deny from all
</Files>


#
# CacheNegotiatedDocs: By default, Apache sends "Pragma: no-cache" with each
# document that was negotiated on the basis of content. This asks proxy
# servers not to cache the document. Uncommenting the following line disables
# this behavior, and proxies will be allowed to cache the documents.
#
#CacheNegotiatedDocs


#
# UseCanonicalName:  (new for 1.3)  With this setting turned on, whenever
# Apache needs to construct a self-referencing URL (a URL that refers back
# to the server the response is coming from) it will use ServerName and
# Port to form a "canonical" name.  With this setting off, Apache will
# use the hostname:port that the client supplied, when possible.  This
# also affects SERVER_NAME and SERVER_PORT in CGI scripts.
#
UseCanonicalName On


#
# TypesConfig describes where the mime.types file (or equivalent) is
# to be found.
#
TypesConfig conf/mime.types


#
```

```
# DefaultType is the default MIME type the server will use for a document
# if it cannot otherwise determine one, such as from filename extensions.
# If your server contains mostly text or HTML documents, "text/plain" is
# a good value.  If most of your content is binary, such as applications
# or images, you may want to use "application/octet-stream" instead to
# keep browsers from trying to display binary files as though they are
# text.
#
DefaultType text/plain


#
# The mod_mime_magic module allows the server to use various hints from the
# contents of the file itself to determine its type.  The MIMEMagicFile
# directive tells the module where the hint definitions are located.
# mod_mime_magic is not part of the default server (you have to add
# it yourself with a LoadModule [see the DSO paragraph in the 'Global
# Environment' section], or recompile the server and include mod_mime_magic
# as part of the configuration), so it's enclosed in an <IfModule> container.
# This means that the MIMEMagicFile directive will only be processed if the
# module is part of the server.
#
<IfModule mod_mime_magic.c>
    MIMEMagicFile conf/magic
</IfModule>


#
# HostnameLookups: Log the names of clients or just their IP addresses
# e.g., www.apache.org (on) or 204.62.129.132 (off).
# The default is off because it'd be overall better for the net if people
# had to knowingly turn this feature on, since enabling it means that
# each client request will result in AT LEAST one lookup request to the
# nameserver.
#
HostnameLookups Off


#
# ErrorLog: The location of the error log file.
# If you do not specify an ErrorLog directive within a <VirtualHost>
# container, error messages relating to that virtual host will be
# logged here.  If you *do* define an error logfile for a <VirtualHost>
# container, that host's errors will be logged there and not here.
#
ErrorLog logs/error.log


#
# LogLevel: Control the number of messages logged to the error.log.
# Possible values include: debug, info, notice, warn, error, crit,
# alert, emerg.
#
LogLevel warn
```

```
#
# The following directives define some format nicknames for use with
# a CustomLog directive (see below).
#
LogFormat "%h %l %u %t \"%r\" %>s %b \"%{Referer}i\" \"%{User-Agent}i\""
   combined
LogFormat "%h %l %u %t \"%r\" %>s %b" common
LogFormat "%{Referer}i -> %U" referer
LogFormat "%{User-agent}i" agent

#
# The location and format of the access logfile (Common Logfile Format).
# If you do not define any access logfiles within a <VirtualHost>
# container, they will be logged here.  Contrariwise, if you *do*
# define per-<VirtualHost> access logfiles, transactions will be
# logged therein and *not* in this file.
#
CustomLog logs/access.log common

#
# If you would like to have agent and referer logfiles, uncomment the
# following directives.
#
#CustomLog logs/referer.log referer
#CustomLog logs/agent.log agent

#
# If you prefer a single logfile with access, agent, and referer information
# (Combined Logfile Format) you can use the following directive.
#
#CustomLog logs/access.log combined

#
# Optionally add a line containing the server version and virtual host
# name to server-generated pages (error documents, FTP directory listings,
# mod_status and mod_info output etc., but not CGI generated documents).
# Set to "EMail" to also include a mailto: link to the ServerAdmin.
# Set to one of:  On | Off | EMail
#
ServerSignature On

#
# Aliases: Add here as many aliases as you need (with no limit). The format is
# Alias fakename realname
#
# Note that if you include a trailing / on fakename then the server will
# require it to be present in the URL.  So "/icons" isn't aliased in this
# example, only "/icons/"..
#
Alias /icons/ "/Apache2.0/icons/"
```

```
#
# ScriptAlias: This controls which directories contain server scripts.
# ScriptAliases are essentially the same as Aliases, except that
# documents in the realname directory are treated as applications and
# run by the server when requested rather than as documents sent to the client.
# The same rules about trailing "/" apply to ScriptAlias directives as to
# Alias.
#
ScriptAlias /cgi-bin/ "/Apache2.0/cgi-bin/"


#
# "/Apache2.0/cgi-bin" should be changed to whatever your ScriptAliased
# CGI directory exists, if you have that configured.
#
<Directory "/Apache2.0/cgi-bin">
    AllowOverride None
    Options None
</Directory>


#
# Redirect allows you to tell clients about documents which used to exist in
# your server's namespace, but do not anymore. This allows you to tell the
# clients where to look for the relocated document.
# Format: Redirect old-URI new-URL
#


#
# Directives controlling the display of server-generated directory listings.
#


#
# FancyIndexing is whether you want fancy directory indexing or standard
#
IndexOptions FancyIndexing


#
# AddIcon* directives tell the server which icon to show for different
# files or filename extensions.  These are only displayed for
# FancyIndexed directories.
#
AddIconByEncoding (CMP,/icons/compressed.gif) x-compress x-gzip

AddIconByType (TXT,/icons/text.gif) text/*
AddIconByType (IMG,/icons/image2.gif) image/*
AddIconByType (SND,/icons/sound2.gif) audio/*
AddIconByType (VID,/icons/movie.gif) video/*

AddIcon /icons/binary.gif .bin .exe
AddIcon /icons/binhex.gif .hqx
AddIcon /icons/tar.gif .tar
AddIcon /icons/world2.gif .wrl .wrl.gz .vrml .vrm .iv
```

```
AddIcon /icons/compressed.gif .Z .z .tgz .gz .zip
AddIcon /icons/a.gif .ps .ai .eps
AddIcon /icons/layout.gif .html .shtml .htm .pdf
AddIcon /icons/text.gif .txt
AddIcon /icons/c.gif .c
AddIcon /icons/p.gif .pl .py
AddIcon /icons/f.gif .for
AddIcon /icons/dvi.gif .dvi
AddIcon /icons/uuencoded.gif .uu
AddIcon /icons/script.gif .conf .sh .shar .csh .ksh .tcl
AddIcon /icons/tex.gif .tex
AddIcon /icons/bomb.gif core

AddIcon /icons/back.gif ..
AddIcon /icons/hand.right.gif README
AddIcon /icons/folder.gif ^^DIRECTORY^^
AddIcon /icons/blank.gif ^^BLANKICON^^

#
# DefaultIcon is which icon to show for files which do not have an icon
# explicitly set.
#
DefaultIcon /icons/unknown.gif

#
# AddDescription allows you to place a short description after a file in
# server-generated indexes.  These are only displayed for FancyIndexed
# directories.
# Format: AddDescription "description" filename
#
#AddDescription "GZIP compressed document" .gz
#AddDescription "tar archive" .tar
#AddDescription "GZIP compressed tar archive" .tgz

#
# ReadmeName is the name of the README file the server will look for by
# default, and append to directory listings.
#
# HeaderName is the name of a file which should be prepended to
# directory indexes.
#
# The server will first look for name.html and include it if found.
# If name.html doesn't exist, the server will then look for name.txt
# and include it as plaintext if found.
#
ReadmeName README
HeaderName HEADER

#
# IndexIgnore is a set of filenames which directory indexing should ignore
# and not include in the listing.  Shell-style wildcarding is permitted.
```

```
#
IndexIgnore .??* *~ *# HEADER* README* RCS CVS *,v *,t

#
# AddEncoding allows you to have certain browsers (Mosaic/X 2.1+) uncompress
# information on the fly. Note: Not all browsers support this.
# Despite the name similarity, the following Add* directives have nothing
# to do with the FancyIndexing customisation directives above.
#
AddEncoding x-compress Z
AddEncoding x-gzip gz tgz

#
# AddLanguage allows you to specify the language of a document. You can
# then use content negotiation to give a browser a file in a language
# it can understand.
#
# Note 1: The suffix does not have to be the same as the language
# keyword --- those with documents in Polish (whose net-standard
# language code is pl) may wish to use "AddLanguage pl .po" to
# avoid the ambiguity with the common suffix for perl scripts.
#
# Note 2: The example entries below illustrate that in quite
# some cases the two character 'Language' abbreviation is not
# identical to the two character 'Country' code for its country,
# E.g. 'Danmark/dk' versus 'Danish/da'.
#
# Note 3: In the case of 'ltz' we violate the RFC by using a three char
# specifier. But there is 'work in progress' to fix this and get
# the reference data for rfc1766 cleaned up.
#
# Danish (da) - Dutch (nl) - English (en) - Estonian (et)
# French (fr) - German (de) - Greek-Modern (el)
# Italian (it) - Norwegian (no) - Korean (kr)
# Portugese (pt) - Luxembourgeois* (ltz)
# Spanish (es) - Swedish (sv) - Catalan (ca) - Czech(cz)
# Polish (pl) - Brazilian Portuguese (pt-br) - Japanese (ja)
# Russian (ru)
#
AddLanguage da .dk
AddLanguage nl .nl
AddLanguage en .en
AddLanguage et .et
AddLanguage fr .fr
AddLanguage de .de
AddLanguage el .el
AddLanguage it .it
AddLanguage ja .ja
AddLanguage pl .po
AddLanguage kr .kr
AddLanguage pt .pt
```

```
AddLanguage no .no
AddLanguage pt-br .pt-br
AddLanguage ltz .ltz
AddLanguage ca .ca
AddLanguage es .es
AddLanguage sv .se
AddLanguage cz .cz
AddLanguage ru .ru
AddLanguage tw .tw
AddLanguage zh-tw .tw


# LanguagePriority allows you to give precedence to some languages
# in case of a tie during content negotiation.
#
# Just list the languages in decreasing order of preference. We have
# more or less alphabetized them here. You probably want to change this.
#
LanguagePriority en da nl et fr de el it ja kr no pl pt pt-br ru ltz ca es sv tw


# Specify a default charset for all pages sent out. This is
# always a good idea and opens the door for future internationalisation
# of your web site, should you ever want it. Specifying it as
# a default does little harm; as the standard dictates that a page
# is in iso-8859-1 (latin1) unless specified otherwise i.e. you
# are merely stating the obvious. There are also some security
# reasons in browsers, related to javascript and URL parsing
# which encourage you to always set a default char set.
#
AddDefaultCharset       ISO-8859-1


#
# Commonly used filename extensions to character sets. You probably
# want to avoid clashes with the language extensions, unless you
# are good at carefully testing your setup after each change.
# See ftp://ftp.isi.edu/in-notes/iana/assignments/character-sets for
# the official list of charset names and their respective RFCs
#
AddCharset ISO-8859-1   .iso8859-1 .latin1
AddCharset ISO-8859-2   .iso8859-2 .latin2 .cen
AddCharset ISO-8859-3   .iso8859-3 .latin3
AddCharset ISO-8859-4   .iso8859-4 .latin4
AddCharset ISO-8859-5   .iso8859-5 .latin5 .cyr .iso-ru
AddCharset ISO-8859-6   .iso8859-6 .latin6 .arb
AddCharset ISO-8859-7   .iso8859-7 .latin7 .grk
AddCharset ISO-8859-8   .iso8859-8 .latin8 .heb
AddCharset ISO-8859-9   .iso8859-9 .latin9 .trk
AddCharset ISO-2022-JP .iso2022-jp .jis
AddCharset ISO-2022-KR .iso2022-kr .kis
AddCharset ISO-2022-CN .iso2022-cn .cis
AddCharset Big5         .Big5       .big5
# For russian, more than one charset is used (depends on client, mostly):
```

```
AddCharset WINDOWS-1251 .cp-1251    .win-1251
AddCharset CP866        .cp866
AddCharset KOI8-r       .koi8-r .koi8-ru
AddCharset KOI8-ru      .koi8-uk .ua
AddCharset ISO-10646-UCS-2 .ucs2
AddCharset ISO-10646-UCS-4 .ucs4
AddCharset UTF-8        .utf8


# The set below does not map to a specific (iso) standard
# but works on a fairly wide range of browsers. Note that
# capitalization actually matters (it should not, but it
# does for some browsers).
#
# See ftp://ftp.isi.edu/in-notes/iana/assignments/character-sets
# for a list of sorts. But browsers support few.
#
AddCharset GB2312       .gb2312 .gb
AddCharset utf-7        .utf7
AddCharset utf-8        .utf8
AddCharset big5             .big5 .b5
AddCharset EUC-TW       .euc-tw
AddCharset EUC-JP       .euc-jp
AddCharset EUC-KR       .euc-kr
AddCharset shift_jis    .sjis


#
# AddType allows you to tweak mime.types without actually editing it, or to
# make certain files to be certain types.
#
# For example, the PHP3 module (not part of the Apache distribution)
# will typically use:
#
#AddType application/x-httpd-php3 .phtml
#AddType application/x-httpd-php3-source .phps

AddType application/x-tar .tgz


#
# AddHandler allows you to map certain file extensions to "handlers",
# actions unrelated to filetype. These can be either built into the server
# or added with the Action command (see below)
#
# If you want to use server side includes, or CGI outside
# ScriptAliased directories, uncomment the following lines.
#
# To use CGI scripts:
#
#AddHandler cgi-script .cgi


#
# To use server-parsed HTML files
```

```
#
#AddType text/html .shtml
#AddHandler server-parsed .shtml

#
# Uncomment the following line to enable Apache's send-asis HTTP file
# feature
#
#AddHandler send-as-is asis

#
# If you wish to use server-parsed imagemap files, use
#
#AddHandler imap-file map

#
# To enable type maps, you might want to use
#
#AddHandler type-map var

#
# Action lets you define media types that will execute a script whenever
# a matching file is called. This eliminates the need for repeated URL
# pathnames for oft-used CGI file processors.
# Format: Action media/type /cgi-script/location
# Format: Action handler-name /cgi-script/location
#

#
# MetaDir: specifies the name of the directory in which Apache can find
# meta information files. These files contain additional HTTP headers
# to include when sending the document
#
#MetaDir .web

#
# MetaSuffix: specifies the file name suffix for the file containing the
# meta information.
#
#MetaSuffix .meta

#
# Customizable error response (Apache style)
#   these come in three flavors
#
#     1) plain text
#ErrorDocument 500 "The server made a boo boo."
#
#     2) local redirects
#ErrorDocument 404 /missing.html
#  to redirect to local URL /missing.html
```

```
#ErrorDocument 404 "/cgi-bin/missing_handlder.pl"
#    i.e. any string which starts with a '/' and has
#    no spaces.
# N.B.: You can redirect to a script or a document using server-side-includes.
#
#    3) external redirects
#ErrorDocument 402 http://some.other_server.com/subscription_info.html
#    i.e. any string whichis a valid  URL.
# N.B.: Many of the environment variables associated with the original
#  request will *not* be available to such a script.
#
#    4) borderline case
#ErrorDocument 402 "http://some.other_server.com/info.html is the place to look"
#    treated as case '1' as it has spaces and thus is not a valid URL
#
# The following directives disable keepalives and HTTP header flushes.
# The first directive disables it for Netscape 2.x and browsers which
# spoof it. There are known problems with these.
# The second directive is for Microsoft Internet Explorer 4.0b2
# which has a broken HTTP/1.1 implementation and does not properly
# support keepalive when it is used on 301 or 302 (redirect) responses.
#
BrowserMatch "Mozilla/2" nokeepalive
BrowserMatch "MSIE 4\.0b2;" nokeepalive downgrade-1.0 force-response-1.0


#
# The following directive disables HTTP/1.1 responses to browsers which
# are in violation of the HTTP/1.0 spec by not being able to grok a
# basic 1.1 response.
#
BrowserMatch "RealPlayer 4\.0" force-response-1.0
BrowserMatch "Java/1\.0" force-response-1.0
BrowserMatch "JDK/1\.0" force-response-1.0


#
# Allow server status reports, with the URL of http://servername/server-status
# Change the ".@@DomainName@@" to match your domain to enable.
#
#<Location /server-status>
#    SetHandler server-status
#    Order deny,allow
#    Deny from all
#    Allow from .@@DomainName@@
#</Location>


#
# Allow remote server configuration reports, with the URL of
#  http://servername/server-info (requires that mod_info.c be loaded).
# Change the ".your_domain.com" to match your domain to enable.
#
#<Location /server-info>
```

```
#     SetHandler server-info
#     Order deny,allow
#     Deny from all
#     Allow from .@@DomainName@@
#</Location>

#
# There have been reports of people trying to abuse an old bug from pre-1.1
# days.  This bug involved a CGI script distributed as a part of Apache.
# By uncommenting these lines you can redirect these attacks to a logging
# script on phf.apache.org.  Or, you can record them yourself, using the script
# support/phf_abuse_log.cgi.
#
#<Location /cgi-bin/phf*>
#     Deny from all
#     ErrorDocument 403 http://phf.apache.org/phf_abuse_log.cgi
#</Location>

#
# Proxy Server directives. Uncomment the following line to
# enable the proxy server:
#
#ProxyRequests On

#
# Enable/disable the handling of HTTP/1.1 "Via:" headers.
# ("Full" adds the server version; "Block" removes all outgoing Via: headers)
# Set to one of: Off | On | Full | Block
#
#ProxyVia On

#
# To enable the cache as well, edit and uncomment the following lines:
# (no cacheing without CacheRoot)
#
#CacheRoot "/Apache2.0/proxy"
#CacheSize 5
#CacheGcInterval 4
#CacheMaxExpire 24
#CacheLastModifiedFactor 0.1
#CacheDefaultExpire 1
#NoCache a_domain.com another_domain.edu joes.garage_sale.com

### Section 3: Virtual Hosts
#
# VirtualHost: If you want to maintain multiple domains/hostnames on your
# machine you can setup VirtualHost containers for them. Most configurations
# use only name-based virtual hosts so the server doesn't need to worry about
# IP addresses. This is indicated by the asterisks in the directives below.
#
# Please see the documentation at <URL:http://www.apache.org/docs/vhosts/>
```

```
# for further details before you try to setup virtual hosts.
#
# You may use the command line option '-S' to verify your virtual host
# configuration.

#
# Use name-based virtual hosting.
#
#NameVirtualHost *

#
# VirtualHost example:
# Almost any Apache directive may go into a VirtualHost container.
# The first VirtualHost section is used for requests without a known
# server name.
#
#<VirtualHost *>
#    ServerAdmin webmaster@dummy-host.example.com
#    DocumentRoot /www/docs/dummy-host.example.com
#    ServerName dummy-host.example.com
#    ErrorLog logs/dummy-host.example.com-error_log
#    CustomLog logs/dummy-host.example.com-access_log common
#</VirtualHost>
```

Once the ServerName directive is defined to match the name of the Apache 2 Web server, the Apache service needs to be started. The service can be started at the command line by executing the following:

```
net start apache
```

The name of the service is the same as what was used when the service was installed. You can also start (and stop) Apache 2 from the Services menu option under the Administrative Tools menu. To stop the service from the command line, execute the following:

```
net stop apache
```

If the net start command is able to start the Web service, a successful message is displayed at the command prompt.

Does It Work?

Once you have compiled, installed, configured, and started the Apache 2 service on your Linux and/or Windows 2000 systems, it's time to see if it works and can service browser requests. In a browser window, enter in the name or IP address of your Apache 2 Web server. Assuming everything is functioning properly, the default index page should look similar to Figure 11.1.

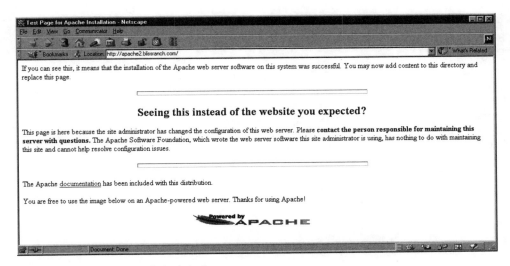

Figure 11.1   Apache 2 default index page.

NOTE   The procedures for compiling and installing Apache 2 may change as the development of Apache 2 continues. In addition, the contents of the Apache 2 httpd.conf file for Linux and Windows may also change. All examples in this chapter were based on Apache 2.0.16 beta for Linux and Windows.

Index